FINDING WHAT YOU NEED

Quick Access Brief will help you become a better writer by answering the questions that come up as you write. Use the following tools to quickly find the information you need:

- The **Brief Contents** on the facing page and this page lists all the parts and chapters in *Quick Access Brief*.

- The **Detailed Contents** on pages vi–xvii lists the parts, chapters, and chapter sections in this book.

- The **Index** at the end of the book lists all handbook topics in alphabetic order. Find your topic, note the page number, and then turn to that page to locate your information quickly.

- The **page elements** such as tabs and section numbers help you navigate (see pages xx–xxi for sample pages with annotations that highlight each item).

- **Quick Boxes** throughout the book give you an easy way to skim and access the most common and important issues that will come up as you write.

- The **Terms Glossary** at the end of the book defines important terms related to writing and grammar. Every word printed in small capital letters in *Quick Access Brief* is defined in the Terms Glossary.

- **Proofreading Marks** and **Response Symbols** that your instructor may use to mark your writing appear on the inside back cover. Refer to these lists to find the section of the handbook that will help you edit and proofread your work.

D0142434

Quick Access
Brief

THIRD EDITION

LYNN QUITMAN TROYKA

DOUGLAS HESSE

Boston   Columbus   Indianapolis   New York   San Francisco   Upper Saddle River
Amsterdam   Cape Town   Dubai   London   Madrid   Milan   Munich   Paris   Montréal   Toronto
Delhi   Mexico City   São Paulo   Sydney   Hong Kong   Seoul   Singapore   Taipei   Tokyo

Vice President and Editor in Chief: Joseph Terry
Senior Development Editor: Marion B. Castellucci
Senior Marketing Manager: Roxanne McCarley
Project Manager: Savoula Amanatidis
Project Coordination, Text Design, and Electronic Page Makeup: Laserwords Private Ltd.
Cover Designer/Manager: John Callahan
Cover Image: © SuperStock
Photo Researcher: Integra
Senior Manufacturing Buyer: Dennis J. Para
Printer and Binder: R. R. Donnelley and Sons Company–Crawfordsville
Cover Printer: Lehigh-Phoenix Color Corporation–Hagerstown

For permission to use copyrighted material, grateful acknowledgment is made to the copyright hold-ers on pp. 511–512, which are hereby made part of this copyright page.

Cataloging-in-Publication Data is on file at the Library of Congress

10 9 8 7 6 5 4 3 2 1—DOC—17 16 15 14

www.pearsonhighered.com

ISBN-10: 0-321-91407-4
ISBN-13: 978-0-321-91407-1

In memory of David Troyka,
my sweetheart and
husband of 47 years

LYNN QUITMAN TROYKA

To Don and Coral Hesse

DOUG HESSE

DETAILED CONTENTS

INTRODUCTION TO STUDENTS

As writers, many of you have much in common with both of us. Sure, we've been at it longer, so we've had more practice, and most rules have become cemented in our heads. However, we share with you a common goal: to put ideas into words worthy of someone else's reading time. So that you can know us better as practicing writers, we'd each like to share a personal story with you.

From Doug: I first glimpsed the power of writing in high school, when I wrote sappy—but apparently successful—love poems. Still, when I went to college, I was surprised to discover all I didn't know about writing. Fortunately, I had good teachers and developed lots of patience. I needed it. I continue to learn from my colleagues, my students, and my coauthor, Lynn.

From Lynn: When I was an undergraduate, questions about writing nagged at me. One day, browsing in the library, I found a dust-covered book with the words *handbook* and *writing* in its title. Such books weren't common in those days, so I read it hungrily. Back then, I never imagined that someday I might write such a book myself. Now that we've completed the third edition of *Quick Access Brief,* I'm amazed that I ever had the nerve to begin. This proves to me—and I hope to you—that anyone can write. Students don't always believe that. I hope you will.

We welcome you as our partners in the process of writing. We hope that the pages of this handbook will help you give voice to your thoughts, in school and in life. Please know that you're welcome always to write us at LTROYKA2@gmail.com or dhesse@du.edu with comments about this handbook and about your experiences as a writer. We promise to answer.

Lynn Quitman Troyka
Doug Hesse

FINDING WHAT YOU NEED ON A PAGE

The running head shows the last section on the current page.

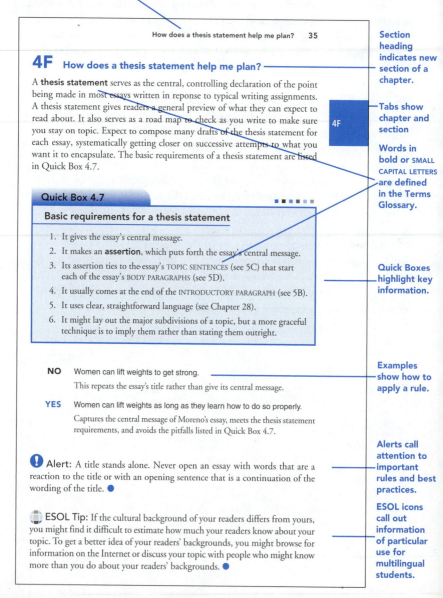

4F How does a thesis statement help me plan?

A **thesis statement** serves as the central, controlling declaration of the point being made in most essays written in reponse to typical writing assignments. A thesis statement gives readers a general preview of what they can expect to read about. It also serves as a road map to check as you write to make sure you stay on topic. Expect to compose many drafts of the thesis statement for each essay, systematically getting closer on successive attempts to what you want it to encapsulate. The basic requirements of a thesis statement are listed in Quick Box 4.7.

Section heading indicates new section of a chapter.

Tabs show chapter and section

4F

Words in bold or SMALL CAPITAL LETTERS are defined in the Terms Glossary.

Quick Box 4.7

Basic requirements for a thesis statement

1. It gives the essay's central message.
2. It makes an **assertion**, which puts forth the essay's central message.
3. Its assertion ties to the essay's TOPIC SENTENCES (see 5C) that start each of the essay's BODY PARAGRAPHS (see 5D).
4. It usually comes at the end of the INTRODUCTORY PARAGRAPH (see 5B).
5. It uses clear, straightforward language (see Chapter 28).
6. It might lay out the major subdivisions of a topic, but a more graceful technique is to imply them rather than stating them outright.

Quick Boxes highlight key information.

NO   Women can lift weights to get strong.

This repeats the essay's title rather than give its central message.

YES   Women can lift weights as long as they learn how to do so properly.

Captures the central message of Moreno's essay, meets the thesis statement requirements, and avoids the pitfalls listed in Quick Box 4.7.

Examples show how to apply a rule.

🛈 **Alert:** A title stands alone. Never open an essay with words that are a reaction to the title or with an opening sentence that is a continuation of the wording of the title. ●

Alerts call attention to important rules and best practices.

🌐 **ESOL Tip:** If the cultural background of your readers differs from yours, you might find it difficult to estimate how much your readers know about your topic. To get a better idea of your readers' backgrounds, you might browse for information on the Internet or discuss your topic with people who might know more than you do about your readers' backgrounds. ●

ESOL icons call out information of particular use for multilingual students.

11A What is an essay that analyzes literary or other works?

An **analysis essay** explains the meaning of a work by breaking it down into its component parts and showing how it is put together. To write an analysis essay, you begin by closely reading, observing, or looking at the specific work you intend to discuss. You consider the whole work as well as its component parts.

In your written analysis, you use your THESIS STATEMENT to present the point of view you intend to explain and support by referring specifically to parts of the work and to the work as a whole. You want to start with a SUMMARY of the whole work, but never stop there. You must go far beyond your summary to analyze the work. You're expected to explain your point of view about the whole work and/or its separate parts. This explanation is your interpretation of the work, through which you display your ability to engage in CRITICAL THINKING and avoid LOGICAL FALLACIES (see Chapter 2).

11A

Frame for an Informative Essay

Introductory paragraph(s)

- **Capture your readers' interest** by using one of the strategies for writing effective introductory paragraphs (see 5B).
- **Present your thesis statement**, making sure it gives the central point of the essay (see 4F).

Body paragraph(s): background information

- **Start with a topic sentence** that clearly relates to your thesis statement and leads logically to the information in the paragraph (see 5C).
- **Provide background** for the information in your essay. This might follow the introductory paragraph or come later in the essay at a point when the background is more relevant.

Sentence and Paragraph Guides

- People experienced with _____ advise that the public needs to know _____ so that everyone can _____.
- _____ captured my interest because _____.
- People generally consider _____, _____, and _____ as the major components of information about _____.

Section heading indicates new section of a chapter.

FRAMES charts show you how to organize typical college papers.

Sentence and paragraph guides help you think out moves writers make.

PREFACE

This third edition of *Quick Access Brief* gives "quick access" to essential information students need about writing, from writing college papers to using and documenting sources, from writing online to writing using visuals, and from mastering grammar to using correct punctuation. We designed *Quick Access Brief* for easy use and speedy entreé into all topics, welcoming students into a conversation about becoming better writers.

WHAT'S NEW IN THE THIRD EDITION?

- **Five new chapters, "Frames for College Writing,"** advise students on commonly assigned papers. Guidance on the personal essay, informative writing, argument, proposal and solution, and analysis of literary and other texts includes a discussion of audience and purpose, a frames chart illustrating a typical organization, sentence/paragraph guides that help develop common writing moves, and an annotated sample student paper (Part 3).

- **A new chapter, "Ten Troublesome Mistakes Writers Make,"** highlights for students the most common grammar and punctuation mistakes, alerting them to key areas that they might otherwise overlook in what can seem a sea of grammar rules. This overview of common mistakes provides additional examples to help students identify and correct these errors in their own writing (Ch. 1).

- **Streamlined and updated coverage of researched writing** includes new material on evaluating and synthesizing sources and organizing a research paper using frames and sentence guides (Chs. 12 and 13).

- **New annotated source illustrations** show students how to identify citation information in a range of typical sources—journal articles, web pages, and books—and how to arrange that information into correct MLA and APA citations.

- **MLA and APA documentation examples** have been completely updated, and examples of electronic sources like e-readers and wikis help students accurately cite increasingly common types of new sources. Author, title, and publication elements of citation examples are now highlighted so students can easily see how to put together a correct citation (Chs. 14 and 15).

- **The new Terms Glossary** provides a convenient cross-referencing system: key terms are boldfaced and defined where they first appear in this book, and are thereafter presented in small capital letters—providing visual cues to readers when more complete definitions can be found in the Terms Glossary.

OTHER FEATURES OF *QUICK ACCESS BRIEF*

- **Authoritative advice about grammar, punctuation, and mechanics** based on the coverage of *Quick Access Reference for Writers* provides condensed and clear explanations with plentiful examples of correct usage.

- **Quick Boxes** highlight and summarize key content throughout the text, providing quick access to important strategies, suggestions, and examples to improve student writing.

- **Extensive samples of student writing** include eight full academic essays and four complete workplace documents to illustrate key elements of various types of writing and help students apply them in their own writing.

- **Support for multilingual writers** includes six stand-alone chapters devoted to areas of special concern as well as ESOL Tips integrated throughout the handbook and embedded within specific grammar, research, and writing topics.

- **Contemporary emphasis on visual and media literacy** includes coverage of reading visuals critically (Ch. 3), using multimedia in presentations (Ch. 52), and writing in online environments such as blogs and wikis (Ch. 53).

- **Thoughtful, up-to-date documentation** coverage includes more MLA and APA example citations than most other comparable titles.

SUPPLEMENTS

- **Instructor's Manual.** *Instructor's Resource Manual to accompany Quick Access Reference for Writers, Seventh Edition* offers practical, hands-on advice for new and experienced composition instructors for organizing their syllabi, planning, and teaching.

- ***Quick Access* Exercise Answer Key**. Contains answers to the many exercises and activities in Quick Access.

- **Student Workbook.** *Workbook for Writers* has additional instruction and exercises for the writing, research, and grammar sections.

If you would like additional information about supplements for your composition course(s), please contact your Pearson sales representative.

MyWritingLab™ NOW AVAILABLE FOR COMPOSITION

Integrated solutions for writing

MyWritingLab is an online homework, tutorial, and assessment program that provides engaging experiences for today's instructors and students.

New features, built on MyWritingLab's hallmark foundation, offer composition instructors:

- A new writing space for students
- Customizable rubrics for assessing and grading student writing
- Multimedia instruction on all aspects of composition, not just grammar
- Advanced reporting to analyze class performance

Instructors can customize the rubrics for assessing student writing.

Adaptive learning powered by multimedia instruction

MyWritingLab offers preassessments and personalized remediation. MyWritingLab continuously adjusts its recommendations based on student activity, so students see improved results and instructors spend less time in class reviewing the basics.

Rich multimedia resources are built in to engage students and support faculty throughout the course.

Visit www.mywritinglab.com for more information.

Students' personalized learning paths are continuously customized to help improve their writing.

ACKNOWLEDGMENTS

With this third edition of *Quick Access Brief*, we heartily thank all those students who, to our great luck, have landed in our writing courses. We yearly learn from them how to stay up to date with students' needs and concerns as writers. We greatly admire how they strive to write skillfully, think critically, and communicate successfully. We especially thank the individual students who have given us permission to make them "published authors" by including their exemplary writing in this handbook.

We also are grateful to our many colleagues who have helped us with their criticisms, suggestions, and encouragement. In particular, we thank: Francesco Ancona, Sussex County Community College; Diana I. Badur, Black Hawk College; Anne Balay, Indiana University Northwest; Evan Balkan, Community College of Baltimore County; Martin Brick, Ohio Dominican University; Ginny Buccelli, Contra Costa College; Ann Marie Bukowski, Bluegrass Community and Technical College; William Carney, Cameron University; Daniel J. Cleary, Lorain County Community College; Anthony Collins, Inver Hills Community College; Shaun D. Curran, Quincy College; Richard Davis, Grayson County College; Marya Davis Turley, Western Kentucky University; Emily Dial-Driver, Rogers State University; Envera Dukaj, The Ohio State University; Fawcett Dunstan, Community College of Baltimore County; Anne Dvorak, Metropolitan Community College–Longview; Ginger S. Fox, Rowan-Cabarrus Community College; Jennifer Gatto, Tunxis Community College; Esther Godfrey, University of South Carolina Upstate; Kim Greenfield, Lorain County Community College; Diana Clark Grumbles, Southern Methodist University; Darin L. Hammond, Brigham Young University–Idaho; Danielle Houck, University of Miami; Christine Howell, Metropolitan Community College, Penn Valley; Cheryl Hunter, NHTI–Concord's Community College; Roberta Kelly, Washington State University; Melinda Knight, Montclair State University; Shanon Lawson, Pikes Peak Community College; Joy Eichner Lynch, Contra Costa College; David MacWilliams, Adams State College; Brandy Meyers, The Art Institute of Philadelphia; Lisa Moreno, Los Angeles Trade-Technical College; Michael N. Morris, Eastfield College; Roxanne F. Munch, Joliet Junior College; D. Erik Nielson, Northern Virginia Community College; Erika Olsen, New Hampshire Technical Institute; Laura Peet, California State University, Bakersfield; Louise Polistena-D'Agosto, Tunxis Community College; Julie A. Ptacek-Wilkey, Northeast Community College; James Rawlins, Sussex County Community College; Deana St. Peter, Guilford Technical Community College; Jean Sorensen, Grayson College; Virginia Tucker, Old Dominion University; Carole Denise Wright, Mineral Area College; and Madeline Yonker, York College of Pennsylvania.

A project as complicated as *Quick Access Brief* cannot be completed without the expertise and dedication of many professionals. We thank all the exceptional people at Pearson who facilitated this new edition. We're especially endebted to Marion Castellucci, Senior Development Editor, for her splendid vision and disciplined leadership; we thank also Joe Opiela, Senior Vice President and Editorial Director for English. We greatly admire the work of Michael Montagna, a fellow faculty member, for reviewing, clarifying, and streamlining our grammar sections.

Doug values Lynn Troyka's vast knowledge, skill, dedication to teaching, and patience. He appreciates the support of all his colleagues in the writing program at the University of Denver, the knowledge and dedication embodied in the memberships of CCCC and WPA, and the hardworking team at Pearson. He further states, "My children, Monica, Andrew, and Paige, amaze me with their creativity, as does the very best writer I know: Becky Bradway, my wife."

Lynn wishes first to pay tribute to David Troyka, her beloved husband of 47 years, who inspired her to enjoy teaching and writing along with their amazing adventures in barely explored parts of the world. She thanks also her coauthor Doug Hesse for his gentle friendship while working on this newest edition of the *Quick Access Brief.* For their unwavering support and love, Lynn also thanks the following: Ida Morea, her steadfast friend and Administrative Assistant for 18 years; Kristen Black, her adored daughter, Dan Black, Kristen's superb husband and their delightful children Lindsey and Ryan; Bernice Joseph, her "adopted" sister and anchor of an amazing family: Mauricia Joseph, and Rachael and Eric Thomas, along with their gifted, enchanting children Nickyla, Nicholas, and Nehemiah; Lynn's "adopted" brother Douglas Young III, his wife Anna, and young "Little" Doug IV; Michael Burns and his wife, Janelle James; and her grand pals Alice, Melanie, Avery, Jimmy, Gitam, Susan, Rose, and Amanda.

Lynn Quitman Troyka
Doug Hesse

ABOUT THE AUTHORS

Lynn Quitman Troyka

Lynn Quitman Troyka, Adjunct Professor of English in the MA Program in Language and Literature at the City College (CCNY) of the City University of New York (CUNY), taught freshman English and basic writing for many years at Queensborough Community College. Dr. Troyka is a past chair of the Conference on College Composition and Communication (CCCC); the College Section of the National Council of Teachers of English (NCTE); and the Writing Division of the Modern Language Association (MLA). She has won many awards for teaching, scholarship, and service, and has conducted hundreds of faculty workshops about teaching writing and its relation to college-level reading.

"This information," says Dr. Troyka, "tells what I've done, not who I am. I am a teacher. Teaching is my life's work, and I love it."

Doug Hesse

Doug Hesse is Professor of English and Executive Director of Writing at the University of Denver, one of only thirty writing programs to receive the CCCC Certificate of Excellence. Dr. Hesse is a past chair of the CCCC, the nation's largest association of college writing instructors. A past president, as well, of the Council of Writing Program Administrators (WPA), Dr. Hesse edited *WPA: Writing Program Administration*. He has served on the NCTE executive committee, chaired the MLA Division on Teaching as a Profession, and served on the MLA Committee on Contingent Labor. Author of nearly sixty articles and book chapters, he has been named University Distinguished Scholar at the University of Denver.

"Of various awards I've received," says Dr. Hesse, "the one that matters most is Distinguished Humanities Teacher. That one came from my students and suggests that, in however small a way, I've mattered in their education and lives."

Part 1
Foundations for Writers

CHAPTERS
1–3

1 Ten Troublesome Mistakes Writers Make

■ ■ ■ ■ ■ ■

Quick Points You will learn to

➤ Recognize and correct ten common errors in writing.

MyWritingLab™ Visit mywritinglab.com for more resources on ten trouble-some mistakes writers make.

Ten troublesome mistakes tend to pop up frequently in college students' writing because students often forget what they learned years before. Most of these errors stand out more in written than in spoken English. If any of these ten errors gives you trouble, try to put aside some time right away to learn how to recognize and eliminate them. Later in this handbook, we include a full chapter on each error (see the chapter numbers in parentheses in Quick Box 1.1).

Quick Box 1.1   ■ ■ ■ ■ ■ ■

Ten troublesome mistakes in writing

1. Sentence fragments instead of complete sentences (see Chapter 21)
2. Comma-spliced sentences and run-on sentences (see Chapter 22)
3. Subject–verb disagreement (see Chapter 18)
4. Pronoun–antecedent disagreement (see Chapter 19, sections 19A–19E)
5. Pronoun references unclear (see Chapter 19, sections 19F–19I)
6. Sentences shift illogically (see Chapter 23)
7. Modifiers placed incorrectly (see Chapter 24)
8. Homonyms misused (see Chapter 29, section 29D)
9. Commas misused (see Chapter 30)
10. Apostrophes misused (see Chapter 33)

■ 1. Sentence fragments

A **sentence fragment** is a written mistake that looks like a sentence but isn't one. Even though it starts with a capital letter and ends with a period, it's not a sentence. It's only a group of words. Sentence fragments are commonly caused by four types of incomplete word groups. Chapter 21 lists them and shows how to turn them into complete sentences.

NO **When** companies show employees respect.

The fragment starts with *when*, a SUBORDINATING CONJUNCTION, and is only a group of words.

YES **When** companies show employees respect, the best workers rarely quit.

The fragment is joined with a complete sentence.

NO A positive working atmosphere most employees productive and happy.

The fragment lacks a VERB and is only a group of words.

YES A positive working atmosphere **keeps** most employees productive and happy.

Keeps, a verb, completes the sentence.

■ 2. Comma splices and run-on sentences

Comma splices and run-on sentences are written mistakes that look almost alike. A **comma-spliced sentence** uses only a comma between two complete sentences. A **run-on sentence** uses no punctuation between two complete sentences. These errors disappear with any one of three fixes: placing a period or semicolon between the two sentences; writing a CONJUNCTION* and any needed punctuation between the two sentences; or turning one of the sentences into a DEPENDENT CLAUSE. Chapter 22 explains how to identify and correct comma splices and run-on sentences.

COMMA SPLICES

NO Bad bosses quickly stand out in workplaces, they scream impatiently at everyone.

YES Bad bosses quickly stand out in workplaces. They scream impatiently at everyone.

A period replaces the comma, which corrects the error. A semicolon also works.

YES Bad bosses quickly stand out in workplaces, **for** they scream impatiently at everyone.

Inserting the COORDINATING CONJUNCTION *for* corrects the error.

YES Bad bosses quickly stand out in workplaces **because** they scream impatiently at everyone.

The SUBORDINATING CONJUNCTION *because* turns the second sentence into a dependent clause, which corrects the error. The comma is dropped.

---

*Words printed in SMALL CAPITAL LETTERS are discussed elsewhere in the text and are defined in the Terms Glossary at the back of the book.

YES   **Because** they scream impatiently at everyone, bad bosses quickly stand out in workplaces.

The SUBORDINATING CONJUNCTION *because* turns the second sentence into a dependent clause, which corrects the error. Now the dependent clause comes before the complete sentence, so the comma is retained.

RUN-ON SENTENCES

NO   Bad bosses quickly stand out in workplaces they scream impatiently at everyone.

YES   Bad bosses quickly stand out in workplaces. They scream impatiently at everyone.

A period or semicolon between the two sentences corrects the error.

YES   Bad bosses quickly stand out in workplaces, **for** they scream impatiently at everyone.

A comma and the COORDINATING CONJUNCTION *for* correct the error.

YES   Bad bosses quickly stand out in workplaces **because** they scream impatiently at everyone.

The SUBORDINATING CONJUNCTION *because* turns the second sentence into a dependent clause, which corrects the error.

YES   **Because** they scream impatiently at everyone, bad bosses quickly stand out in workplaces.

The SUBORDINATING CONJUNCTION *because* turns the second sentence into a dependent clause, which corrects the error. Now the dependent clause comes before the complete sentence and is followed by a comma.

■ 3. Mistakes in subject–verb agreement

A mistake in subject–verb agreement occurs when a VERB and its SUBJECT are mismatched, often within one sentence. This error, in written as well as spoken English, most often occurs when singulars and plurals are mixed incorrectly. Chapter 18 explains all causes of subject–verb agreement errors and how to correct them.

NO   **Effective leaders** in business **knows** how to motivate people to excel.

YES   **Effective leaders** in business **know** how to motivate people to excel.

The plural subject *Effective leaders* matches the plural verb *know*.

YES   **An effective leader** in business **knows** how to motivate people to excel.

The singular subject *Effective leader* matches the singular verb *knows*.

■ 4. Mistakes in pronoun–antecedent agreement

Pronoun–antecedent agreement errors occur when a PRONOUN and its ANTECEDENT are mismatched, usually because one is singular and the other plural. Errors in pronoun–antecedent agreement occur in written as well as spoken English. Chapter 19, sections 19A–19E, explains all causes of mistakes in pronoun–antecedent agreement and how to correct them.

NO My office partner admired my new computer **monitors** for **its** sleek design.

YES My office partner admired my new computer **monitors** for **their** sleek design.

The plural antecedent *monitors* matches the plural pronoun *their*.

YES My office partner admired my new computer **monitor** for **its** sleek design.

The singular subject *monitor* matches the singular pronoun *its*.

■ 5. Unclear pronoun reference

Unclear pronoun reference, in written as well as spoken English, occurs when the noun to which a pronoun—often *it, they, them*—refers is not obvious. Chapter 19, sections 19F–19I, describes the sentence structures that often lead to unclear pronoun reference problems and explains how to correct them.

NO The construction supervisors paid little attention to the bricklayers when **they** were distracted.

They is an unclear pronoun reference. Who is distracted, the *construction supervisors* or the *bricklayers*?

YES When the construction supervisors were distracted, **they** paid little attention to the bricklayers.

They clearly refers to the *construction supervisors*.

NO Experienced bricklayers waste little motion to preserve their energy so that they can finish an entire section of wall without taking a break. **This** creates a sturdy wall.

This is an unclear pronoun reference. Is the wall sturdy because the bricklayers wasted little motion to preserve their energy or because the bricklayers finished an entire section without taking a break?

YES So that the wall they build is sturdy, experienced bricklayers waste little motion to preserve their energy so that they can finish an entire wall section without taking a break.

This is eliminated when the revised sentence makes clear how bricklayers can create a sturdy wall.

■ 6. Illogical shifts within sentences

Illogical shifts within sentences are mistakes, in written as well as spoken English, that occur midsentence when a category of words, such as the verbs, changes form for no reason. All categories of words need to remain consistent within sentences as well as in groups of sentences. Chapter 23 shows how shifts create unclear writing and how they can be avoided.

> **NO**   Our union representative **explained** the new salary schedule and then **allows** time for questions.

> **YES**   Our union representative **explained** the new salary schedule and then **allowed** time for questions.

> **YES**   Our union representative **explains** the new salary schedule and then **allows** time for questions.

> In the correct sentences, both verbs are in the same tense, either PAST TENSE or PRESENT TENSE.

■ 7. Mistakes with modifiers

Mistakes with MODIFIERS are more obvious in written than spoken English. Such errors happen when a modifier is placed in a wrong spot in a sentence so that the meaning becomes muddled. Misplaced modifiers and dangling modifiers are two of four types of incorrect placements for modifiers. Chapter 24 explains all four and how to correct them.

MISPLACED MODIFIER

> **NO**   The consultant who observed our meeting **only** took notes with a pen.

> **YES**   The consultant who observed our meeting took notes **only** with a pen.

> The modifier *only* belongs with *pen* to clarify that nothing else was used to take notes.

> **NO**   The consultant took notes with a pen **sporting a large handlebar mustache**.

> **YES**   The consultant **sporting a large handlebar mustache** took notes with a pen.

> The mustache belongs to the consultant, not the pen.

DANGLING MODIFIER

> **NO**   Studying our company's budget projection, the numbers predicted bankruptcy.

> *Numbers* after the comma says that numbers can study.

> **YES**   Studying our company's budget projection, I saw that the numbers predicted bankruptcy.

> *I saw* after the comma says that a person is studying.

■ 8. Mistakes with homonyms

Homonyms are words that sound alike but have different meanings and spellings. Mistakes with homonyms are obvious in written English more than in spoken English. If you compile your own personal list of the homonyms that you habitually mix up, you can set aside time to master them so that you will avoid many errors. Chapter 29, section 29D, lists the homonym sets most frequently confused.

> **NO** **Its** important **too** lock **you're** office door and **right** a note **four** the guards if you have **all ready** turned off the heat.
>
> Simply to illustrate common homonym errors, we exaggerate how many show up in one sentence.

> **YES** **It's** important **to** lock **your** office door and **write** a note **for** the guards if you have **already** turned off the heat.

■ 9. Comma errors

Comma errors are written, not spoken, mistakes. Commas clarify meaning for readers, especially when a sentence contains both major and minor information. As a writer, resist the suggestion to insert a comma whenever you pause. After all, everyone speaks and thinks at different rates. This fact is particularly noticeable when people gather from different parts of the United States and Canada, or when a person's native language isn't English. Chapter 30 presents and explains all rules for comma use in written English.

We suggest that you copy and carry with you the major rules for using commas, listed in Quick Box 30.1 on pages 376–377. The more you refer to your list of rules, the more quickly you'll know it by heart. To help you start, here's a list you can master quite quickly—the five spots where a comma *never* belongs.

- Never after *such as* but before it, it's fine: *Our office staff enjoyed perks, **such as** free coffee, tea, and hot chocolate.*

- Never before *than* in a comparison: *That company's truck was safer **than** ours.*

- Never between a subject and verb written close together. *Our **company offers** a generous sick leave policy.*

- Never immediately after a subordinating conjunction. ***Because** I developed a nasty cold, I left work early.*

- Never before an opening parentheses; fine after a closing one: *Although some of us always route our phone calls to voicemail **(we don't like constant interruptions)**, our supervisor strongly disapproves.*

2A

■ **10. Apostrophe errors**

Apostrophe errors are written, not spoken, mistakes. Apostrophes serve only two purposes: they indicate possession (*the president's car*), and they indicate missing letters in contractions (*isn't* for *is not*). Chapter 33 explains all uses of the apostrophe and how to avoid errors with them.

NO   The main **office's** are closed for the evening.

YES   The main **offices** are closed for the evening.

Apostrophes never create plural words.

NO   The security guard **patrol's** the building every hour.

YES   The security guard **patrols** the building every hour.

Apostrophes are never involved with verbs.

NO   The security guards **do'nt** need dogs to help them.

YES   The security guards **don't** need dogs to help them.

If you write a contraction, place an apostrophe only where a letter is omitted.

2 Thinking Critically
■ ■ ■ ■ ■ ■

Quick Points   You will learn to

➤ Use critical thinking when examining ideas (section 2A).
➤ Recognize and use the logical, ethical, and emotional appeals (p. 10).
➤ Reason inductively and deductively (pp. 11–13).
➤ Recognize logical fallacies (pp. 14–16).

MyWritingLab™ Visit mywritinglab.com for more resources on thinking critically.

2A   How do I engage in critical thinking?

Thinking isn't something people choose to do, any more than fish choose to live in water. To be human is to think. Thinking comes naturally. **Critical thinking** means you deliberately think about your thinking by asking yourself the questions in Quick Box 2.1.

Quick Box 2.1

■ ■ ■ ■ ■ ■

Questions critical thinkers ask themselves

- Do I insist on hearing "the whole story," not just one point of view?
- Do I insist on factual accuracy?
- Do I resist easy solutions that are being pushed at me?
- Do I remain open to ideas that don't fit with what I'm used to believing?
- Do I insist on clarity when confronted with vague language?
- Do I resist being hurried to make up my mind?

The word *critical* here has a neutral meaning. It doesn't mean taking a negative view or finding fault, as when someone criticizes another person. Critical thinking requires time because you need to pause and reflect on your thoughts. For a systematic process when you encounter new ideas or want to reexamine familiar ideas more deeply, use the four-step sequence of the critical reading process described in Quick Box 2.2.

Quick Box 2.2

■ ■ ■ ■ ■ ■

Steps in the critical thinking process

1. **Summarize.** Whenever you encounter ideas, first make sure you understand them. Check yourself by restating the ideas accurately and objectively. Add nothing. Resist inserting your feelings or opinion into your summary.

2. **Analyze.** Break ideas into their component parts. Figure out how each part contributes to the overall meaning. Think about what is implied by the ideas.

3. **Synthesize.** Use your summary from Step 1 and analysis from Step 2 to connect to other ideas or perspectives that you have encountered. Consider other ideas you've learned, thought about, and/or experienced. Synthesizing is a recursive activity that often circles back on itself. Give yourself time to do this.

4. **Evaluate.** Form an early judgment about the ideas, knowing you need to take time to reach a final conclusion. As you do so, remain resolutely open-minded about others' points of view, avoiding **biases** and prejudices you might have accepted without question before.

2B   How do the rhetorical appeals help me think critically?

Rhetoric is the art and skill of speaking and writing effectively. If you understand three central principles of rhetoric—the persuasive appeals— you can greatly enhance your ability to think critically. Today, these appeals extend far beyond persuasion. They turn up in most material you read, see in movies and on television and the Internet, and in everyday life. For examples of these three principles in action, see the student essays in Chapters 7 through 11 in this handbook: Each shows extensive, hands-on applications of rhetorical appeals. Often the three are called by their Greek names: *logos*, meaning logic; *ethos*, meaning credibility; and *pathos*, meaning empathy or compassion. To recognize them in action and to use them in your writing, see Quick Box 2.3.

Quick Box 2.3   ■ ■ ■ ■ ■ ■

Three central principles of rhetoric: the persuasive appeals

- **Use the logical appeal** (*logos*) to evoke a rational response:
  - Demonstrate sound reasoning.
  - Define terms.
  - Give accurate facts, statistics, and evidence.
  - Use relevant quotations from experts and authorities.

- **Use the ethical appeal** (*ethos*) to evoke confidence in your credibility, reliability, and trustworthiness:
  - Show respect by using appropriate language and tone.
  - Show that you are fair-minded and open to a variety of perspectives.
  - Be well informed and sincere.
  - Give reliable information (see Chapter 12).

- **Use the emotional appeal** (*pathos*) to evoke empathy and compassion:
  - Add a sense of humanity and reality.
  - Appeal to hearts more than minds, but never manipulate.
  - Communicate values that call on one's "better self."
  - Use descriptive language and concrete details to create mental pictures.
  - Never use biased or slanted language (see Chapter 28).

2C   How do inductive and deductive reasoning help me think critically?

Inductive reasoning moves from the specific to the general. In contrast, **deductive reasoning** moves from the general to the specific. Taken together, these two major reasoning processes can help you think critically by distinguishing sound reasoning from faulty reasoning.

■ Inductive reasoning

Inductive reasoning moves from specific, explicit facts or instances to broad general principles. For example, suppose at the Registry of Motor Vehicles closest to your home you stand in line for 2 hours to renew your driver's license. A few months later, you return to the same location to get new license plates and again stand in a 2-hour line. You conclude that all offices of the Registry of Motor Vehicles serve the public inefficiently. Your conclusion is based on inductive reasoning, from your specific experiences of being in line for 2 hours twice.

As a critical thinker, you need to ask whether the conclusion is an absolute truth. It is not. The conclusion is only a statement of probability. After all, perhaps the Registry of Motor Vehicles office farthest from your home is so well run that no one ever stands in line for more than 10 minutes. Therefore, inductive reasoning is based on probability, not absolute truth. Quick Box 2.4 lists the characteristics of inductive reasoning.

Quick Box 2.4   ■ ■ ■ ■ ■ ■

Features of inductive reasoning

- Inductive reasoning begins with specific **evidence**—facts, observations, or experiences—and moves to a general conclusion.

- Inductive reasoning is based on a sampling of facts, not on the whole universe of related facts.

- The advantage of inductive reasoning is that you can speculate on the unknown based on what's known.

- The conclusions in inductive reasoning are considered reliable or unreliable, but never true or false.

■ Deductive reasoning

Deductive reasoning moves from general claims, called premises, to a specific conclusion. The three-part structure of two premises and a conclusion is known as a **syllogism**.

PREMISE 1	Students who don't study fail Professor Sanchez's exams.
PREMISE 2	My friend didn't study.
CONCLUSION	My friend failed Professor Sanchez's exams.

Premises in syllogism can be facts or **assumptions**. Assumptions need close scrutiny because they're statements assumed to be true but with no concrete evidence to support them. Because some assumptions are based on incorrect information, a critical thinker needs to evaluate each premise carefully.

The conclusion in a syllogism is judged to be either valid or invalid. When the conclusion logically follows from the premises, a deductive argument is valid. When the conclusion doesn't logically follow from the premises, a deductive argument is invalid.

VALID—DEDUCTIVE REASONING EXAMPLE 1

PREMISE 1	When it snows, the streets get wet. [fact]
PREMISE 2	It is snowing. [fact]
CONCLUSION	Therefore, the streets are getting wet. [valid]

INVALID—DEDUCTIVE REASONING EXAMPLE 2

PREMISE 1	When it snows, the streets get wet. [fact]
PREMISE 2	The streets are getting wet. [fact]
CONCLUSION	Therefore, it is snowing. [invalid]

Deductive argument 2 is invalid because even though the two premises are facts, the conclusion is wrong because the streets can be wet for many reasons such as rain, street-cleaning trucks that spray water, or people washing their cars.

INVALID—DEDUCTIVE REASONING EXAMPLE 3

PREMISE 1	Learning a new language takes hard work.
PREMISE 2	Nicholas has learned to speak Spanish.
CONCLUSION	Nicholas worked hard to learn Spanish.

Deductive argument 3 is invalid because it rests on a wrong assumption: not everyone has to work hard to learn a new language; some people—for example, young children—learn new languages easily.

As a critical thinker, whenever you encounter an assumption, either stated or unstated, you need to check whether it's true. If it isn't, the reasoning is flawed. Quick Box 2.5 lists the characteristics of deductive reasoning.

Quick Box 2.5

■ ■ ■ ■ ■ ■

Features of deductive reasoning

- Deductive reasoning moves from the general to the specific. Its three-part structure, called a syllogism, consists of two premises and a conclusion drawn from them.

- Deductive reasoning is valid if its conclusion follows logically from its premises.

- In deductive reasoning, the conclusion can be judged either true or false: If both premises are true, the conclusion is true. If either premise is false, the conclusion is false.

- Deductive reasoning is based on what a person already knows, so it doesn't yield new information.

- The advantage of deductive reasoning is it builds a stronger argument than inductive reasoning because its conclusions can be either true or false.

● **EXERCISE 2-1**   Determine whether each conclusion here is valid or invalid. Be ready to explain your answers. For help, consult section 2C.

1. Faddish clothes are expensive.

   This shirt is expensive.

   This shirt must be part of a fad.

2. When a storm is threatening, small-craft warnings are issued.

   A storm is threatening.

   Small-craft warnings will be issued.

3. The Pulitzer Prize is awarded to outstanding literary works.

   The Great Gatsby never won a Pulitzer Prize.

   The Great Gatsby isn't an outstanding literary work.

4. All states send representatives to the United States Congress.

   Puerto Rico sends a representative to the United States Congress.

   Puerto Rico is a state.

5. Finding a good job requires patience.

   Sherrill is patient.

   Sherrill will find a good job. ●

2D   How do I avoid logical fallacies to think critically?

Logical fallacies are statements with defective reasoning based on irrational ideas. Critical thinkers want to avoid them. Many logical fallacies aren't obvious. Critical thinking calls for analyzing statements carefully to make sure they're not based on logical fallacies. Unfortunately, many people use logical fallacies intentionally to sway audiences toward certain actions or beliefs. This often happens in debates, on public blogs, in newspaper editorials, on radio talk shows, in advertisements, in political speeches, in informal conversations, and in dozens of others places. To avoid falling prey to the thought manipulations of logical fallacies, study the list in Quick Box 2.6 and the longer explanations that follow.

Quick Box 2.6   ■ ■ ■ ■ ■ ■

Common logical fallacies

FALLACIES THAT USE SHORT-SIGHTED THINKING

Either-or thinking: X and Y are the only choices.

False analogy: X and Y are completely different, but A claims they're alike.

False cause: X always causes Y, with no exceptions.

Hasty generalization: All As are the same, with no exceptions.

Stereotyping: Because A was born in B, A is no good.

FALLACIES THAT USE DISTRACTIONS

Attacking the person: A is a sloppy dresser, so A's opinions are worthless.

Bandwagon effect: A does it, so we all can do it.

Begging the question: A avoids the topic by repeating it in different words.

False authority: A is a celebrity, so A is an expert on all topics.

Irrelevant argument: What A says has nothing to do with the topic.

Red herring: A uses an emotional topic to distract everyone from the main topic.

Slippery slope: If A does one thing wrong, A will surely progress to doing much worse things.

- **Attacking the person**: Criticizing a person's appearance, personal life, or conduct instead of dealing with the merits of the individual's opinion. Example: *If Senator Williams had children of his own, he'd understand why we oppose his support of a proposed law to give short prison sentences to child abusers.* This is a fallacy because even if the man were a parent, he might still support the proposed law. (This fallacy has a Latin name: *ad hominem*, meaning "attacking a man's character rather than his argument.")

- **The bandwagon effect:** Asserting that something is right because everyone else is doing it. Example: *"Why can't we go to tonight's rap concert? All our friends are going."* This is a fallacy because "going along with the crowd" isn't a reason to justify an action. (This fallacy has a Latin name: *ad populum*, meaning "appeal to popularity.")

- **Begging the question**, also called **circular reasoning:** Restating the main issue using supporting reasons for it, instead of focusing on the main issue itself. Example: *We shouldn't increase our workers' salaries because then our payroll would be larger.* This is a fallacy because "increased salaries" means the same thing as "a larger payroll"; the issue is whether the workers deserve larger salaries or whether the company can afford to pay larger salaries.

- **Either-or thinking**, also called **false dilemma:** Limiting choices to only two alternatives when more exist. Example: *Either stop criticizing our president or move to another country.* This is a fallacy because these two extremes aren't the only options in democratic countries where people are free to criticize elected officials.

- **False analogy:** Claiming that two ideas or items are alike when they're more different than similar. Example: *If we can put someone on the moon, we should be able to find a cure for cancer.* This is a fallacy because space science is very different from biological science.

- **False authority:** Accepting the opinion of someone who isn't an expert on the topic. Example: *I want to wear XYZ running shoes because my favorite comedian says they're the best.* This is a fallacy because comedians aren't experts about running shoes; in our society, celebrities receive large sums of money to endorse products they know nothing about.

- **False cause:** Asserting that one event leads to another when the two events aren't related, even though they might happen at the same time. Example: *After we opened the new municipal park, the city's crime rate increased.* This is a fallacy because crime rates can rise for many reasons, including joblessness and gang activity. (This fallacy has a Latin name: *post hoc, ergo propter hoc*, meaning "after this, therefore because of this.")

- **Hasty generalization:** Drawing conclusions based on insufficient evidence. Example: *All college students leave bad tips at restaurants.* This is a fallacy because some students leave proper tips.

- **Irrelevant argument:** Using unrelated information to form a conclusion. Example: *Ms. Chu is a forceful speaker, so she will be an outstanding mayor.* This is a fallacy because Ms. Chu's speaking style does not reflect her administrative abilities. (This fallacy has a Latin name: *non sequitur*, meaning the premise doesn't support the conclusion.)

- **Red herring:** Sidetracking attention to an issue by bringing up unrelated issues to distract people from thinking about the core issue. Example: *Why worry about the homeless when we should really be concerned with global warming?* This is a fallacy because the topic of global warming is introduced to divert attention from the issue of the problem of homelessness.

- **Slippery slope assumption:** Believing that one small first step will inevitably lead to a chain of related actions that will terminate in a significant event. Example: *Anyone who shoplifts will soon turn to more serious crimes and eventually become a murderer.* This is a fallacy because shoplifters don't always continue to commit crimes and become murderers.

- **Stereotyping:** Holding close-minded notions about people, beliefs, or ideas based on race, religions, philosophies, etc.: *Everyone who belongs to religion X hates to dance.* This is a fallacy because (a) "everyone" excludes even one exception, and (b) "hatred" is an emotion, not part of a religious philosophy.

● **EXERCISE 2-2**   Following are comments posted to a newspaper Web site. Do a critical analysis of each, paying special attention to logical fallacies.

1. I oppose the plan to convert the abandoned railroad tracks into a bicycle trail. Everyone knows that the only reason the mayor wants to do this is so that she and her wealthy friends can have a new place to play. No one I know likes this plan, and if they did, it would probably be because they're part of the wine and cheese set, too. The next thing you know, the mayor will be proposing that we turn the schools into art museums or the park into a golf course. If you're working hard to support a family, you don't have time for this bike trail nonsense. And if you're not working hard, I don't have time for you.

   —Mike1218

2. I encourage everyone to support the bicycle trail project. Good recreation facilities are the key to the success of any community. Since the bike trail will add more recreation opportunities, it will guarantee the success of our town. Remember that several years ago our neighbors over in Springfield decided not to build a new park, and look what happened to their economy, especially that city's high unemployment rate. We can't afford to let the same thing happen to us. People who oppose this plan are narrow-minded, selfish, and almost unpatriotic. As that great patriot John Paul Jones said, "I have not yet begun to fight."

   —Bikerdude ●

3 Reading Critically

■ ■ ■ ■ ■ ■

Quick Points You will learn to

➤ Use the critical reading process (see below).
➤ Use techniques for close, active reading (see pp. 19–20).
➤ Read images critically (see pp. 20–22).

MyWritingLab™ Visit mywritinglab.com for more resources on reading critically.

3A How do I read written material critically?

Reading critically is similar to thinking critically: you take time to think about what the reading says as well as what it implies. You do this while you're engaged in reading but mostly after you finish reading, whether you pause to consider a particular passage or all the material. Here are four steps you might use as you engage with written material. They are parallel to the steps suggested for critical thinking in Chapter 2.

STEPS IN THE CRITICAL READING PROCESS

1. **Summarize** the material by looking for its **literal meaning**, sometimes called reading "on the line." You absorb what the words say, no more, and resist adding your own thoughts or feelings. This takes disciplined practice because you need to resist the common reaction of wanting immediately to debate material or jump to conclusions. (One challenging way to see how well you read for literal meaning is to choose and read a newspaper article with a friend. Then tell each other exactly what it says to see whether you can filter out your own reactions.)

2. **Analyze** the material by thinking about its **implied meaning**, sometimes called "reading between the lines" by thinking about what the writer hopes you'll infer from the material. Thinking about inferences requires time for reflection so that you can examine why you think what you do about the material. To do this, you'll need to re-read the material, ideally allowing time to pass between readings because you'll see that you sometimes revise your initial inferences after thinking critically about them. Here are some features to look for:

- Does the writer make assumptions that you're expected to accept as true without proof? If so, do you resist them and decide what this implies about the material and about you as a reader?

- Does the writer clearly differentiate between opinions and facts? If not, what does this imply about the quality of the writer's thinking and of the material?

- Does the writer assert strong viewpoints without any support? In the writer's choice of words and examples, do you discern prejudice toward certain groups of people or particular ideas or actions? If so, what does this imply about the reliability of the writer and the material?

- Does the TONE of the writer's words suggest respect for you as a reader? Is the writer's choice of words suited to the material: a more formal tone when the content is serious and weighty but a less formal tone when the content is relatively more informal and conversational? If not, what does this imply about the writer's attitudes and credibility?

(An effective way to examine and solidify your inferences is to share and debate them with others because people frequently disagree about the inferences they make from a reading. Talking them through has a clarifying effect, although you still might not agree on all points.)

3. **Synthesize** your reading by associating it with other material you have read, thought about, and experienced. This is sometimes called "reading beyond the lines." Now is your chance to move freely from the material's literal and inferential meaning to allow yourself to connect any new thoughts or ideas you discovered from reading the material to ones you already have. (One way to increase the richness of this experience is by sharing your synthesis with others who have read the same material. Being forced to articulate your ideas and thoughts so that others understand them, and listening to the thinking of others, can stimulate and expand your synthesis.)

4. **Evaluate** the material by forming an opinion about it or by exploring your subjective, personal response to it. Note that evaluation is the final step in critical reading, which means that you resist forming an opinion about what you have read until you have systematically summarized, analyzed, and synthesized the material. This takes mental discipline because people often reject or embrace an idea before they truly examine it critically.

3B   How do I read closely and actively as a critical reader?

Reading closely and actively involves writing notes to yourself as you read. Brain studies show that the act of annotating anchors written material in the mind of the reader. When readers read print on paper with pen or pencil in hand, they absorb and remember far more of the material than if they only read it. You might first prefer to read through the material without annotating it and then immediately go back and make your annotations.

Specifically, **close reading** means jotting down notes on key content; **active reading** means jotting down notes on the reader's thoughts and reactions. Figure 3.1 shows a reading selection on which a student reader has used lowercase letters for close reading (content notes) and ALL-CAPITAL LETTERS for active reading (notes of personal thoughts and reactions). Using two styles keeps your annotations differentiated from each other. Besides cementing the information more firmly in your mind, the major bonus from these activities is when you re-read the material, you can easily find the sections that were important to you the first time—and you can then decide whether to change your mind or confirm your thinking.

Figure 3.1   A student's annotations on a Web page showing close and active reading.

WHY & WHATEVER
BLOG

ACTIVE READING (CAPITAL LETTERS)

Close reading (lowercase letters)

important fact: car crashes when driver is using a phone, 3 times as likely.

Ever explain to an 18-year-old **WHY** it's dangerously distracting to use a cell phone while driving? And then to a 40-year-old? Turns out, in my admittedly limited sample, that both teens and adults say they know the risks but—and here's the surprise—they insist they are the exceptions who can handle cell phones safely while driving. Most have heard about the National Highway Traffic Safety Administration (NHTSA) study that shows "visual-manual tasks associated with <u>hand-held phones and other portable devices increased the risk of getting into a crash by three times</u>" (www.distraction.gov, April 2013). **WHATEVER** is it that allows magical thinking to override reality? I always thought that we live in a rational society, but I'm changing my mind: most people prefer to dwell in their cocoons of fairy-tale thinking, certain nothing bad will happen to them or their loved ones.

← DRIVERS WHO TALK ON CELL PHONES SCARE ME!!

← WILL WE EVER UNDERSTAND PEOPLE'S STUPIDITY?

With print material, if you do not want to write in or on printed material, you can create a "Double Entry Notebook": draw a line to create three columns on a notebook page; use the first column on the left to write the title, page, or section of what you are reading; the middle column for close reading (content notes); and the right column for active reading (notes of personal thoughts and reactions). Don't expect to fill all columns; simply write notes when you think the material is significant.

For electronic material, you have choices: you can print the material and write on the printout; you can create a "Double Entry Notebook" as described in the previous paragraph; you can activate a computer program that lets you write in comment clouds, attached sticky notes, comment columns, and so on.

● **EXERCISE 3-1**   Decide which of the following statements are facts and which are opinions. For help, consult section 3A.

1. The fast food industry pays the minimum wage to a higher proportion of its workers than any other American industry.

—Eric Schlosser, *Fast Food Nation*

2. Grief, when it comes, is nothing we expect it to be.

—Joan Didion, *The Year of Living Dangerously*

3. A mind is a terrible thing to waste.

—United Negro College Fund

4. In 1927, F. E. Tylcote, an English physician, reported in the medical journal *Lancet* that in almost every case of lung cancer he had seen or known about, the patient smoked.

—William Ecenbarger, "The Strange History of Tobacco"

5. A critical task for all of the world's religions and spiritual traditions is to enrich the vision—and the reality—of the sense of community among us.

—Joel D. Beversluis, *A Sourcebook for Earth's Community of Religions* ●

3C   How do I "read" images critically?

Images surround us—in publications, on computer screens, on smart phones. You can "read" images critically in the same way that you can read critically (see Quick Box 2.2 and section 3A). As you study the following list, look at Figure 3.2.

Summarize: On a literal level, you can see—at a minimum—a street full of older houses with modern skyscrapers in the distance.

Figure 3.2   Images help us think visually.

Analyze: Make inferences to "read between the lines" to see that it's fairly rich with layers of meaning. You can think about the meanings conveyed by the condition of the houses versus those of the modern buildings, or about the lives of the people who live and work in each place. You can focus on the message of the comparative sizes of the houses and skyscrapers; on the contrast between this street and those you imagine at the base of the skyscrapers; on why the photographer chose this perspective; on how different captions might give the picture different meanings. For example, consider the difference between three different captions: "Progress," "Inequality," or "The Neighborhood."

Synthesize to associate "beyond the lines" to other photographs as well as other artworks you've seen, your reading, and your experiences. This imparts deeper, more richly complex connections to your thoughts about the photograph.

Evaluate the quality and impact of the message of the photograph. Resist evaluating prematurely because by going through the earlier steps of thinking and reading critically, your evaluation becomes informed by more than a noncritical personal reaction such as "I like the picture" or "I don't like the picture."

In "reading" a visual critically, you might start by speaking of how the visual "struck" you at first glance and then narrating how it did or did not gain depth of meaning as you drew inferences and engaged in synthesis within the realms of your personal experience and education.

● **EXERCISE 3-2** Use critical thinking to consider the photograph in Figure 3.3. Write either informal notes or a mini-essay, according to what your instructor requires. Refer to section 3C to generate your summary, analysis, synthesis, and evaluation of the photograph(s).

Figure 3.3 Photo of barrels in a natural setting.

Part 2
Writing Processes

CHAPTERS
4–6

4 Ten Steps for Writing Essays

4A

Quick Points   You will learn to

- ➤ Adapt writing processes for yourself (see 4A).
- ➤ Think like a writer (see 4B).
- ➤ Decide each essay's purpose and audience (see 4C).
- ➤ Plan a writing portfolio (see 4D).
- ➤ Develop ideas about your topic (see 4E).
- ➤ Use a thesis statement to help you plan (see 4F).
- ➤ Use outlining to help you plan (see 4G).
- ➤ Get started on a first draft (see 4H).
- ➤ Revise effectively (see 4I).
- ➤ Edit and proofread effectively (see 4J).

My WritingLab™   Visit mywritinglab.com for more resources on writing essays.

This chapter explains ten steps for writing an essay. They're designed to be flexible so that you can adjust the order according to your needs for each different writing assignment.

4A   How do I adapt writing processes for myself?

Many people assume that a real writer can magically write a finished product, word by perfect word. Experienced writers know that each piece of writing is a process, a series of activities that starts the moment they begin thinking about a topic and ends when they complete a final draft. All writers adapt their **writing processes** to suit their personalities as well as the special demands of the different writing projects they undertake. For the usual major stages in the writing process, see Quick Box 4.1. Although the steps are listed separately, few real writers work in lockstep order. They know that the steps overlap and double back on themselves, as the circles and arrows in Figure 4.1 show.

Figure 4.1   Visualizing the writing process.

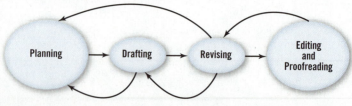

Quick Box 4.1

The writing process

- **Planning** means you think like a writer (see 4B); determine your purpose and audience (see 4C); plan a writing portfolio (see 4D); develop ideas about your topic (see 4E); compose a tentative thesis statement (see 4F); consider using an outline (see 4G).

- **Drafting** means you write a first pass by composing your ideas into sentences and paragraphs (see 4H).

- **Revising** means you rewrite your drafts, often more than once, for the purpose of expanding and/or tightening them; rearranging and/or deleting parts; checking that you've stayed on your topic; and perhaps drafting needed new material (see 4I).

- **Editing** means you check for the correctness of your surface-level features, including grammar, spelling, punctuation, and mechanics. **Proofreading** means you carefully scrutinize your final draft to fix typing errors and missing/repeated small words (see 4J).

What is the major difference between weak writers and successful ones? The good ones refuse to give up. Good writing takes time. We urge you to be patient with yourself. Remember that experienced writers sometimes struggle with ideas that are difficult to express, sentences that won't take shape, and words that aren't precise. When that becomes frustrating, they put their writing aside for a while, do something unrelated to writing, and return with the "new eyes" that only distance makes available.

4B   How do I think like a writer?

Writers begin by thinking the way writers do. They engage in the habits of mind of effective writers, as explained in Quick Box 4.2.

Quick Box 4.2

How to think like a writer

Think *by Engaging in Writers' Habits of Mind*
  - Realize that writing takes time.
  - Know that writing requires focused attention free of distractions.
  - Recognize that all writing involves rewriting, often many times (see 4I).

continued >>

4B

Quick Box 4.2   Think Like a Writer (continued)   ■ ■ ■ ■ ■ ■

- Believe that the physical act of writing helps fresh ideas spring to mind (see 4E).
- Think critically (see Chapter 2).

Think *by Completely Understanding Each Task at Hand*

- Read writing assignments completely. Then reread them.
- Approximate the length of a suitable final draft.
- Estimate how long you'll need for
  - Planning (see 4C, 4E, 4F, and 4G)
  - Drafting (see 4H)
  - Revising (see 4I)
  - Editing (see 4J)
  - Proofreading (see 4J)
- Calculate and set aside the total time you'll need to complete the assignment.
- Find out if you need to plan for a writing portfolio.

Think *About Your Topic*

- Does your assignment state a topic explicitly? If so, focus on it exclusively without going off the topic.
- Does your assignment give a general topic and expect you to think of a suitable subtopic? If so, make sure your chosen topic isn't too broad or too narrow:

GENERAL TOPIC	Marriage
TOO BROAD	What makes a successful marriage?
TOO NARROW	Couples can go to a municipal hall to get married.
JUST RIGHT	Compromise is vital for a happy marriage.

- Does your assignment say you're free to choose an essay topic? If so, think of one suitable for academic writing.

  - Topic needs to demonstrate your intellectual and writing abilities.
  - Topic needs sufficient specific details to back up each general statement.

Think *About Typical Purposes for Your Writing (see 4C)*

Think *About the Audience for Your Writing (see 4C)*

Think *of Ways to Develop Your Topic (see 4E)*

Think *About Your Thesis Statement (see 4F)*

Consider *Outlining (see 4G)*

4C How do I decide on the purpose and audience for each essay?

■ Purpose

Behind each writing project lies the reason, or **purpose**, for its being undertaken. Purposes for writing vary, and each makes its own demands on the writer. This handbook includes six full chapters of targeted discussions about different writing purposes, as listed in Quick Box 4.3. Each chapter explores its purpose in depth, offers ways to imagine your probable audience, presents a suggested essay frame along with sentence and/or paragraph guides, and gives a complete annotated student essay.

4C

Quick Box 4.3 ■ ■ ■ ■ ■ ■

Typical purposes for writing

- **To narrate** something about your life or ideas that's worth knowing (see Chapter 7)

- **To give information** (see Chapter 8)

- **To analyze** a text (see Chapter 11)

- **To argue or persuade**
  - In favor of a point of view on a debatable issue (see Chapter 9)
  - In favor of a proposal or a solution to a problem (see Chapter 10)

- **To evaluate** the quality of a text, object, individual, or event

---

 ESOL Tip: If you're from another culture, you might be surprised—even offended—by the directness with which people speak and write in the United States. If so, we hope you'll read our open letter to multilingual writers that introduces Part Six in this handbook. We want you to know how much we honor your native culture. Some cultures might expect writing to contain elaborate, ceremonial language, or to introduce your central point in an essay's middle, or to engage in tactful and indirect discussions. However, when you write for U.S. readers, you need to adapt to U.S. writing style, which is direct and straightforward, as the annotated essays in Chapters 7 to 11 in this handbook demonstrate. ●

■ Audience

The **audience** for your writing are your readers. In planning and writing each essay, the more specifically you can imagine who your readers will be, the more likely your chances for engaging their attention. To begin constructing a portrait of your probable readers, try the ideas listed in Quick Box 4.4.

Quick Box 4.4

Ways to imagine your audience

- **Their level of knowledge.** Do your readers have a general idea of your topic, to the extent that nonspecialized educated readers might? Or are your readers specialists in your topic? The answer influences the level of information you provide in your essay.

- **Their interests.** How interested or uninterested in your topic are your readers likely to be? Can you assume your readers are probably enthusiastic about it, resistant to it, or open to it? The answer influences the techniques you use for discussing your topic.

- **Their beliefs.** Do your readers probably agree or disagree with your point of view, or have no opinion about it? The answer influences the degree to which you need to try to convince your readers to change their minds about a debatable topic.

- **Their backgrounds.** Which background characteristics are important to consider in relation to your topic and the purpose you want to achieve with your writing? How much shared background do you have with them?
  - Age, gender, economic situation, ethnic origin?
  - Roles in life, such as student, instructor, business owner, worker, parent, voter, veteran, property owner, etc.?
  - Interests or hobbies?

- **Relation to you.** Are your readers your personal friends, family, coworkers, and others you know? Or are they strangers in whom you want to build trust about your credibility, reliability, and accuracy in presenting your topic (see ETHICAL APPEAL* in 2B)? The answer influences the LEVEL OF FORMALITY in the language (see 4I) you use in presenting your material.

ESOL Tip: If the cultural background of your readers differs from yours, you might find it difficult to estimate how much your readers know about your topic. To get a better idea of your readers' backgrounds, you might browse for information on the Internet or discuss your topic with people who might know more than you do about your readers' backgrounds. ●

---

*Words printed in SMALL CAPITAL LETTERS are discussed elsewhere in the text and are defined in the Terms Glossary at the back of the book.

YOUR INSTRUCTOR AS AUDIENCE

Of course, one specific audience for your college writing is always your instructor (and often your peers, as discussed later). The instructor who gave you a particular writing assignment plays three roles:

- As a stand-in for readers with general or specialized knowledge of your topic
- As your writing coach with experience in guiding students to write well
- As the evaluator of your final draft

Instructors expect each writing project to show that the students took serious time to go through their writing process deliberately and respectfully, even though your teachers know that few students are experienced writers or experts on their topics. Instructors recognize a minimal effort at once.

Be careful never to assume that your instructor will mentally fill in information you haven't taken the time to write about. You're expected to delve deeply into your topic, develop it beyond its obvious, bare-bones basics, and write about it fully.

YOUR PEER-RESPONSE GROUP AS AUDIENCE

A PEER-RESPONSE GROUP consists of other students in your class. Many writing classes today assign peer groups to gather together and react to each others' writing. Participating in a peer-response group makes you part of a respected academic tradition of colleagues helping colleagues. Professional writers often seek comments from other writers to improve their rough drafts. In many business areas, final drafts almost always emerge after many people have shared their thoughts and ideas.

As a member of a peer-response group in a college writing course, you're expected to offer your peers as thorough and specific responses as you can. The guidelines in Chapter 55 can help you do this.

4D How do I plan a writing portfolio?

Many instructors require a **writing portfolio** from each student, so it's wise to plan for it from the beginning of each writing course. To do so, keep all writing you've done in response to all your assignments, including any drafts commented on during your writing process as well as your final papers and exams. Throw away nothing. Date each item. If you work on more than one computer, carry and clearly label a thumb drive set aside expressly for collecting your writing.

A writing portfolio can be paper or digital, depending on your instructor's requirements. A **paper portfolio** consists of your writings collected in a folder or a binder. A **digital portfolio** is like a paper one but in electronic format. It can contain links between—and within—individual texts. Your digital portfolio might be an upload from your work into an online course management program, such as BlackBoard. More sophisticated digital portfolios involve your own design efforts, including images, sounds, and video. For more specific advice about how to create a writing portfolio, see Quick Box 4.5.

4D

Most writing portfolios include a self-reflection essay or letter. Feel free to use the first person ("I") since it's about you as a writer. Here are guidelines for such an essay.

1. Start with a paragraph in which you introduce yourself as a writer and state the criteria for selecting the writings you've used in your portfolio.

2. Compose a set of body paragraphs in which you give the title and date to refer in exact date sequence to each separate piece of writing in your portfolio. Explain why you chose to include it.

Quick Box 4.5

■ ■ ■ ■ ■

How to create a writing portfolio

1. Choose your writing for inclusion according your instructor's directions. Here are three typical portfolio assignments.

   - "Present three works that best display your strengths as a writer." (Here, you want to choose writings that display the range of your abilities.)

   - "Create a portfolio of three works that demonstrates how you're able to write for different AUDIENCES and PURPOSES." (Here, you want to choose examples that respond to more than one **writing situation** and one FRAME.)

   - "Select four examples of your writing from this semester that demonstrate how your writing has developed." (Here, you want to show that you've improved over the semester, so you might choose writings from the beginning, middle, and end of the course. Alternatively, you might choose a few examples of the same paper in early and revised drafts.)

2. Write an essay or letter of self-reflection in response to your specific portfolio assignment and by using the suggestions in section 4D.

3. List all the items in your portfolio with page numbers for your instructor's reference.

   - Write a page number in the upper right corner on each sheet of paper, to conform to the list of items.

   - Enter the date of each piece of writing.

4. Use an appealing format.

3. Write a paragraph, either here or before item 2 in this list, that discusses how you as a writer have evolved (or have not evolved) during the course.

4. Conclude with a paragraph to wrap up your self-reflection. You might also mention your future goals for yourself as a writer.

Here is an excerpt from a reflective essay for a portfolio.

EXCERPT FROM A REFLECTIVE ESSAY

During the 2013 fall semester, I completed five papers in English 101, revising each of them several times based on responses from my peers and feedback from my instructor. In the beginning, I was very frustrated. I was getting low grades, but I had been told in high school my writing was excellent. After a few weeks, I came to realize my critical thinking about our topics was too superficial and my peers didn't always understand what I thought was clear in my writing. I'm leaving this course with more confidence as a writer, based on the strengths the three papers in this portfolio demonstrate.

One quality apparent in these papers is my ability to adjust writings for different audiences, both academic and general. For example, "Analyzing the Merits of Organic Produce" addresses academic readers, specifically members of the scientific community. This can be seen in my use of APA citation style and a scholarly tone suitable for experts, as in my opening sentence. The paper begins bluntly and directly because I decided scholars would require little orientation and would value my getting right to the point. . . . In contrast, my paper "Is That Organic Apple Really Worth It?" is aimed at a general audience, such as readers of a news magazine. That paper uses scenes and examples to engage readers with a friendly tone. . . .

Generalization

Specific example

Explanation of the tone

Transition to another specific example

4E   How do I expand my ideas about my topic?

Strategies popular with experienced writers when they want to extend their ideas on a topic are listed in Quick Box 4.6 and explained after it. Experiment to find out which strategies you find most helpful, adapting to your PURPOSE and AUDIENCE for each new writing assignment.

4E

Quick Box 4.6   ■ ■ ■ ■ ■ ■

Strategies for developing ideas about topics

- Freewriting and focused freewriting
- Brainstorming
- Asking and answering structured questions
- Clustering (also called "mapping")
- Writing in a journal or a blog
- Chatting with other people

■ Freewriting

Freewriting calls for you to write whatever comes into your mind without stopping. Freewriting uses the physical act of writing to trigger brain processes that uncover ideas that don't come to mind by conscious thinking. It means you don't think about whether your ideas are good or your spelling is correct. **Focused freewriting** means starting with a favorite word or sentence from your journal, a quotation you like, or perhaps a topic you're studying for a course, and then freewriting with that focus in mind. When you freewrite, don't interrupt the flow. Keep writing. Don't censor your thoughts or insights. Don't review or cross out. Such writing is a voyage of discovery in which you allow your thoughts to emerge as you write.

After a session of freewriting, look over your material for ideas. At times you may find your material isn't helpful, but on other occasions, your insights may startle or delight you.

■ Brainstorming

Brainstorming means listing everything that comes to mind about your topic. Don't censor your thoughts. Let your mind roam, and jot down all ideas that flow logically or that simply pop into your head. After you've brainstormed for a while, look over your lists for patterns. If you don't have enough to work with, choose one item in your list and brainstorm from there.

Next, move the items into groups even if loosely related. Discard items that don't fit into any group. You'll probably find that the groups with the most items turn out to be most effective for developing your topic.

Here's some brainstorming by student Carol Moreno, whose essay about the benefits for women of learning to lift weights appears in Chapter 8. Carol grouped the items marked here with an asterisk and used them in her second paragraph.

*women don't want masculine-looking muscles; how much weight is safe for a woman to lift?; *women's muscles grow long, not bulky; how to bend down for lifting?; *firm muscles are attractive; free weights or machines?; *exercise type—anaerobic exercise; *exercise type—aerobic exercise; injuries; *toning the body

■ Asking and answering structured questions

Asking and answering structured questions can stimulate you to think of ideas for developing your topic. One popular question set consists of those journalists use: *Who? What? Where? When? Why? How?*

Here's how Alex Garcia used the journalists' questions to start writing about why organic foods are worth the cost, shown in Chapter 9:

> Who are the people who care about the benefits of eating organic foods?
>
> What are typical foods people prefer to be organically grown?
>
> Where did the idea of organic foods originate?
>
> When did organic foods become popular?
>
> Why do organic foods cost more than conventionally grown foods?
>
> How are organic foods processed?

■ Clustering

Clustering, also called *mapping*, is a visual form of brainstorming. Write your topic in the middle of a sheet and then circle it. Next, move out from the middle circle by drawing lines with circles at the end of each line. Put in each circle a subtopic or detail related to the main topic. If a subtopic or detail in a given circle has further subtopics, draw lines and circles fanning out from that circle. Continue using this method as far as it can take you. Though you might not include in your essay all the subtopics and details in your map, chances

are that some of the material might come in handy. For example, see page 33 for the map that Miquel Sanz drew to help him think of ideas for the second paragraph of his essay about auditioning to be in a musical.

■ Writing every day in a journal or blog

Writing in a journal or blog every day for 5 to 10 minutes is like having a conversation with yourself. It gets you into the habit of productivity so that when handling a writing assignment, your routine of writing flows more smoothly. The more you write, the more you get used to expressing yourself through words.

Write about whatever's on your mind. Draw on your thoughts, experiences, observations, dreams, reactions to your course work, or responses to something you've read recently. Use a paper notebook or computer document, depending on what's most handy and pleasurable for you. Often your journal or blog can serve as a source of topics for essays as well as related supporting specifics.

■ Chatting

Chatting with others means talking with them—but with a targeted purpose. Talk about your topic and toss around ideas. Keep paper, or your journal or computer, at hand so that you'll be sure to jot down the ideas as they come to mind. Research shows that new lines of thoughts and ideas slip people's minds rather quickly. Little is as frustrating as remembering you had thought of a good idea, but now you forget what it was.

"Chatting" today has come to mean more than only talking. You can chat online with instant messaging, e-mail, and other electronic forums. Exchanging ideas online not only stimulates your thinking but also acts like a warm-up for putting ideas into words.

● **EXERCISE 4-1** Here's a list brainstormed for a writing assignment. The topic was "Ways to promote a new movie." Look over the list and group the ideas. You'll find that some ideas don't fit into a group. Then, add any other ideas you have to the list.

previews in theaters	suspense	director
TV ads	book the movie was based on	topical subject
provocative ads	locations	special effects
movie reviews	Internet trailers	dialogue
how movie was made	adventure	excitement
sneak previews	newspaper ads	photography
word of mouth	stars	Facebook page ●

4F   How does a thesis statement help me plan?

A **thesis statement** serves as the central, controlling declaration of the point being made in most essays written in reponse to typical writing assignments. A thesis statement gives readers a general preview of what they can expect to read about. It also serves as a road map to check as you write to make sure you stay on topic. Expect to compose many drafts of the thesis statement for each essay, systematically getting closer on successive attempts to what you want it to encapsulate. The basic requirements of a thesis statement are listed in Quick Box 4.7.

"Play" with your thesis statement patiently; indeed, many writers discover their best thesis statements emerge only after they've written their concluding paragraph. As you revise your essay, continually check your thesis statement to make sure that it goes well with the content of your essay. If you find a mismatch, revise one or the other—or perhaps both.

In her essay "Weight Lifting for Women," shown in Chapter 8, Carol Moreno describes how, with the right training, women can become strong by lifting free weights. She uses the idiom "pumping iron," a commonly used term in gyms. Her thesis statement evolved from a thin assertion to a full one that makes her message clear.

Quick Box 4.7   ■ ■ ■ ■ ■ ■

Basic requirements for a thesis statement

1. It gives the essay's central message.

2. It makes an **assertion**, which puts forth the essay's central message.

3. Its assertion ties to the essay's TOPIC SENTENCES (see 5C) that start each of the essay's BODY PARAGRAPHS (see 5D).

4. It usually comes at the end of the INTRODUCTORY PARAGRAPH (see 5B).

5. It uses clear, straightforward language (see Chapter 28).

6. It might lay out the major subdivisions of a topic, but a more graceful technique is to imply them rather than stating them outright.

7. Avoid these common mistakes in writing a thesis statement:

   a. Don't use it to give a fact that leads nowhere.

   b. Don't say you're not an expert in your topic; your readers expect you to have learned enough about it to write your essay.

   c. Don't announce your essay's PURPOSE with words such as "The purpose of this essay is . . ."

   d. Don't refer back to your essay's title using words such as "This is an important issue . . ." or "My essay is called 'XYZ' because . . ."

NO   Women can lift weights as well as men do.

This has too little information.

NO   If trained, any woman can get strong.

The concept of lifting weights is gone; "any" is too broad.

4G

NO   Women can lift weights to get strong.

This repeats the essay's title rather than give its central message.

YES   Women can lift weights as long as they learn to do so properly.

Captures the central message of Moreno's essay, meets the thesis statement requirements, and avoids the pitfalls listed in Quick Box 4.7.

● **EXERCISE 4-2**   Each set of the following sentences offers several versions of a thesis statement. Within each set, the thesis statements progress from weak to strong. The fourth thesis statement in each set is the best. Referring to requirements listed in Quick Box 4.7, explain why the first three choices in each set are weak and the last is best.

A. 1. Advertising is complex.
2. Magazine advertisements appeal to readers.
3. Magazine advertisements must be creative and appealing to all readers.
4. To appeal to readers, magazine advertisements must skillfully use language, color, and design.
B. 1. Soccer is a widely played sport.
2. Playing soccer is fun.
3. Soccer requires various skills.
4. Playing soccer for fun and exercise requires agility, stamina, and teamwork.
C. 1. *Hamlet* is a play about revenge.
2. Hamlet must avenge his father's murder.
3. Some characters in the play *Hamlet* want revenge.
4. In the play *Hamlet*, Hamlet, Fortinbras, and Laertes all seek revenge. ●

4G   How does outlining help me write?

An **outline** is a structured, sequential list of the contents of a text. Some instructors require an outline with assignments, but others don't. Always ask. When given a choice, some students never outline, whereas others find that outlining helps them write. You might find that outlining helps at different stages of your writing process: perhaps before DRAFTING to help you flesh out, pull together, and arrange material; or perhaps during REVISION to help you check your flow of thought or make sure you haven't gone off the topic. Figure out what works best for you by experimenting.

An **informal outline** does not follow the numbering and lettering conventions of a formal outline. It often looks like a brainstorming list (see 4E), with ideas jotted down in a somewhat random order. Here's an informal outline for the second paragraph of Yanggu Cui's solution essay, "A Proposal to Improve Fan Behavior at Children's Games" (see Chapter 10).

4H

SAMPLE INFORMAL OUTLINE

little league games

parents on sidelines

parents yell at officials

insult opposing team

A **formal outline**, in contrast, follows long-established conventions for using numbers and letters to show relationships among ideas. No one outline format is endorsed for MLA STYLE, but instructors generally prefer the format used in Quick Box 4.8. Outlines usually don't show the content of introductory and concluding paragraphs, but some instructors want them included, so always ask.

To compose a formal outline, always use at least two subdivisions at each level—no I without a II, no A without a B, etc. All subdivisions need to be at the same level of generality, so don't pair a main idea with a subordinate idea or a subordinate idea with a supporting detail. In format, use PARALLELISM so that each outline item starts with the same PART OF SPEECH.

A formal outline can be a **sentence outline**, of only complete sentences, or a **topic outline**, of only words and PHRASES. Be careful never to mix the two styles in one outline. Quick Box 4.8 shows both types.

4H   How do I get started on a first draft?

Here are three ways to write a first draft. You will probably discover others as you write more frequently.

- **Write a discovery draft.** Put aside any planning notes (see 4E) and use FOCUSED FREEWRITING about your topic. Chances are you'll remember many of the ideas you thought of. When you finish the first draft, you can consult your notes.

- **Write a structured draft.** Consult your planning notes (see 4E) as you write, but don't allow yourself to stall at a part you don't like. Use a signal to tell yourself you want to return to that part, and keep on going.

- **Combine using a discovery draft and a structured draft.** Start with a discovery draft, and when stalled, switch to a structured draft. Or do the reverse.

The direction of drafting is forward. Keep pressing ahead. If a spelling, a word choice, or a sentence bothers you, use a signal that says you want to check it later—underline it, highlight it in a color, or switch it to capital letters.

4H

Quick Box 4.8   ▪ ▪ ▪ ▪ ▪ ▪

Outline formats

FORMAT OF TRADITIONAL FORMAL OUTLINE

Thesis statement: Present the entire thesis statement.

  I. First main idea

    A. First subordinate idea

      1. First reason or example

      2. Second reason or example

        a. First supporting detail

        b. Second supporting detail

    B. Second subordinate idea

  II. Second main idea

EXAMPLE: FORMAL SENTENCE OUTLINE

This outline goes with the second paragraph of Yanggu Cui's solution essay, "A Proposal to Improve Fan Behavior at Children's Games" (see Chapter 10).

Thesis statement: The league organizers need to bring an end to this kind of abuse, and the best way to do so is by requiring parents to sign a code of good behavior.

  I. For decades, parents have proudly watched their sons and daughters play little league softball, baseball, soccer, and other sports.

    A. In recent years, the parents who attend little league games have become more vocal on the sidelines.

    B. Parents who used to shout encouragement and congratulations to their children and the teams are now rude.

      1. They scream protests about the coaches' decisions.

      2. They yell insults at the opposing team.

      3. They hurl threats at officials, many of whom are young.

EXAMPLE: FORMAL TOPIC OUTLINE

This outline goes with the second paragraph of Yanggu Cui's solution essay, "A Proposal to Improve Fan Behavior at Children's Games" (see Chapter 10).

Thesis Statement: The league organizers need to bring an end to this kind of abuse, and the best way to do so is by requiring parents to sign a code of good behavior.

continued >>

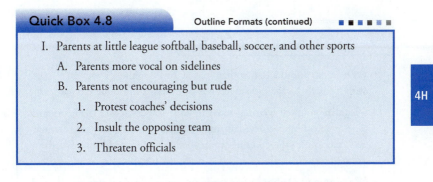

Quick Box 4.8   Outline Formats (continued) ■ ■ ■ ■ ■ ■

I. Parents at little league softball, baseball, soccer, and other sports

  A. Parents more vocal on sidelines

  B. Parents not encouraging but rude

    1. Protest coaches' decisions

    2. Insult the opposing team

    3. Threaten officials

4H

Research proves that the physical act of writing without pausing makes ideas and the connections among them "pop into people's heads unbidden."

Writers vary in how they're most comfortable drafting. Some finish their first draft in one sitting. Others draft a few paragraphs, take a break, and come back later. Resist being tempted to revise before you finish the first draft. Do these drafting problems sound familiar?

MY DRAFTING PROBLEM	I open a blank document, write a few words, don't like them, delete them, and start again, repeatedly.
SOLUTION	Darken your computer screen, and type without stopping. Save your work. Then lighten your computer screen to find an early draft.
MY DRAFTING PROBLEM	I start out well, but soon I'm going off the topic.
SOLUTION	Mark the spot with a highlighter, and pull yourself back to the topic. Don't stop. You can revise later.

As you draft, delete nothing. Throw away nothing. You might use some parts of your first draft as shown in Figure 4.2.

■ Writer's block

Writer's block is the condition that shuts off writers from their ability to write. Even expert writers sometimes hit a writer's block. If you get blocked, use the suggestions in Quick Box 4.9.

Figure 4.2 Using a first draft for later revising, editing, and proofreading.

Write first draft. → Save and keep it as its own document. → Copy and paste it into a new document. → Use the new document for revising, editing, and proofreading.

Quick Box 4.9

■ ■ ■ ■ ■ ■

Ways to overcome writer's block

- **Start in the middle.** Rather than start at the beginning of your essay, start with the body paragraph you feel will be easiest or most interesting to write.

- **Visualize yourself writing, moving your fingers across the keyboard.** Top athletes always use visualizing, imagining themselves going though each motion involved in their sport. Before you start writing, visualize yourself writing easily.

- **Write an e-mail about your topic to a friend, even if you don't send it.** Write informally. Be playful with your language or ideas. Loosen up.

- **Call a friend or relative to chat about your topic.** When you chat with friends about your topic, you are also inviting them to disagree or argue with you. Keep paper and pen at hand because this exchange can spark ideas and get your enthusiasm going.

- **Play the role of someone else and write to yourself about your topic.** Take on someone else's identity—a famous person alive now or in the past, for example—and imagine that person listening to you talk about your topic and disagreeing or agreeing with you.

- **Imagine a scene or sound that relates to your topic.** Start to write by describing what you see or hear. Allow yourself to sink into the environment of that scene or sound.

41   How do I revise effectively?

To **revise**, you work on your first draft systematically to rewrite it so that you get the content into the best shape you can. You do this by adding, cutting, replacing, and rearranging material.

While DRAFTING, you suspended judgment of your writing; for revision, you need to switch to making judgments. As you revise, keep all your drafts and notes as you rewrite because you might want to go back to an earlier revision and use part of it.

Here's an important point: although you know your topic well, your reader might be encountering it for the first time. This means you need to strive during revision for clarity, often by defining and explaining any terms or processes that might be unfamiliar to them. Work on the overarching elements of your essay. Save the last two steps—editing and proofreading—until you've finished revising the draft. This tactic is important: "premature editing" distracts writers too soon from the content of their material.

Quick Box 4.10

■ ■ ■ ■ ■ ■

Revision checklist

Section numbers in parentheses refer to more about each topic.

1. Does your introductory paragraph (see 5B) clearly lead into your topic, thesis statement, and essay?

2. Does your thesis statement clearly focus on your topic and tie into your topic sentences (see 4F)?

3. Do your topic sentences flow logically from your thesis statement (see 5C) and tie into the content of each paragraph?

4. Do your topic sentences, which are your generalizations, contain sufficient support with reasons, examples, and other types of details (see 5C)?

5. Is the sequence of your paragraphs logically arranged (see Chapter 7–11)?

6. Have you used appropriate transitions to connect ideas within and between paragraphs (see 5D)?

7. Have you used deliberate repetition and parallelism, when possible, to enhance the flow in your paragraphs and essay (see 5D)?

8. Does your conclusion complete your essay logically (see 5F)?

As you revise, work through the questions in Quick Box 4.10, or use revision guidelines supplied by your instructor. When you make a change, evaluate it on its own and also in the context of the surrounding material. Also, as you work, check your THESIS STATEMENT so that you update it to fit well with your newly evolved essay. Continue revising until you're satisfied that your essay is ready for editing.

As you start to revise your essay, avoid being impressed by the clean, well-formatted appearance of your draft as it looks on the screen or printed on paper. Drafts are meant to be revised, so during revision expect to add and delete words or longer passages. Neatness is crucial only after you've finished proofreading (see 4J).

■ Revisit your thesis statement

In working through your essay draft to revise it, revisit your THESIS STATEMENT, which you wrote for your earlier draft, to make sure that it fits well with your newly evolved essay. Use your thesis statement also as a check at the end of each body paragraph to make sure that the paragraph's topic sentence and content ties clearly with your thesis statement.

4J

■ Consider your essay's title

Your title needs to be an integral part of your entire essay. Never simply tack on a title at the last minute. Check your title if you created one for your draft, or write one for the first time, making sure that you've stayed on your topic. As you work systematically through your revision, keep reconsidering your title for its fit with your essay.

Alert: A title stands alone. Never open an essay with words that are a reaction to the title or with an opening sentence that is a continuation of the wording of the title. ●

■ Review your level of formality

You want to maintain a consistent level of formality throughout your essay. As you revise, make sure you haven't slipped from one level to another without realizing the switch. Levels of formality are generally divided into three categories. The "Semiformal Level" of writing is most appropriate for college essays, BUSINESS WRITING, public writing such as in newspapers, published opinion pieces, and the like.

- **Semiformal level of style** in writing has these characteristics: (1) Its presentation is reasonable and evenhanded, without pretension or highly informal word choice; (2) the sentence style is direct, clear, and concise.

- **Informal level of style** in writing is not appropriate for college essays, unless you use dialogue for specific effect. It's appropriate for personal—not business—e-mails, for Facebook postings, tweets, personal blogs, and the like.

- **Formal level of style** in writing is appropriate for formal occasions such as official ceremonies and for the language in contracts, policy statements, and the like.

4J   How do I edit and proofread effectively?

Editing, which comes after revision, means finding and fixing errors you've made in grammar, spelling, punctuation, capitals, numbers, italics, and abbreviations. Some instructors call these *surface-level features*. These are considered very important.

You may also want to ask friends, classmates, or colleagues with a good "editing eye" to read your paper and circle anything they think you need to check for correctness.

You want to hand in writing that shows you've paid close attention to the small errors that can ruin a paper's clarity and shows a respectful stance toward your assignment, yourself, and your instructor. Edit slowly and methodically.

Whenever you question a rule or a writing technique, use the Index at the back of this handbook to find the page for the exact information you want, and use it carefully.

■ Editing software

Editing features in software can lead you to make mistakes instead of helping you to correct your writing. Use it very cautiously. Microsoft® Word, for example, flags contractions and suggests incorrect alternatives: if you write "they're," the flags suggest you use "their" or "there," neither of which is correct. Also, most word processing software suggests rules of sentence structure and grammar that are extremely old fashioned and sometimes incorrect.

■ Spell check software

Software that claims to check your spelling is highly unreliable. While it can flag a serious typo ("hte" for "the"), it does not warn you that "form" is wrong when you meant to type "from."

■ Thesaurus software

Thesaurus software, often built into word processing programs, gives you SYNONYMS for words. While those synonyms might seem appealing, they often have slightly different meanings from what you intend to say. If you're not completely sure of the definition of a suggested synonym, always look it up in a dictionary or online. If you use the wrong, but seemingly impressive, word, your instructor will know you're either trying to show off or have not taken the time to check its meaning.

■ Strategies for proofreading

PROOFREADING means a careful, line-by-line reading of a final, clean version of your writing. If you find errors during proofreading, always print a fresh, clean copy of your work.

Almost all writers proofread more effectively on a printed page rather than on a screen, so print your pages whenever possible for proofreading. If you cannot avoid working onscreen, try highlighting a small section at a time so that you are visually separating it from the rest of the writing on the screen. This helps reduce the tendency to read too quickly and overlook errors.

Here are some effective proofreading strategies.

- Consult your lists of spelling, punctuation, or grammar errors that you often make. (For example, you may have trouble keeping *to, too*, and *two* straight.) Consult your lists before you proofread to look specifically for your personal troublemakers.

- Proofread with a ruler held just under the line you are reading so that you can focus on one line at a time.
- Start at the end of a paragraph or the end of your essay, and read each full sentence in reverse order or word by word, to avoid being distracted by the content.
- Read your final draft aloud so that you see and/or hear errors.
- Look especially for omitted letters and words.
- Watch out for repeated words ("the" or "and" are common repeats).

5 Composing Paragraphs

Quick Points   You will learn to

- ➤ Write effective introductory paragraphs (sec 5B).
- ➤ Write effective body paragraphs (pp. 48–51).
- ➤ Write effective concluding paragraphs (pp. 57–58).

MyWritingLab™   Visit mywritinglab.com for more resources on composing paragraphs.

5A   What is a paragraph?

A **paragraph** is a group of sentences that work together to develop a unit of thought. Paragraphs help you divide material into manageable parts and arrange the parts in a unified whole. College essays typically consist of an introductory paragraph, a group of body paragraphs, and a concluding paragraph; each type is described in this chapter.

5B   How can I write effective introductory paragraphs?

Introductory paragraphs point to what lies ahead and seek to arouse readers' interest. For strategies for composing effective introductory paragraphs, consult Quick Box 5.1. The paragraph's final sentence usually presents the essay's

Quick Box 5.1

■ ■ ■ ■ ■ ■

Strategies for writing introductory paragraphs

STRATEGIES FOR CAPTURING YOUR READER'S INTEREST

- Provide relevant background information about your topic.
- Relate a brief, interesting anecdote that applies to your topic.
- Give pertinent, perhaps surprising statistics about your topic.
- Ask a provocative question or two to lead in to your topic.
- Use a quotation that relates closely to your topic.
- Draw an analogy to clarify or illustrate your topic.
- Define a key term you use throughout your essay.

STRATEGIES TO AVOID

- Never make obvious statements about the essay's topic or purpose, such as "I am going to discuss some facts about animation."
- Never apologize, as in "I'm not sure I'm right, but here's what I think."
- Never use overworked expressions, such as "Haste does make waste, as I recently discovered."

THESIS STATEMENT (see 4F and Quick Box 4.7). Sample paragraphs 1 and 2 use different strategies to arouse interest; both conclude with a thesis statement.

For six additional examples of introductory paragraphs, see the student essays in sections 7E, 8E, 9E, 10E, 11E, and 11F.

1 Alone one is never lonely, May Sarton says in her essay "The Rewards of Living a Solitary Life." Most people, however, are terrified of living alone. They are used to living with others—children with parents, roommates with roommates, friends with friends, husbands with wives. When the statistics catch up with them, therefore, they are rarely prepared. Chances are high that most adult men and women will live alone, briefly or longer, at some time.

Paraphrase of quotation

Thesis statement

—Tara Foster, student

Arguably the greatest mysteries in the universe lie in the three-pound mass of cells, approximately the consistency of oatmeal, that reside in the skull of each of us. It has even been

Surprising fact to arouse interest

2 suggested that the brain is so complex that our species is smart enough to fathom everything except what makes us so smart; that is, the brain is so cunningly designed for intelligence that it is too stupid to understand itself. We now know that is not true. The mind is at last yielding its secrets to persistent scientific investigation. We have learned more about how the mind works in the last twenty-five years than we did in the previous twenty-five hundred.

Thesis statement

—Daniel T. Willingham, *Why don't students like school?*

5C   How can I write effective topic sentences?

A **topic sentence** contains the main idea of a BODY PARAGRAPH and controls its content. Main ideas are usually GENERALIZATIONS. The connection needs to be clear between the main idea and its supporting details in the sentences that follow it. Topic sentences usually come at the beginning of a paragraph, but putting them at the end or implying them can be effective depending on how you want your sentences to flow.

For additional examples of topic sentences, see the body paragraphs in the student essays in sections 7E, 8E, 9E, 10E, 11E, and 11F.

Starting with a topic sentence

When a topic sentence starts a paragraph, readers immediately know what topic will be discussed.

3 Family businesses are discovering a new venue where they can work out their problems: the classroom. Over the past few years, more family-firm leaders have been turning to executive-education courses tailored to their needs. Instead of just teaching the best way to run a business, the courses focus on overcoming the unique obstacles that family ties can pose—such as succession planning and poor communication among relatives. Several company executives are encouraged to attend at the same time, and a large part of the courses involves getting everyone at the company on the same page, often through team exercises like role playing. The instructors act partly as professors and partly as counselors, giving advice on navigating current family conflicts as they teach business theory.

—Alina Dizik, "The Family That Goes to School Together . . ."

Ending with a topic sentence

When a topic sentence ends a body paragraph, you want all sentences leading to it to flow into it smoothly.

4 The third most popular language in America—after English and Spanish—is American Sign Language (ASL). It is a visual-gestural language composed of a collection of coded gestures based on a system developed in France in the eighteenth century. It was brought to the United States by Thomas Hopkins Gallaudet, a young Congregational minister from Connecticut. After traveling to France and learning about this system of signing, Gallaudet returned to the United States, bringing a young French deaf-signing teacher, Laurent Clerc, with him. Together they developed a sign language system that blended French signs with American signs. As a legacy, today deaf people in both France and the United States can recognize similarities in the signs they use.

—Roger E. Axtell, *Gestures: The Do's and Taboos of Body Language around the World*

■ Implying a topic sentence

When a paragraph conveys a main idea without a specific topic sentence, you want to be sure that the details clearly add up to a main idea. The implied topic sentence of paragraph 5, if it were stated explicitly, might be something like "To lure buyers into the local clothing store, the manager engaged in false advertising, but not everyone caught on."

5 Customers used to wait at the cash register for minutes before a checker would finally pay attention. Of course, the wait happened only when they actually had found the item they had come to buy. Most customers went away empty-handed. The manager had a practice of running ads for products that were just about sold out. I would watch people pick through piles of shirts in a fruitless search for something other than an extra-small or an extra-extra-large.

—Armstrong Washington, student

● **EXERCISE 5-1**   Identify the topic sentences in the following paragraphs. If the topic sentence is implied, write the point the paragraph conveys. For help, consult section 5C.

A.   A good college program should stress the development of high-level reading, writing, and mathematical skills and should provide you with a broad historical, social, and cultural perspective, no matter what subject you choose as your major. The program should teach you not only the most current knowledge in your field but also—just as important—prepare you to keep learning throughout your life. After all, you'll probably change jobs, and possibly even careers, at least six times, and you'll have other responsibilities, too—perhaps as a spouse and as a parent and certainly as a member of a community whose bounds extend beyond the workplace.

—Frank T. Rhodes, "Let the Student Decide"

B.   The once majestic oak tree crashes to the ground amid the destructive flames, as its panic-stricken inhabitants attempt to flee the fiery tomb. Undergrowth that formerly flourished smolders in ashes. A family of deer darts furiously from one wall of flame to the other, without an emergency exit. On the outskirts of the inferno, firefighters try desperately to stop the destruction. Somewhere at the source of this chaos lies a former campsite containing the cause of this destruction—an untended campfire. This scene is one of many that illustrate how human apathy and carelessness destroy nature.

—Anne Bryson, student

C.   Rudeness isn't a distinctive quality of our own time. People today would be shocked by how rudely our ancestors behaved. In the colonial period, a French traveler marveled that "Virginians don't use napkins, but they wear silk cravats, and instead of carrying white handkerchiefs, they blow their noses either with their fingers or with a silk handkerchief that also serves as a cravat, a napkin, and so on." In the 19th century, up to about the 1830s, even very distinguished people routinely put their knives in their mouths. And when people went to the theater, they would not just applaud politely—they would chant, jeer, and shout. So, the notion that there's been a downhill slide in manners ever since time began is just not so.

—"Horizons," *U.S. News & World Report* ●

5D   How can I write effective body paragraphs?

Body paragraphs in an essay come after the introductory paragraph. Its sentences support the generalization in the TOPIC SENTENCE. **What separates most good writing from bad is the writer's ability to move back and forth between generalizations and specific details**.

■ Specific details

For help in thinking of details, try using **RENNS**, a memory device summarized in Quick Box 5.2. You need not expect to use all the RENNS in each of your body paragraphs. Choose whichever RENNS details work for your paragraphs or think of others.

Paragraph 6 contains many specific details that support the opening topic sentence.

Between 1910 and 1920, "The Rubber Capital of the World" was the fastest-growing city in the nation, thanks to a booming automobile industry. Akron, Ohio, had a few crucial features that helped it thrive as a hub. It was not only located close to auto makers, it also had water power and cheap coal to

| Numbers |
| Names |
| Reasons |

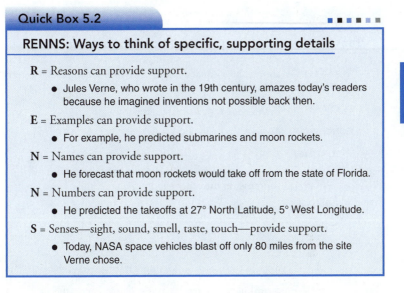

Quick Box 5.2

RENNS: Ways to think of specific, supporting details

R = Reasons can provide support.

- Jules Verne, who wrote in the 19th century, amazes today's readers because he imagined inventions not possible back then.

E = Examples can provide support.

- For example, he predicted submarines and moon rockets.

N = Names can provide support.

- He forecast that moon rockets would take off from the state of Florida.

N = Numbers can provide support.

- He predicted the takeoffs at 27° North Latitude, 5° West Longitude.

S = Senses—sight, sound, smell, taste, touch—provide support.

- Today, NASA space vehicles blast off only 80 miles from the site Verne chose.

5D

6   draw on. During the peak years, more than 300 rubber companies called the city home, but most died off in the fierce pricing competition. Then, in the 1970s, French manufacturer Michelin introduced the longer-lasting radial tire. In Akron, profits slipped and plants closed. Goodyear Tire & Rubber Co. is now the only major tire company that still has headquarters in Akron.

Examples

Numbers

Names

—*Wall Street Journal* research "Akron, Ohio"

● **EXERCISE 5-2**   Look again at the paragraphs in Exercise 5-1. Identify the RENNS in each paragraph. For help, consult 5D. ●

▉ Transitions

Transitions are words that express connections among ideas. Such connections are links that create **coherence**, a smooth flow of thoughts within paragraphs and from one paragraph to another in essays. The most commonly used transitions are listed in Quick Box 5.3.

Here are some tips for using transitions effectively.

- Vary the transitions you use within a category. For example, avoid using *for instance* every time you give an example.

- Use each transition precisely, according to its exact meaning. For example, the expression *in contrast* signals that you will be discussing something that's unlike what you just discussed.

5D

Quick Box 5.3

Transitions: words to express relationships among ideas

ADDITION	also, besides, equally important, furthermore, in addition, moreover, too
COMPARISON	in the same way, likewise, similarly
CONCESSION	granted, naturally, of course
CONTRAST	at the same time, certainly, despite the fact that, however, in contrast, instead, nevertheless, on the contrary, on the other hand, otherwise, still
EMPHASIS	indeed, in fact, of course
EXAMPLE	a case in point, as an illustration, for example, for instance, namely, specifically
PLACE	here, in the background, in the front, nearby, there
RESULT	accordingly, as a result, consequently, hence, then, therefore, thus
SUMMARY	finally, in conclusion, in short, in summary
TIME SEQUENCE	eventually, finally, meanwhile, next, now, once, then, today, tomorrow, subsequently, yesterday

NO   The jewels were valuable. Otherwise, the carpets were not.

Otherwise makes no sense.

YES   The jewels were valuable. In contrast, the carpets were not.

This comparison makes sense.

Paragraph 7 contains four transitions, highlighted here to stand out.

7   Jaguars, **for example**, were **once** found in the United States from southern Louisiana to California. Today they are rare north of the Mexican border, with no confirmed sightings since 1971. They are rare, **too**, in Mexico, where biologist Carl Koford estimated their population at fewer than a thousand in a 1972 survey. Some biologists think the number is even smaller today. **Similarly**, jaguars have disappeared from southern Argentina and Paraguay.

—Jeffrey P. Cohen, "Kings of the Wild"

■ **Deliberate repetition and parallelism**

Deliberate repetition means you intentionally repeat key words to achieve coherence within and between paragraphs. Used well, it moves readers along gracefully. Overused, its monotony dulls your impact. Paragraph 8 uses deliberate repetition well. The word *it* is repeated throughout, each time clearly referring to the skin; midway, the word *skin* recurs once, but it is also reinforced by *it* and *it's*. **Parallelism** enhances coherence with the rhythms of language (see Chapter 27). In paragraph 8, one sentence uses the rhythm of matching phrases: *gives us, protects us, cools us, heats us*. Another sentence twice employs "of" phrasing: *organ of the body, organ of sexual attraction*.

5D

8   Our skin is what stands between us and the world. If you think about it, no other part of us makes contact with something not us, but the skin. It imprisons us, but it also gives us individual shape, protects us from invaders, cools us down or heats us up as need be, produces vitamin D, holds in our body fluids. Most amazing, perhaps, is that it can mend itself when necessary, and it is constantly renewing itself. Weighing from six to ten pounds, it's the largest organ of the body, and the key organ of sexual attraction. Skin can take a startling variety of shapes: claws, spines, hooves, feathers, scales, hair. It's waterproof, washable, and elastic. Although it may cascade or roam as we grow older, it lasts surprisingly well. For most cultures, it's the ideal canvas to decorate with paints, tattoos, and jewelry. But, most of all, it harbors the sense of touch.

Deliberate repetition

Parallelism

Parallelism

—Diane Ackerman, *A Natural History of the Senses*

● **EXERCISE 5-3** Locate the coherence techniques in the following paragraph. Look for transitional expressions, deliberate repetition, and parallel structures. For help, consult 5D.

Kathy sat with her legs dangling over the edge of the side of the hood. The band of her earphones held back strands of straight copper hair that had come loose from two thick braids that hung down her back. She swayed with the music that only she could hear. Her shoulders raised, making circles in the warm air. Her arms reached out to her side; her open hands reached for the air; her closed hands brought the air back to her. Her arms reached over her head; her opened hands reached for a cloud; her closed hands brought the cloud back to her. Her head moved from side to side; her eyes opened and closed to the tempo of the tunes. Kathy was motion.

—Claire Burke, student ●

5E How can I use rhetorical strategies to develop effective body paragraphs?

Rhetorical strategies are patterns for presenting ideas effectively. You can choose to use each strategy depending on what you want to accomplish.

Here we show you rhetorical strategies one at a time. In real writing, however, no paragraph is isolated, so rhetorical strategies often overlap in one paragraph. For example, in a paragraph explaining how to prepare a slide to study under a microscope, you would likely use the process pattern along with definition and description.

■ Narration

Narrative writing tells what is happening or what has happened, as in Paragraph 9. It is storytelling. For an example of narration in an essay, see the story about what happened when friends went skiing in "Saved by Technology—Or Distracted by It?" the student essay in section 7E.

9   We walked down the path to the well-house, attracted by the fragrance of the honeysuckle with which it was covered. Someone was drawing water and my teacher placed my hand under the spout. As the cool stream gushed over one hand she spelled into the other the word *water*, first slowly, then rapidly. I stood still, my whole attention fixed upon the motions of her fingers. Suddenly I felt a misty consciousness as of something forgotten—a thrill of returning thought; and somehow the mystery of language was revealed to me. I knew then that "water" meant the wonderful cool something that was flowing over my hand. That living word awakened my soul, gave it light, hope, joy, set it free! There were barriers still, it is true, but barriers that could in time be swept away.

—Helen Keller, *The Story of My Life*

■ Description

Descriptive writing paints a picture in words. To impose a logical sequence on your **description**, you might work from the general to the specific, as in paragraph 10. Other effective sequences include top to bottom; from least to most important, building to a climax; or any other sequence that works well with your topic. Description is often used in college essays, as many of the student essays in Chapters 7–11 demonstrate. The most striking examples are in the sixth paragraph of "Saved by Technology—Or Distracted by It?" in section 7E and in the third paragraph of "Weight Lifting for Women" in section 8E.

Paragraph 10 uses specific details to expand our understanding of a common object: the yo-yo. To see description functioning in essays, consult the student essays at the end of each chapter in Part Three.

10 The common yo-yo is crudely made, with a thick shank between two widely spaced wooden disks. The string is knotted or stapled to the shank. With such an instrument nothing can be done except the simple up-down movement. My yo-yo, on the other hand, was a perfectly balanced construction of hard wood, slightly weighted, flat, with only a sixteenth of an inch between the halves. The string was not attached to the shank, but looped over it in such a way as to allow the wooden part to spin freely on its own axis. The gyroscopic effect thus created kept the yo-yo stable in all attitudes.

—Frank Conroy, *Stop Time*

■ Process

Process writing presents instructions; lays out steps in a procedure; explains how objects work; or describes human behaviors, as in paragraph 11 about people's reactions in a plane crash. To see process writing in an essay, look at "Weight Lifting for Women," the student essay in section 8E.

11 In the precious first moments after a plane crash, when experts say a half-second head start can get you to an aisle first, the most basic elements of human character are revealed. Some instincts help survival and others hinder escape. Some people are panicked into pushing, shoving and fighting. For many, the brain shuts down and they are slow to react. That's why practice and familiarity can help. Balking at the top of a three-story evacuation slide can lead to a push, sending you cart-wheeling down and resulting in broken ankles. Research shows even practicing with the seat belt latch can help quicken escape. On average, six percent of passengers in an evacuation get delayed by seat-belt struggles, the Civil Aeronautics Administration study found.

—Scott McCartney, "British Airways Puts Fliers in Mock Disasters: How to Get a Head Start"

■ Examples or illustrations

Examples and **illustrations** provide concrete, specific support for the main idea. Paragraph 12 presents in rapid succession several types of "metamessages" so that taken together the examples create a coherent picture. All the student essays at the ends of Chapters 7–11 make abundant use of examples.

12 Another way to think about metamessages is that they frame a conversation, much as a picture frame provides a context for the images in the picture. Metamessages let you know how to interpret what someone is saying by identifying the activity that is going on. Is this an argument or a chat? Is it helping, advising, or scolding? At the same time, they let you know what position the speaker is assuming in the activity, and what position you are being assigned.

—Deborah Tannen, *You Just Don't Understand*

■ Extended definition

Definition calls for clarifying the meaning of a word or concept in more detail than a dictionary definition. Extended definitions are often included in paragraphs that are developed in other ways. Paragraph 13 offers an extended definition of the term "soft skills," using examples that progress from the somewhat less important to the more dramatic, crucially important point. Within essays, extended definitions clarify concepts that might not be familiar to the writer's probable audience.

When it comes to soft skills, most people think they are all about those warm-and-fuzzy people skills. Yes, it's true that people skills are a part of the equation, but that's just for starters. While hard skills refer to the technical ability and the factual knowledge needed to do the job, soft skills allow you to more effectively use your technical abilities and knowledge. Soft skills encompass personal, social, communication, and self-management behaviors. They cover a wide spectrum of abilities and traits: being self-aware, trustworthiness, **13** conscientiousness, adaptability, critical thinking, attitude, initiative, empathy, confidence, integrity, self-control, organizational awareness, likeability, influence, risk taking, problem solving, leadership, time management, and then some. Quite a mouthful, eh? These so-called soft skills complement the hard ones and are essential for success in the rough-and-tumble workplace. You can have all the technical expertise in the world, but if you can't sell your ideas, get along with others, or turn your work in on time, you'll be going nowhere fast.

—Peggy Klaus, *The Hard Truth About Soft Skills*

■ Comparison and contrast

Comparisons deal with similarities; *contrasts* deal with differences. **Comparison and contrast** writing is usually organized in one of two ways. **Point-by-point organization** moves back and forth between the items being compared, as in paragraph 14. **Block organization** discusses one item completely before discussing the next, as in paragraph 15 (sporting games are covered completely before anything is said about business). These organizational patterns can be extended into essays, adapting them as suits the topic. For example, see the comparisons in the student essay "Rhetorical Strategies in Two Airport Security Web Sites" in section 11F.

I retain only one confused impression from my earliest years: it's all red, and black, and warm. Our apartment was red: the upholstery was of red moquette, the Renaissance dining-room was red, the figured silk hangings over the stained-glass doors were red, and the velvet curtains in Papa's study **14** were red too. The furniture in this awful sanctum was made of black pear wood; I used to creep into the kneehole under the desk and envelop myself in its dusty glooms; it was dark and warm, and the red of the carpet rejoiced my eyes. That is how I seem to have passed the early days of infancy. Safely ensconced, I watched, I touched, I took stock of the world.

—Simone de Beauvoir, *Memoirs of a Dutiful Daughter*

Games are of limited duration, take place on or in fixed and finite sites and are governed by openly promulgated rules that are enforced on the spot by neutral professionals. Moreover, they are performed by relatively evenly matched teams that are counseled and led through every move by seasoned hands. Scores are kept, and at the end of the game, a winner is declared. Busi-**15** ness is usually a little different. In fact, if there is anyone out there who can say that the business is of limited duration, takes place on a fixed site, is governed by openly promulgated rules that are enforced on the spot by neutral professionals, competes only on relatively even terms, and performs in a way that can be measured in runs or points, then that person is either extraordinarily lucky or seriously deluded.

—Warren Bennis, "Time to Hang Up the Old Sports Clichés"

■ Analysis

Analysis examines and discusses separate parts of a whole. Paragraph 16 offers an analysis of how to create strong passwords for your computer's protected files. Many of the student essays in Chapters 7–11 use analysis to discuss their topics; a particularly good example is the analysis of organic foods in "Why Organic Foods Are Worth the Cost," in section 9E.

For a pretty strong password, think 10. If your password contains 10 characters, you should be able to sleep well at night—perhaps for 19.24 years. That's how long it would take hackers to try every combination of 10 characters, assuming that the password is encrypted and that the hackers have enough **16** computing power to mount a 100-billion-guesses-a-second effort to break the encryption. But if your user names and passwords are sitting unencrypted on a server, you may not be able to sleep at all if you start contemplating the potential havoc ahead.

—Randall Stross, "Digital Domain"

5E

■ Classification

Classification groups items according to a shared characteristic. In paragraph 17, three types of signals used by some baseball coaches are explained.

17 Many different kinds of signals are used by the coaches. There are flash signals, which are just what the name implies: The coach may flash a hand across his face or chest to indicate a bunt or hit-and-run. There are holding signals, which are held in one position for several seconds. There might be the clenched fist, bent elbow, or both hands on knees. Then there are the block signals. These divide the coach's body into different sections, or blocks. Touching a part of his body, rubbing his shirt, or touching his cap indicates a sign. Different players can be keyed to various parts of the block so the coach is actually giving several signals with the same sign.

—Rockwell Stensrud, "Who's on Third?"

■ Analogy

Analogy is a kind of comparison, identifying similarities between objects or ideas that are not usually associated with each other. Essays that explain complicated processes or examples often benefit when the writer uses an analogy to a more familiar idea. Paragraph 18 discusses word choices in writing by drawing analogies to choices of dress.

18 Casual dress, like casual speech, tends to be loose, relaxed, and colorful. It often contains what might be called "slang words": blue jeans, sneakers, baseball caps, aprons, flowered cotton housedresses, and the like. These garments could not be worn on a formal occasion without causing disapproval, but in ordinary circumstances they pass without remark. "Vulgar words" in dress, on the other hand, give emphasis and get immediate attention in almost any circumstances, just as they do in speech. Only the skillful can employ them without some loss of face, and even then they must be used in the right way. A torn, unbuttoned shirt, or wildly uncombed hair can signify strong emotions: passion, grief, rage, despair. They are most effective if people already think of you as being neatly dressed, just as the curses of well-spoken persons count for more than those of the customarily foul-mouthed.

—Alison Lurie, *The Language of Clothes*

■ Cause and effect

Cause and effect paragraphs examine outcomes and reasons for outcomes. *Causes* lead to an event or an effect; *effects* result from causes. For an example of using cause and effect in an essay, see section 10E for the solution essay "A Proposal to Improve Fan Behavior at Children's Games."

Paragraph 19 discusses the effect of ecological problems.

Many collapses of the past appear to have been triggered, at least in part, by ecological problems: people inadvertently destroyed their environmental resources. But societies are not doomed to collapse because of environmental damage. Some societies have coped with their problems, whereas others have

19 not. But I know of no case in which a society's collapse can be attributed simply to environmental damage; there are always complicating factors. Among them are climate change, the role of neighbors (who can be friendly or hostile), and, most important, the ways people respond to their environmental problems.

5F

—Jared Diamond, "Collapse: Ecological Lessons in Survival"

5F How can I write effective concluding paragraphs?

Concluding paragraphs of essays need to follow logically from the THESIS STATEMENT and BODY PARAGRAPHS. Your concluding paragraph provides a sense of completion, a finishing touch that enhances the whole essay. Never merely tack on a conclusion. Quick Box 5.4 suggests ways for writing conclusions. The

---

Quick Box 5.4   ■ ■ ■ ■ ■ ■

Strategies for writing concluding paragraphs

STRATEGIES FOR CAPTURING YOUR READER'S INTEREST

- Use one of the strategies suggested for introductory paragraphs (see Quick Box 5.1), but always choose a different one than you used in the introduction.

- Ask the reader for awareness, action, or a similar outcome.

- Project into the future.

- Summarize the main points of the essay but only if it is particularly long.

STRATEGIES TO AVOID

- Never introduce new ideas or facts that belong in the body of the essay.

- Never merely reword the introduction.

- Never announce what you have done, as in "In this paper, I have explained Japanese animation."

- Never make absolute claims, as in "In this essay, I have proved that anime deserves our attention."

- Never apologize, as in "Even though I am not an expert, I feel the points I have made are valid."

conclusion in paragraph 20 is from the essay whose introductory paragraph was shown in paragraph 1. It poses a challenging question and asks the reader to prepare for the future. For six additional examples of concluding paragraphs, see the student essays in sections 7E, 8E, 9E, 10E, 11E, and 11F.

6A

20 You need to ask yourself, "If I had to live alone starting tomorrow morning, would I know how?" If the answer is no, you need to become conscious of what living alone calls for. If you face up to life today, you will not have to hide from it later on.

—Tara Foster, student

6 Designing Documents

■ ■ ■ ■ ■ ■

Quick Points   You will learn to

➤ Design documents effectively (see section 6A).
➤ Use photographs and graphs effectively (see section 6B).

My**Writing**Lab™   Visit mywritinglab.com for more resources on document design.

6A   How can I design documents effectively?

Document design refers to the format and physical appearance of your written work. It deals with how a document looks, not what it says, including elements such as text, headings, highlighting, and layout of pages when they include graphics or photographs.

🛈 **Alert:** As you read this chapter, check to see if your instructors have specific format requirements for student work and if so, follow them, not the principles in this chapter. ●

■ Text

College essays usually call for one-inch margins all around, double spacing, and 12-point type in the font called "Times New Roman." For emphasis, use WORD CHOICE, not ITALICS, although of course use *italics* for names of sources, such as books (see Chapters 28 and 39).

For posters, newsletters, and brochures you can choose among many fonts, but make sure that your material is easy to read by using only one or, if absolutely necessary, two fonts. Select a font that conveys a **tone** suitable for your message. For example, avoid handwriting fonts, unless for a signature or in a formal invitation.

■ Lists

Lists rarely have a place in an essay. However, they're usually permitted in research papers, science reports, posters, and the like. Use numbers or small bullets to set off each item. For the first word in each item, use the same PART OF SPEECH, as explained below under "headings"

■ Highlights

Highlights, such as **boldface**, *italics*, and background colors, call attention to key words in a document. In essays, your word choice rather than a highlight creates emphasis. In posters, newsletters, and brochures, use highlights in moderation so that they clarify rather than complicate.

■ Headings

Headings allow writers to break long passages into chunks, thereby making complex material easier to understand. In your non-research essays, avoid headings unless they are permitted by your instructor. For research papers, MLA STYLE discourages headings, while APA STYLE favors them (compare the MLA-style student research paper in section 14H and the APA-style student research paper in section 15G). In posters, newsletters, and brochures, headings can serve an essential role by directing the reader's eye to key material. Here are guidelines for using headings:

- Maintain the same size as the text font in research papers and science reports. Slightly increase their size and consider using boldface in posters and the like.

- Keep the wording brief and informative.

- Use PARALLELISM for the first word of each heading. You can use VERBS, NOUNS, ADJECTIVES, ADVERBS, or PREPOSITIONS as long as you're consistent.

6B

■ Color

Use only black for the text in your college essays. The use of other colors becomes important when you want to insert color photographs and/or graphics (see 6B) into your document. Color can add an attractive dimension, but use it sparingly for the best effect. In posters, newsletters, and brochures, you can call attention to your key words or elements by changing the text color or using a tinted colored background over them.

■ Page layout

Page layout refers to the arrangement of text, visuals (drawings, photographs, and graphics), color, and white space in a document. You want to arrange your elements so that the document is easy to read or look at, with key words or elements immediately obvious to your audience. Attention to page layout becomes especially important when you insert graphics and photographs into your documents (see 6B). Consider these principles of document design in illustrated essays, posters, newsletters, brochures, and the like.

- **Unity:** strive for harmony among all elements, such as print, visuals, color, and white space.
- **Variety:** use headings, boldface, and color to break up monotony.
- **Balance and emphasis:** give your main message prominence in the document, and place the related material so that the whole document is appealing to the eye. To test this, look at the document from a distance or reduce it to page view on your computer, asking yourself whether the presentation seems lopsided or too busy.

6B   How do I use photographs and graphics effectively?

■ Photographs

Photographs that illustrate content can add a dynamic dimension to written material, such as essays, posters, newsletters, and brochures. However, before you insert photographs in your essays, check that your instructor permits them.

In selecting photographs, make sure that they tie directly to the content of your material. When necessary for clarity, write a caption to place below the photograph. Try to place the photograph close to the text to which it applies. If this is impossible, put it in an appendix and refer to it clearly in your writing.

Sharp focus is important in choosing photographs. If you use your personal photograph, you'll need it to be in digital form so that it prints clearly in your paper. Take care if you find a photograph on a Web site because while it might look clear on your computer screen, it often becomes fuzzy when extracted and inserted into a document. To be assured of clarity, you might choose a "stock photo" from the Web site of a stock photo agency, each of which has hundreds of thousands of images; however, in some cases a small fee is required.

Copyright laws are important to keep in mind when you use a photograph other than your own or one a friend gives you. Generally you may use an image once for a class assignment since the use is not for profit, and—most important—you will never post your paper online or anywhere else. To ask permission to use an image more extensively, e-mail the source for reprint rights. For a student project, sometimes the fee will be waived, but this is happening less often today because of the widespread misuse of others' "intellectual property," including images and music. Your instructors are aware of copyright laws, so never plagiarize a photo or other image.

As long as you don't distort the truth, you can adjust a photograph by making it lighter or darker, sharpening colors, getting rid of red eye, and other minor changes. You can even crop an image so that it focuses on the point you want to make. For example, Figure 6.1 shows a complete scene of a woman driving her young child while using her phone; Figure 6.2 is cropped so that the focus is only on the woman talking on her phone.

DOCUMENTATION of sources, including photographs and other visuals, is a central academic responsibility of all students. This applies even if a photograph is yours or belongs to a friend. For essays, research papers, science reports, and the like, use the documentation style required in your course, listing your sources on a separate end page: in MLA STYLE on the WORKS CITED page, or in APA STYLE, the REFERENCES page. On posters, the source information can be entered in small print at the bottom; in brochures and newsletters, the source information can be placed in small print either near the material or at the end of the document, as long as you make clear what information came from which source.

Graphics

Graphics serve to display factual and numeric information by visually condensing it, comparing it, and otherwise laying it out so that it delivers a clear message. If you create a graphic yourself, you need only to document the source of the information you used. If you copy a graphic from a source, you need to document it; if the graphic gives a source for its information, be sure to document that also. The most typical varieties of graphics appear on page 63: a bar graph, a line graph, a pie chart, and a table.

6B

Figure 6.1 Original full version of photograph.

Figure 6.2 Cropped version of the same photograph.

- **Bar graphs** compare values, such as the number of different majors at a college, as shown in the graph at right.

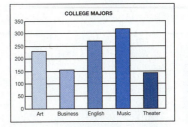

6B

- **Line graphs** indicate changes over time. For example, advertising revenue is shown over an eight-month period in the graph at left.

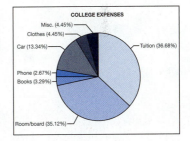

- **Pie charts** show the relationship of each part to a whole, such as a typical budget for a college student, as shown in the chart at right.

- **Tables** present data in list form, as shown in the following, to allow readers to grasp a lot of information at a glance.

TABLE 1   STUDENT RATINGS OF SUSTAINABILITY, BY TERM

Semester	Students Rating Sustainabilily as Important	Percentage of All Students
Fall 2011	2,321	65.8%
Spring 2012	2,892	72.3%
Fall 2012	3,425	78.1%

Part 3
Frames for College Writing

CHAPTERS
7–11

What are frames for college writing?

Essay **frames** are guides that suggest how to develop and structure an effective college essay. We offer frames for five types of essays, the ones most frequently assigned in college writing courses. Each frame lays out the elements of essays that combine to create the greatest possible unity, clarity, and impact. Each frame is followed by a complete student essay, with annotations to show how the essay works, along with the writer's thinking that includes integrating the three persuasive appeals of logical reasoning (*logos*), ethical credibility (*ethos*), and compassionate emotions (*pathos*), as explained in Quick Box 2.3.

Because using the writing process is so important, for each frame, we explain how the writing process works for that type of essay. We discuss that type's PURPOSE* and probable AUDIENCE and then list specific strategies for planning and revising it. Following each frame is a collection of sentence and paragraph guides that offer you hands-on experience with the sorts of language moves expected in **academic writing**.

In using the frames and guides, you need to adapt them to the specifics of each of your writing assignments. Although we place the five essay types in separate chapters, we hope you use them flexibly and creatively.

7 Personal Essays

■ ■ ■ ■ ■ ■

Quick Points   You will learn to

➤ Describe key elements of a personal essay (see section 7A).
➤ Apply the writing process to a personal essay (p. 68).
➤ Adapt frames and guides for a personal essay to your own needs (pp. 68–69).

MyWritingLab™ Visit mywritinglab.com for more resources on personal essays.

*Words printed in SMALL CAPITAL LETTERS are discussed elsewhere in the text and are defined in the Terms Glossary at the back of the book.

7A   What is a personal essay?

Personal essays narrate one or more true experiences to reveal something worth knowing about their writers' lives or ideas. Personal essays often use stories and explain what they mean. The trick in writing a personal essay for audiences wider than your family and friends is to narrate your experiences so that readers care about not only what happened but also what you thought about it.

What makes a personal essay effective is how you present it. Your word choice, level of openness, and use of the three persuasive appeals of logic (*logos*), ethical credibility (*ethos*), and compassion and empathy (*pathos*)—see 2B—can combine to deliver an engaging essay. Consider the following example. The YES version is a detailed, thorough description about a pleasant memory from the 1950s.

7A

> **NO**   I can remember my father driving our car into a filling station at the edge of Birmingham. Two miles after we passed a particular motel, he would turn onto Callahan drive, which was a gravel road.
>
> This provides uninteresting facts and description.

> **YES**   After lunch, our father would fold up his map and tuck it in the felt visor until we pulled into the filling station on the outskirts of Birmingham. Are we there yet? We had arrived when we saw the Moon Winx Motel sign—a heart-stopping piece of American road art, a double-sided neon extravaganza; a big taxicab-yellow crescent with a man-in-the-moon on each side, a sly smile, a blue eye that winked, and that blatant misspelling that "x" that made us so happy.
>
> —Emily Hiestand, *Angela the Upside-Down Girl*

■ Purpose

Personal essays mainly have an expressive or literary purpose that's designed to engage and enlighten readers. The best personal essays have a message or point. Sometimes they lead readers to learn things about their lives that they might not have otherwise recognized. Your self-discovery, revealed candidly to the readers, can add to the impact of personal essays. (For more about purposes for writing, see 4C.)

■ Audience

People tend to read personal essays for "serious pleasure." They want to be entertained by true stories, especially by the engaging way the writer tells them, but they also want to encounter thoughts and ideas. (For more about audience, see 4C.)

7B   How do I plan and revise personal essays?

Generating ideas

- Concentrate first on getting the basic story down. Imagine you're a reader who's eager to read your story.
- Try next to create detailed scenes. Work on describing the physical setting in detail and perhaps use some dialogue so that readers can get a sense of being there. If you recreate the place, time, and people who were involved, you allow your readers to form their opinion of the scene.

Revising

- Does your story "show, not tell" so that its details convey your impression of the experience?
- Do you need more specific details (see "RENNS," 5D)?
- Would your essay benefit if you included some dialogue?

7C   What is a frame for a personal essay?

The basic shape of a personal essay is a story, but it will probably also have some commentary or reflection (when you "step back" and explain what it all means). Here is a possible frame for a personal essay to adapt to the specifics of your assignment.

Frame for a Personal Essay

Introductory paragraph(s): Dramatic scene from the story

- **Capture your readers' attention** with an event or significant detail by (1) describing a specific scene or action at the start of your story, (2) beginning with the end of the story, OR (3) beginning at a dramatic point in the middle of the story. Each way creates a different kind of suspense.
- **Use your** THESIS STATEMENT to give readers a preview of the central point of your narrative.

Background

- **Explain the background of the story**, the general setting, the time and place it happened. Start each paragraph with a TOPIC SENTENCE.
- **Include some reflection or the point of your experience** or save it for later in your essay.

Rest of the story

- **Tell what happened** in several paragraphs, starting each with a topic sentence.

Personal Essay Frame (cont.)

- **Keep going** if you started at the beginning of your story. If you started at the middle or end, return to the beginning so that you tell the whole story. Use a mixture of SUMMARY (covering time in a few sentences) and scene (slowing down and including details and dialogue).
- **Use topic sentences** to sequence your story.

Reflection or analysis

- **Explain what readers can learn from this event**—about you, about other people or human nature, about situations, ideas, institutions, etc.
- **Use topic sentences**.

Optional: Include a related experience or event

- **Include a second experience or story** that relates to your main one, or an event in the news, someone else's story, or a historical situation.
- **Include your reflection or analysis** of the related material.
- **Connect any related material** to your main story.

Conclusion

- **Include a final detail, a final observation, a restatement of the main message of your story, or relate what happened after your story ended** as long as it flows smoothly with the rest of your paragraph.

7D What sentence and paragraph guides can help generate ideas?

Adapt these sentence and paragraph guides to your PURPOSE and AUDIENCE.

Sentence and Paragraph Guides

- One day [incident, event, experience, etc.] in particular stands out because _____.
- The experience of _____ ultimately taught me [helped me realize, illustrated how] _____.
- At first, this event might have seemed _____, but on deeper reflection it was _____.
- The most interesting [strangest, disturbing, humorous, perplexing, etc.] thing about the experience was _____. That was because _____. Furthermore, _____.

7E   A student's personal essay

Samantha Neuchterlein

WRIT 1622

Dr. Hesse

2 Feb. 2013

Dramatic opening starts mysteriously in the middle of the story.

7E

Saved by Technology—or Distracted by It?

In the late afternoon of a cold January day, Kurt and I were struggling through deep snow. We had slung our skis over our shoulders and had spent the past hour hiking up the face of a mountain, searching for familiar territory. It would be getting dark soon, and we were lost.

Ethical appeal (*ethos*) hints at the character and human side of the writer. Paragraph of reflection.

I have often exaggerated that my smartphone has "saved my life." Usually these perilous moments happen when, for example, a calendar notice pops up to remind me that I have a meeting with a teacher in fifteen minutes that I had totally forgotten. Recently though, my friend and his iPhone actually saved my life. Well, maybe that's a little extreme, but the phone certainly helped. In the process, however, I had a disturbing realization about the way technology has infiltrated our lives.

Paragraph explains context, introducing the people and setting the background.

A few Saturdays ago, I joined two friends, Kurt and Carter, for a day of skiing. We left our dorms at the University of Denver before dawn to drive two hours west, to the Arapahoe Basin ski area. The sun came up as we neared the Continental Divide, bathing the high peaks in pink and gold light. It was a spectacular cloudless morning with temperatures in the teens, and the brilliant skies promised a great day on the slopes.

By early afternoon we had completed several runs and had just taken the lift up to the top of the mountain. Standing at 12,000 feet, we stared at the backside, considering several

continued >>

Neuchterlein 2

options in the Montezuma Bowl. One was the tempting area out of bounds, the unpatrolled and unofficial slopes where signs warned us of dangers, including death. Most skiers have a love affair with untouched powder, fluffy snow with no tracks that surrounds you in a shimmering white cocoon as you swoosh through it. Any powder had long since been packed down on Arapahoe's ski runs, but out of bounds everything was still clean and pure. So, naturally (and foolishly) the three of us ducked under the ropes and hurtled down uncharted territory.

Writer summarizes the day and focuses on the most dramatic events.

At first it was terrific. The fresh snow squeaked with each turn that sent up white sparkling waves as we dodged boulders and looked for a path down. We called to each other in delight. But after about fifteen turns, things changed. Carter got split off from Kurt and me, and suddenly the untouched terrain became unskiable, over sixty degrees steep, with cliffs and drop-offs. Although we had started above the tree line, our path was now blocked with lodgepole pines. Going further would have been even more suicidal, so we stopped.

Writer evokes an emotional reaction (pathos).

Details give a clear picture of the situation. The writer combines a logical appeal (logos) with emotional (pathos) and ethical (ethos) appeals to capture the reader's attention.

"What's our plan?" Kurt asked.

"Our best hope is hiking up."

So we took off our skis and began trudging back up toward the edge of the boundary. Ski boots, deep snow, and thin air are a bad combination, especially when you're trying to climb a thousand feet and it's getting late. After nearly an hour and a half, we were exhausted. It was around five o'clock, well after the lifts had closed, dusk was falling, and it was getting colder. Suddenly, Kurt's cell phone rang. He quickly ripped off his gloves, thinking it was Carter. However, it was the ski patrol. Kurt told them that we had climbed back to the edge of bounds and would be back at the bottom momentarily. Two ski

7E

continued >>

Neuchterlein 3

Dialogue creates immediacy and the story uses all three appeals: emotional (*pathos*), ethical (*ethos*), and logical (*logos*).

patrollers met us near the lift, which they started to get us out of the back bowl. One said, "We got your phone numbers from your friend. He's OK. He's skiing down with other patrollers."

Forty-five minutes later, when we finally all met at the car, Carter explained more or less how he and his iPhone had saved us from a cold night in the middle of the woods. When he had realized that he was lost and much too far away from the resort, he took out his iPhone to check if there was 3G. There was. The first thing he Googled was when the sun would set at his location. 5:30. He had about an hour and a half of sunlight left. He then Googled the phone number for Arapahoe Basin ski patrol, called them, and said he was in the middle of the woods, split from his friends. He gave them our phone numbers,

Dialogue shows Carter's character, rather than telling us about it.

e-mailed his coordinates, and sat down to wait. "So I was sitting in the snow in the middle of the woods, waiting for them, going through my iTunes library trying to decide which song I'd like to die listening to." The three of us got a laugh out of this, but later I got thinking.

This paragraph begins the writer's reflection by thinking back on her friend's comment and what it might signify.

Carter's comment is the epitome of how technology has infiltrated our daily life. At all times, even a situation where someone is contemplating his "pre-death ritual," technology affects our decisions. Rather than thinking of his family or his life's accomplishments, Carter was caught between Dr. Dre and Eminem's "Forgot About Dre" and the classic by Kanye West, "Higher." Our unique thoughts and experiences are overshadowed by a small rectangle of plastic and metal. Even in an extreme moment, we're not entirely in that moment. Although this technology certainly holds the power to take us out of danger, as that day on the mountain showed, it also can distract us from our very lives.

continued >>

Neuchterlein 4

That night on the dark drive back to Denver, we listened to music. We told each other the story of that afternoon over and over, remembering details, sharing thoughts. We knew that our irresponsibility in going out of bounds had cost others trouble and effort, but we also knew we got a great story out of it. It was a story we would tell with some guilt, but we would happily tell it anyway. Beyond that, I knew that I had seen two sides of our reliance on technology, which can both save us and distract us from ourselves.

Concluding paragraph includes the story's end and more reflection; ending powerful sentence makes a logical statement (logos).

8A

8 Informative Essays

■ ■ ■ ■ ■ ■

Quick Points   You will learn to

➤ Describe key elements of informative essays (see section 8A).
➤ Apply the writing process to an informative essay (p. 74).
➤ Adapt frames and guides for an informative essay to your own needs (pp. 74–76).

MyWritingLab™   Visit mywritinglab.com for more resources on informative essays.

8A   What are informative essays?

When you write an informative essay, you play the role of an expert on the topic you're assigned or you choose.

■ Purpose

Your PURPOSE in writing an informative essay is solely to give your readers information about your topic in a logical sequence, written clearly and engagingly. If the assignment asks only for information, don't add an opinion or argument. Although assignments might not include the word *informative*, you can usually figure out the purpose from the wording. (For more about purposes, see 4C.)

■ Audience

To give information, you want to consider whether your readers might be specialists on your topic. If you can't know this, you're safest in assuming that your audience consists of nonspecialists, which means you need to present full information for people who have no background in your topic. Your readers hope to learn not only the basics of your topic but also sufficient, interesting specifics to hold their interest. (For more about audience, see 4C.)

8B   How do I plan and revise informative essays?

Generating ideas

- Read or talk to people knowledgeable about your topic.
- Search the Internet for useful, interesting information about your topic, but use only reliable, credible sources, quote them carefully, and avoid PLAGIARISM (see Chapter 13).

Revising

- Have you included the right amount of information if your readers are specialists in your topic? Conversely, if your readers aren't specialists on your topic, have you provided sufficient information for them?
- Have you used specific details to make the information come alive (see 5D)?
- Have you explained why this information is important or significant?

8C   What is a frame for an informative essay?

Informative essays can be organized in many ways. Here's a frame you can adapt to the specifics of your assignments.

Frame for an Informative Essay

Introductory paragraph(s)

- **Capture your readers' interest** by using one of the strategies for writing effective introductory paragraphs (see 5B).
- **Present your thesis statement**, making sure it gives the central point of the essay (see 4F).

Body paragraph(s): background information

- **Start with a topic sentence** that clearly relates to your thesis statement and leads logically to the information in the paragraph (see 5C).
- **Provide background** for the information in your essay. This might follow the introductory paragraph or come later in the essay at a point when the background is more relevant.

Body paragraph(s)

- **Present sections of information**, divided into logical groups, generally one to a paragraph, starting each paragraph with a topic sentence that clearly relates to the essay's thesis statement and leads logically into the paragraph (see 5C).
- **Support each topic sentence with specific details**, such as RENNS (see 5D).

Conclusion

- **Bring the essay to a logical conclusion**, using one of the strategies for writing effective concluding paragraphs (see 5F).

8D

8D What are sentence and paragraph guides for an informative essay?

Adapt these sentence and paragraph guides to your PURPOSE and AUDIENCE.

Sentence and Paragraph Guides

- People experienced with _____ advise that the public needs to know _____ so that everyone can _____.
- _____ captured my interest because _____.
- People generally consider _____, _____, and _____ as the major components of information about _____.

(continued)

Informative Guides (cont.)

- In addition to _____, _____ plays a major role in _____.
- For many people, the most compelling information about _____ is _____. However, they often overlook _____. That aspect is important because _____.
- Other important information about _____ is _____.
- In conclusion, _____.
- After considering all the information available about _____, we can conclude that _____.

8E   A student's informative essay

Moreno 1

Carol Moreno

English 1122

Professor Fleming

12 Feb. 2013

Weight Lifting for Women

Introductory paragraph uses ethical and emotional appeals (*ethos* and *logos*) with a story to lead into the thesis statement that presents the writer's point of view about the topic.

Last summer, after my grandmother fell and broke her hip, I wanted to help care for her. Because she was bedridden, she needed to be lifted at times. I was shocked to discover that I could not lift her fragile frame of 90 pounds without my brother's help. At least I could tend to her in other ways, especially by reading aloud to her, which she loved. Still, my pride was hurt, so I signed up for a Physical Education class at the local community college in weight lifting for women. The course brochure captured my interest immediately. It said that women can lift weights as long as they learn how to do so properly.

Topic sentence about the writer's career goal.

What excited me the most about the weight lifting course for women was that my career goal was to be a nurse. Once my two children were old enough to go to school all day, I intended

continued >>

Moreno 2

to start my studies. Nursing care for the elderly had always appealed to me. My experience with my grandmother proved how important physical strength would be in nursing. Although in the United States the elderly usually are not revered as much as they are in Asian countries, I had great respect for my grandparents. They all lived nearby, and I would seek them out to tell me their life stories. For example, my grandmother who had broken her hip had lived in Nairobi, Kenya, for ten years as a U.S. Trade Representative to various African countries. She had to have been a strong, resourceful woman. Not being able to lift her when she was ill really upset me.

Specific details name a location and job.

8E

The first fact that I learned in my course for women lifting weights was we can rely on our biology to protect us from developing masculine-looking muscle mass. Women's bodies produce only small amounts of the hormones that enlarge muscles in men. If women want to be bodybuilders and compete for titles such as Ms. Olympia and Ms. International, they need to take supplements to alter their body chemistry so that their muscles become bulkier rather than longer. The students in my class did not want that look. We wanted smooth, firm muscles, not massive bulges. Aside from gaining nicer looking muscles, some students said from the start that they expected the course to help them lose weight. Our teacher had disappointing news for them. Muscles actually weigh more than fat. The good news was that when our flab turned into muscle, we would lose inches from our limbs and waist. Those students might not weigh less, but they would look slimmer.

Topic sentence ties into thesis statement and starts biology information.

Specific details name two titles.

Specific details give factual information.

Striving for strength can end in injury unless weight lifters learn the safe use of free weights and weight machines. Free weights are barbells, the metal bars that round metal

continued >>

Writer uses logical appeal (*logos*).

weights can be attached to at each end. To be safe, no matter how little the weight, lifters must never raise a barbell by bending at the waist. Instead, they should squat, grasp the barbell, and then use their leg muscles to straighten into a standing position. To avoid a twist that can lead to serious injury, lifters must use this posture: head erect and facing forward, back and neck aligned. The big advantage of weight machines, which use weighted handles and bars hooked to wires and pulleys, is that lifters must use them sitting down. Therefore, machines like the Nautilus and Universal actually force lifters to keep their bodies properly aligned, which drastically reduces the chance of injury.

8E

Once a weight lifter understands how to lift safely, she needs a regimen personalized to her physical needs. Because benefits come from "resistance," which is the stress that lifting weight puts on a muscle, no one has to be strong to get started. A well-planned, progressive weight-training program begins with whatever weight a person can lift comfortably and gradually adds to the base weight as she gets stronger. What builds muscle strength is the number of repetitions, or "reps," the lifter does, not necessarily the addition of weight.

Writer uses specific details for an emotional appeal (*pathos*).

Our instructor helped the women, who ranged from 18 to 43, scrawny to pudgy, and couch potato to superstar, to develop a program that was right for our individual weight, age, and overall level of conditioning. Everyone's program differed in how much weight to start out with and how many reps to do for each exercise. Our instructor urged us to not try more weight or reps than our programs called for, even if our first workouts seemed too easy. This turned out to be good advice because

continued >>

Moreno 4

those of us who did not listen woke up the next day feeling as
though evil forces had twisted our bodies.

In addition to fitting a program to her physical
capabilities, a female weight lifter needs to design an
individual routine to fit her personal goals. Most students
in my class wanted to improve their upper body strength, so
we focused on exercises to strengthen our arms, shoulders,
abdomens, and chests. Each student worked on specifically
tailored exercises to isolate certain muscle groups. Because
muscles toughen up and grow when they are rested after a
workout, our instructor taught us to alternate muscle groups
on different days. For example, a student might work on her
arms and abdomen one day and then her shoulders and
chest the next day. Because I had had such trouble lifting
my grandmother, I added exercises to strengthen my legs
and back. Another student had hurt her neck in a car crash,
so she added exercises that focused exclusively on her neck
and upper shoulders. Someone else who was planning to be
a physical therapist added finger and hand-strengthening
routines. By the middle of the term, we each had our specific,
personal routine to use during class and continue once the term
ended.

At the end of our 10 weeks of weight training, we had
to evaluate our progress. Was I impressed! I felt ready to lift
the world. If my grandmother were still bedridden, I could lift
her with ease. When I started, I could not lift 10 pounds over
my head twice. Midterm, I could lift that much only for four
repetitions. By the end of the course, I could lift 10 pounds over
my head for 15 repetitions, and I could lift 18 pounds for two

8E

Writer uses humor for ethical appeal (*ethos*).

Topic sentence ties back to essay's thesis statement and uses transition "in addition."

Specific details (RENNS, see 5D) combine with an ethical appeal (*ethos*).

Last sentence leads into the concluding paragraph.

Topic sentence starts drawing the essay to a logical end.

Specific detail ties into the introductory paragraph's story.

continued >>

Moreno 5

Specific details wrap up the student's experience.

Concluding sentences tie to essay's thesis statement and end with humor.

repetitions. Also, I could swim laps for 20 sustained minutes instead of the five I had barely managed at first. In conclusion, I am so proud of my accomplishments that I still work out three or four times a week. I am proof that any woman can benefit from "pumping iron." After all, there isn't anything to lose— except some flab.

9A

9 Arguments

■ ■ ■ ■ ■

Quick Points   You will learn to

➤ Describe key elements of arguments (see 9A).
➤ Apply the writing process to an argument (pp. 82–83).
➤ Adapt frames and guides for an argument to your own needs (pp. 83–85).

MyWritingLab™ Visit mywritinglab.com for more resources on arguments.

9A What is an argument?

A written ARGUMENT consists of

- A THESIS STATEMENT (also called a *claim*) that clearly presents the debatable topic and sets forth the writer's opinion regarding that topic
- Support for the debatable topic, consisting of EVIDENCE, EXAMPLES, and reasons, with logical explanations to back them up

If you were to judge the nature of arguments only by the popular media, you might think arguments are simply name-calling or fighting. For college-level writing, however, arguments need to demonstrate CRITICAL THINKING and sound reasoning as explained in Chapter 2.

■ Purpose

The goal of argument essays is to try to convince readers to believe or do something. If you can't reasonably expect to change a person's mind, especially on highly controversial issues like capital punishment or a woman's right to choose, your purpose is to demonstrate a thoughtful point of view that has good reasoning behind it.

Sometimes instructors assign students a position to argue. In such cases, even if you personally disagree with it, you need to reason logically and effectively. If instructors assign you to select your own topic, choose one suitable for college writing. For example, "Should public libraries block certain Web sites?" is worthy of a college-level essay.

Purposes for arguments fall into four general categories, as explained in Quick Box 9.1.

9A

Quick Box 9.1   ■ ■ ■ ■ ■ ■

Purposes and categories of arguments

- **Definition arguments** persuade readers to interpret a term or concept. Is assisted suicide "murder," "a medical procedure," or an "act of kindness"? What characteristics must a film have to be called a romantic comedy?

- **Evaluation arguments** persuade readers that something is good or bad or worthwhile or a waste of time, compared to other things like it.

- **Cause and effect arguments** take two different forms. One argues that a situation results from a particular cause, such as causes most responsible for homelessness. Another argues that an action will have a specific effect, such as more nuclear power plants would reduce global warming.

- **Proposal or solution arguments**, covered in detail in Chapter 10, convince readers that a particular solution to a problem or a particular way of addressing a need is best.

■ Audience

Arguments require the writer to be highly sensitive to readers' interests and needs. You want to analyze what your readers know and what they already believe about the topic. What are their values, viewpoints, and assumptions?

The approach most commonly used for arguments is known as **classical argument**. Section 9C offers you a frame for it.

When your readers hold extreme or one-sided opinions, your arguments can rarely change their minds, but you're expected to demonstrate that you can use sound reasoning when you address them. In such cases, consider using the approach to argument known as **Rogerian argument.** It's based on psychologist Carl Rogers's communication principles, which suggest that even strong opponents can respect your position, if you show that you understand their viewpoint and treat it with respect. Section 9C offers you a frame for a Rogerian argument.

9B How do I plan and revise arguments?

Generating ideas

- Make sure your topic is open to debate. For example, "We will eventually run out of fossil fuels" is not a debatable topic. "We should require car makers to increase mileage by 50 percent" is.

- Test that your topic is open to debate by asking if it answers a question open to more than one possible answer. The following list shows you an example.

TOPIC	Students at Mitchler College must study a foreign language.
DEBATABLE QUESTION	Should Mitchler College require students to study a foreign language?
FIRST ANSWER	Mitchler College should not require students to study a foreign language.
SECOND ANSWER	Mitchler College should require students to study a foreign language.
THIRD ANSWER	Mitchler College should require all business majors to study a foreign language.

- Ask yourself *why* you take the position you do on your debatable topic. When you respond, "Because . . . ," you're ready to offer reasons.

- List the pros (in favor of) and cons (against) your position.

- Arrange your possible reasons in logical order, which might suitably become TOPIC SENTENCES of your paragraphs.

- Decide whether support for your position involves research. (See Chapters 12–15.)

- Use the three persuasive appeals, explained in 2B: logical appeal (*logos*), ethical appeal (*ethos*), and emotional appeal (*pathos*).

Alex Garcia, who wrote the argument essay that appears in section 9E, was interested in whether organic food was really better. Here's how Alex progressed from topic to claim to thesis statement.

TOPIC	Organic food
DEBATABLE QUESTION	Are organic foods better than regular foods?
MY POSITION	I think people should buy organic foods when they can.
THESIS STATEMENT (FIRST DRAFT)	It is good for people to buy organic foods. This preliminary thesis statement clearly states the writer's position, but the word *good* is vague.
THESIS STATEMENT (SECOND DRAFT)	To achieve health benefits and improve the quality of the environment, organic foods should be purchased by consumers. This revised thesis statement is better because it states the writer's point of view, but it suffers from a lack of conciseness and from the passive construction "should be purchased."
THESIS STATEMENT (FINAL DRAFT)	Research shows that the health and environmental benefits of organic foods outweigh their extra costs. This final version works well because it states the writer's point of view clearly and concisely, with verbs all in the active voice. It also meets the requirements for a thesis statement given in Quick Box 4.8.

9C

Revising

- Does your essay take a clear position on a debatable topic?

- Have you stayed on your topic?

- Do your reasons and evidence support your argument well?

- Have you anticipated and responded to objections or counterarguments that others might have?

- Is your tone reasonable, thoughtful, and fair?

- Have you used logical, emotional, and ethical appeals (*logos, pathos,* and *ethos*) appropriately to convince your audience (see 2B)?

- Have you avoided logical fallacies (see 2D)?

9C What are frames for arguments?

Successful arguments can take many forms. We present here two possible frames—one for classical argument and one for Rogerian argument—to adapt to the specifics of your assignments.

Frame for a Classical Argument

Introductory paragraph(s)

- **Capture your readers' interest** by using one of the strategies for writing effective introductory paragraphs (see 5B).
- **Present your THESIS STATEMENT**, making sure it gives the central point that you will argue.

Body paragraph(s): background information

- **Start with a TOPIC SENTENCE** that clearly relates to your thesis statement and leads logically to the information in the paragraph.
- **Provide background** for the information in your essay. This might follow the introductory paragraph or come later in the essay at a point when the background is more relevant.

Body paragraphs: Reasons to support your claim

- **Present reasons for your argument**, one to a paragraph. If a reason is very complicated, use two paragraphs divided at a logical point.
- **Start each paragraph with a topic sentence** that states your reason.
- **Support each topic sentence** with evidence, examples, and reasoning.

Body Paragraphs: Rebuttal

- **Present objections and answer them**. State the major objections that someone might give against your position. Answer those criticisms by explaining why your position is stronger.
- **Start each paragraph with a topic sentence** that helps your readers follow your line of reasoning.

Conclusion

- **Wrap up the essay** with a brief summary of the argument.
- **Present an elaboration of the argument's significance**, or give a call to action for the readers, or use one of the strategies for an effective concluding paragraph listed in Quick Box 5.4.

Frame for a Rogerian Argument

Introductory paragraph(s)

- **Capture your readers' interest** by using one of the strategies for writing effective introductory paragraphs (See 5B).
- **Present your thesis statement**, making sure it gives the central point that you will argue.

Rogerian Argument Frame (cont.)

Body paragraph(s): Establish common ground with readers

- **Explain the issue**, acknowledging that some readers probably don't agree with you.
- **Explain the points of agreement** you and your readers share concerning underlying problems or issues.
- **Summarize opposing positions** and acknowledge ways, if any, that some of them may be desirable. This may take one paragraph or several, depending on the complexity of the issue.
- **Start each paragraph with a** TOPIC SENTENCE that ties into your thesis statement and previews the content of the paragraph.

Body paragraphs: Reasons to support your claim

- **Present reasons for your claim**, one to a paragraph.
- **Start each paragraph with a topic sentence** that states your reason.
- **Support each topic sentence** with evidence, examples, and reasoning.

Conclusion

- **Use an engaging strategy** for a concluding paragraph (see 5F).
- **Summarize why your position is preferable** to your opponent's. Use a reasonable tone.

9D

9D What are some sentence and paragraph guides for arguments?

Adapt these guides to your PURPOSE and AUDIENCE.

Sentence and Paragraph Guides

- The main reason [the most compelling argument] is _____. Recent statistics show that _____. These statistics are important because _____.
- Many experts support this position. For example, _____, who is _____, has argued "_____." _____ makes a similar point by explaining _____. The significance of this quotation is _____.
- I understand that my opponents believe _____. I respect their reasoning that _____ and also that _____. In fact, one thing we have in common is _____.

(continued)

> Argument Guides (cont.)

- Some people might oppose my position by arguing that _____. They might explain that _____, and they might point to support such as _____. However, this argument fails to take into account _____. Furthermore, other evidence suggests a different conclusion, namely _____. Ultimately, this opposing argument is unconvincing because _____.

9E   A student's argument essay

9E

Garcia 1

Alex Garcia

Professor Brosnahan

WRIT 1122

4 Oct. 2012

Why Organic Foods Are Worth the Cost

A mainstay of televised cooking programs and

Writer uses a popular reference to get readers' attention, introduces a key debatable question, and states the thesis of the paper in his last sentence.

competitions, from Top Chef to Iron Chef, is an emphasis on fine ingredients. Beyond the caviar, truffles, and lobster, however, one small feature gets big attention: organic. Increasingly, that word matters in supermarkets where displays of similar fruits and vegetables differ by cost and a sticker saying "organic." Are organics worth the extra money, especially when budgets are tight? After all, even the United States Department of Agriculture (USDA) "makes no claims that organically produced food is safer or more nutritious than

Writer uses a logical appeal (*logos*), even though he intends to disagree with it.

conventionally produced food." Despite all the confusion, current research shows that the health and environmental benefits of organic foods outweigh their extra costs.

Organic foods are produced without using most chemical pesticides, without artificial fertilizers, without genetic

continued >>

Garcia 2

engineering, and without radiation (USDA). In the case of organic meat, poultry, eggs, and dairy products, the animals are raised without antibiotics or growth hormones. As a result, people sometimes use the term "natural" instead of "organic," but "natural" is less precise. Before 2002, people could never be quite sure what they were getting when they bought supposedly organic food, unless they bought it directly from a farmer they knew personally. In 2002, the USDA established standards that food must meet in order to be labeled and sold as organic.

Writer provides background information and defines "organic."

9E

Organic foods do cost up to 50% more than nonorganic (Zelman) mainly because they are currently more difficult to mass-produce. Artificial fertilizers tend to increase the yield, size, and uniformity of fruits and vegetables, and herbicides kill weeds that compete with desirable crops for sun, nutrients, and moisture. Animals that routinely receive antibiotics and growth hormones grow more quickly and produce more milk and eggs. In contrast, organic farmers have lower yields and, therefore, higher costs. These get passed along as higher prices to consumers.

A second paragraph of background information. Cost is a key issue, so this paragraph explains why organic foods are expensive.

Still, the extra cost is worthwhile in terms of health benefits. Numerous studies have shown the dangers of pesticides for humans. An extensive review of research by the Ontario College of Family Physicians concludes that "Exposure to all the commonly used pesticides . . . has shown positive associations with adverse health effects" (Sanborn et al. 173). The risks include cancer, psychiatric effects, difficulties becoming pregnant, miscarriages, and dermatitis. Carefully washing fruits and vegetables can remove some of these dangerous chemicals, but according to the prestigious journal *Nature*, even this does not remove all of them (Giles 797). An extensive review of research by

Writer uses an ethical appeal (*ethos*) to arouse readers' concern for their health.

Writer supports argument by citing three experts.

continued >>

Garcia 3

Writer uses an emotional appeal (*pathos*) and gives the first main reason in support of the thesis.

medical professor Denis Lairon found that "the vast majority (94–100%) of organic food does not contain any pesticide residues" (38). Certainly, if there's a way to prevent these poisons from entering our bodies, we should take advantage of it. The few cents saved on cheaper food can quickly disappear in doctors' bills needed to treat conditions caused or worsened by chemicals.

A second reason in favor of organic foods. The writer uses careful reasoning to explain it.

Organic meat, poultry, and dairy products can address another health concern: the diminishing effectiveness of antibiotics. In past decades, many kinds of bacteria have become resistant to drugs, making it extremely difficult to treat some kinds of tuberculosis, pneumonia, staphylococcus infections, and less serious diseases ("Dangerous" 1). Routinely giving antibiotics to all cows and chickens means that these drugs enter our food chain early, giving bacteria lots of chances to develop resistance. A person who switches to organic meats won't suddenly experience better results from antibiotics; the benefit is a more gradual one for society as a whole. Buying organic is a way to persuade more farmers to adopt this practice.

Writer uses logical, ethical, and emotional appeals (*logos, ethos,* and *pathos*).

Writer explains a third reason, again using an expert source in support.

Another benefit of organic foods is a societal one: Organic farming is better for the environment. In his review of several studies, Colin Macilwain concluded that organic farms nurture more and diverse plants and animals than regular farms (797). Organic farms also don't release pesticides and herbicides that can harm wildlife and run into our water supply, with implications for people's health, too. Macilwain notes that those farms also can generate less carbon dioxide, which will help with global warming. Also, many scientists believe that organic farming is more sustainable because it results in better soil quality (798). While these benefits are not ones that people will personally experience right away, a better natural

continued >>

Garcia 4

environment means a better quality of living for everyone and for future generations.

Some critics point out that organic products aren't more nutritious than regular ones. Four years ago, media star and physician Sanjay Gupta, for example, found the medical evidence for nutritional advantages is "thin" (60), and the *Tufts University Health and Nutrition Letter* reported that the research on nutritional benefits is mixed ("Is Organic" 8). However, other studies differ. For example, research shows that organically raised tomatoes have higher levels of flavonoids, nutrients that have many health benefits (Mitchell et al.). More recently, both Denis Lairon and Walter J. Crinnion found higher levels of several nutrients in organic food. Nutritional value, including vitamins and other beneficial substances, is a different measure than food safety. Even if the nutritional evidence is uncertain, the argument that farmers improve food safety by avoiding chemicals remains convincing.

Despite the considerable benefits of purchasing organic products, there are no simple ways to measure that spending fifty cents more on a cantaloupe will improve someone's quality of life by fifty cents. However, there is a position between all organics and none. The nonprofit Environmental Working Group identifies a dozen types of organic produce (including apples, strawberries, and spinach) as safer and worth the extra cost, but they conclude another dozen are not, including bananas, pineapples, and onions (Zelman). Overall, the long-term benefits of buying organic, for anyone who can reasonably afford to, far outweigh the short-term savings in the checkout line.

By arousing the "better self" of readers, the writer uses an ethical appeal (*ethos*).

Writer mentions objections that contradict his argument.

9E

Writer counters objections and strongly favors organic foods.

Writer uses logical and emotional appeals (*logos* and *pathos*) to try to convince his readers.

Concluding paragraph returns to issues of cost in the thesis statement, summarizes paper's reasoning and gives a strong call for action.

Ends by appealing to logic, ethics, and emotions (*logos*, *ethos*, and *pathos*).

continued >>

9E

Garcia 5

Works Cited

In an actual paper, the Works Cited starts on a new page.

"Dangerous Bacterial Infections Are on the Rise." *Consumer Reports on Health* (Nov. 2007): 1–4. Print.

Crinnion, Walter J. "Organic Foods Contain Higher Levels of Certain Nutrients, Lower Levels of Pesticides, and May Provide Health Benefits for the Consumer." *Alternative Medicine Review* 15.1 (Apr. 2010): 4–12. Web. 14 Sept. 2011.

Giles, Jim. "Is Organic Food Better for Us?" *Nature* 428.6985 (2004): 796–97. Print.

Gupta, Sanjay, and Shahreen Abedin. "Rethinking Organics." *Time* (20 Aug. 2007): 60. Print.

"Is Organic Food Really More Nutritious?" *Tufts University Health and Nutrition Letter* (Sept. 2007): 8. Web. 25 Sept. 2011.

Lairon, Denis. "Nutritional Quality and Safety of Organic Food. A Review." *Agronomy for Sustainable Development* 30 (2010): 33–41. Web. 14 Sept. 2011.

Macilwain, Colin. "Is Organic Farming Better for the Environment?" *Nature* 428.6985 (2004): 797–98. Print.

Mitchell, Alyson E., et al. "Ten-Year Comparison of the Influence of Organic and Conventional Crop Management Practices on the Content of Flavonoids in Tomatoes." *Journal of Agricultural Food Chemistry* 55.15 (2007): 6154–59. Web. 30 Sept. 2011.

United States. Dept. of Agriculture. "Organic Food Labels and Standards: The Facts." *National Organic Program*. Jan. 2007. Web. 26 Sept. 2011.

continued >>

Garcia 6

Sanborn, Margaret, et al. *Pesticides Literature Review:*
   Systematic Review of Pesticide Human Health Effects.
   Toronto: Ontario College of Family Physicians, 2004. Web.
   28 Sept. 2011.

Zelman, Kathleen M. "Organic Food—Is 'Natural' Worth the
   Extra Cost?" *WebMD*. 2007. Web. 17 Sept. 2011.

10A

10 Proposal or Solution Essays
■ ■ ■ ■ ■ ■

Quick Points   You will learn to

➤ Describe key elements of a proposal or solution essay (see 10A).
➤ Apply the writing process to a proposal or solution essay (pp. 92–93).
➤ Adapt frames and guides for a proposal or solution essay to your own needs (pp. 93–95).

MyWritingLab™ Visit mywritinglab.com for more resources on proposal or
solution essays.

10A What are proposal or solution essays?

Proposal or **solution essays** are specific types of ARGUMENTS (see Chapter 9) that require you to do three things: (1) Convince readers that a particular problem exists and requires action. (2) Propose a specific solution or course of action and offer reasons for proposing it. (3) Defend your solution or proposal as better than others.

■ Purpose

The purpose of proposal or solution essays is to persuade readers to act on a solution. You need to address the problem you are writing about, your proposed solution(s), and the beliefs your readers hold about them. Here are two examples of problems and possible solutions, one of which you might choose to write about.

A. Problem: Students can't get the classes they need to graduate on time.

   Solution 1: The college should offer more courses by hiring more faculty or having faculty teach more students.

   Solution 2: The college should increase the number of popular or required courses it offers by cutting elective courses.

   Solution 3: The college should change graduation requirements.

B. Problem: Unemployment is high.

   Solution 1: The government should hire unemployed people to build roads, bridges, parks, and other public projects.

   Solution 2: The government should reward businesses that hire people to work in this country or penalize businesses that send jobs overseas.

   Solution 3: Workers should be less choosey about the jobs they will accept, or they should start their own businesses.

No doubt you can think of other solutions. Which solution would be best? Why?

■ Audience

In both the above examples A and B, some readers may deny a problem exists. They might think that delays for graduation aren't a problem. They might not realize how many people are unemployed or consider high unemployment troublesome. You need to address these possibilities (or others) in your essay.

For more about audience, see 4C.

10B How do I plan and revise proposal or solution arguments?

In writing proposal or solution essays, you might use these questions.

• What caused the problem? Complex problems usually have many possible causes so take time to brainstorm a list.

• What are possible solutions? Because each cause might have a different solution, don't rush into settling on one of them. Allow yourself time to be creative.

- Why is your solution effective? Who needs to be involved? What do they need to do? When? How? Why?

- Why is your solution feasible? A solution is feasible when it is practical and affordable. For example, we could solve poverty by giving every poor person $50,000 a year, but that's not feasible.

- What are drawbacks of other solutions? Apply questions of effectiveness and feasibility to all solutions to reveal weaknesses in alternative proposals. Also, you might consider unintended effects or results.

- What will happen if people don't act? This question can generate an effective conclusion and be a good source of emotional appeals (*pathos*).

Revising

- Have you established that there's a problem that needs a solution?

- Is your solution effective, feasible, well-reasoned, and preferable to others?

- Have you used evidence that is sufficient, representative, relevant, and accurate (see 12G)?

- Have you used appropriate logical, emotional, and ethical appeals (*logos, pathos,* and *ethos;* see 2B)?

- Is your TONE reasonable, thoughtful, and fair?

10C   What is a frame for a proposal or solution essay?

Here is a possible proposal/solution essay frame to adapt to the specifics of your assignments.

Frame for a Proposal or Solution Essay

Introductory paragraph(s)

- **Capture your readers' interest** in your topic by using one of the strategies for writing effective introductory paragraphs (see 5B).
- **Introduce** a problem or opportunity and present your THESIS STATEMENT, making sure it proposes a solution (see 4F).

Body paragraph(s): Background information

- **Start each paragraph with a TOPIC SENTENCE** that clearly relates to your thesis statement and leads logically to the information in the paragraph (see 5C).
- **Provide background information.** If the background isn't complicated, your essay might move directly to persuading readers that a problem exists.

(continued)

| Frame for a Proposal or Solution Essay (cont.) |

Body paragraphs: Persuade readers that a problem exists

- **Explain the problem that exists**, grouping the parts of the problem effectively within separate paragraphs.
- **Start each paragraph with a** TOPIC SENTENCE and support each topic sentence with evidence, examples, and reasoning.
- **If your emphasis is on the solution** because the problem is well known, keep this section short.

Solution paragraph(s)

- **Divide parts of your solution** into sensible paragraphs, starting each with a topic sentence.
- **Explain why your solution will be effective and feasible**.
- **If your emphasis is on the problem**, keep this section short.

Rebuttal paragraph(s): Place here or immediately before your solution

- **Present alternative solutions and refute them**. Explain other possible solutions and why they aren't as good as yours. Use topic sentences to clarify your line of reasoning.
- **If your emphasis is on the problem**, keep this section short.

Conclusion

- **End with a strategy** for concluding paragraphs (see 5F).
- **Summarize** your problem briefly and portray the negative consequences of not adopting your solution.

10D   What are some sentence and paragraph guides for proposal/solution essays?

Adapt these guides to your PURPOSE and AUDIENCE.

| Sentence and Paragraph Guides |

- The best way to solve the problem of _____ is by _____.
- To address the problem of _____, _____ (we, you, the city council, the board, parking services, etc.) should _____.
- There are _____ reasons the current situation is a problem. The first is _____. The second is _____. However, the most important is _____.

> **Proposal or Solution Guides (cont.)**
>
> - The most effective and practical solution to this problem is
>   _____. One result of implementing this solution would be
>   _____. That's because _____. Another outcome would
>   be _____. A potential difficulty of this solution is _____.
>   However, we can overcome that difficulty by _____.
> - Some other possible solutions would be to _____ or to
>   _____. The first is problematic because _____. The
>   second is impractical because _____. My solution is preferable
>   to both alternatives because _____.
> - Failing to take this action will have several negative consequences.
>   First, _____. Furthermore, _____.

10E

10E   A student's solution essay

Cui 1

Yanggu Cui

Professor Leade

Writing 102

10 Dec. 2013

A Proposal to Improve Fan Behavior at Children's Games

"Ref, you're an idiot!"

"You're blind as a bat and twice as stupid!"

"Get a life, ref!"

"I'll see you after the game!"

Those were just a few yells I heard from the sidelines of
a soccer game last Saturday. I wasn't watching a professional
match or even a high school one. Instead, it was my eight-year-
old cousin's game in the Arapahoe Recreation League. The
referee wasn't a 30-year-old professional but, rather, a skinny
high school girl who seemed to be fifteen or sixteen. The people
yelling weren't drunken guys in sweatshirts or even coaches

**Quotations
get readers'
attention and
lead to the
introduction.**

**Details create
emotional
appeals
(*pathos*)
by giving a
picture of the
events.**

continued >>

Cui 2

Introductory paragraph sets up the problem. In the thesis sentence at the end of the paragraph, the writer presents a solution.

with red faces and bulging neck veins; instead, they were moms and dads drinking lattes. The league organizers need to bring an end to this kind of abuse, and the best way to do so is by requiring all parents to sign a code of good behavior.

Mentioning parents appeals to emotions (*pathos*) and provides context.

Parents for decades have proudly watched their sons and daughters play little league softball, baseball, soccer, and other sports. In recent years, these sports have gotten more competitive, with more games, longer seasons, more practices, and greater expectations for winning. One result is that parents have gotten more vocal on the sidelines, not only yelling encouragement for Julio and Jenny but also screaming protests at coaches, the opposing team, and officials. Almost every call against their team is greeted by loud disbelief, at best, and insults or threats, at worst.

Topic sentence announces four reasons for convincing readers that a problem exists and is a logical appeal (*logos*).

Each reason receives a brief explanation. Numbering creates clarity.

The current level of fan abuse is troubling for at least four reasons. First, it discourages officials, especially younger ones who are just learning the job themselves. No one fears making a wrong call more than someone who is just gaining experience as a referee. If parents make the job so unpleasant that kids making minimum wage stop doing it, the games will come to a halt. Second, it makes what should be a fun recreational experience for all into an ordeal. Rather than paying attention to the game, players and spectators alike get distracted by the drama on the sidelines, even getting nervous that a physical confrontation or fight might occur. Third, it embarrasses the kids themselves. Parents might feel like their kids appreciate and value someone sticking up for them, but the truth of the matter is that most children would rather not have that particular kind of attention.

10E

continued >>

Cui 3

The fourth, and most distressing, problem is that fan abuse warps the nature of the game itself. At a time when participating, having fun, and learning new skills should be primary, young players get the clear message that only winning matters, winning at all costs. Rather than assuming that officials and others are trying their best to be impartial and fair, kids are being taught that people are incompetent and malicious. Rather than assuming that sometimes in life we make mistakes that get penalized, but life goes on, kids learn that they are rarely, if ever, at fault. Rather than accepting adversity, even if sometimes it's wrong, kids learn to dwell on every hardship. The result is that instead of learning lessons valuable for a happy life, kids learn to be intolerant and bitter, and they learn it from their parents.

It would be nice to assume that merely talking to parents would control the situation, but the situation actually requires a more active solution. The Arapahoe Recreational League should adopt a code of conduct for all parents, in the form of an agreement they must sign. This code should indicate fan behaviors that are approved and encouraged; these would include yelling encouragement or congratulations for all players. The code would also specify behaviors that are banned; these would include taunting or criticizing players, coaches, and officials. Children whose parents refuse to sign would not be allowed to participate.

Granted, merely signing a code of conduct will not prevent all abuse. However, it gives a clear mechanism to end it once it happens. If there's a violation, officials can stop the game, and ask the coach of the team with offending parents to remind them of the code they signed. If extreme behavior

Writer presents most important reason last.

10E

Writer explains the negative influence on children.

Writer introduces the solution and provides an explanation using a logical appeal (logos).

Writer strengthens her ethical appeal (ethos) by recognizing some limitations. She goes on to explain how the solution would be effective.

continued >>

Cui 4

continues, the official can stop the game for an extended period, and if it still persists, he or she can declare a forfeit and end the game. This series of events puts responsibility on the parents, who cannot claim they didn't understand the consequences, and it puts a clear end to the abuse.

10E

This paragraph acknowledges other possible solutions and explains their shortcomings.

Other solutions have been proposed in different leagues. The most extreme is to ban spectators from even attending games. While a ban would surely prevent fan abuse, it would unfairly penalize those many parents who are good sports and supportive spectators. Plus, who wants to deprive people from seeing an important part of their children, grandchildren, and friends' childhood? Another solution has been to require spectators to be absolutely silent during games. This solution, while also potentially successful, deprives players and parents alike of the joys of praise and encouragement.

The essay concludes with a call to action that has a logical appeal (*logos*). It shows the benefits of the solution and portrays the consequences of not adopting it.

I urge you, then, to adopt my solution. Having a code of conduct will reduce fan abuse, restore some of the fun to our games, and keep them in perspective as fun, not battles. Failing to take this action would worsen the attitude that winning is everything and leave children even less prepared for the inevitable disappointments and struggles of life. Ultimately, it might eventually result in empty fields with no one willing to endure threats and insults from spectators who lack the discipline and perspective to behave in ways that their own children deserve.

Essays Analyzing Literary or Other Works

Quick Points You will learn to

➤ Describe key elements of an analysis essay (see section 11A).
➤ Apply the writing process to an analysis essay (pp. 101–102).
➤ Adapt frames and guides for an analysis essay to your own needs (pp. 102–104).

MyWritingLab™ Visit mywritinglab.com for more resources on analyzing literary and other works.

11A What is an essay that analyzes literary or other works?

An analysis essay explains the meaning of a work by breaking it down into its component parts and showing how it is put together. To write an analysis essay, you begin by closely reading, observing, or looking at the specific work you intend to discuss. You consider the whole work as well as its component parts.

In your written analysis, you use your THESIS STATEMENT to present the point of view you intend to explain and support by referring specifically to parts of the work and to the work as a whole. You want to start with a SUMMARY of the whole work, but never stop there. You must go far beyond your summary to analyze the work. You're expected to explain your point of view about the whole work and/or its separate parts. This explanation is your interpretation of the work, through which you display your ability to engage in CRITICAL THINKING and avoid LOGICAL FALLACIES (see Chapter 2). You employ SYNTHESIS to relate what you're discussing to ideas, concepts, feelings, or incidents you have experienced, read about, or learned about through other means.

These processes of summary followed by interpretation take time so plan your schedule with room to re-read, re-observe, or re-examine the work you've chosen to write about. The time to think and reflect is crucial if you want your essay to be thorough, fair-minded, and have a sound line of reasoning. Craft your essay's THESIS STATEMENT with special care so that it clearly states your central position concerning the work.

Literary works include fiction (novels and stories), drama (plays, scripts, and some films), and poetry (poems and lyrics), as well as nonfiction with artistic qualities (memoirs, personal essays, and so on). Often assignments for a literary analysis ask you to focus on one element in a work or to discuss how a writer develops a theme through several elements. Quick Box 11.1 describes the major literary elements you might be asked to examine.

Works other than literary ones that you might be assigned to analyze include films; works of art (paintings, sculptures, and murals); Web sites; television programs; or any of a wealth of other creative processes.

Quick Box 11.1

■ ■ ■ ■ ■ ■

11A

Major elements to analyze in literary works

PLOT	Events and their sequence
THEME	Central idea or message
STRUCTURE	Organization and relationship of parts to each other and to the whole
CHARACTERIZATION	Traits, thoughts, and actions of the people in the work
SETTING	Time and place of the action
POINT OF VIEW	Perspective or position from which a narrator or a main character presents the material
STYLE	Word choice and sentence structures that author uses: the "how," not the "what."
IMAGERY	Descriptive language that creates mental pictures for the reader
TONE	Attitude toward the subject of the work—and sometimes toward the reader as shown by author—as expressed through choice of words, imagery, and point of view
FIGURES OF SPEECH	Unusual use or combination of words, such as METAPHOR or SIMILE, for enhanced vividness or effect
SYMBOLISM	Using a specific object or event to represent a deeper, often abstract, meaning or idea
RHYTHM	Beat, meter
RHYME	Repetition of similar sounds for their auditory effect

In this chapter we show two very different, complete student essays of analysis. One analyzes a literary work, a poem by Paul Laurence Dunbar (see 11E). The other analyzes two contrasting Web sites about the US government's Transportation Safety Administration (TSA) (see 11F).

■ Purpose

The purpose of analysis essays is to invite your reader into the discussion of your selected work. You want to explain the features or patterns you've discovered and present your view of what they mean or how they operate. Analysis essays offer either a content analysis (explaining the meaning of a work) or a rhetorical analysis (explaining how the work operates to achieve its effect). Many analysis essays are expected to include both types. Both student essays in this chapter use a combination of the two types of analysis.

If your assignment asks you to evaluate the work, include that in your essay. In your evaluation, you want to convince your readers that your point of view is reasonable and accurate. Both essays in this chapter include evaluation, though less extensively so in the literary analysis.

■ Audience

Academics tend to be the primary readers of your analysis. This can include your instructor, other students, people who read scholarly journals, and the like. Before you start, try to learn whether your readers are specialists in the area of the work you're analyzing, in which case you can assume that they're somewhat more familiar with the work you're discussing compared to general readers. If your audience is more general, you'll need to describe the work more fully. Both student essays in this chapter assume nonspecialist readers. No matter who your readers are, they probably won't have the written text or the visual in front of them as they read your essay. Nor will they be as familiar with the work as you are, so write your opening summary in as much detail as you think your readers will need to follow your line of reasoning.

11B   How do I plan and revise an analysis essay?

Generating ideas for an analysis

- For content analysis, think about the meaning of the work by focusing on the "what" and how it creates its meaning—images? repetition of words or phrases? other features?

- For content analysis, let your reader know what part of the work you're discussing (line numbers for poems, chapter numbers or titles for books, etc.).

- For content analysis, consider what the author or artist does or does not include and why.

11B

- For rhetorical analysis, think about the "how" of the work by focusing on the devices the author or artist uses to influence readers.
- For rhetorical analysis, use the three principles of persuasion discussed in 2B: logic (*logos*), ethical stance of the writer (*ethos*), and methods of eliciting compassion or sympathy (*pathos*).
- Combine content and rhetorical analysis by focusing on both the "what" and the "how."
- Craft a thesis statement that makes a claim about the work's central point or points.
- Use the body of your essay to explain and support your claim, with one or two rationales per paragraph.
- Support your claims with evidence from the work, using RENNS (see 5D) and, if allowed by the assignment, reporting on research you conduct to survey opinions of experts on the work or the topic of the work.

11C

Revising

- Is the internal logic of your analysis sound so that it convincingly supports the claim you made in your thesis statement?
- Does the progression of ideas within and between your paragraphs follow a clear line of reasoning?
- Have you checked that any quotations, paraphrases, or summaries based on the work are accurately presented?
- If you've conducted research, have you provided full source information in the documentation style required in your course?
- Have you used correct verb tenses?
- Did you use the PRESENT TENSE when you describe or discuss a literary work or any of its elements: *Watter* [a character] **makes** *a difficult decision when he* **turns down** *Linder's offer to buy the house.* In addition, did you use the present tense for discussing what an author has done in a specific work: *Lorraine Hansberry, author of* A Raisin in the Sun, **explores** *not only powerful racial issues but also common family dynamics.* Finally, have you used a PAST-TENSE VERB to discuss historical events or biographical information: *Lorraine Hansberry's* A Raisin in the Sun **was** *the first play by an African American woman to be produced on Broadway.*

11C   What is a frame for an analysis essay?

Here is a possible frame for an analysis essay for you to adapt to the specifics of your assignment.

Frame for an Analysis of Literary or Other Works

Introductory paragraph

- **Capture your readers' interest** by using one of the strategies for writing effective introductory paragraphs (see 5B).
- **Present your thesis statement**, making sure it states the point of your analysis and offers your readers a concise preview of your essay (see 4F).

Paragraph(s) summarizing the work

- **Summarize the work** you're analyzing concisely; if the work is long, focus especially on the material you're discussing.
- **Mention the source of the work** and, as needed, where it was published or presented, its purpose, and its intended audience
- **Start each paragraph with a topic sentence** that leads clearly to the paragraph's content.

11C

Body paragraphs analyzing the work

- **Focus on separate sections or elements of the work**, usually one at a time, with specific identifying information so that your reader can follow your line of reasoning.
- **Give your analysis of the material along with your rationale for it**, using description, quotation, summary, or paraphrase, as appropriate.
- **Include an explanation** of why you've chosen what you've focused on.
- **Start each paragraph with a topic sentence** that leads clearly to the paragraph's content.

Evaluative paragraph(s)—if assigned

- **Present your evaluation of the work by** judging the success of the material.
- **Convince your readers that your judgment is reasonable**, using critical thinking and avoiding logical fallacies.
- **Start each paragraph with a topic sentence** that leads clearly to the paragraph's content.

Conclusion

- **Wrap up the essay** by helping your readers review the points you've made and stating why your analysis matters.

WORKS CITED (MLA STYLE) or REFERENCES (APA STYLE)

- **Include a separate DOCUMENTATION page** in the style required in your course.

11D   What are some sentence and paragraph guides for analysis essays?

Adapt these guides to your PURPOSE and AUDIENCE.

Sentence and Paragraph Guides

- The writer attempts to _____ primarily by using the strategy of _____.

- The most significant feature (interesting aspect/important quality/etc.) of this text is _____ because _____.

- The writer uses emotional [or logical or ethical] appeals to create a sense of _____ in readers. Consider for example the statement that "_____" or the statement that "_____." The language of these passages suggests _____ because _____. Consider, for example, how different the emotional appeals would be if the wording had been _____.

- A noteworthy pattern in the text is _____. For example, at one point the writer states _____. At another she asserts _____. At a third, she claims _____. This pattern is significant because _____.

- Reading this text through _____'s theory that _____ reveals a key meaning.

11E   A student's essay analyzing a literary work

■ Working on the assignment

Samantha Wilson, a student in first-year English, fulfilled an assignment to write an analysis of Paul Laurence Dunbar's poem "Sympathy." In the process of drafting her paper, Samantha decided to read about the poet's life.

■ Learning about the poet, Paul Laurence Dunbar

She learned that Paul Laurence Dunbar was perhaps the first African American poet to receive wide critical acclaim. He was born in 1872, in Dayton, Ohio, to a mother who was a former slave and a father who had escaped slavery to fight in the Civil War. Supporters of his work included the famous abolitionist Frederick Douglass. Dunbar worked briefly at the Library of Congress and lived in various cities in the United States and in England. After producing twelve books of poetry, four books of short stories, a play, and five novels, he died in 1906, at the tragically early age of only 33.

■ The poem

SYMPATHY

Paul Laurence Dunbar

I know what the caged bird feels alas!
When the sun is bright on the upland slopes;
When the wind stirs soft through the springing grass,
And the river flows like a stream of glass;
When the first bird sings and the first bud opes,   5
And the faint perfume from its chalice steals—
I know what the caged bird feels!

I know why the caged bird beats his wing
Till its blood is red on the cruel bars;
For he must fly back to his perch and cling   10
When he fain would be on the bough a-swing;
And a pain still throbs in the old, old scars
And they pulse again with a keener sting—
I know why he beats his wing!

I know why the caged bird sings, ah me,   15
When his wing is bruised and his bosom sore,—
When he beats his bars and he would be free;
It is not a carol of joy or glee,
But a prayer that he sends from his heart's deep core,
But a plea, that upward to Heaven he flings—   20
I know why the caged bird sings!

■ Student's essay about literature

Wilson 1

Samantha Wilson

Professor Parrish

English 100

4 Mar. 2013

Images, Progression, and Meaning in "Sympathy"

How can a writer artfully convey the despair of not

having freedom? Paul Laurence Dunbar faces that challenge

Introduction asks attention-getting question.

continued >>

Wilson 2

in his poem "Sympathy," which uses the central image of a bird in a cage. By choosing a creature that did nothing to deserve its imprisonment, Dunbar invites readers to empathize with anyone who has experienced a similar fate by artfully building its message through precise images and a meaningful procession of ideas.

Thesis statement gives clear preview of essay.

"Sympathy" appears in three seven-line stanzas that closely match each other. The rhyme scheme in each is ABAABCC, and the first and seventh lines of each stanza begin with "I know what" or "I know why." Those lines, in fact, are nearly identical, and the result is a tightly compressed, even repetitive poem that makes readers pay close attention to any changes. Those changes create a dramatic progression in the poem.

11E

This paragraph analyzes poem's key features.

The imagery in the first stanza focuses on the world beyond the cage. It's a world of strong visual senses, the sun "bright upon the upland slopes" (line 2) and the river flowing "like a stream of glass" (4). But Dunbar also invokes smell, with the flower's perfume, and he invokes sounds, including the wind softly stirring the grass (3) and a bird singing (5). (In the third stanza, that singing becomes a key idea—and a much different one.) References to the sun on the hills and to the "first bird" and "first bud" suggest dawn and possibilities, with potential that is almost holy. After all, the flower bud is a "chalice," a sacred vessel holding communion wine (6). However, the caged bird is removed from this world, and while the poet says, "I know what the caged bird feels" (7), he does not specifically name or describe that feeling. Instead, we are left to draw our own conclusions, comparing the limits of the cage to the possibilities of nature.

Topic sentence invites readers to walk through the poem with writer.

Using line references and quoted words, the writer stays on the topic and with the thesis.

continued >>

Wilson 3

The imagery in the second stanza is much harsher and more concrete. Instead of the internal state of the bird's feeling, the poet describes an external, physical action, the bird's wings beating against the cage "Till its blood is red on the cruel bars" (9). Clearly this is a futile, painful, and ongoing action. The bird's "pain still throbs" (12), even "When his wing is bruised and his bosom sore" (16). Yet the bird persists, desperately longing to fly from branch to branch rather than to sit on a single artificial perch, in a cage that denies flight to a creature whose nature is to fly.

11E

The brutal images of the second stanza give way to the surprising insights of the third one, which also have a physical action but of a different sort. We generally think of bird songs as pretty sounds, conveying happiness. However, "Sympathy" makes them "not a carol of joy or glee" (18) but, rather, something mournful and somber. The song is an extension of and accompaniment to the self-torture of wings beating against the cage. By calling that song a "prayer" and a "plea" (20), the poet transforms the bird from a mere animal behaving instinctively to a being with consciousness performing intentionally, calling to heaven. By separating one of heaven's creatures from nature, whoever has imprisoned the bird has violated not only its freedom but also the divine order. Further, it makes listening to and enjoying the bird's song almost a perverse act, since the bird sings out of torment. The poem's progression from feeling to beating to singing, then, traces a progression from instinct to action to hope.

Of course, the poem is about more than birds in cages. The key refrain is "I know why," which emphasizes the poet's clear identification with the bird. He can know why the bird

Topic sentence transitions nicely to the writer's next point.

Writer harks back to the "sympathy" concept in her first paragraph.

Topic sentence focuses on analysis, using clear reasoning (*logos*).

continued >>

Wilson 4

feels, acts, and prays because he experiences the same loss
of freedom; he feels, acts, and prays for similar reasons.
Given Dunbar's autobiography, it's obvious that this poem
comments directly on the treatment of African Americans in
the nineteenth century, even after the Civil War, as attitudes
and events continued to restrict former slaves. The images
powerfully support that interpretation.

However, Dunbar is brilliantly artful in not restricting the
poem only to people in one time and situation. By choosing the
common image of a bird in a cage, he succeeds by inviting his
readers to identity with anyone who has lost his or her freedom,
for reasons beyond their control. Some of those people—and
readers may be among them—may be physically separated
from the world, but for others, the "imprisonment" may be
more emotional or metaphorical. Dunbar was free to write and
publish this poem, but that does not diminish his sympathy
with the caged bird—or our own sympathy with it.

Writer ends with analysis of the larger meaning of the poem.

Wilson 5

Works Cited

Dunbar, Paul Laurence, "Sympathy." *The Collected Poetry
of Paul Laurence Dunbar*. Ed. Joanne M. Braxton.
Charlottesville: UP of Virginia, 1993. 102. Print.

Works Cited appears alone on the next page in the actual paper.

11F   A student's analysis of two Web sites

Matt Gotlin-Sheehan

Professor Hesse

WRIT 1622

17 Nov. 2013

Rhetorical Strategies in Two Airport Security Web Sites

Is the current level of security screening at American airports a patriotic way to safeguard travelers, or is it a ruthless assault by power-crazed bureaucrats? Most people stand somewhere between these two positions: annoyed by what they have to do to board a plane, but convinced the experience serves a good purpose. Other people, though, hold an extreme view. For example, the group We Won't Fly protests, "We will not be treated like criminals," while the federal government's Transportation Security Administration (TSA) soothes, "Your safety is our priority." Analyzing the Web sites of these two groups reveals not only contrasting messages but also quite different rhetorical strategies for delivering them.

Airport security measures changed drastically following the September 11, 2001, attacks. Previously, private companies performed airport security and passenger screenings. However, in November 2001 the Transportation Security Administration (TSA) was created to standardize security practices and promote safer travel. Since then, a few incidents and threats persuaded the TSA to enhance their measures, culminating in full-body scanners and passenger pat downs. These practices have been the subject of intense scrutiny, criticism, and ridicule, especially over the Internet.

11F

Thesis statement sets up promise to discuss both the content and the strategies of two different texts.

Paragraph of background information orients readers.

continued >>

Gotlin-Sheehan 2

Writer appeals to logic (*logos*) with information and emotions (*pathos*) by quoting inflammatory language.

Wewontfly.com voices anger over airport security. The site seeks to convince flyers that the TSA security procedures are invasive. Adorned with aggressive imagery, such as mock scanner images underneath a foreboding red "no" symbol, the site has bold headlines: "Act Now. Travel With Dignity" and "Stop Flying Until the Scanners and Gropers are Gone." Characterizing the screening agents as "gropers" associates them with sex offenders and criminals, not public servants, and it casts travelers as innocent victims. This strong language is reinforced by the "distressed" fonts in its headlines, as seen in Figure 1.

11F

Inserting a screen capture of the Web site provides a helpful visual and confirms the writer's credibility (*ethos*) by showing an example.

Figure 1   Heading from the home page for http://wewontfly .com

Emotional appeals (*pathos*) are the focus of this paragraph.

The main rhetorical strategy is to arouse readers' emotions. The page calls the TSA "ineffective and dangerous" as well as a "health risk." The site claims that security scanners may cause radiation poisoning and that screeners don't change gloves between pat-downs increasing the chance of spreading harmful contagions, like lice. The emotional appeals are heightened by passenger stories reported on the site's blog. In one of them, a passenger named Elizabeth narrates in detail how she was "a victim of a government-

continued >>

Gotlin-Sheehan 3

sanctioned sexual assault." An anonymous poster explains that she had once been raped, so that being touched during a search was traumatic. These stories imply that, if disturbing things can happen to others, they can also happen to me, my friends, or family.

Two specific examples arouse readers' sense of compassion, an aspect of an emotional appeal (*pathos*).

In general, the site uses examples and stories rather than statistics or other kinds of evidence. As a result, logical appeals are minimal. Consider the following argument:

11F

> Al-Qaeda is an agile, networked organization. It's peer-to-peer. The TSA is a top-down, lumbering bureaucracy. Al-Qaeda operatives are passionate and motivated. TSA employees are order-takers. There is simply no contest between these two types of organizational structures. It's like David and Goliath, the Viet Cong vs. the US Army, Luke vs. the Death Star. The TSA is structurally incapable of defending against this threat, just as the US Army was structurally incapable of defeating the Viet Cong.

To make the point most clearly, the writer includes an extended block quotation.

Some readers might find the analogies between the TSA and Goliath, the American Army in Vietnam, and the Death Star clever, perhaps even convincing. However, this paragraph provides no facts or evidence for readers to make an informed judgment about the truth of this claim.

Writer explains and analyzes the long quotation. Thus, the writer uses a logical appeal (*logos*).

The TSA (www.tsa.gov) site also uses emotional and ethical appeals, but to a very different effect. Featuring smooth, clean lines, soothing shades of blue, and calming photos of empty airports, the site implies "It's all cool. Relax!" The site's banner features the slogan "Your Safety Is Our Priority." Information for travelers and the media, along with

Transitional sentence to the next Web site also serves as a topic sentence for the paragraph.

continued >>

Gotlin-Sheehan 4

explanations of "Our Approach," suggest that the TSA has nothing to hide. The site is easy to navigate and presents visitors with extensive information in a systematic manner, as Figure 2 shows.

11F

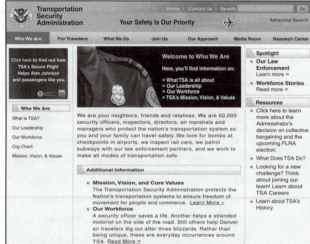

Screen capture of Web site provides a helpful visual element and confirms the writer's credibility (*ethos*).

Figure 2   Page from TSA Web site: www.tsa.gov/who_we_are/index.shtm

Topic sentence announces the theme of the paragraph, and provides examples, quotations, and discussion.

The TSA tries to project a personality of friendship and common purpose. It identifies employees as "your neighbors, friends, and relatives" who work hard so that "you and your family can travel safely." The site portrays TSA workers as they "look for bombs," "inspect rail cars," and "patrol subways." A worker "saves a life" or "helps a stranded motorist," suggesting that the TSA goes beyond faithfully performing assigned airport duties to help people in need.

However, the most striking rhetorical strategy on the TSA site is the extensive use of logical appeals. The information ranges from poll results and surveys to news articles and

continued >>

Gotlin-Sheehan 5

television reports from credible sources like *USA Today*. An entire tab is devoted to "Research," which is divided into three main headings and fourteen subheadings, each of which lists numerous facts. "Screening Statistics," for example, notes that, "We screened 708,400,522. The average wait time was 3.79 minutes and the average peak wait time was 11.76 minutes." Clearly, then, the TSA site puts a strong emphasis on knowledge. For example, "What to know before you go" explains various traveling scenarios, and a search bar tells passengers whether they can take particular items through a checkpoint. The strategy seems to be one of overwhelming travelers with mountains of information so that the TSA looks like it's thorough, open, and cooperative, and that travelers have nothing to fear.

> Writer uses logic (*logos*) and enlivens the material with specific details (RENNS, see 5D).

11F

These two Web sites will probably succeed with different types of visitors. Chances are that an anti-government activist will distrust the extensive information on the TSA site. Likewise, a staunch supporter of US security measures after 9/11 would likely scoff at *We Won't Fly's* emotional outbursts. The two sites employ rhetorical strategies that reinforce their audience's biases. Sites like *www.wewontfly.com* succeed when they make readers feel threatened and angry. They fail when they lack the evidence of how legitimate and widespread concerns are. Sites like *www.tsa.gov* succeed when they reassure readers with information and facts. They may be less successful when they fail to demonstrate whether they can truly prevent all dangerous situations.

> Once again, the writer goes beyond simply summarizing to include discussion of meaning.

> The writer gives a balanced conclusion that uses a logical appeal (*logos*) and fair-minded emotional appeal (*ethos*).

continued >>

Gotlin-Sheehan 6

Works Cited appears alone on the next page in the actual paper.

Works Cited

Transportation Security Administration. "Who We Are."

Transportation Security Administration, 2011. Web. 15 Nov.

2011.

Wewontfly.com. 2011. Web. 15 Nov. 2011.

11F

Part 4
Research Writing and Documentation

CHAPTERS
12–15

12 Finding and Evaluating Sources

Quick Points You will learn to

➤ Explain the different types of sources and search tools (see below).
➤ Find sources for a research project (see pp. 119–131).
➤ Evaluate sources for reliability (see pp. 131–142).
➤ Do field research (see pp. 143–145).

MyWritingLab™ Visit mywritinglab.com for more resources on finding and evaluating sources.

12A What are sources and what tools do I use to find them?

A **source** is any form of information that provides data, ideas, examples, concepts, and evidence. Sources are either primary or secondary.

- A **primary source** is original work that can take one of two forms. One form is original documents such as letters, diaries, novels, poems, short stories, autobiographies, original reporting, findings from a research study, speeches, journals, or so on. In addition to physical copies in libraries or elsewhere, copies of original documents often exist online in digital form. The second form is FIELD RESEARCH* (see 12H) that you carry out yourself, such as experiments, observations, interviews, or surveys.

- A **secondary source** reports, describes, comments on, or analyzes someone's original work. That is, someone other than the primary source relays the information, adding a layer between you and the original material. Much of your college-level research depends on secondary sources. Works of literary criticism, which provide expert commentary on literary works, are secondary sources, while the literary works themselves are primary sources. Newspaper and magazine articles are secondary sources because they report on events or situations.

Suppose you wish to research student attitudes toward US policy in the Middle East. Surveying several students would be primary research. Consulting scholars' books and articles about student attitudes toward the Middle East would be secondary research. Your decision to use primary and/or secondary

---

*Words printed in SMALL CAPITAL LETTERS are discussed elsewhere in the text and are defined in the Terms Glossary at the back of the book.

sources depends on your research question or the nature of your assignment. For her APA–style research paper about women playing video games in Chapter 15, Leslie Palm conducted primary research by analyzing several video games and secondary research by reading scholarly articles about them.

■ Differentiating between scholarly and popular sources

Whether you're using primary or secondary sources, you want to know how to distinguish between scholarly, academic sources and popular, commercial sources, as explained in Quick Box 12.1. To locate information suitable for college-level research, you need to focus on scholarly sources because they're much more reliable than most sources you find by simply browsing the Internet.

Quick Box 12.1   ■ ■ ■ ■ ■ ■

Scholarly sources versus popular sources

Scholarly Sources	**Popular Sources**
How you find them: Mainly through DATABASES	**How you find them:** Sometimes through databases; often through SEARCH ENGINES
Examples: Journal articles; books published by university presses; professional organization Web sites	**Examples:** Newspapers and magazines; general Web sites and blogs
Audience: Scholars, experts, researchers, students	**Audience:** General readers; people who may be interested but don't necessarily have specific knowledge or expertise
Purpose: To provide cutting-edge ideas and information supported by research	**Purpose:** To entertain; to translate expert information for general readers; to persuade
Authors: Researchers; professors; content experts; professionals	**Authors:** Journalists or freelance writers; hobbyists or enthusiasts; people from all walks of life
Characteristics: Citations and bibliographies show sources of ideas; sources explain research methods and limitations of conclusions	**Characteristics:** Rarely include citations or bibliographies; might refer to people or sources in the body of the work
Where published: Appear in scholarly books and periodicals or on Web sites maintained by professional organizations	**Where published:** Appear in popular books and periodicals; blogs; personal or informal Web sites

12A

❗ Alert: While Google is a popular Web search engine for general searches, Google Scholar is far better for college-level research when you search for scholarly sources on the Web. ●

■ Using Web search engines, databases, and library catalogs

Most searches for sources start online, whether you're in a library or using the Internet in other locations. In conducting college-level research, you want to be aware of the important differences between the major search tools: Web search engines, subscription **databases**, and **library catalogs**. Each of these is useful for locating different types of sources.

WEB SEARCH ENGINES: World Wide Web pages (www.), popular periodicals, commercial, educational, and government sites

- Available to all Internet users (examples include Google, Yahoo, and Bing). Try using more than one search engine because each provides different results for the same key words.

- List sources in popular, not scholarly, periodicals as well as in all Web pages that have been uploaded to the Web.

- Offer a search bar into which you type words related to the subject you're researching; if many of the links listed for your words are irrelevant, try words with a more narrow focus.

- Contain links unfiltered for content and often created by commercial, political, and other special-interest groups whose intent is to sell or promote products and ideas, not to give objective information.

SUBSCRIPTION DATABASES: Articles in scholarly and serious popular periodicals and databases (see section 12B)

- Available to users through membership in a library, accessible with a college or library ID (examples include EBSCOHost, PsycINFO, InfoTrac).

- List scholarly and serious popular sources organized by subject areas.

- Accept narrowed searches using BOOLEAN EXPRESSIONS (see page 121).

- Judged by librarians and other scholarly experts as worthy of inclusion in the databases.

LIBRARY CATALOGS: Books, periodicals, and multimedia (see section 12C)

- Available to users through membership in a library, accessible with a college or library ID.

12A

- List the library's own holdings, mostly books; sometimes also list holdings of other related libraries.
- Can be searched by author, title, and keyword.

Always remember that anyone can put anything on the Web. While this makes the Web an extensive source of general information, it also makes finding what you're looking for difficult, and—most importantly—it opens the possibility of encountering inaccurate or biased materials. Therefore, before you use any Web (or other) sources, be sure to evaluate their credibility (see section 12G).

12B   How do I search for articles in periodicals?

Periodicals consist of newspapers, magazines, journals, and other documents published regularly, or periodically. For the many types of periodicals available today and their uses, see Quick Box 12.2. You can expect to use subscription databases when you conduct most of your searches for scholarly articles and serious popular articles.

Quick Box 12.2   ■ ■ ■ ■ ■ ■

12B

Types of periodicals

Type	Characteristics	Useful for
Journal	Scholarly articles written by experts for other experts; usually focus on one academic discipline; published relatively infrequently; examples are *College Composition and Communication* and *American Journal of Public Health*	The most reliable expert research on a particular subject; detailed articles and extensive bibliographies that can point to other sources or experts; may also have book reviews
News magazines	Short to medium-length articles on current events or topics of interest to a broad readership; lots of photos and graphics; may have opinions or editorials, as well as reviews; generally are published weekly; examples are *Time* and *Newsweek*	Easily understandable and timely introductions to current topics; often can point to more expert sources, topics, and keywords

continued >>

Quick Box 12.2	Types of periodicals (continued)	■ ■ ■ ■ ■ ■
Type	**Characteristics**	**Useful for**
Special-interest or "lifestyle" magazines	Written for audiences (including fans and hobbyists) interested in a particular topic; include news and features on that topic; generally published monthly, with entertainment as an important goal; examples include *Outside*, *Rolling Stone*, *Wired*	Providing "how-to" information on their topics of focus, as well as technical information or in-depth profiles of individuals, products, or events; many include reviews related to emphasis; the more serious examples are well written and reliable
"Intellectual" or literary magazines	Publish relatively longer articles that provide in-depth analysis of issues, events, or people; may include creative work as well as nonfiction; aimed at a general, well-educated audience; usually published monthly; examples include *The Atlantic*, *Harper's*, *The New Yorker*	Learning about a topic in depth but in a way more accessible than scholarly journals; becoming aware of major controversies and positions; learning who experts are and what books or other sources have been published; reading arguments on topics
Trade magazines	Focus on particular businesses, industries, and trade groups; discuss new products, legislation, or events that will influence individuals or businesses in that area; examples include *National Hog Farmer*, *Sound and Video Contractor*	Specialized information focusing on applying information or research in particular settings; seeing how specific audiences or interest groups may respond to a particular position
Newspapers	Publish articles about current news, sports, and cultural events; contain several sections, including opinions and editorials, lifestyle, sports; most appear daily; examples are *The Washington Post*, *The DeWitt, Iowa, Observer*	Very current information; national newspapers (such as *The New York Times*) cover world events and frequently have analysis and commentary; local newspapers cover small happenings you likely won't find elsewhere; opinion sections and reviews are sources of ideas and positions

12B

■ Using general and specialized databases

Most college libraries subscribe to one or more database services. Your college library's Web site will show the resources it has available. Because the college pays for these services, you don't have to; every student has access with an ID. Check with a librarian to see what's required at your college.

General databases include sources from a broad range of periodicals and books, both popular and scholarly. General databases are suitable for academic research projects. However, take care to focus on scholarly sources and well-regarded popular publications. Large libraries have many general databases. A common one is *Academic Search Premier*.

Specialized databases focus on specific subject areas or disciplines. They list books and articles published by and for expert readers. Some examples include *Art Abstracts*, *MLA International Bibliography*, *PsycINFO*, and *Business Abstracts*. Many specialized databases include the abstract, or summary, that is printed at the beginning of each scholarly article.

Each source in a DATABASE contains bibliographic information, including a title, author, date of publication, and publisher (in the case of books or reports) or periodical (in the case of articles). The entry might also provide a summary or list of contents.

12B

■ Using keywords to search databases

Keywords, also called *descriptors* or *identifiers*, are your pathways to finding sources in databases, catalogs, and Web sites. Keywords are the main words in a source's title or words that an author or editor has identified as most important to its topic and content. Figure 12.1 shows three screens from a keyword search of *PsycINFO* on *déjà vu*. While working on his research paper about *déjà vu* that appears in section 14H, the student consulted this database.

You can search with a single keyword, but usually that generates far too many or far too few "hits." Combinations of keywords using BOOLEAN EXPRESSIONS or ADVANCED SEARCHES can solve both problems.

■ Using Boolean expressions to search databases

Using **Boolean expressions** means that you search online by typing KEYWORD combinations that narrow and refine your search. To combine keywords, use the words *AND, OR*, and *NOT* (or symbols that represent those words). Quick Box 12.3 (p. 123) explains how.

■ Using advanced searches for databases

Advanced searches, sometimes called *guided searches*, allow you to search by entering information in a form online. A typical search involves selecting a range of dates of publication (for example, after 2010 or between 1990 and

Figure 12.1 Keyword search of *déjà vu* in a database.

Keyword search for *déjà vu*

Searching: **PaycINFO** | Choose Databases >>

deja vu	in	Select a Field (optional)	**Search**	**Clear**
AND	in	Select a Field (optional)		
AND	in	Select a Field (optional)	Add Row	

Basic

95 Results for...

Refine your resul
- Linked Full Text
- References Availabl
- Scholarly (Peer Revi Journals
- 2005 Publication Date

7. Déjà vu: Origins and phenomenology: Implications of the four subtypes for future research.
Neppe, Vernon M.; Journal of Parapsychology, Vol 74(1), Spr. 2010. pp. 61-97. [Journal Article]
An analysis of déjà vu subtypes is done in accordance with Neppe's universally accepted operational definition of déjà vu (any subjectively inappropriate impression of familiarity of the present ...
Subjects: Consciousness States; Etiology; Parapsychology; Phenomenology
Database: PsycINFO

Add to folder | Relevancy: ■■■■■■■ | Cited References: (71)

Find this item in Penrose Library | ARTICLE | Check Article Linker

Novel insights into false recollection: A model of déjà vécu.

Authors: O'Connor, Akira R., Washington University in St. Louis, St. Louis, MO, US
Lever, Colin, Institute of Psychological Sciences, University of Leeds, Leeds, United Kingdom
Moulin, Chris J. A., Leeds Memory Group, Institute of Psychological Sciences, University of Leeds, Leeds, United Kingdom, c.j.a.moulin@leeds.ac.uk

Address: Moulin, Chris J. A., Institute of Psychological Sciences, University of Leeds, Leeds, United Kingdom, LS2 9JT, c.j.a.moulin@leeds.ac.uk

Source: Cognitive Neuropsychiatry, Vol 15(1-3), Jan, 2010. pp. 118-144.

Page Count: 27

Publisher: United Kingdom: Taylor & Francis.

ISSN: 1354-6805 (Print)
1464-0619 (Electronic)

Language: English

Keywords: false recollection; cognitive neurosciences; hippocampus; familiarity; dementia; **deja vu**

Abstract: The thesis of this paper is that **déjà** experiences can be separated into two forms: **déjà vu**, arising from the erroneous sensation of familiarity, and **déjà vécu**, arising from the erroneous sensation of recollection. We summarise a series of cases for

Partial result of search of database

One article found in the search

1995) and specifying only a certain language (such as English) or a certain format (such as books). Figure 12.2 shows an example of a search conducted by Andrei Gurov, who wrote the MLA–style research paper shown in Chapter 14. Gurov searched for sources that have *déjà vu* in their titles and use *false memory* as another keyword but exclude *crime*.

Using subject directories

Subject directories provide an alternative to keyword searches. These directories are lists of topics (education, computing, entertainment, and so on) or resources and services (shopping, travel, and so on), with links to sources on

Quick Box 12.3

Boolean expressions for refining keyword searches

AND or the + ("plus") symbol: Narrows the focus of your search because both keywords must be found. If you research the topic of the APA paper in 15G (how women characters are depicted in video games), the expression *video games AND women AND characters* works. Many search engines and databases don't require the word *AND* between terms.

NOT or the – ("minus") symbol: Narrows a search by excluding texts containing the specified word or phrase. If you want to eliminate women playing games from your search, type *video games AND women AND characters NOT players.*

OR: Expands a search's boundaries by including more than one keyword. If you want to expand your search to include sources about women characters who are either heroes or villains in games, try the expression *video games AND women AND characters OR heroes OR villains.*

Quotation marks (" "): Direct the search to match your exact word order. For example, a search for *"role playing games"* will find sources that contain the exact phrase "role playing games." Also, if you search for *James Joyce* without using quotation marks, search engines will return all pages containing the words *James* and *Joyce* anywhere in the document; however, a search using "James Joyce" brings you closer to finding Web sites about the Irish writer.

12B

Figure 12.2 Advanced keyword search.

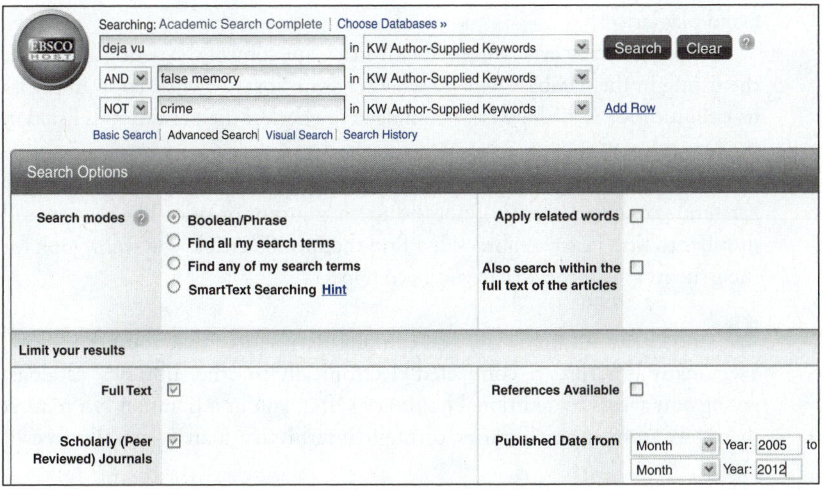

those topics and resources. Most search engines, and some library catalogs or databases, have one or more subject directories. In addition, there are independent subject directories. Some examples are

Educator's Reference Desk

Librarians' Index to the Internet

Library of Congress

Refdesk.com

Clicking on a general category in a subject directory will take you to lists of increasingly specific categories. Eventually, you'll get a list of Web pages on the most specific subtopic you select. These search engines also allow you to click on a category and enter keywords. For example, suppose you're using Google to search for information on organic food. You would first go to Google's general category of "Health" and find the category of "Nutrition." Within "Nutrition" you would find a link to "Organic Food," a page that lists dozens of additional categories and sources.

■ Locating the periodical articles themselves

12B

After databases help you find information about sources, how do you get your hands on the source itself? Often you can find an online full-text version of the article in the database to read, download, or print. A full-text version may be either in HTML format or PDF; the listing will tell you which one. If you have a choice, we recommend using the PDF version, which is easier to cite because it has the layout of a print article. However, if you want to copy a section and paste it in your notes, only HTML allows this (but be careful to avoid plagiarism).

Sometimes, however, you need to find a print copy of the periodical. Often the listing in the database will say whether your library owns a copy and what its **call number** is. Otherwise, you'll need to check if the periodical is listed in the library's CATALOG.

In either case, search for the periodical by name (for example, *American Literature* or *The Economist*), not the article's author or title. Then use its call number to find it in the library. To find the specific article you want, look for the issue in which the article you need appears.

🛈 **Alert:** Almost no library will contain every source that you need. However, many libraries are connected electronically to other libraries' catalogs, giving you access to additional holdings. Often you or a librarian can request materials from other libraries through interlibrary loan (generally free of charge). ●

12C How do I search for books?

In an age when the Web contains billions of pages of information, it might seem almost prehistoric to talk about libraries. After all, the library is where generations of college students have traditionally gone to find books and periodicals, but today much is available online. Still, many sources, especially scholarly ones, are available only through the library. Notice that we've said "through" the library, not "in" it. That's because many library sources and services are available through the Internet to students or authorized others.

If you're a new student at your college, we urge you to take time to become familiar with exactly how your particular college library works before you start your search for books. Although all libraries have basic functions, available in the building and online, each varies in its specific details. Start by looking for a display of written handouts for students to take with them, each one about a different aspect of the specific processes and products at your college library.

Your best allies, online and in person, are the librarians, especially those who work at the Reference Desk. They're usually delighted with students who ask questions. Quick Box 12.4 lists the ten top questions librarians are asked, but other inquiries are welcome.

12C

Quick Box 12.4

Top ten questions to ask a librarian

1. Do I need to log in to use the library's computer system? If so, how?
2. Can I access the library's computer system from home or off campus?
3. How do I search the library's catalog?
4. Can I look for books directly on the shelves, or do I need to request them from a central place? How do I check out materials?
5. How do I use an electronic version of a library book?
6. What databases would you recommend if I'm looking for scholarly sources on topic X?
7. What might be the best keywords or search strategy to use when I'm searching databases for sources on topic X?
8. How can I best keep track of sources I find? Can I e-mail them to myself? Print a list of citations?
9. How can I get copies of articles or other sources I need?
10. If our library doesn't own a source I need, is there a way for me to access or order a copy?

■ Using your library's catalog

A library's CATALOG, which lists its holdings (its entire collection), exists as a computer database in almost every modern library. To find a book, you can search by author, by title, by subject, or by keyword. Figure 12.3 shows the home page for the book catalog at the Library of Congress. Note that it allows you a Basic Search by title, author, subject, CALL NUMBER, or keyword; it also allows you to use a Guided Search to find particular indexes and to search using Boolean expressions.

Suppose a source recommends that you find a book by the author Tim Wu, but you don't know its title. A screen on your library's computer will have a place for you to type *Wu, Tim* in a space for "author." (Usually, you enter last name, then first name, but check which system your library uses.) If your library owns any books by Tim Wu, the computer will display their titles and other bibliographic information, such as the library call number. Then you can use the call number to request the book or to find it yourself. Figure 12.4 shows results from a search for books by author Tim Wu.

Suppose, however, you know a book's title but not its author and want to see if your library owns a copy. Find the place to type in the title.

Perhaps you don't know book titles or authors' names and have only a research topic. In this case, you need to search by subject, using the terms listed in the *Library of Congress Subject Headings* (*LCSH*). The *LCSH* is a multivolume catalog available, primarily in book form, in the reference section of every library. Or, you can search by keyword in your library's holdings. For example, you could find Wu's book using the keywords *information, media, technology*, and so on. Figure 12.5 shows a book catalog search by keyword.

Figure 12.3   Catalog of the Library of Congress online.

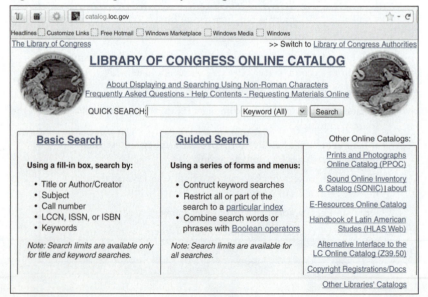

Figure 12.4 Results of an author search for books by Tim Wu.

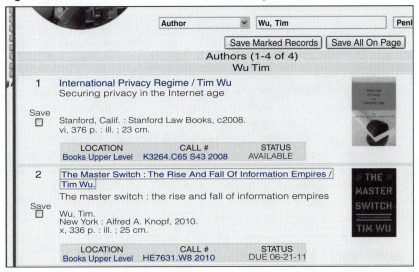

Figure 12.5 A library catalog search using keywords: locates books by Tim Wu.

Keywords: (information) and
(media) and (technology)

Keyword	(information) and (media) and (tec	Penro

Limited to: Year after 2009 *5 results found. sorted*

Save Marked Records   Save All On Page

Keywords (1-5 of 5)

1 Government secrecy [electronic resource] / edited by Susan Maret.
Government secrecy

Save
☐ Bingley, U.K. : Emerald. 2011.
1 online resource (xxx, 434 p.) : multiple formats, ill.
▸ Website

LOCATION	CALL #	STATUS
Internet	JF1525.S4 G68 2011eb	ONLINE

2 The Routledge Companion to Literature and Science [electronic resource].
The Routeledge Companion to Literature and Science

Save
☐ Clarke, Bruce.
Hoboken : Taylor & Francis, 2010
1 online resource (569 p.)
▸ Website

LOCATION	CALL #	STATUS
Internet	PN55.R68 2010eb	ONLINE

3 The master switch : the rise and fall of information empires / Tim Wu.
The master switch : the rise and fall of information empires

Save
☐ Wu, Tim.
New York : Alfred A. Knopf, 2010.
x, 366 p. : ill. ; 25 cm.

Book by Tim Wu

127

Scan the results of your searches to identify promising sources. When you select a record (usually by clicking on it or a box next to it), you encounter detailed information about the source. Some libraries allow you to print out this information, send it to your e-mail account, download it, or use social networking. Whether you choose one of these options or copy the information directly into your **working bibliography** (see 13D), it's crucial to record the CALL NUMBER exactly as it appears, with all numbers, letters, and decimal points. The call number tells where the book is located in the library's stacks (storage shelves). If you're researching in a library with open stacks (shelves that are accessible without special permission), the call number leads you to the area in the library where all books on the same subject can be found.

A call number is especially crucial in a library or special collection with closed stacks, which is a library where you hand in a slip at the call desk (or submit a request online) and wait for the book to arrive. Such libraries don't permit you to browse the stacks, so you have to rely entirely on the book catalog.

■ Using electronic books

You're probably familiar with electronic books on readers like the Kindle, Nook, or iPad. Many books have electronic versions that you can access—and without paying—if you go through a library. Figure 12.6 shows one book found in a library catalog that's available only in an electronic format. Students at this school can log in to read the book online.

Figure 12.6   Electronic book available only online.

Author	Clarke, Bruce.
Title	**The Routledge Companion to Literature and Science [electronic resource].**
Publ Info	Hoboken : Taylor & Francis, 2010.

The links below are for electronic versions of this publication:
Access online: Individual login with EBL required

LOCATION	CALL #	STATUS
Internet	PN55.R68 2010eb	ONLINE

Description	1 online resource (569 p.)
Series	Routledge Literature Companions.
	Routledge Literature Companions.
	Routledge Literature Companions.
Note	Book preview interface supplies PDF, image or read-aloud access. Adobe Digital Editions software required for book downloads.
	Mode of access: World Wide Web.
Note(s)	Description based upon print version of record.
Contents	LITERATURES AND SCIENCES; 1 AI AND ALIFE; 2 ALCHEMY; 3 BIOLOGY; 4 CHAOS AND COMPLEXITY THEORY; 5 CHEMISTRY; 6 CLIMATE SCIENCE; 7 COGNITIVE SCIENCE; 8 CYBERNETICS; 9 ECOLOGY; 10 EVOLUTION; 11 GENETICS; 12 GEOLOGY; 13 **INFORMATION** THEORY; 14 MATHEMATICS; 15 MEDICINE; 16 NANOTECHNOLOGY; 17 PHYSICS; 18 PSYCHOANALYSIS; 19 SYSTEMS THEORY; 20 THERMODYNAMICS; PART II: DISCIPLINARY AND THEORETICAL APPROACHES; 21 AGRICULTURAL STUDIES; 22 ANIMAL STUDES; 23 ART CONNECTIONS; 24 CULTURAL SCIENCE STUDIES; 25 DECONSTRUCTION

12C

Google has scanned many books and put them on the Web. You can find them by searching Google Books. Even if you find a book you want online, unless it's very old, only a portion of it will be available. If you're lucky, it will be the part you want; otherwise, you'll need to find the book through other means such as interlibrary loan.

12D   How do I use reference works?

Reference works include encyclopedias, almanacs, yearbooks, fact books, atlases, dictionaries, biographical reference works, and bibliographies. *General* reference works provide information on a vast number of subjects, but without much depth. *Specialized* reference works provide information on selected topics, often for more expert or professional audiences.

■ Using general reference works

General reference works are the starting point for many college researchers—but they're no more than a starting point. They help researchers identify useful keywords to use to search for subject headings and online catalogs. They're also good for finding examples and verifying facts.

Most widely used general reference works are available online. Check your library's Web site to see what it has subscribed to. For example, you may find a subscription to the *Gale Virtual Reference Library*, which gives libraries access to up to 1,000 reference books online. Alternatively, you can search the Web on your own. Be aware that often you have to pay a fee for works you don't access through a library.

GENERAL ENCYCLOPEDIAS

Articles in multivolume general encyclopedias, such as the *Encyclopaedia Britannica*, can give you helpful background information, the names of major experts in the field, and, often, a brief BIBLIOGRAPHY on the subject.

🛈 **Alert:** A Note on *Wikipedia*: *Wikipedia* is an unedited source that almost anyone can modify. Obviously, then, the accuracy and quality of information it contains isn't always reliable. There's always the possibility that a *Wikipedia* source is flawed. Still, *Wikipedia* can be a useful starting place for some quick information on a topic. For example, like many professionals and professors, we occasionally check *Wikipedia* to learn names, concepts, or basic information on a particular topic. But we know *Wikipedia* is only a starting place, a way to get oriented. Other sources serve us—and you—better for college-level research. When students use *Wikipedia* extensively, readers realize they haven't taken the time or responsibility to find more scholarly sources. ●

12D

ALMANACS, YEARBOOKS, AND FACT BOOKS

Often available both in print and online, almanacs, yearbooks, and fact books are huge compilations of facts and figures. Examples include the *World Almanac, Facts on File*, and the annual *Statistical Abstract of the United States*.

ATLASES AND GAZETTEERS

Atlases, such as the *Times Atlas of the World*, contain maps of our planet's continents, seas, and skies. Gazetteers, such as the *Columbia Gazetteer of the World*, provide comprehensive geographical information on topography, climates, populations, migrations, natural resources, and so on.

DICTIONARIES

Dictionaries define words and terms. In addition to general dictionaries, specialized dictionaries focus exclusively on many academic disciplines.

BIOGRAPHICAL REFERENCE WORKS

Biographical reference books, such as the *Who's Who* series and the *Dictionary of American Biography*, give brief factual information about famous people— their accomplishments along with pertinent events and dates in their lives.

BIBLIOGRAPHIES

12E

BIBLIOGRAPHIES are guides to sources on particular topics. They list books, articles, documents, films, and other resources along with publication information so that you can find them. Annotated or critical bibliographies describe and evaluate the works that they list.

■ **Using specialized reference works**

Specialized reference works provide authoritative, specific information on selected topics, often for more expert researchers. These works are usually appropriate for college-level research because the information is more advanced and detailed. Examples include the *Dictionary of American Biography, Encyclopedia of Banking and Finance, Encyclopedia of Chemistry, Encyclopedia of Religion, Encyclopedia of the Biological Sciences, International Encyclopedia of Film, New Grove Dictionary of Music and Musicians*, and *Oxford Companion to the Theatre*.

12E   How do I search for media?

If you need or want to include images in a research paper, you have three options. A keyword search through the "Images" menu on Google or Yahoo! will generate links to images as they appear in sites and documents across the

Internet. However, there are ethical and, sometimes, even legal concerns in using what you find this way. Although "fair use" means that students can usually use sources once for a classroom project, you are behaving ethically if you get written permission from the photographer or site where you found the image. Always be sure to cite the source properly.

A good alternative is to use a "stock photo" Web site. These are services like iStockphoto or Getty Images that have gathered thousands, even millions, of photographs, which you can browse by category or keyword. For a small fee you can purchase the one-time use of an image from these sites. (There are a few "free" sites, too.)

Finally, your library may provide access to image archives or databases. Ask a librarian. Once again, always cite images properly.

12F   How do I search for government documents?

Government publications are available in astounding variety. You can find information on laws and legal decisions, regulations, population, weather patterns, agriculture, national parks, education, and health, to name just a few topics. Most are available online.

- The Government Printing Office maintains its searchable *Catalog of U.S. Government Publications.*

- THOMAS, a service of the Library of Congress, offers information about legislation.

- A directory of all US federal government sites provides statistical information.

- The LexisNexis database service provides access to a huge number of other governmental reports and documents. For example, the Congressional Information Service indexes all papers produced by congressional panels and committees.

12G   How do I evaluate the sources I find?

Not all sources are created equal. We don't only mean the differences between books, periodicals, and Web sites, or between scholarly and popular sources. Sources differ also in quality. Some present information that has been carefully gathered and checked. Others report information, even rumor, that is secondor thirdhand or, worse, perhaps not even based in fact.

Some sources make claims that are accompanied by strong evidence and reasoning. Others make claims based only on opinion, or they use information illogically. Some are written by experts wanting to advance

12G

knowledge. Others are produced by people wanting to promote special interests however they can, even if it means ignoring data, oversimplifying issues, or overpromising results. Some sources have been reviewed by experts and published only after passing standards. Others appear without anyone judging their quality.

As a college writer, you don't want to use weak sources that hurt your ETHOS and ruin your paper. Therefore, evaluate each source you find by asking the questions in Quick Box 12.5.

Quick Box 12.5

Five questions for evaluating sources

1. Where did you find the source?
2. Is the publisher authoritative?
3. Is the author qualified to write about the topic?
4. Does the source have sufficient and credible evidence?
5. Does the source pass other critical thinking tests?

12G

■ Where did I find the source?

Sources that you find through DATABASES, especially databases you access through a library Web site (see 12C), are more likely to be useful than sources found through a general Google or Yahoo! search. A source in a database has been edited and checked for quality. The more scholarly a database is, the more confident you can be that its sources are reliable.

For example, suppose you want to research the safety of vaccines. (We illustrate the range of options on this topic in Figure 12.7, where a student has done four different searches.) A Google search produces thousands of sources. Some of them are reliable; many are not. If you search a library database like Academic Search Premier, you'll find hundreds of sources, mainly of higher quality. Still, the most authoritative sources come from a college library's CATALOG or a scholarly database like Medline, which is created for physicians, researchers, and other medical professionals. (Of course, some highly advanced expert sources can be hard to understand.)

Figure 12.7 Four searches with less to more reliable results.

Least Reliable:
A general Google search

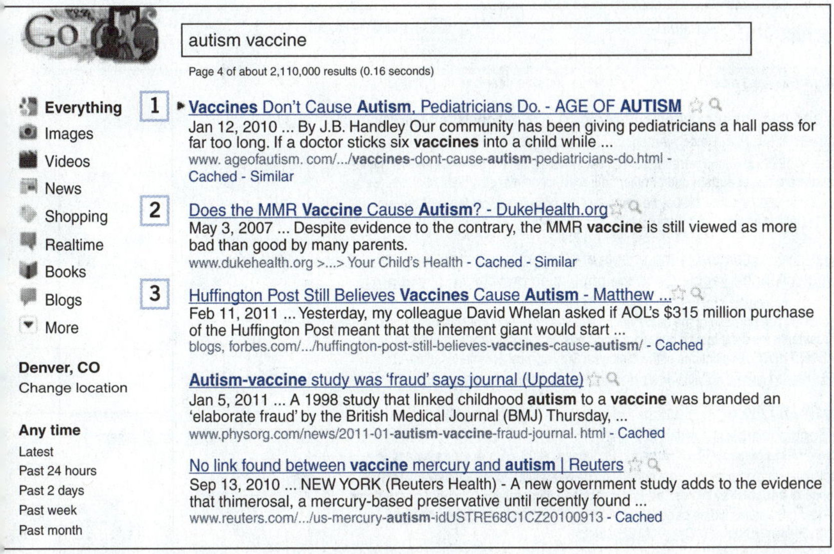

autism vaccine

Page 4 of about 2,110,000 results (0.16 seconds)

Everything
Images
Videos
News
Shopping
Realtime
Books
Blogs
More

Denver, CO
Change location

Any time
Latest
Past 24 hours
Past 2 days
Past week
Past month

1 **Vaccines** Don't Cause **Autism**, Pediatricians Do. - AGE OF **AUTISM**
Jan 12, 2010 ... By J.B. Handley Our community has been giving pediatricians a hall pass for far too long. If a doctor sticks six **vaccines** into a child while ...
www. ageofautism. com/.../**vaccines**-dont-cause-**autism**-pediatricians-do.html - Cached - Similar

2 Does the MMR **Vaccine** Cause **Autism**? - DukeHealth.org
May 3, 2007 ... Despite evidence to the contrary, the MMR **vaccine** is still viewed as more bad than good by many parents.
www.dukehealth.org >...> Your Child's Health - Cached - Similar

3 Huffington Post Still Believes **Vaccines** Cause **Autism** - Matthew ...
Feb 11, 2011 ... Yesterday, my colleague David Whelan asked if AOL's $315 million purchase of the Huffington Post meant that the intement giant would start ...
blogs, forbes.com/.../huffington-post-still-believes-**vaccines**-cause-**autism**/ - Cached

Autism-vaccine study was 'fraud' says journal (Update)
Jan 5, 2011 ... A 1998 study that linked childhood **autism** to a **vaccine** was branded an 'elaborate fraud' by the British Medical Journal (BMJ) Thursday, ...
www.physorg.com/news/2011-01-**autism-vaccine**-fraud-journal. html - Cached

No link found between **vaccine** mercury and **autism** | Reuters
Sep 13, 2010 ... NEW YORK (Reuters Health) - A new government study adds to the evidence that thimerosal, a mercury-based preservative until recently found ...
www.reuters.com/.../us-mercury-**autism**-idUSTRE68C1CZ20100913 - Cached

1 Title suggests that this site expresses the strong opinion that doctors cause autism. You'd have to check this one carefully for bias.

2 The name and the .org domain suggests that it might be associated with Duke University.

3 Blogs can have opinions unsupported by facts. Check carefully.

Figure 12.7 Four searches with less to more reliable results (continued).

More Reliable:
A Google Scholar search

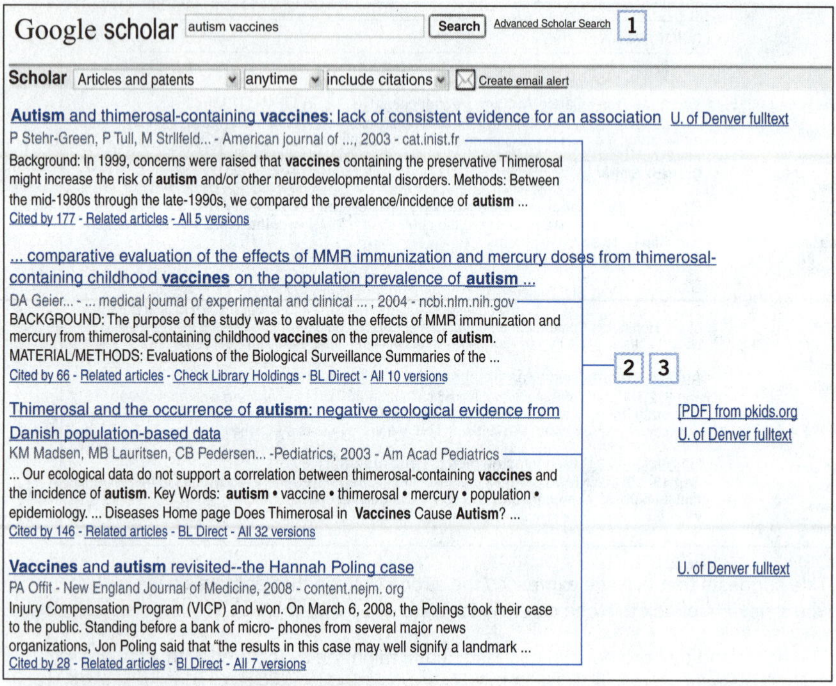
Google scholar autism vaccines Search Advanced Scholar Search 1

Scholar Articles and patents anytime include citations Create email alert

Autism and thimerosal-containing vaccines: lack of consistent evidence for an association U. of Denver fulltext
P Stehr-Green, P Tull, M Strllfeld... - American journal of ..., 2003 - cat.inist.fr
Background: In 1999, concerns were raised that vaccines containing the preservative Thimerosal might increase the risk of autism and/or other neurodevelopmental disorders. Methods: Between the mid-1980s through the late-1990s, we compared the prevalence/incidence of autism ...
Cited by 177 - Related articles - All 5 versions

... comparative evaluation of the effects of MMR immunization and mercury doses from thimerosal-containing childhood vaccines on the population prevalence of autism ...
DA Geier... - ... medical journal of experimental and clinical ... , 2004 - ncbi.nlm.nih.gov
BACKGROUND: The purpose of the study was to evaluate the effects of MMR immunization and mercury from thimerosal-containing childhood vaccines on the prevalence of autism. MATERIAL/METHODS: Evaluations of the Biological Surveillance Summaries of the ...
Cited by 66 - Related articles - Check Library Holdings - BL Direct - All 10 versions

2 3

Thimerosal and the occurrence of autism: negative ecological evidence from Danish population-based data [PDF] from pkids.org U. of Denver fulltext
KM Madsen, MB Lauritsen, CB Pedersen... -Pediatrics, 2003 - Am Acad Pediatrics
... Our ecological data do not support a correlation between thimerosal-containing vaccines and the incidence of autism. Key Words: autism • vaccine • thimerosal • mercury • population • epidemiology. ... Diseases Home page Does Thimerosal in Vaccines Cause Autism? ...
Cited by 146 - Related articles - BL Direct - All 32 versions

Vaccines and autism revisited--the Hannah Poling case U. of Denver fulltext
PA Offit - New England Journal of Medicine, 2008 - content.nejm. org
Injury Compensation Program (VICP) and won. On March 6, 2008, the Polings took their case to the public. Standing before a bank of micro- phones from several major news organizations, Jon Poling said that "the results in this case may well signify a landmark ...
Cited by 28 - Related articles - Bl Direct - All 7 versions

1 Sources on this page come from journals in the field, which are edited and written by experts.

2 Full text versions show that these are articles, not Web sites.

3 All sources on this page are somewhat old for current medical research.

Figure 12.7 Four searches with less to more reliable results (continued).

Reliable:
A search using a common college library database

5. <u>Refusing kids' vaccine more common</u>
   By: Liz Szabo, *USA Today,* 05/04/2010
   Database: Academic Search Complete —————————— **1**

   Add to folder

   HTML Full Text   Find this items in Penrose Library   ARTICLE Linker   Check Article Linker

6. <u>3 Rulings Find No Link to **Autism** in a Mercury Preservative in **Vaccines.**</u>
   By: McNEIL, Jr., DONALD G., *New York Times,* 3/13/2010, p11, 0p
   Subjects: VACCINATION; AUTISM; DEVELOPMENTAL disabilities; UNITED States; UNITED States. Court of Federal Claims;
   Administration of Public Health Programs

   Database: Academic Search Complete

   Add to folder

   Find this items in Penrose Library   ARTICLE Linker   Check Article Linker

2 7. <u>Lancet retracts 12-year-old article linking **autism** to MMR **vaccines.**</u>
   By: Eggertson, Laura, *CMAJ: Canadian Medical Association Journal,* 3/9/2010 Supplement, Vol. 182, pE199-E200, 2p, 1 Color
   Photograph; DOI: 10.1503/cmaj.109-3179
   Subjects: VACCINATION of children; AUTISM in children; GREAT Britain; LANCET, The (Periodical); MMR vaccine;
   WAKEFIELD, Andrew

   Database: Academic Search Complete

1 Database includes popular sources like newspaper articles, which will be easier to understand.

2 Database also includes scholarly sources like journal articles. These PRIMARY SOURCES will have the most authoritative research but can sometimes be difficult for nonspecialists to understand.

Figure 12.7 Four searches with less to more reliable results (continued).

Expert:
A search using a database designed for experts in a field

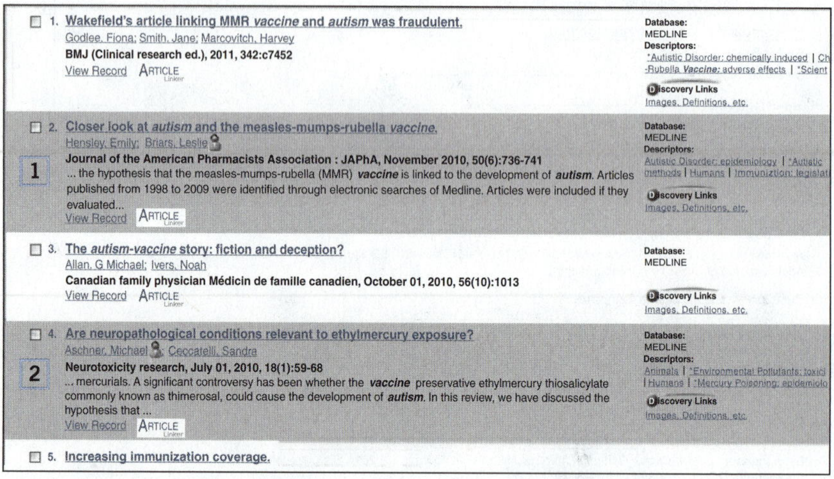

1. Wakefield's article linking MMR *vaccine* and *autism* was fraudulent.
Godlee, Fiona; Smith, Jane; Marcovitch, Harvey
BMJ (Clinical research ed.), 2011, 342:c7452
View Record ARTICLE Linker
Database: MEDLINE
Descriptors: *Autistic Disorder: chemically induced | Ch -Rubella *Vaccine:* adverse effects | *Scient
Discovery Links
Images, Definitions, etc.

2. Closer look at *autism* and the measles-mumps-rubella *vaccine*.
Hensley, Emily; Briars, Leslie
Journal of the American Pharmacists Association : JAPhA, November 2010, 50(6):736-741
... the hypothesis that the measles-mumps-rubella (MMR) ***vaccine*** is linked to the development of ***autism***. Articles published from 1998 to 2009 were identified through electronic searches of Medline. Articles were included if they evaluated...
View Record ARTICLE Linker
Database: MEDLINE
Descriptors: Autistic Disorder: epidemiology | *Autistic methods | Humans | Immuniztion: legislat
Discovery Links
Images, Definitions, etc.

3. The *autism-vaccine* story: fiction and deception?
Allan, G Michael; Ivers, Noah
Canadian family physician Médicin de famille canadien, October 01, 2010, 56(10):1013
View Record ARTICLE Linker
Database: MEDLINE
Discovery Links
Images, Definitions, etc.

4. Are neuropathological conditions relevant to ethylmercury exposure?
Aschner, Michael; Ceccatelli, Sandra
Neurotoxicity research, July 01, 2010, 18(1):59-68
... mercurials. A significant controversy has been whether the ***vaccine*** preservative ethylmercury thiosalicylate commonly known as thimerosal, could cause the development of ***autism***. In this review, we have discussed the hypothesis that ...
View Record ARTICLE Linker
Database: MEDLINE
Descriptors: Animals | *Environmental Pollutants: toxici | Humans | *Mercury Poisoning: epidemiolo
Discovery Links
Images, Definitions, etc.

5. Increasing immunization coverage.

1 All articles in this database come from scholarly journals, and many report fairly recent research.

2 Short descriptions provide some information about article contents.

■ Is the publisher authoritative?

The publisher is the company or group ultimately responsible for a book, periodical, or Web site.

Is the Publisher Authorative?

Reliable sources are . . .	Questionable sources are . . .
• **From reputable publishers.** Generally, encyclopedias, textbooks, and academic journals, such as the *Journal of Counseling and Development*, are authoritative. Books from university and other established presses are authoritative. Sources published in major newspapers such as *The Washington Post* and in general-readership magazines such as *Time* and *Harper's*, and textbooks, such as those from Pearson, are reliable, too. See Figure 12.8.	• **From special-interest groups.** Some groups exist only to advance a narrow interest or political viewpoint. Examples would be a group existing only to legalize marijuana or one to stop all immigration. Special-interest groups might publish useful sources, but you want to check their facts and reasoning by asking "Why does the group exist?" Be sure to question its motives, especially if it asks you to take a specific action, such as donate money. See if materials published by the group are included in scholarly databases, and apply other tests listed in this chapter.
• **Web sites from educational, not-for-profit, or government organizations.** Web sites from professional associations, such as the National Council of Teachers of English or The American Medical Association, are reliable. If you don't recognize an organization, you need to investigate how long it has existed, whether it is not-for-profit, who its members and leaders are, and so on.	• **Web sites from commercial enterprises** may or may not provide evidence or list sources for claims they make. If they fail to do so, or if the evidence and sources seem weak, don't use them. Be sure the Web site is not one that encourages illegal activities. See Figure 12.9.
• **Direct online versions of authoritative print sources.** Many journals, newspapers, and book publishers release online versions of print publications. Online versions of authoritative publications are reliable.	• **Secondhand excerpts, quotations, and references.** Materials that appear in a source that is not the official site of the publisher (such as a quotation taken from a magazine) may have been edited in a biased or inaccurate manner. Always check the original. Figure 12.10 illustrates a problem that can occur with secondhand materials.

12G

Figure 12.8   A commercial (nonscholarly) book and a scholarly book.

Commercial Book

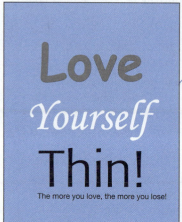

A self-help book that gives diet and relationship advice and promises results. The publisher also sponsors a commercial Web site focusing on spin-off products. Therefore, this is not a scholarly source.

McIntire, Marilyn. *Love Yourself Thin!* Ankeny, IA: Maddie, 2012. Print.

12G   **Scholarly Book**

A scholarly book that reports findings from a research study of body image and relationships among young college graduates. The publisher is a university press, which makes the work authoritative.

Neufeld, Sarah. *Body Image, Relationships, and the Influence of Popular Culture.* Evergreen, CO: Evans UP, 2012. Print.

Figure 12.9 An authoritative Web site and a questionable Web site.

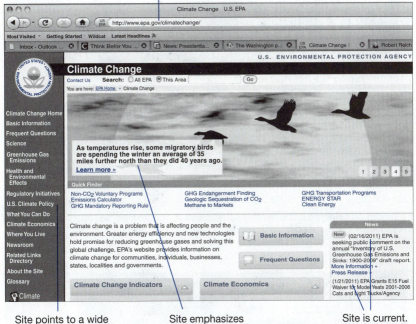

An authoritative Web site   A .gov URL signals government sponsorship.

Site points to a wide
range of information.

Site emphasizes
facts.

Site is current.

A .com URL means it is commercial, so you want to
check the nature and motives of the group.

A questionable Web site

Advertising.

Chat box contains information
that hasn't been reviewed.

Figure 12.10   A section from an original article and a misused quotation from that article.

THURSDAY, MARCH 10, 2011

SEARCH OUR SITE

the *Atlantic*

POLITICS | BUSINESS | CULTURE | INTERNATIONAL |

APRIL 2011 ATLANTIC MAGAZINE

At an individual level, I think the "distracted Americans" scare will pass. Either people who manage to unplug, focus, and fully direct their attention will have an advantage over those constantly checking Facebook and their smart phone, in which case they'll earn more money, get into better colleges, start more successful companies, and win more Nobel Prizes. Or they won't, in which case distraction will be a trait of modern life but not necessarily a defect. At the level of national politics, America is badly distracted, but that problem long predates Facebook and requires more than a media solution.

Fallows, James. "Learning to Love the (Shallow, Divisive, Unreliable) New Media." *Atlantic.* Atlantic Monthly Group, Apr. 2011. Web.10 Mar. 2011.

Comment on original: In the original full article from *The Atlantic*, a serious magazine for general readers, James Fallows agrees that Americans are distracted when it comes to politics, but he does not blame the Internet for that situation.

CIVILIZATION
The Truth about Our Declining World
About / Links / Campaigns / Donations

James Fallows complains about the effects of the internet on democracy when he says that, "At the level of national politics, America is badly distracted."

Comment on misused quotation: The Civilization Web site misrepresents Fallows. By using only part of his quotation, it makes him express exactly the opposite of what he actually wrote. It would be a serious mistake to quote this site.

■ Is the author qualified to write about the topic?

Anyone can express an opinion or argue for an action, but the only writers worth quoting or summarizing in your writing have knowledge and expertise about their topics. Often, their credentials appear in a note in an introduction, at the bottom of the first page, or at the end of an article. In a book, look for an "About the Author" statement, on a Web site, a short biography or a "Contributors" note (see Figure 12.11). Sometimes you might need to do some research to learn about the author.

Figure 12.11　Authors with and without scholarly credentials.

Start Loving Life!

Hi! I'm **Marilyn McIntire**, motivational speaker, fitness guru, relationship coach, and author. My life has been an astonishing adventure, and yours can be, too. Let's walk this journey together! Check me out whenever you need inspiration, advice, and a good laugh.
—Rainbow joys, Marilyn

If you were writing an academic paper on dieting and evaluating the two books in Figure 12.8 (page 138), the credentials of Sarah Neufeld would be much more credible. (Marilyn McIntire's credentials would be suitable for other purposes, perhaps, but not for an academic paper.)

Sarah Neufeld

Psychology Department Chair

Dr. Sarah Neufeld, Professor of Psychology at Evans University, was named chair of the department in 2011. She joined the faculty after receiving her Ph.D. from New York University in 1998 and has published over 35 articles in her area of research: the effects of popular culture on self-esteem and interpersonal behavior.

12G

Is the Author Qualified to Write About the Topic?

Reliable sources are . . .	Questionable sources are . . .
• **From expert authors**. Experts have degrees or credentials in their field. Biographical material in the source may list these credentials. If in doubt, look up the author in a biographical dictionary, search online for a resume or bio, or search a database. Check if the author's name appears in other reliable sources. Check whether there is contact information for questions or comments.	• **From authors with fuzzy credentials**. A warning sign should flash when you can't identify who has produced a source. Discussion threads, anonymous blogs, and similar online postings are questionable when they don't give information about the writer's qualifications. Check to make sure that listed credentials fit the topic. Just because someone has a graduate degree in history, for example, doesn't qualify the person to give medical advice.

ESOL Tip: The definition of "authority" can differ across cultures. In the United States, a source has authority only if it meets specific criteria. It must appear in a scholarly book or journal; its author must have a degree, title, or license; or other authorities must seek his or her knowledge. A source is not reliable simply because the author or speaker is an influential or well-known member of the community; claims to have knowledge about a topic but has no credentials related to the topic; or publishes material in print or online on the topic without being qualified to do so. You are expected to judge the authority of sources in a US college. ●

Does the source have sufficient and accurate evidence?

If an author expresses a point of view but offers little evidence to back up that position, reject the source. See Figure 12.12 for an example of how sources use evidence.

Figure 12.12 Sources that do and do not cite evidence.

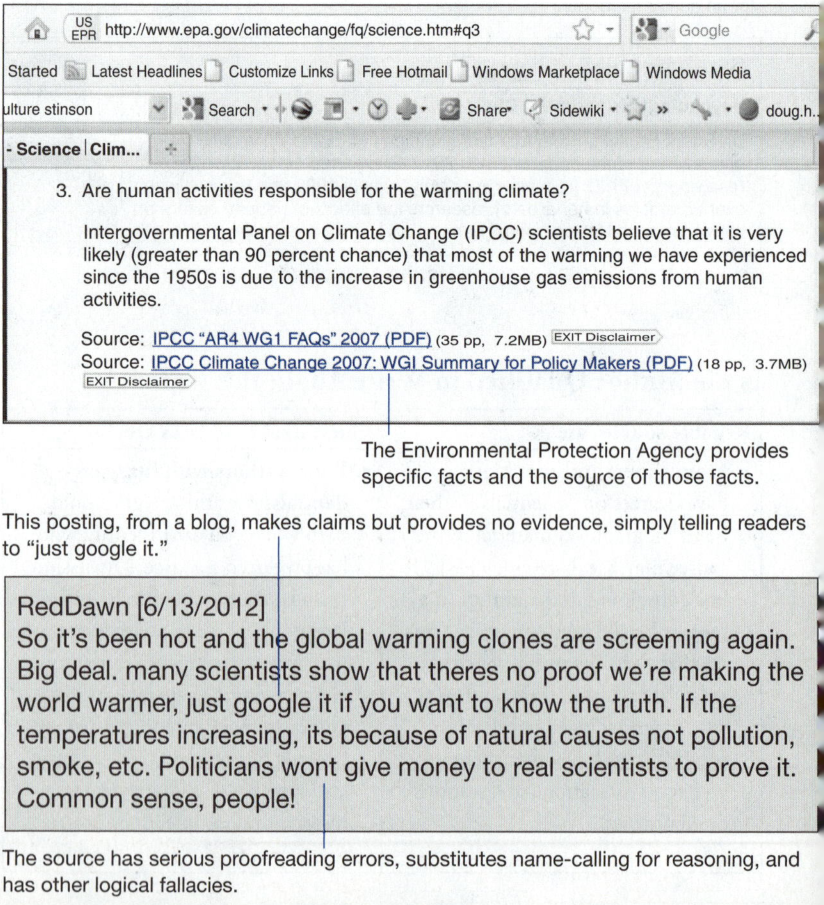
US EPA http://www.epa.gov/climatechange/fq/science.htm#q3
Google
Started Latest Headlines Customize Links Free Hotmail Windows Marketplace Windows Media
ulture stinson
Search
Share
Sidewiki
doug.h..
- Science | Clim...
3. Are human activities responsible for the warming climate?
Intergovernmental Panel on Climate Change (IPCC) scientists believe that it is very likely (greater than 90 percent chance) that most of the warming we have experienced since the 1950s is due to the increase in greenhouse gas emissions from human activities.
Source: IPCC "AR4 WG1 FAQs" 2007 (PDF) (35 pp, 7.2MB) EXIT Disclaimer
Source: IPCC Climate Change 2007: WGI Summary for Policy Makers (PDF) (18 pp, 3.7MB) EXIT Disclaimer
The Environmental Protection Agency provides specific facts and the source of those facts.
This posting, from a blog, makes claims but provides no evidence, simply telling readers to "just google it."
RedDawn [6/13/2012]
So it's been hot and the global warming clones are screeming again. Big deal. many scientists show that theres no proof we're making the world warmer, just google it if you want to know the truth. If the temperatures increasing, its because of natural causes not pollution, smoke, etc. Politicians wont give money to real scientists to prove it. Common sense, people!
The source has serious proofreading errors, substitutes name-calling for reasoning, and has other logical fallacies.

Does the Source Have Sufficient and Accurate Evidence?

Reliable sources are . . .	Questionable sources are . . .
• **Well supported with evidence.** The source's writer provides clear and plentiful facts and reasons to support assertions.	• **Unsupported or biased.** They carry assertions that have little or no supporting evidence.
• **Factually accurate.** The sources for statistics, quotations, and other information are listed. You or anyone can look them up to check their accuracy.	• **Factually questionable.** They may include statistics or other information, but they fail to identify who generated them. You have no way to check facts.
• **Current.** Information is recent or, in the case of Web sites, regularly updated.	• **Outdated.** This is 20-year-old medical advice. The political situation is based on a Web site last updated in 2009.

■ **Does the source pass other critical thinking tests?**

Use CRITICAL THINKING skills when you evaluate a source (see Chapter 2). Figure 12.13 shows one Web site that shows critical thinking in its fairly balanced tone and one that is more biased in tone.

12G

Does the Source Pass Other Critical Thinking Tests?

Reliable sources are . . .	Questionable sources are . . .
• **Balanced in tone.** The source is respectful of others and creates a sense of fairness.	• **Biased in tone.** Some warning signs of biased tone are name-calling, sarcasm, stereotyping, or absolute assertions about matters that are open to interpretation. For example, if a source declares, "Television programs are never worth watching" or that "women are always better than men at writing," you are encountering bias.
• **Balanced in treatment.** The author advocates a credible position but also acknowledges different viewpoints. For example, they summarize contradictory evidence.	• **One-sided.** The author omits any mention or fair summary of competing views or gives unreliable information, especially if openly ridiculing competing positions.
• **Logical.** The source draws fair conclusions from evidence. The reasoning is clear.	• **Full of LOGICAL FALLACIES.**
• **Well-edited.** The source has been proofread and is free of grammatical errors.	• **Marked by errors.** Beware of any source that has typos or sloppy errors.

Figure 12.13   A source with balanced tone and a source with biased tone.

Balanced tone   The writer acknowledges there is a difference of opinion.

| Home | What is Global Warming | News | For Children | Solutions | Business | About |

What is global warming ?

What is global warming?

While some would call global warming a theory, others would call it a proven set of facts. Opinions differ vehemently. Let us consider global warming to be both a premise that the enviroment of the world as we know it is slowly, but very surely increasing in overall air and water temperature, and a promise that if whatever is causing this trend is not interrupted or challenged life on earth will dynamically be affected.

The prevailing counter opinion is that all that is presently perceived to be global warming is simply the result of a normal climactic swing in the direction of increased temperature. Many proponents of this global warming ideology have definitive social and financial interests in these claims.

The writer summarizes the point of view with which he or she disagrees.

There is, however, a slight element of bias in saying that people have an "ideology."

The writer relies on name-calling rather than acknowledging others.

The comparison to "vampires avoid silver bullets" gets readers' attention, but it's hardly respectful.

Biased tone

OVERVIEW OF THE GLOBAL WARMING MYTH

Print

April 4, 2012 **Posted by Renee Locke at 10:45 p.m.**

"The world is getting warmer, and humans are responsible." If that basic myth of global warming weren't so dangerous, it would be downright laughable. After all, it's nearly inconceivable that so many people could be deluded by pseudo-scientists who avoid truth like vampires avoid silver bullets. But there's nothing funny about totalitarian politicians seeking to wrap our freedoms in chains. The rigorous but accessible <u>Scientists for Sense</u> website provides evidence against global warming, and I distill this evidence below.

Earn your Master of Science in Management-Sustainability

The writer promises to send readers to a "rigorous but accessible" informational site. However, you need to evaluate that site to be sure.

12H What is field research?

Field research is a term that refers to ways to create new knowledge. You explore real-life situations to observe, survey, interview, or participate in some activity firsthand. As a field researcher, you might go to a factory, a lecture, a day-care center, or a mall—anywhere that people engage in everyday activities. You might also interview experts and other relevant individuals. You might observe and describe objects, such as paintings or buildings, or performances and events, such as concerts or television shows.

■ Observing

Anthropologists, education and marketing researchers, sociologists, and other scholars conduct research by observing people and situations. For observations of behavior (for example, fans at a game or tourists at a museum), take notes during the activity. Try to remain objective so that you can see things clearly. One strategy for recording your observations is to take notes in a two-column format. On the left, record only your objective observations; on the right, record your comments or interpretations. Figure 12.14 is an example of a double-column note strategy.

12H

Figure 12.14 A double-column set of notes on observations.

Notes	Comment/Analyses
Small conference room; round table covered with papers	
JP suggests fundraising plan	JP seems nervous. Her normal behavior, or is it this situation?
AR and CT lean forward; SM leans back	
SM interrupts JP's plan, asks for more; CT silent	The fact that JP and AR are women might explain SM's response. Or is it that he's more senior?
JP continues proposal	
SM looks out window, taps pencil	Seems to have made up his mind. A power move?

■ Surveying

Surveys use questions to gather information about people's experiences, situations, or opinions. Multiple-choice or true/false questions are easy for people to complete and for researchers to summarize and report. Open-ended questions, in which people are asked to write responses, require more effort to summarize. However, they sometimes provide more complete or accurate information. For advice on developing a survey, see Quick Box 12.6.

When you report findings from a survey, keep within your limitations. For example, if the only people who answer your survey are students at a particular campus, you can't claim they represent "all college students."

❶ **Alert:** Online tools can help you distribute and analyze surveys easily. Two popular free services for small surveys are Zoomerang and Survey-Monkey. You go to the service's Web site, enter your survey questions, and then receive a URL to send to participants. After you receive responses, you can go back to the Web site to download the results or do some analysis. ●

12H

Quick Box 12.6   ■ ■ ■ ■ ■ ■

Guidelines for developing a survey

1. Define what you want to learn.
2. Identify the appropriate types and numbers of people to answer your survey so that you get the information you need.
3. Write questions to elicit the information.
4. Phrase questions so that they are easy to understand.

   NO   Recognizing several complex variables, what age generally do you perceive as most advantageous for matrimony?

   YES What do you think is the ideal age for getting married?

5. Make sure that your wording doesn't imply what you want to hear.

   NO   Do irresponsible and lazy deadbeats deserve support from hardworking and honest taxpayers?

   YES Should we provide benefits to unemployed people?

6. Decide whether to include open-ended questions that allow people to write their own answers.
7. Test a draft of the questionnaire on a small group of people. If any question is misinterpreted or difficult to understand, revise and retest it.

■ Interviewing

Instead of surveying, you might interview people in the general population to gather data or opinions. You might also interview experts, who can offer valuable information and viewpoints. One good place to start is with the faculty at your college, who may also suggest additional sources. Also, corporations, institutions, or professional organizations often have public relations offices that can answer questions or make referrals.

Make every attempt to conduct interviews in person so that you can observe body language and facial expressions. However, if distance is a problem, you can conduct interviews over the phone or online. Quick Box 12.7 provides suggestions for conducting interviews.

Quick Box 12.7 ■ ■ ■ ■ ■ ■

Conducting research interviews

- Arrange the interview well in advance, do background research, prepare specific questions, and arrive on time.

- Rehearse how to ask your questions without reading them (perhaps highlight the key words). Looking your interviewee in the eye as you ask questions establishes ease and trust. If you're interviewing on the telephone, be organized and precise.

- Never depend on recording an interview because people have become reluctant to be recorded.

- Take careful notes, listening especially for key names, books, Web sites, or other sources.

- Create a shortcut symbol or letter for key terms you expect to hear during the interview. This cuts down on the time needed to look away from your interviewee.

- Use standard paper so that you have room to write. (Many people are annoyed when others type while they're talking.)

- Bring extra pens or pencils.

12H

Ten Steps for Writing a Research Paper

Quick Points   You will learn to

➤ Plan your research (see below).

➤ Conduct research (see pp. 151–159).

➤ Organize your research paper (see pp. 159–161).

➤ Synthesize your sources (see pp. 161–172).

➤ Avoid plagiarism by quoting, paraphrasing, and summarizing sources correctly (see pp. 172–185).

➤ Draft and revise your research paper (see pp. 185–187).

MyWritingLab™   Visit mywritinglab.com for more resources on writing a research paper.

13A   How do I plan my college-level research paper?

Research is a systematic process of gathering information to answer a question. You're doing research when you're trying to decide which college to attend or which smartphone to buy. Even these everyday tasks have things in common with college research: finding, evaluating, and synthesizing information. Research can be a creative, absorbing activity. When you write a college-level research paper, you come to know a subject deeply, gain fresh insights, and become a self-reliant learner.

Here are some major reasons for conducting research:

- To find how important facts and information have changed over time

  How does the cost of college today compare to the cost twenty years ago?

- To understand an issue or situation in today's world

  What is the effect of globalization on today's political systems?

- To gather information and present a comprehensive synthesis of the latest knowledge

  What are the major current treatments for diabetes?

- To identify opinions or points of view about a debatable topic and to agree or disagree with one of them using an effective defense

  Should college students be permitted to use smartphones during class?

- To create new knowledge by conducting field research

  During a national election, what are the political views of 18–24-year-olds on this campus?

Understanding the processes involved in writing a research paper

Research writing layers additional activities on top of the ten usual steps in the writing process explained in Chapter 4 of this handbook. Keep those steps in mind as you focus on the research-based aspects of writing your research paper. Quick Box 13.1 summarizes the basic steps involved in writing a research paper.

Quick Box 13.1

The research writing process

- **Planning** your research means choosing a good topic, posing a research question about it, choosing a documentation style, planning a search strategy and timeline, and setting up a research log (see 13A, 13B).
- **Conducting research** involves finding and evaluating sources (Chapter 12), taking notes (13C), and developing a bibliography (13D).
- **Organizing** your research paper involves adapting a frame to suit your project (13E).
- **Synthesizing** your sources means you weave their ideas together with your own (13F).
- **Quoting, paraphrasing, and summarizing** sources correctly will help you **avoid plagiarism** (13G, 13H, 13I).
- **Writing** your research paper involves drafting, revising, and editing (13I).

13A

Choosing a topic worthy of a college research paper

Sometimes college instructors assign specific topics; other times you get to choose. When you need to select your own research topic:

- Select a topic that interests you. It will be your companion for quite a while, perhaps most of a term.
- Choose a sufficiently narrow topic that will allow you to be successful within the time and length given by the assignment. Avoid topics that are too broad.

NO Emotions

YES How people respond to anger in others

NO Social networking

YES The effect of Facebook on job applications

- Choose a topic that your readers will perceive as significant. Avoid trivial topics that prevent you from investigating ideas, analyzing them critically, or synthesizing complex concepts.

NO Kinds of fast food

YES The relationship between fast food and obesity

If you're unsure of taking a chance to select your research topic, you might have research–topic block. Don't panic. Instead, try some of the following strategies for generating ideas.

- **Talk with others.** Ask instructors or other experts in your area of interest what issues currently seem important to them. Ask them to recommend readings or the names of authorities on those issues.
- **Browse the Internet.** Some Web search engines provide SUBJECT DIRECTORIES (see 12B). Browsing those, you can use their categories and subcategories to turn up an interesting topic.
- **Pay attention to news and current events.** Regularly browsing newspapers or magazines (print or online), blogs, or social network channels can furnish a wealth of issues and topics.
- **Browse textbooks in your area of interest.** Read the table of contents and major headings in a textbook related to your topic. Note the names of important books and experts, often mentioned in reference lists at the ends of chapters or at the back of the book.
- **Read encyclopedia articles.** Read online and, if available, print encyclopedias about your area of interest. Notice its subcategories for possible ideas for investigation. Never, however, stop with encyclopedias—they are too basic for college-level research. Be very cautious about using information from Wikipedia because it can be seriously unreliable (see the Alert in 12D).
- **Browse the library or a good bookstore.** Stroll through the shelves to find subjects that interest you. Look at books as well as popular magazines. Skim academic journals in fields that interest you.

■ Turning a topic into a research question

A **research question** provides a clear focus for your research and a goal for your WRITING PROCESS. Without such a question, your research writing can become an aimless search for a haphazard collection of facts and opinions. For example, you can more successfully research the question "How do people become homeless?" than you can research the broad topic of "homelessness." Some questions can lead to a final, definitive answer (for example, "How does penicillin destroy bacteria?"). Others can't because they involve an argument that has two or more sides (for example, "Is softball a better sport than volleyball?").

The answer to your research question usually, but not always, appears in the THESIS STATEMENT of your research essay. Sometimes the thesis statement simply alludes to your answer, especially when the answer is long or complicated.

■ Knowing what documentation style to use

A DOCUMENTATION STYLE is a system for providing information to your readers about each source you use. Documentation styles vary from one academic discipline to another.

MLA (Modern Language Association) STYLE (Chapter 14): Humanities

APA (American Psychological Association) STYLE (Chapter 15): Social
sciences

If you don't know which style to use, ask your instructor. Use only one documentation style in each piece of writing.

Determine the required documentation style at the start so that you keep a list of the exact details you need to document your sources. You need to document all PRIMARY SOURCES and SECONDARY SOURCES. If you're doing primary research, your instructor may ask you to submit notes or results from observations, questionnaires, surveys, or interviews.

13B How do I use a search strategy to find sources for my research paper?

A **search strategy** is an organized procedure for locating and gathering sources to answer your research question. Using a search strategy helps you work more systematically and quickly. Here are three frequently used search strategies.

QUESTIONING METHOD	Useful when you have a topic. Think of a research question and brainstorm to break it into several smaller questions. Then find sources to answer each of them. This allows you to see if your sources cover all the areas important to your research question.
EXPERT METHOD	Useful when your topic is specific and narrow. Start with articles or books by an expert in the field. You might want to interview an expert on the topic. Then pursue key sources mentioned.
CHAINING METHOD	Useful when your topic is general. Start with reference books and bibliographies in current articles or WEB SITES. Use them to link to additional sources. Keep following the links until you reach increasingly expert sources. You might also talk with people who have general knowledge of your topic and ask them to refer you to experts and/or sources they might know.

13B

■ Planning a timeline

Efficient writers of college research papers plan the time they need by dividing the work into segments. Use Quick Box 13.2 and note the steps and decisions needed for writing your paper. Next to each one, write down how much time you'll need to accomplish the task. Always add a few extra days for the more complex tasks (such as finding sources, taking notes, and drafting and revising the paper). Starting from the day you are given the assignment, use a calendar to lay out when you must complete each step. Stick to that schedule with tenacity.

■ Starting my research log

A **research log**—a diary of your research process—is essential for keeping yourself organized and on track. With long projects, it's easy to waste time retracing what you've done and figuring out where you're headed next. Research logs can also show instructors and others how carefully you've worked. Here's how to set one up:

- Create a "Research Log" file or folder on your computer or notebook.
- Record each step in your search for information. Enter the date, your search strategies, the gist of the information you discovered, the documentation details of exactly where you found it, and exactly where you have filed your detailed notes, if any, on the source.

Quick Box 13.2

Timeline plan for my research paper

Use a calendar to plan your research project from start to finish. Write the dates on the chart below.

_____ Date I received my research paper assignment

_____ Date first draft due

_____ Date final draft due

Number of days from start to finish _____

PLANNING

_____ Research topic and research question (13A)

_____ Primary or secondary sources or both

_____ Documentation style (13A)

_____ Choose search strategy (13B)

_____ Start research log (13B)

FINDING SOURCES OR SETTING UP FOR FIELD RESEARCH

_____ Periodicals (12B)

_____ Books (12C)

_____ Planning and writing documents for field research (12H)

COLLATING FOR WRITING: NOTES, BIBLIOGRAPHY, FRAME

_____ Take notes (13C)

_____ Compose working bibliography (13D)

_____ Compose annotated bibliography (if required) (13D)

_____ Adapt a frame (13E)

WRITING FIRST DRAFT

_____ Synthesize material in notes (13F)

_____ Avoid plagiarism (13G)

_____ Integrate quotations (13H)

_____ Use summary (13I)

_____ Use paraphrase (13I)

WRITING FINAL DRAFT

_____ Revise first draft (13J)

_____ Edit final draft (13J)

13B

Figure 13.1   A selection from the research log of Andrei Gurov, the student whose research paper on *déjà vu* appears in Chapter 14.

> *November 17:* Finished reading Brown's book, <u>The Déjà Vu Experience</u>. Great source. I wonder if he's published anything more recently. Will meet with reference librarian this afternoon to identify sources.
>
> *November 18:* Followed librarian's suggestion and searched the PsycINFO database for more recent articles. Found a chapter by Brown in a 2010 book that looks promising.

- Decide on the next step you should take with your research.
- Realize when you're ready to move away from gathering material to organizing it or writing about it.
- Keep notes on your thoughts and insights as you move through the research, organizing, and writing processes.

Although much of what you write in your research log will never find its way into your paper, it will greatly increase your efficiency. Figure 13.1 shows a section from Andrei Gurov's research log for his MLA-style research paper in Chapter 14.

13C   How do I take effective notes while conducting my research?

Taking notes effectively is at the core of your research process. The more detailed your notes, the better they will serve you as you write your research paper. Here is specific advice:

- For notes on index cards, put a heading (title and author) on each card that gives a precise link to one of your bibliography items.
- For notes on your computer, keep careful track of what ideas came from each source. One strategy is to open a new file for each source. Later, after you determine what topics are important for your paper, open a new file and type a heading for each topic. Copy and paste notes from all your sources under the headings they best fit.
- For all notes, record all documentation information so that you never need to return to a source. Always include the page numbers from which you're taking notes. If an electronic source has no page numbers, use chapter, section, or paragraph numbers, if any.

Figure 13.2 Content note card in MLA style.

> Brown, Alan S. "The Déjà Vu Illusion." *Current Directions in*
>   *Psychological Science* 13.6 (2004): 256–59. Print.
>
> Summary: Recent advances in neurology and the study of cognitive illusions
> reveal that two seemingly separate perceptual events are indeed one.
>
> Comment: This is the part that grabs my attention. How could this be?

- For every note, do one of three things: (1) copy the exact words from a source, enclosing them in overlarge quotation marks so that you can't miss them when you're writing your research paper; (2) write a paraphrase; (3) write a summary. Keep track of the kind of note you're taking: *Q* for QUOTATION, *P* for PARAPHRASE, and *S* for SUMMARY. This helps you avoid PLAGIARISM.

- As you take notes, separately record your own reactions and ideas. Use critical thinking skills. For example, what are the strengths and weaknesses of the source? What are its implications? Also include a note about what might be useful from the source. Does it provide an example? An idea? A fact? Take care to differentiate your ideas from those in your sources. You might write your own thoughts in a different color ink (note card) or font (computer); you might use a computer program's "Comment" feature.

Figure 13.2 shows one of Andrei Gurov's note cards for his research paper about *déjà vu* in 14H.

13D ## How do I develop a working and an annotated bibliography?

■ Preparing a working bibliography

A WORKING BIBLIOGRAPHY is a preliminary list of the sources you gather in your research. It contains information about each source and where your readers can find it. As a rough estimate, your working bibliography needs to be about twice as long as the list of sources you end up using. Here is a list of basic elements to include.

13D

ELEMENTS OF A CITATION TO RECORD

Books	Periodical Articles	Online Sources
Author(s)	Author(s)	Author(s) (if available)
Title of book	Title of article; digital object identifier (doi), if any	Title of document
Edition, if any		
Publisher and place of publication	Name of periodical, volume number, issue number	Name of Web site or database; editor or sponsor of site
Year of publication	Date of issue	Date of electronic publication
Call number	Page numbers of article	Electronic address (URL)
Print or Web version?	Print or Web version?	Date you accessed the source

13D

Begin your working bibliography as soon as you start identifying sources. If your search turns up only a very few sources, you may want to change your topic. If it reveals a vast number, you'll want to narrow your topic or choose a different one. Expect to add and drop sources throughout the research process.

You can record your working bibliography on note cards or on a computer. On the one hand, note cards are easy to sift through and rearrange. At the end of your WRITING PROCESS, you can easily alphabetize them to prepare your final bibliography. Write only one source on each card (see Figure 13.3) or Word document. Putting your working bibliography on a computer saves having to type your list of sources later. If you do this, clearly separate one entry from another alphabetically, by author, or by subtopics.

Figure 13.3 Bibliographic entry in MLA format.

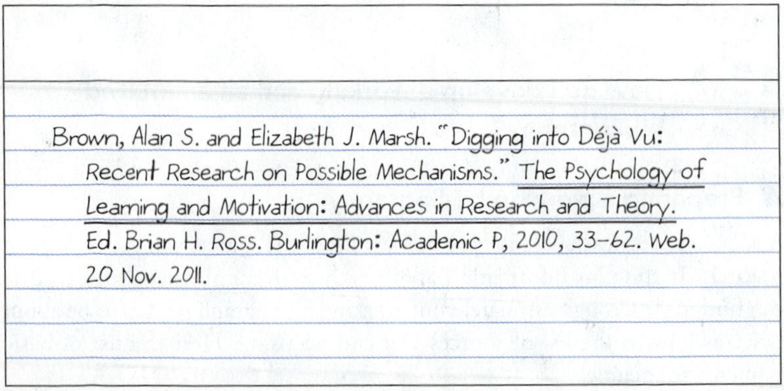

Brown, Alan S. and Elizabeth J. Marsh. "Digging into Déjà Vu: Recent Research on Possible Mechanisms." The Psychology of Learning and Motivation: Advances in Research and Theory. Ed. Brian H. Ross. Burlington: Academic P, 2010, 33–62. Web. 20 Nov. 2011.

Whichever method you use, when you come across a potential source, immediately record the information exactly as you need it to fulfill the requirements of the DOCUMENTATION STYLE your assignment requires. Spending a few extra moments at this stage can save you hours of work and frustration retracing your steps later on.

■ Using social networking software to create or organize bibliographies

Several software programs allow you to store bibliographic information about your sources and then access this information to organize it in many ways. For example, a program like NoodleBib or RefWorks lets you type in information (author, title, publisher, and so on) about each source you find. Then, with a click of a button, you can generate an MLA-style "Works Cited" page, an APA-style "References" page, or a bibliography in many other formats. You can export the bibliography into the paper you're writing, without having to retype. Of course, you're still responsible for the accuracy of any bibliography you generate with this software.

These programs also allow you to import citations directly from many databases, which means you never have to type them. Because you store your source information online, you can access it from any computer. Check to see if your library gives you access to bibliographic software. See Figure 13.4 for an example of one of these programs.

13D

Figure 13.4 Web page showing the start of a project in NoodleBib.

NoodleTools

Projects   Dashboard   Bibliography   Notecards

My Projects > Create a New Project

Welcome, mcluser | Sign Out | My Account | Help

📑 Create a New Project

Select a citation style (MLA, APA, or Chicago), then enter a short description of your topic.

Citation style:

○ **MLA**
  • follows the *MLA Handbook*, 7th ed.

○ **APA**
  • follows the *APA Publication Manual*, 6th ed.

○ **Chicago/Turabian**
  • bibliography and footnotes
  • follows *The Chicago Manual of Style*, 16th ed.

Description: Science 5A Project
For example, "History 101 report on George Washington"
[Cancel]   [Create Project]

Other online tools can help you collect, store, access, and organize materials you find on the Web. For example, Diigo allows you to store URLs or even copies of Web pages so you always have access to them from any device that connects to the Internet. You can tag each entry by adding descriptive words so that you can search for particular topics later. You can also highlight or add notes. You can share your bibliographics with others, which can be helpful for group projects.

There's one disadvantage, however. Because this software makes it so easy to gather materials, it can be tempting to merely record information and avoid analysis. Analysis is vital to making sources your own.

Figure 13.5 Section from an annotated bibliography in MLA style.

Brown, Alan S., and Elizabeth J. Marsh. "Digging into Déjà Vu: Recent
Research on Possible Mechanisms." *The Psychology of Learning
and Motivation: Advances in Research and Theory*. Ed. Brian
H. Ross. Burlington: Academic P, 2010, 33–62. Web. 20 Nov. 2011.

> This chapter summarizes laboratory research that tried
> to explain déjà vu. The authors discuss three theories.
> "Split perception" refers to people seeing part of a scene
> before seeing the whole. "Implicit memory" refers to people
> having had a previous experience that, however, is stored in
> their memories imprecisely, so they remember only the
> sensation and not the scene. "Gestalt familiarity" refers to
> having experienced something very familiar to the present
> setting.

Carey, Benedict. "Déjà Vu: If It All Seems Familiar, There May Be
a Reason." *New York Times* 14 Sept. 2004: F1+. *LexisNexis*.
Web. 11 Nov. 2011.

> Scientific research shows that déjà vu is a common and real
> phenomenon, even if its causes are unclear. Perhaps the best
> explanation is that people have had a similar previous
> experience that they have since forgotten.

13D

■ Creating an annotated bibliography

An **annotated bibliography** includes not only documentation information about your sources but also a commentary. Instructors sometimes require annotated bibliographics as a step in research projects, or they sometimes assign them as separate projects in their own right.

Most annotations contain

1. The thesis or a one-sentence summary

2. The main points or arguments in support of the thesis

3. The kinds of evidence used in the source (For example, does the source report facts or results from formal studies? Are these primary or secondary? Does source contain stories? Interviews?)

Figure 13.5 shows part of an annotated bibliography using MLA-style documentation.

13E   What are frames for research papers?

Frames are presented for five types of college essays in Part 3 of the handbook (Chapters 7 through 11). Each frame is accompanied by advice on planning and revising the essay type as well as a complete, annotated student essay. As partners to those five frames, we suggest here two frames that might fit the specifics of your research-writing assignment. Adapt them freely to fit your effective answer to your RESEARCH QUESTION.

The first frame is for an informative research paper. A complete example of such a paper, written in MLA style, appears in section 14H.

Frame for an Informative Research Paper

Introductory paragraph(s)

• **Establish why your topic is important or interesting**. Consider, "Why does this matter? To whom does this matter? What might happen if we resolve this issue one way versus another?"

• **Your THESIS STATEMENT** needs to make clear how you will answer your research question.

(continued)

Informative Research Frame (cont.)

Body paragraph(s): Background information

- **Provide the history or background of your topic.** Why is it a problem or concern at this time?

Body paragraphs: Explanations of topics

- **Discuss the main subtopics** of your general topic in a paragraph with a clear TOPIC SENTENCE.
- If a subtopic is lengthy, it may require more than one paragraph.

Body paragraphs: Complications

- **Discuss what is controversial or in dispute.** What do people disagree about? Why? Do they dispute facts? Interpretations? Causes? Effects or implications? Solutions?

Conclusion

- **Wrap up your topic.** What questions or issues remain? What are areas for further research or investigation? What might readers do with this information?

Works Cited or References

- If you are using MLA style, include a list of Works Cited (Chapter 14); if you are using APA style, include a References list (Chapter 15).

13E

The second frame is for an argumentative research paper. A complete example of such a paper, written in APA style, appears in section 15G.

Frame for an Argumentative Research Paper

Introductory paragraph(s)

- **Establish why your topic is important or interesting.** Consider, "Why does this matter? To whom does this matter? What might happen if we resolve this issue one way versus another?"
- **Your THESIS STATEMENT** needs to make clear how you will answer your research question.

Body paragraph(s): Background information

- **Provide the history or background of your topic.** Why is it a problem or concern at this time?

Argumentative Research Frame (cont.)

Body paragraph(s): Agreement among sources

- **Discuss points of agreement**. What is uncontroversial or widely accepted?
- Depending on the size or nature of the topic, this may be one or several paragraphs.

Body paragraph(s): Complications

- **Discuss what is controversial or in dispute**. What do people disagree about? Why? Do they dispute facts? Interpretations? Causes? Effects or implications? Solutions?

Body paragraph(s): Arguments

- **Present your arguments**. What reasons do you have for your position or proposed action? State each reason as a TOPIC SENTENCE, and provide evidence and support in the paragraph.
- If you have extensive support for a particular reason, you might need more than one paragraph.

Conclusion

- **Wrap up your argument**. Why is your position or proposal best? What actions should follow?

Works Cited or References

- If you are using MLA style, include a list of Works Cited (Chapter 14); if you are using APA style, include a References list (Chapter 15).

13F

13F How do I synthesize sources when writing my research paper?

A SYNTHESIS weaves ideas together. Unsynthesized ideas and information are like separate spools of thread, neatly lined up, possibly coordinated, but not woven together or integrated. Synthesized ideas and information are like threads woven into a tapestry. By synthesizing, you show evidence of your ability to bring ideas together.

Your goal in synthesizing information you find in your sources is to join two or more ideas, concepts, or examples together into a single piece of writing that is your own. The resulting text needs to be more than just a succession of summaries. Therefore, avoid merely listing who said what about a topic because you're not creating new connections.

Quick Box 13.3 suggests additional approaches for writing a synthesis.

13F

Quick Box 13.3   ■ ■ ■ ■ ■

Effective synthesis

- Make comparisons with—or contrasts between—ideas and information. Do the sources generally agree or generally disagree? What are the bases of their agreement or disagreement? Are there subtle differences or shades of meaning or emphasis?
- Create definitions that combine and extend definitions you encounter in the separate sources.
- Use examples or descriptions from one source to illustrate ideas in another.
- Use processes described in one source to explain those in others.

The following example shows how a student synthesized two sources. Read source 1 and source 2 to familiarize yourself with the information the student read. Then study the synthesis of the two sources.

SOURCE 1

Shishmaref is melting into the ocean. Over the past 30 years, the Inupiaq Eskimo village, perched on a slender barrier island 625 miles north of Anchorage, has lost 100 ft. to 300 ft. of coastline—half of it since 1997. As Alaska's climate warms, the permafrost beneath the beaches is thawing and the sea ice is thinning, leaving its 600 residents increasingly vulnerable to violent storms. One house has collapsed, and 18 others had to be moved to higher ground, along with the town's bulk-fuel tanks.   [from page 68]

—Margot Roosevelt, "Vanishing Alaska"

SOURCE 2

Hard winters with cold temperatures can kill beetle eggs and larvae wintering under a tree's outer bark. Related to general climate warming, average winter temperatures in the Rocky Mountains have been higher than normal over the past ten years. Trees have also been weakened by a prolonged period of low precipitation. The combination of milder temperatures and low precipitation has aided a vast outbreak of beetles.

—*National Park Service, Forest Health: Mountain Pine Beetle*

EXAMPLE OF A SYNTHESIS OF TWO SOURCES

Global warming is affecting both the natural and artificial worlds. Less severe temperatures in the Rocky Mountains in recent years have allowed pine beetles to survive winters, which has led to overpopulation of these insects that devour trees ("Forest Health"). Climate change has also altered life for residents of Arctic regions. For example, eighteen families in Shishmaref, Alaska, had to move their houses away from the coast because the permafrost under the beaches had thawed (Roosevelt 68).

—Devon Harris, student

Notice in the student's synthesis how he used SUMMARY and PARAPHRASE to synthesize the two sources. Also observe how the first sentence in his synthesis weaves the sources together with a new concept. The student also used in-text citations (in MLA STYLE) to signal to the reader which information he borrowed from each of the two sources. In his Works Cited list at the end of his paper, he listed full source information for both sources as shown below.

SOURCES LISTED ON DEVON'S WORKS CITED PAGE

"Forest Health: Mountain Pine Beetle." *National Park* Service.
 US Department of the Interior, n.d. Web. 24 Sept. 2013.

Roosevelt, Margot. "Vanishing Alaska." *Time* 4 Oct. 2004: 68–70. Print.

● **EXERCISE 13-1**   Write a one-paragraph synthesis of the summary of the Barry Schwartz passage and the following opening to a short online article by Ronni Sandroff, editor of *Consumer Reports on Health*.

13F

Last time I dropped by my pharmacy in search of a decongestant, I was stopped cold by the wall-sized display of remedies. The brands I had used in the past had multiplied into extended families of products. Yes, I saw *Contac, Excedrin, Tylenol,* and *Vicks,* but each brand came in multiple versions. Products for severe colds, coughs and colds, and headache and flu abounded, and there were further choices: gels, tablets, capsules, extended release, extra strength. I was eager to just grab a product and go, but to find the right one I had to dig out my reading glasses and examine the fine print.   [from page 3]

—Ronni Sandroff, "Too Many Choices"

SUMMARY OF BARRY SCHWARTZ

Research finds that people with large numbers of choices are actually less happy than people with fewer choices. Although the amount of wealth and number of choices have increased during the past thirty years, fewer Americans report themselves as being happy, and depression, suicide, and mental health problems have increased. Although some choice is good, having too many choices hinders decision making, especially among "maximizers," who try to make the best possible choices. Research in shopping, education, and medical settings shows that even when people eventually decide, they experience regret, worrying that the options they didn't choose might have been better (Schwartz).

SOURCE

Schwartz, Barry. "The Tyranny of Choice." *Chronicle of Higher Education* (23 Jan. 2004): B6. Web. 3 Apr. 2013. ●

■ Determining the relationships between sources

A major challenge when trying to synthesize sources effectively for your research paper is discerning the relationships between what you find in two or more sources. Your chances of writing synthesis rather than mere summary greatly increase once you become familiar with the five most common relationships between sources. The discussion that follows walks you through source material illustrating each of the five relationships and provides you with a student-written synthesis of each set of source material. The five relationships are

- **Different Subtopic:** Sources share the same broad subject but are about different subtopics.

- **Agreement:** Two sources make the same basic point, though perhaps in different words.

- **Part Agreement:** Two sources mostly agree but differ a little bit.

- **Disagreement:** Two sources disagree.

- **General and Specific:** One source offers specific information that either supports or contradicts a more general point in another source.

13F

SYNTHESIZING SOURCES WITH DIFFERENT SUBTOPICS

You will likely find sources that present different subtopics of the same broad subject. For example, as you research career options, one source might discuss salaries, another might discuss workplace environments, and a third might discuss expectations for job openings. Here is an example of two different subtopics relating to information in our digital age.

Source A	Source B
"While new technology eases connections between people, it also, paradoxically, facilitates a closeted view of the world, keeping us coiled tightly with those who share our ideas. In a world that lacks real gatekeepers and authority figures . . . conspiracy theories, myths, and outright lies may get the better of many of us." (17–18)	"CNN used to be a twenty-four-hour news outlet shown only on TV. The *New York Times* and the *Wall Street Journal* were simply newspapers. But on the Internet today, they are surprisingly similar. . . . Online, the lines between television and newspapers have blurred—and soon the same will be said about books, movies, TV shows, and more." (14)

Source A	Source B
Manjoo, Farhad. *True Enough: Learning to Live in a Post-Fact Society.* Hoboken, NJ: Wiley. 2008. Print.	Bilton, Nick. *I Live in the Future & Here's How It Works.* New York: Crown Business, 2010. Print.
Student's Content Note	**Student's Content Note**
Manjoo 17–18 —although technology can connect us to others, it can also allow us to communicate only with people that agree with us; we might be susceptible to lies [paraphrase]	Bilton 14 —TV network and newspaper sites have become similar on the Internet. Examples: CNN and *NY Times, WSJ* [summary]

Notice in the student's CONTENT NOTES, he included the type of note (paraphrase or summary) he took in brackets (see 13C). Here is a possible sentence/paragraph guide for sources on different subtopics:

13F

Sentence and Paragraph Guides

There are (one, two, or however many) important considerations for (aspects of, reasons for, etc.) _____ . One is _____ [from Source A] _____ . A second is _____ [from Source B] _____ .

EXAMPLE OF SYNTHESIS

There are two important developments in the way we receive news online. One is that, even though it is easier to connect to information, we tend to seek people with whom we already agree (Manjoo 17–18). A second, as Nick Bilton notes, is that distinctions between types of news sources on the Internet are disappearing (14).

SYNTHESIZING SOURCES THAT AGREE

Sources agree when they present similar information or make the same point. If sources are truly repetitious, you might use only one. Sometimes, however, including multiple similar sources strengthens your point. Here is an example:

Source A	Source B
"Our study confirmed the well-known gender gap in gaming, verifying that this overall trend also occurs among college students. Seventy percent of male undergraduates had played a digital game the week of the survey, compared to only one quarter of the females. The majority of women fell in the category of non-gamers, those who had not played a game in over 6 months, or never." (Winn 10)	"Women proportionally were more likely than men to only play an hour or less per week. . . . Twenty-one percent of the women and 68% of the men played two or more hours per week." (Ogletree 539)
Winn, Jillian, and Carrie Heeter. "Gaming, Gender, and Time: Who Makes Time to Play?" *Sex Roles* 61 (2009): 1–13. Web. 9 May 2011.	Ogletree, Shirley Matile, and Ryan Drake. "College Students' Video Game Participation and Perceptions: Gender Differences and Implications." *Sex Roles* 56 (2007): 537–42. Web. 9 May 2011.
Student's Content Notes	**Student's Content Notes**
Winn 10 —70% of male and 25% of female students played video games [summary]	Ogletree —68% of men and 21% of women played 2 or more hours per week [summary]

Here is a possible sentence/paragraph guide for synthesizing sources that agree:

Sentence and Paragraph Guides

A and B reach the same conclusion (provide similar information, argue the same point, etc.) about _____. A explains that _____. B found that _____.

EXAMPLE OF SYNTHESIS

Two studies show that men play video games more extensively than women. Winn and Heeter found that 70% of male students but only 25% of females regularly play games (10). In a study of how many hours per week students play, Ogletree learned that 68% of men and only 21% of women play two or more hours per week (539).

SYNTHESIZING SOURCES THAT PARTLY AGREE

Often sources generally agree with each other but use different evidence or emphasize slightly different conclusions. Here is an example:

Source A	Source B
"[M]ore males reportedly developed leadership skills as a result of playing video games as opposed to females. More males also reported that playing video games helped them develop skills that will help them in the workplace, such as the ability to work as a team member, to collaborate with others and the ability to provide directions to others." (Thirunarayanan, 324) Thirunarayanan, M. O., Manuel Vilchez, Liala Abreu, Cyntianna Ledesma, and Sandra Lopez. "A Survey of Video Game Players in a Public, Urban Research University." *Educational Media International* 47.4 (2009): 311–27. Web. 9 May 2011.	"Games make it easy to build stronger social bonds with our friends and family. Studies show that we like and trust someone better after we play a game with them—even if they beat us. And we're more likely to help someone in real life after we've helped them in an online game." (McGonigal) McGonigal, Jane. "Be a Gamer, Save the World." wsj.com. *Wall Street Journal*, 22 Jan 2011. Web. 9 May 2011.
Student's Content Note	**Student's Content Note**
Thirunarayanan, 324 —more men said they learn leadership and team-member skills than women said they did [summary]	McGonigal —games build social connections like trust and willingness to help others [summary]

13F

Here is a possible sentence or paragraph guide to use when sources partly agree:

Sentence and Paragraph Guides

Scholars generally agree (conclude, share the opinion, demonstrate, etc.) that _____. However, a difference between them is _____. A emphasizes (asserts, believes, etc.) _____. B, on the other hand, emphasizes _____.

EXAMPLE OF SYNTHESIS

Scholars generally agree that playing video games can have some positive social effects. However, they differ as to who benefits most. Jane McGonigal asserts that games build social connections such as trust and the willingness to help others, suggesting this is true for all players. Thirunarayanan et al., on the other hand, found that men believe they learn leadership and team-member skills more than women say they do (324).

SYNTHESIZING SOURCES THAT DISAGREE

Because people can disagree on everything from whether certain laws should be passed to whether certain movies are any good, it's no surprise that sources can disagree, too. Here is an example:

13F

Source A	Source B
"Imagine that everything stays 99 percent the same, that people continue to consume 99 percent of the television they used to, but 1 percent of that time gets carved out for producing and sharing. The connected population still watches well over a trillion hours of TV a year; 1 percent of that is more than one hundred Wikipedias' worth of participation per year." (Shirky 23)	"With hundreds of thousands of visitors a day, Wikipedia has become the third most visited site for information and current events; a more trusted source for news than the CNN or BBC Web sites, even though Wikipedia has no reporters, no editorial staff, and no experience in news-gathering. It's the blind leading the blind—infinite monkeys providing infinite information for infinite readers, perpetuating the cycle of misinformation and ignorance." (Keen 4)
Shirky, Clay. *Cognitive Surplus, Creativity and Generosity in a Connected Age.* New York: Penguin, 2010. Print.	Keen, Andrew. *The Cult of the Amateur.* New York: Doubleday, 2007. Print.
Student's Content Note	**Student's Content Note**
Shirky 23	Keen 4
—If people used even 1% of time they spend watching TV instead to produce content for the Web, they'd create "one hundred Wikipedia's worth" each year [paraphrase and quotation]	—Wikipedia used more for information and current events than CNN or the BBC —no professionals writing for W. —writers are "infinite monkeys" who create "misinformation and ignorance" [summary and quotation]

Here is a possible sentence/paragraph guide to use for sources that disagree:

Sentence and Paragraph Guides

There are two different perspectives (positions, interpretations, opinions, etc.) about _____. A says _____. B, on the other hand, says _____.

Particularly when sources disagree, your writing will be stronger if you go a step further and use critical thinking to understand the nature of the disagreement. For example:

- Writers might disagree because they use different facts or information (or no information at all!).
- Writers might disagree when they use the same information but interpret it differently.
- Writers might operate with different assumptions or perspectives.

Here is a stronger sentence/paragraph guide for sources that disagree:

13F

Sentence and Paragraph Guides

There are two different perspectives (positions, interpretations, opinions, etc.) about _____. A says _____. B, on the other hand, says _____. They disagree mainly because they cite different facts (interpret information differently, operate with different assumptions, etc.). A points to _____, while B _____. On this point, B's [or A's] perspective is more convincing because _____.

EXAMPLE OF SYNTHESIS

Some writers find Wikipedia a reason for celebration, while others declare it a cause for despair. Clay Shirky hopes people will divert just 1% of their TV watching time to writing for the Web, which could generate "one hundred Wikipedia's worth" of content each year (23). That possibility would trouble Andrew Keen, who characterizes those writers as "infinite monkeys" who only spread "misinformation and ignorance" (4). They assume quite different things about the quality of the knowledge on Wikipedia. Keen has considerably less faith in the ability of people to write accurate information.

SYNTHESIZING SOURCES THAT AREN'T EQUALLY SPECIFIC

Sometimes sources aren't equally specific when one provides examples, illustrations, or evidence and the other makes a more general point. Here is an example:

Source A	Source B
"Old media is facing extinction." (Keen 9)	"In 2008, paid newspaper circulation in the United States fell to 49.1 million, the lowest number since the late 1960s and well below the peak of 60 million reached in the 1990s, when the internet was just starting to come into its own." (Bilton 6)
Keen, Andrew. *The Cult of the Amateur.* New York: Doubleday, 2007. Print.	Bilton, Nick. *I Live in the Future & Here's How It Works.* New York: Crown Business, 2010. Print.
Student's Content Note	**Student's Content Note**
Keen 9 "Old media is facing extinction" [quotation]	Bilton 6 —newspaper circulation was 60 million in the 1990s, 49.1 million in 2008 [summary]

13F

Here are useful sentence/paragraph guides when a specific source supports a general one:

Sentence and Paragraph Guides

A observes (claims, argues, concludes, etc.) that _____.
B provides an example (a set of data, some information, etc.) to support this observation. B states that _____.

or

According to B, _____. This illustrates A's concept (point, claim, conclusion, etc.) that _____.

EXAMPLE OF SYNTHESIS

According to Nick Bilton, newspaper circulation declined over ten million between the 1990s and 2008, from 60 million to 49.1 million subscribers (6). His figures illustrate Andrew Keen's observation that "Old media is facing extinction" (9).

Sometimes one source contradicts a more general idea in another source. Sources can often disagree with each other obviously at the level of ideas or claims. Sometimes, however, the disagreement is more subtle. Specific information in one source can contradict a more general point made in another. This can happen when writers make a claim but offer no proof or when they offer partial or different evidence. Here's an example:

Source A	Source B
"But college students are, in fact, getting lazier. 'Aggregate time spent studying by full-time college students declined from about 24 hours per week in 1961 to about 14 hours per week in 2004,' Babcock writes, citing his own research." (de Vise)	"Nationally, approximately 80 percent of community college students work, and they work an average of 32 hours per week. Research indicates that working a few hours each week is actually beneficial to students' persistence and success, provided that they are in school full time and attending consistently. However, to succeed academically, experts suggest working no more than 15–20 hours per week." (Zomer 2)
de Vise, Daniel. "Grade Inflation Is Making Students Lazier." washingtonpost.com/college-inc. *Washington Post*, 22 July 2010. Web. 9 May 2011.	Zomer, Saffron. *Working Too Hard to Make the Grade*. Sacramento, CA: California Public Interest Research Group, 2009. Web. 9 May 2011.
Student's Content Note	Student's Content Note
de Vise	Zomer 2
—college students getting "lazier"; they studied 10 hours a week less in 2004 than in 1961 [summary]	—80% of CC students work average of 32 hours/week —some work is good, but should be no more than 15–20 hours [summary]

13F

Here is a useful sentence/paragraph guide when specific information contradicts a general claim:

Sentence and Paragraph Guides

> Evidence suggests (proves, demonstrates, etc.) that A's claim that _____ is wrong (incomplete, overstated, etc.). B shows that _____.

EXAMPLE OF SYNTHESIS

Daniel de Vise's claim that college students are getting lazier fails to recognize complete information. De Vise points to students studying ten hours per week less in 2004 than in 1961. However, he fails to take into account how much students are now working. For example, 80% of community college students now work an average of 32 hours per week, even though experts recommend working no more than 20 hours per week (Zomer 2). Far from being lazy, college students are working hard, perhaps with less time for studying.

13G   How do I avoid plagiarism in writing my research paper?

Plagiarism is using someone else's words in your writing without giving credit to that person. Plagiarizing means you are stealing someone else's words. Plagiarism is a form of academic dishonesty or cheating. It's a serious offense that can be grounds for a failing grade or expulsion from a college. Beyond that, you're hurting yourself. If you're plagiarizing, you're not learning.

Plagiarism isn't just something that college instructors get fussy about. In the workplace, it can get you fired. Plagiarism at work also has legal implications because using someone else's intellectual property without permission or credit is a form of theft that may land you in court. Furthermore, plagiarism in any setting—academic, business, or civic—hurts your credibility and reputation. Become familiar, therefore, with all types of plagiarism so that you can be sure to avoid them.

■ Types of plagiarism

You're plagiarizing if you . . .

- Buy a paper from an Internet site, another student or writer, or any other source.
- Turn in any paper that someone else has written, whether the person has given it to you, you've downloaded it from the Internet, or you've copied it from any other source.
- Change selected parts of an existing paper and claim the paper as your own.
- Neglect to put quotation marks around words that you quote directly from a source, even if you list the source in your Works Cited or References.
- Type or paste into your paper any key terms, phrases, sentences, or longer passages from another source without using documentation to tell precisely where the material came from.
- Use ideas or reasoning from a source without correctly citing and documenting that source, even if you put the ideas into your own words.

- Combine ideas from many sources and pass them off as your own without correctly citing and documenting the sources.

- Use photographs, charts, figures, or other visual images from anyone (colleagues, organizations, Web sites, and so on) without crediting and documenting them.

ESOL Tip: Perhaps you come from a country or culture that considers it acceptable for students to copy the writing of experts and authorities. Some cultures, in fact, believe that using another's words, even without citing them, is a sign of respect or learning. However, this practice is unacceptable in American colleges. ●

Avoiding plagiarism

The two keys to avoiding plagiarism are

- Never copy material directly from a SOURCE; use the techniques in Quick Box 13.4.

- Always use complete, detailed documentation information in the style required by your course (for MLA style, see Chapter 14; for APA style,

---

Quick Box 13.4

Strategies for avoiding plagiarism

- Become thoroughly familiar with the documentation style your instructor requires you to use. For MLA style, see Chapter 14. For APA style, see Chapter 15.

- Immediately when you expect to quote, paraphrase, or summarize from a source in your draft, include the appropriate in-text citation, and add the source to your Works Cited or References. Don't wait to do this later. The danger of forgetting or making a mistake is too great.

- Use a consistent notetaking system. Use different colors, or some other coding system, to distinguish three different types of material.

  1. For **quotations** from a source; write clear, even oversized quotation marks so you can't miss them later

  2. For **material you have summarized** or **paraphrased** from a source

  3. Not for **your own thoughts**, triggered by what you have read or experienced

- When editing and proofreading, look carefully at your paper for any places you might have overlooked that need documentation.

- Consult your instructor if you're unsure about any aspect of the documentation process.

see Chapter 15). Many instructors require students to hand in a WORKING BIBLIOGRAPHY or ANNOTATED BIBLIOGRAPHY (see 13D). Your instructor may ask to see your research log (see 13B), your working notes, copies of your sources, or working drafts of your paper. Quick Box 13.4 suggests practical steps for avoiding plagiarism.

■ Avoiding plagiarism when using Internet sources

When you use Internet sources, take special care concerning plagiarism. You might be tempted to download a paper from the Internet. Don't. That kind of intellectual dishonesty can get you into real trouble. Some students believe if they buy a paper or hire someone else to write it, the paper is "theirs." No. It's not. This is clearly plagiarism, and teachers can easily trace it.

Even if you have absolutely no intention of plagiarizing, be extraordinarily careful as you consult online sources. Quick Box 13.5 suggests some ways you can avoid plagiarism when you're working on the Internet.

13G

Quick Box 13.5   ■ ■ ■ ■ ■ ■

Guidelines for avoiding plagiarism when using Internet sources

- Be careful how you manage copied files. Use another color or a much larger font as a visual reminder when material isn't your work.

- Never copy material from an online source and paste it directly into your paper. You can too easily lose track of which language is your own and which comes from a source.

- Keep material that you downloaded or printed from the Internet completely separate from your own writing, whether you intend to quote, summarize, or paraphrase the material.

- Be sure to record documentation information about the source at the same time as you're copying or pasting the quotation into your file.

- Summarize or paraphrase materials *before* you include them in your paper. Document the sources of summarized passages at the same time as you insert them in your paper.

- Use Google or Yahoo! to search one or two sentences that you think you might have plagiarized. To make this work, always place quotation marks around the sentences you want to check when you type them into the search window.

■ Knowing what you don't have to document

You don't have to document common knowledge or your own thinking. Common knowledge is information that most educated people know, although they might need to remind themselves of certain facts by looking them up in a reference book. For example, you would not need to document statements like these:

- George W. Bush was the US president before Barack Obama.
- Mercury is the planet closest to the sun.
- Water boils at 212°F.
- All the oceans on our planet contain saltwater.

■ Using verbs to help weave source material into sentences

Use the verbs in Quick Box 13.6 appropriately according to their meanings in your sentences. For example, *says* and *states* are fairly neutral introductory verbs; you're just reporting the source's words. On the other hand, while still fairly neutral, *claims* or *contends* introduces a slight skepticism; you're suggesting that you may not share the source's certainty. *Demonstrates* or, even stronger, *proves* indicates that you find the source conclusive on a particular point.

13G

Quick Box 13.6

Useful verbs for integrating quotations, paraphrases, and summaries

acknowledges	contrasts	illustrates	recommends
agrees	declares	implies	refutes
analyzes	demonstrates	indicates	rejects
argues	denies	insists	remarks
asserts	describes	introduces	reports
begins	develops	maintains	reveals
believes	discusses	means	says
claims	distinguishes	notes	shows
comments	between	notices	specifies
compares	among	observes	speculates
complains	emphasizes	offers	states
concedes	establishes	points out	suggests
concludes	explains	prepares	supports
confirms	expresses	promises	supposes
considers	finds	proves	wishes
contends	focuses on	questions	writes
contradicts	grants	recognizes	

13H   How do I use quotations correctly in my research paper?

In research writing, a well-chosen **quotation** can lend a note of authority and enliven a document with someone else's voice. When you use a quotation, be sure it is the exact words of a source enclosed in quotation marks (see Chapter 34).

Avoid using too many quotations. If more than a quarter of your paper consists of quotations, you've probably written what some people call a "cut-and-paste special." Doing so gives your readers—including instructors—the impression that you haven't bothered to develop your own thinking and that you're letting other people do your talking. Quick Box 13.7 provides guidelines for using quotations.

Quick Box 13.7   ■ ■ ■ ■ ■ ■

Guidelines for using quotations

- Select quotations that fit your message. Choose a quotation only for the following reasons.

   Its language is particularly appropriate or distinctive.

   Its idea is particularly hard to paraphrase accurately.

   The source's authority is especially important for support.

   The source's words are open to interpretation.

- Use quotations only from reliable authorities on your subject to support or refute what you've written.

- Never use a quotation to present your THESIS STATEMENT or a TOPIC SENTENCE.

- Never allow quotations to make up a quarter or more of your paper. Instead, rely on paraphrase and summary (see 13I).

- Quote accurately. Always check a quotation against the original source—and then recheck it.

- Integrate quotations smoothly into your writing.

- Avoid plagiarism (see 13G).

- Document quotations carefully.

■ Fitting quotations smoothly into your sentences

When you use quotations, the greatest risk you take is that you'll end up with incoherent, choppy sentences. You can avoid this problem by making the words you quote fit smoothly with three aspects of your writing: grammar, style, and logic. These three problems are shown below, followed by revised versions. All examples are in MLA documentation style.

SOURCE

Turkle, Sherry. *Alone Together: Why We Expect More from Technology and Less from Each Other*. New York: Basic, 2011. Print.

ORIGINAL (TURKLE'S EXACT WORDS)

Digital connections and the sociable robot may offer the illusion of companionship without the demands of friendship. Our networked life allows us to hide from each other, even as we are tethered to each other.   [from page 1]

GRAMMAR PROBLEM

Turkle explains how relying on network communication "illusion of companionship without the demands of friendship" (1).

STYLE PROBLEM

Turkle explains that the digital connections and lives of robots "offer the illusion of companionship without the demands of friendship" (1).

LOGIC PROBLEM

Turkle explains networked connections "without the demands of friendship" (1).

ACCEPTABLE USE OF THE QUOTATION

Turkle explains that networked connections "may offer the illusion of companionship without the demands of friendship" (1).

13H

BRACKETS TO ADD WORDS

You can add a word or very brief phrase to the quotation, in brackets—[ ]—so that the meaning fits seamlessly with the rest of your sentence. Make sure that your bracketed additions don't distort the meaning of the quotation.

ORIGINAL (TURKLE'S EXACT WORDS)

If we divest ourselves of such things, we risk being coarsened, reduced.   [from page 292]

QUOTATION WITH EXPLANATORY BRACKETS

"If we divest ourselves of such things [as caring for the sick], we risk being coarsened, reduced" (Turkle 292).

ELLIPSIS TO DELETE WORDS

You can use ellipsis to fit a quotation smoothly into your sentence. For the words in the quotation that seem to be causing the problem, substitute ELLIPSIS POINTS for them. When you use ellipses to delete troublesome words, make sure that the remaining words accurately reflect the source's meaning and that your sentence still flows smoothly.

ORIGINAL (TURKLE'S EXACT WORDS)

The idea of addiction, with its one solution that we know we won't take, makes us feel hopeless.   [from page 294]

QUOTATION USING ELLIPSIS

Turkle notes that "the idea of addiction . . . makes us feel hopeless" (294).

AUTHOR NAMES, SOURCE TITLES, AND OTHER INFORMATION

Without context-setting information about your quotation, your readers can't know exactly why you included a particular quotation. Never drop a quotation into your writing without a specific reason that you make clear to your reader. Furthermore, your readers need to know who said each group of quoted words.

13H

SOURCE

Wright, Karen. "Times of Our Lives."*Scientific American* Sept. 2002: 58–66.
   Print.

AUTHOR'S NAME

Karen Wright explains that "in human bodies, biological clocks keep track of seconds, minutes, days, months and years" (66).

AUTHOR'S NAME AND SOURCE TITLE

Karen Wright explains in "Times of Our Lives" that "in human bodies, biological clocks keep track of seconds, minutes, days, months and years" (66).

AUTHOR'S NAME AND CREDENTIALS

Karen Wright, an award-winning science journalist, explains that "in human bodies, biological clocks keep track of seconds, minutes, days, months and years" (66).

AUTHOR'S NAME WITH STUDENT'S INTRODUCTORY ANALYSIS

Karen Wright reviews evidence of surprising subconscious processes, explaining that "in human bodies, biological clocks keep track of seconds, minutes, days, months and years" (66).

■ Adding explanation for a quotation

ORIGINAL (WRIGHT'S EXACT WORDS)

In human bodies, biological clocks keep track of seconds, minutes, days, months and years.   [from page 66]

QUOTATION UNEXPLAINED

The human body has many subconscious processes. People don't have to make their hearts beat or remind themselves to breathe. "In human bodies, biological clocks keep track of seconds, minutes, days, months and years" (Wright 66).

QUOTATION EXPLAINED

The human body has many subconscious processes. People don't have to make their hearts beat or remind themselves to breathe. However, other processes are less obvious and perhaps more surprising. Karen Wright observes, for example, "In human bodies, biological clocks keep track of seconds, minutes, days, months and years" (66).

● **EXERCISE 13-2**   Read the following original material, from page 295 of *Deep Water: The Gulf Oil Disaster and the Future of Offshore Drilling*, published in 2011 by the National Commission on the BP Deepwater Horizon Oil Spill and Offshore Drilling. Then, read items 1 through 4 and explain why each is an incorrect use of a quotation. Next, revise each numbered sentence so that it correctly uses a quotation. End each quotation with this MLA-style parenthetical reference: (National 295).

13H

> Yet growing demand for oil around the world, particularly in the huge and rapidly developing economies of Asia, ensures heightened competition for supplies, putting upward pressure on oil prices. That poses a long-term challenge for the United States, which is not and cannot be self-sufficient in oil supply.

EXPLAIN THESE UNACCEPTABLE USES OF QUOTATIONS

1. Demand for oil is increasing globally. "That poses a long-term challenge for the United States, which is not and cannot be self-sufficient in oil supply" (National 295).
2. One obvious cause is that "the huge economies of Asia are putting upward pressure on prices" (National 295).
3. A difficult situation, "that poses a long-term challenge for the United States" (National 295).
4. In the 1990s, "that poses a long-term challenge for the United States" (National 295). ●

13I   How do I use summary and paraphrase in my research paper?

■ Using a summary

SUMMARY and paraphrase differ in important ways: Whereas a paraphrase restates the original material in its entirety, a summary states only the main points of the original source in a much briefer fashion. Summarizing is the technique you'll probably use most frequently to integrate sources. A summary doesn't include supporting evidence or details. It's the gist, the nub, the seed of what the author is saying. As a result, a summary is much shorter than a paraphrase. Quick Box 13.8 explains how to summarize effectively.

Quick Box 13.8   ■ ■ ■ ■ ■ ■

Guidelines for summarizing

- Identify the main points, and take care not to alter the meaning of the original source.
- Don't be tempted to include your opinions; they don't belong in a summary.
- Never use a summary to present your THESIS STATEMENT or a TOPIC SENTENCE.
- Keep your summary as short as possible to accomplish your purpose.
- Integrate summarized material smoothly into your writing.
- Use your own words. If you need to use key terms or phrases from the source, include them in quotation marks, but otherwise put everything into your own words.
- Document the original source accurately.
- Avoid PLAGIARISM (13G).

Here's an example of a summary that is unacceptable due to plagiarism and an acceptable one.

SOURCE

Tanenbaum, Leora. *Catfight: Women and Competition*. New York: Seven Stories, 2002. Print.

ORIGINAL (TANENBAUM'S EXACT WORDS)

Until recently, most Americans disapproved of cosmetic surgery, but today the stigma is disappearing. Average Americans are lining up for procedures—two-thirds of patients report family incomes of less than $50,000 a year—and many of them return for more. Younger women undergo "maintenance" surgeries

131

in a futile attempt to halt time. The latest fad is Botox, a purified and diluted form of botulinum toxin that is injected between the eyebrows to eliminate frown lines. Although the procedure costs between $300 and $1000 and must be repeated every few months, roughly 850,000 patients have had it performed on them. That number will undoubtedly shoot up now that the FDA has approved Botox for cosmetic use. Even teenagers are making appointments with plastic surgeons. More than 14,000 adolescents had plastic surgery in 1996, and many of them are choosing controversial procedures such as breast implants, liposuction, and tummy tucks, rather than the rhinoplasties of previous generations.   [from pages 117–118].

UNACCEPTABLE SUMMARY (HIGHLIGHTED WORDS ARE PLAGIARIZED)

Average Americans are lining up for surgical procedures. The latest fad is Botox, a toxin injected to eliminate frown lines. This is an insanely foolish waste of money. Even teenagers are making appointments with plastic surgeons, many of them for controversial procedures such as breast implants, liposuction, and tummy tucks (Tanenbaum 117–18).

The unacceptable summary has several major problems: It doesn't isolate the main point. It plagiarizes by taking much of its language directly from the source. It includes the writer's interpretation ("This is an insanely foolish waste of money") rather than objectively representing the original. The acceptable summary concisely isolates the main point, puts the source into the writer's own words, calls attention to the author by including her name in the summary, and remains objective throughout.

131

ACCEPTABLE SUMMARY

Tanenbaum explains that plastic surgery is becoming widely acceptable, even for Americans with modest incomes and for younger women. Most popular is injecting the toxin Botox to smooth wrinkles. She notes that thousands of adolescents are even requesting controversial surgeries (117–18).

■ Degrees of summary

The degree to which your summary compresses the original source depends on your assignment. For example, you can summarize an entire 500-page book in a single sentence, in a single page, or in five or six pages. Here are two different levels of summary based on the same source, a 3,000-word article too long to reprint here.

SOURCE

Schwartz, Barry. "The Tyranny of Choice." *Chronicle of Higher Education* (23 Jan. 2004): B6. Web. 3 Apr. 2011.

SUMMARY IN A SINGLE SENTENCE

Research finds that people with large numbers of choices are actually less happy than people with fewer choices (Schwartz).

SUMMARY IN 50 TO 100 WORDS

Research finds that people with large numbers of choices are actually less happy than people with fewer choices. Although the amount of wealth and number of choices have increased during the past thirty years, fewer Americans report themselves as being happy, and depression, suicide, and mental health problems have increased. Although some choice is good, having too many choices hinders decision making, especially among "maximizers," who try to make the best possible choices. Research in shopping, education, and medical settings shows that even when people eventually decide, they experience regret, worrying that the options they didn't choose might have been better (Schwartz).

Notice that the longer summary begins with the same sentence as the short one. This is done because leading a summary with the reading's main idea is effective. Notice that both summaries put ideas in the student's own words, thereby avoiding plagiarism. Notice that the short summary captures only the main idea.

131

● **EXERCISE 13-3** Read the original material from pages 23–24 of *Diversity: The Invention of a Concept* by Peter Wood (San Francisco: Encounter, 2003). Then, read the unacceptable summary. Note each example of plagiarism. Finally, write your own summary, starting it with a phrase mentioning Wood and ending it with this parenthetical reference: (23–24).

ORIGINAL (WOOD'S EXACT WORDS)

Among the many meanings of diversity, let's for the moment distinguish two: the actual racial and ethnic condition of America, which I will call *diversity I*, and the diversiphile ideal of how American society should recognize and respond to its racial and ethnic composition, which I will call *diversity II*. In principle, it ought to be easy to distinguish between these two meanings. One refers to the facts, the other to hopes or wishes. *Diversity I* is the sort of thing that we might expect could be counted, or at least approximated, with wide agreement. We know with reasonable certainty, for example, that about 13 percent of the U.S. population considers itself of African descent. We can and do argue with one another over the significance of this fact, but the fact itself is not seriously in dispute.

Diversity II, by contrast, is an ideal. It expresses a vision of society in which people divide themselves into separate groups, each with profound traditions of its own, but held together by mutual esteem, respect and tolerance. It would be futile, however, to look for general agreement about the exact details of this ideal.

UNACCEPTABLE SUMMARY (HIGHLIGHTED WORDS ARE PLAGIARIZED)

Peter Wood distinguishes between *diversity I*, the actual racial and ethnic condition of America, and *diversity II*, the diversiphile ideal of how American society should recognize and respond to its racial and ethnic composition. *Diversity I* could be counted or approximated with wide agreement. *Diversity II* is an ideal vision of society, but there can be no general agreement about the exact nature of this ideal (23–24). ●

■ Using a paraphrase

A **paraphrase** precisely restates in your own words the words of someone else. Use paraphrase only for passages that carry ideas you need to reproduce in detail to explain a point or support an argument. Avoid trying to paraphrase more than a paragraph or two; for longer passages, use summary. Quick Box 13.9 offers advice for paraphrasing.

Quick Box 13.9   ■ ■ ■ ■ ■ ■

Guidelines for writing paraphrases

- Never use a paraphrase to present your THESIS STATEMENT or a TOPIC SENTENCE.
- Say what the source says, but no more.
- Reproduce the source's sequence of ideas and emphases.
- Use your own words, phrasing, and sentence structure to restate the material. If some technical words in the original have only awkward synonyms, quote the original words—but do so sparingly.
- Read your sentences over to make sure they don't distort the source's meaning.
- Expect your material to be as long as the original or even slightly longer.
- Integrate your paraphrase into your writing so that it fits smoothly.
- Avoid PLAGIARISM (13G).
- Document your paraphrase carefully.

13I

Here is an example of a paraphrase that is unacceptable because of plagiarism and an acceptable one.

SOURCE

Hulbert, Ann. "Post-Teenage Wasteland?" *New York Times Magazine* 9 Oct. 2005: 11–12. Print.

ORIGINAL (HULBERT'S EXACT WORDS)

[T]he available data suggest that the road to maturity hasn't become as drastically different as people think—or as drawn out, either. It's true that the median age of marriage rose to 25 for women and almost 27 for men in 2000, from 20 and 23, respectively, in 1960. Yet those midcentury figures were record lows (earnestly analyzed in their time). Moreover, Americans of all ages have ceased to view starting a family as the major benchmark of grown-up status. When asked to rank the importance of traditional milestones in defining the arrival of adulthood, poll respondents place completing school, finding full-time employment, achieving financial independence and being able to support a family far above actually wedding a spouse or having kids. The new perspective isn't merely an immature swerve into selfishness; postponing those last two steps is good for the future of the whole family.   [from page 11]

UNACCEPTABLE PARAPHRASE (HIGHLIGHTED WORDS ARE PLAGIARIZED)

Data suggest that the road to maturity hasn't changed as much as people think. True, the median age of marriage was 25 for women and 27 for men in 2000, up from 20 and 23 in 1960. Yet those 1960 figures were record lows. Furthermore, Americans have stopped regarding beginning a family as the signpost of grown-up status. When they were asked to rank the importance of traditional benchmarks for deciding the arrival of adulthood, people rated graduating from school, finding a full-time job, gaining financial status, and being a breadwinner far above marrying or having kids. This new belief isn't merely immature selfishness; delaying those last two steps is good for the future of the whole family (Hulbert 11).

ACCEPTABLE PARAPHRASE

According to Ann Hulbert, statistics show that people are wrong when they believe our society is delaying maturity. She acknowledges that between 1960 and 2000, the median age at which women married rose from 20 to 25 (for men it went from 23 to 27), but points out that the early figures were extreme lows. Hulbert finds that Americans no longer equate adulthood with starting a family. Polls show that people rank several other "milestones" above marriage and children as signaling adulthood. These include finishing school, securing a full-time job, and earning enough to be independent and to support a family. Hulbert concludes that we should regard postponing marriage and children not as being selfish or immature but as investing in the family's future (11).

● **EXERCISE 13-4**   Read the original material, a paragraph from page 49 of *Uniforms: Why We Are What We Wear* by Paul Fussell (Boston: Houghton, 2002). Then, read the unacceptable paraphrase, and point out each example of plagiarism. Finally, write your own paraphrase, starting it with a phrase naming Fussell and ending it with this parenthetical reference: (49).

ORIGINAL (FUSSELL'S EXACT WORDS)

Until around 1963, part of the routine for Levi's wearers was shrinking the trousers to fit, and the best way to do that was to put them on wet and let them dry on your body. This gave the wearer the impression that he or she was actually creating the garment, or at least emphasizing one's precious individuality, and that conviction did nothing to oppose the illusion of uniqueness precious to all American young people.   [from page 49]

UNACCEPTABLE PARAPHRASE

Paul Fussell says that until around 1963 Levi's wearers used to shrink new trousers to fit. The best way to do that was to put them on wet and let them dry while wearing them. Doing this created the impression that wearers were actually creating the garment or emphasizing their precious individuality. It reinforced the illusion of uniqueness precious to all American teens (49). ●

13J   How do I draft, revise, and edit my research paper?

■ Drafting

Expect to write several drafts of your research paper. The first draft is a chance to discover new insights and fresh connections. Here are some suggestions to write your first draft based on ways experienced researchers write.

- **Some researchers work from a source map or cluster diagram.** They organize their notes into topics and determine the relationship between sources. They use frames and sentence and paragraph guides to generate a first draft.

- **Some research writers work with their notes at hand.** They organize the notes into broad categories so that each category becomes a section of the first draft. This method can reveal any gaps in information that call for additional research. It can also show that some research doesn't fit into their paper. However, they don't throw it out because it might be useful in a later draft.

- **Some research writers generate a list of questions that their paper needs to address.** Then they answer each question, one at a time, looking for the content notes that will help them. For example, on the topic of déjà vu (see the student paper in 14H), some possible questions might be, "What is déjà vu? What are possible explanations for it? Does everyone experience it the same way or with the same frequency?" Generating and answering questions can turn a mass of information into manageable groupings.

- **Some research writers stop at various points and use FREEWRITING to get their ideas into words.** They say that it helps them to recognize when they need to adjust their research question or adjust their search. After a number of rounds of researching and freewriting, they find that they can write their complete first draft relatively easily.

- **Some research writers review their sources and create an OUTLINE before drafting.** Some find a FORMAL OUTLINE helpful, whereas others use a less formal approach.

■ Revising

Before you write each new draft, read your previous draft with a sharp eye. Assess all the features listed in Quick Box 4.10 (see 4I) and Quick Box 13.10. For best results, take a break of a few days (or at least a few hours) before

13J

Quick Box 13.10   ■ ■ ■ ■ ■ ■

Revision checklist for a research paper

WRITING

✓ Do your one or two introductory paragraphs lead effectively into the material? (5B)

✓ Have you met the basic requirements for a thesis statement? (4F)

✓ Do your thesis statement and the content of your paper address your research question(s)? (13A)

✓ Have you developed effective body paragraphs? (5E)

✓ Do your ideas follow sensibly and logically within each paragraph and from one paragraph to the next? (5D)

✓ Does the concluding paragraph end your paper effectively? (5F)

RESEARCH

✓ Have you fully answered your research question? (13A)

✓ Have you evaluated the quality of your sources? Have you used sources that are appropriate for ACADEMIC WRITING? (12G)

✓ Have you used QUOTATIONS, PARAPHRASES, and SUMMARIES well? (13H and 13I)

✓ Have you integrated your source material well without PLAGIARIZING? (13G)

beginning this process to get some distance from your first drafts and a clearer vision of what you need to revise. You might consider asking a few people you respect to read and react to a draft.

One key to revising any research paper is to examine carefully the evidence you've included. EVIDENCE consists of facts, statistics, expert studies and opinions, examples, and stories. Use RENNS (see 5D) to see if you can develop paragraphs more fully. Identify each of the points you have made in your paper, including your THESIS STATEMENT and all your subpoints. Then ask yourself the following questions.

- **Is the evidence sufficient?** To be sufficient, evidence can't be thin or trivial. As a rule, the more evidence you present, the more convincing your thesis will be to readers.

- **Is the evidence representative?** Representative evidence is customary and normal, not based on exceptions.

- **Is the evidence relevant?** Relevant evidence relates directly to your thesis or topic sentence. It illustrates your reasons straightforwardly and never introduces unrelated material.

- **Is the evidence accurate?** Accurate evidence is correct, complete, and up to date. It comes from a reliable source. Equally important, you present it honestly, without distorting or misrepresenting it.

- **Is the evidence reasonable?** Reasonable evidence is not phrased in extreme language and avoids sweeping generalizations. Reasonable evidence is free of LOGICAL FALLACIES (see 2D).

After you've asked the questions above about your evidence, use Quick Box 13.10 to check your work.

■ Editing

Quick Box 13.11 lists questions to ask when you edit your research paper.

Quick Box 13.11   ■ ■ ■ ■ ■ ■

Editing checklist for a research paper

✓ Is the paper free of errors in grammar, punctuation, and mechanics?

✓ Is your format correct in your parenthetical references? (Chapter 14 or 15)

✓ Does each of your parenthetical references tie into an item in your Works Cited list (MLA style) or References list (APA style) at the end of your paper? (Chapter 14 or 15)

✓ Does your format exactly match what you've been assigned to follow? Check margins, spacing, title, headings, page numbers, font, and so on. (Chapter 14 or 15)

13J

14 MLA-Style Documentation and Format

■ ■ ■ ■ ■ ■

Quick Points You will learn to

➤ Cite sources within your sentences using MLA style in-text citations (see pp. 188–194).

➤ Cite sources at the end of your paper in a Works Cited list (see pp. 194–220).

➤ Format your paper according to MLA guidelines (see pp. 223–224).

MyWritingLab™ Visit mywritinglab.com for more resources on MLA-style documentation and format.

14A What is MLA documentation style?

A **documentation style** is a standard format that writers follow to tell readers what SOURCES they used and how to find them. Different disciplines follow different documentation styles. The one most frequently used in the humanities is from the Modern Language Association (MLA).

MLA style requires you to document your sources in two connected, equally important ways.

1. Within the body of the paper, use parenthetical documentation, as described in sections 14B and 14C.

2. At the end of the paper, provide a list of the sources you used in your paper. Title this list "Works Cited," as described in sections 14D and 14E.

The guidelines and examples in this chapter are based on the Seventh Edition of *The MLA Handbook for Writers of Research Papers* (2009). If you need more information regarding MLA style updates, check the MLA Web site. See Quick Box 14.2 on pages 194–196 for more guidance on these requirements.

14B What is MLA in-text parenthetical documentation?

MLA-style **parenthetical documentation** (also called **in-text citations**) places source information in parentheses within the sentences of your research papers. This information—given each time that you quote, summarize, or paraphrase source materials—signals materials used from outside sources and enables readers to find the originals. (See Chapter 13 for information on how to quote, paraphrase, and summarize.)

Author name cited in text; page number cited in parentheses If you include an author's name (or, if none, the title of the work) in the sentence to introduce the source material, you include in parentheses only the page number where you found the material:

> According to Brent Staples, IQ tests give scientists little insight into intelligence (293).

For readability and good writing technique, try to introduce the names of authors (or titles of sources) in your own sentences.

Author name and page number cited in parentheses If you don't include the author's name in your sentence, you need to insert it in the parentheses, before the page number. There is no punctuation between the author's name and the page number:

> IQ tests give scientists little insight into intelligence (Staples 293).

■ Placement of parenthetical reference

When possible, position a parenthetical reference at the end of the quotation, summary, or paraphrase it refers to—preferably at the end of a sentence, unless that would place it too far from the source's material. When you place the parenthetical reference at the end of a sentence, insert it before the sentence-ending period.

If you're citing a quotation enclosed in quotation marks, place the parenthetical information after the closing quotation mark but before sentence-ending punctuation.

> Coleman summarizes research that shows that "the number, rate, and direction of time-zone changes are the critical factors in determining the extent and degree of jet lag symptoms" (67).

Block quotations: Longer than four lines The one exception to the rule of putting parenthetical information before sentence-ending punctuation concerns quotations that you set off in block style, meaning one inch from the left margin. (MLA requires that quotations longer than four typed lines be handled this way.) For block quotations, place the parenthetical reference after the period.

> Bruce Sterling worries that people are pursuing less conventional medical treatments, and not always for good reasons:
>
>> Medical tourism is already in full swing. Thailand is the golden shore for wealthy, sickly Asians and Australians. Fashionable Europeans head to South Africa for embarrassing plastic surgery. Crowds of scrip-waving Americans buy prescription drugs in Canada and Mexico. (92)

If you're quoting part of a paragraph or one complete paragraph, don't indent the first line of quoted words more than an inch. But if you quote more than one paragraph, indent the first line of each paragraph—including the first if it's a complete paragraph from the source—an additional quarter inch.

14C What are MLA examples for parenthetical citations?

The directory in Quick Box 14.1 corresponds to the numbered examples in this section. Most of these examples show the author's name or the title included in the parenthetical citation, but remember that it's usually more effective to include that information in your sentence.

1. One Author—MLA

Give an author's name as it appears on the source: for a book, on the title page; for an article, directly below the title or at the end of the article.

IQ tests give scientists little insight into intelligence (Staples 293).

2. Two or Three Authors—MLA

Give the names in the same order as in the source. Spell out *and*. For three authors, use commas to separate the authors' names.

> As children get older, they begin to express several different kinds of intelligence (Todd and Taylor 23).

> Another measure of emotional intelligence is the success of inter- and intrapersonal relationships (Voigt, Dees, and Prigoff 14).

3. More Than Three Authors—MLA

If your source has more than three authors, you can name them all or use the first author's name only, followed by *et al.*, either in a parenthetical reference or in your sentence. *Et al.* is an abbreviation of the Latin *et alii*, meaning "and others." In MLA citations, don't underline or italicize *et al.* No period follows *et*, but one follows *al.*

> Emotional security varies, depending on the circumstances of the social interaction (Carter et al. 158).

4. More Than One Source by an Author—MLA

When you use two or more sources by the same author, include the relevant title in each citation. In parenthetical citations, use a shortened version of the title. For example, in a paper using two of Howard Gardner's works, *Frames of Mind: The Theory of Multiple Intelligences* and "Reflections on Multiple Intelligences: Myths and Messages," use *Frames* and "Reflections." Shorten the titles as much as you can without making them ambiguous to readers, and start with the word by which the work is alphabetized in your WORKS CITED list. Separate the author's name and the title with a comma, but don't use punctuation between the title and page number.

> Although it seems straightforward to think of multiple intelligences as multiple approaches to learning (Gardner, *Frames* 60–61), an intelligence is not a learning style (Gardner, "Reflections" 202–03).

When you incorporate the title into your own sentences, you can omit a subtitle. After the first mention, you can shorten the main title as well.

5. Two or More Authors with the Same Last Name—MLA

Use each author's first initial and full last name in each parenthetical citation. If both authors have the same first initial, use the full name in all instances.

> According to Anne Cates, psychologists can predict how empathetic an adult will be from his or her behavior at age two (41), but other researchers disagree (T. Cates 171).

MLA
14C

6. Group or Corporate Author—MLA

Use the corporate name just as you would an individual's name.

> A five-year study shows that these tests are usually unreliable (Boston Women's Health Collective 11).

7. Work Cited by Title—MLA

If no author is named, use only the title. If the title is long, shorten it. Here's an in-text citation for an article titled "Are You a Day or Night Person?"

> The "morning lark" and "night owl" descriptions typically are used to categorize the human extremes ("Are You" 11).

8. Multivolume Work—MLA

If you use more than one volume of a multivolume work, include the relevant volume number in each citation. Separate the volume number and page number with a colon followed by a space.

> Although Amazon forest dwellers had been exposed to these viruses by 1900 (Rand 3: 202), Borneo forest dwellers escaped them until the 1960s (Rand 1: 543).

MLA
14C

9. Novel, Play, Short Story, or Poem—MLA

Literary works frequently appear in different editions. When you cite material from literary works, providing the part, chapter, act, scene, canto, stanza, or line numbers usually helps readers locate what you are referring to better than page numbers alone. Unless your instructor tells you not to, use arabic numerals for these references, even if the literary work uses roman numerals. For novels that use them, give part and/or chapter numbers after page numbers. Use a semicolon after the page number but a comma to separate a part from a chapter.

> Flannery O'Connor describes one character in *The Violent Bear It Away* as "divided in two—a violent and a rational self" (139; pt. 2, ch. 6).

For plays that use them, give act, scene, and line numbers. Use periods between these numbers. For short stories, use page numbers.

> Among the most quoted of Shakespeare's lines is Hamlet's soliloquy beginning "To be, or not to be: that is the question" (3.1.56).

> The old man in John Collier's "The Chaser" says about his potions, "I don't deal in laxatives and teething mixtures . . . " (79).

For poems and songs, give canto, stanza, and/or line numbers. Use periods between these numbers.

> In "To Autumn," Keats's most melancholy image occurs in the lines "Then in a wailful choir the small gnats mourn / Among the river swallows" (3.27–28).

10. Bible or Sacred Text—MLA

Give the title of the edition you're using, the book (in the case of the Bible), and the chapter and verse. Spell out the names of books in sentences, but use abbreviations in parenthetical references.

> He would certainly benefit from the advice in Ephesians to "get rid of all bitterness, rage, and anger" (*New International Version Bible*, 4.31).

> He would certainly benefit from the advice to "get rid of all bitterness, rage, and anger" (*New International Version Bible*, Eph. 4.31).

11. Work in an Anthology or Other Collection—MLA

You may want to cite a work you have read in a book that contains many works by various authors and that was compiled or edited by someone other than the person you're citing. Your in-text citation should include the author of the selection you're citing and the page number. For example, suppose you want to cite the poem "Several Things" by Martha Collins, in a literature text edited by Pamela Annas and Robert Rosen. Use Collins's name and the title of her work in the sentence and the line numbers (see item 9) in a parenthetical citation.

> In "Several Things," Martha Collins enumerates what could take place in the lines of her poem: "Plums could appear, on a pewter plate / A dead red hare, hung by one foot. / A vase of flowers. Three shallots" (2–4).

12. Indirect Source—MLA

When you want to quote words that you found quoted in someone else's work, put the name of the person whose words you're quoting into your own sentence. Give the work where you found the quotation either in your sentence or in a parenthetical citation beginning with *qtd. in.*

> Martin Scorsese acknowledges the link between himself and his films: "I realize that all my life, I've been an outsider. I splatter bits of myself all over the screen" (qtd. in Giannetti and Eyman 397).

13. Two or More Sources in One Reference—MLA

If more than one source has contributed to an idea, opinion, or fact in your paper, cite them all. An efficient way to credit all is to include them in a single parenthetical citation, with a semicolon separating each block of information.

> Once researchers agreed that multiple intelligences existed, their next step was to try to measure or define them (West 17; Arturi 477; Gibbs 68).

14. An Entire Work—MLA

References to an entire work usually fit best into your own sentences.

> In *Convergence Culture*, Henry Jenkins explores how new digital media create a culture of active participation rather than passive reception.

MLA
14C

15. Electronic Source with Page Numbers—MLA

When an electronically accessed source identifies its author, use the author's name for parenthetical references. If no author is named, use the title of the source. When an electronic source has page numbers, use them exactly as you would the page numbers of a print source.

> Learning happens best when teachers truly care about their students' complete well-being (Anderson 7).

16. Electronic Source without Page Numbers—MLA

Many online sources don't number pages. Simply refer to those works in their entirety. Include the name of the author, if any, in your sentence.

> In "What Is Artificial Intelligence? John McCarthy notes that the science of artificial intelligence includes efforts beyond trying to simulate human intelligence.

14D   What are MLA guidelines for a Works Cited list?

In MLA-style DOCUMENTATION, the **Works Cited** list gives complete bibliographic information for each SOURCE used in your paper. Include only the sources from which you quote, paraphrase, or summarize. Quick Box 14.2 gives general information about the Works Cited list. The rest of this chapter gives models of many specific kinds of Works Cited entries.

Quick Box 14.2

Guidelines for an MLA-style Works Cited list

See 14H, pages 233–234, for a sample student Works Cited list.

TITLE
Use "Works Cited" (without quotation marks), centered, as the title.

PLACEMENT OF LIST
Start a new page numbered sequentially with the rest of the paper, following the Notes pages, if any.

CONTENT AND FORMAT
Include all sources quoted from, paraphrased, or summarized in your paper. Start each entry on a new line and at the regular left margin. If the entry uses more than one line, indent the second and all following lines one-half inch from the left margin. Double-space all lines.

SPACING AFTER PUNCTUATION
Use one space after a period, unless your instructor asks you to use two. Always put only one space after a comma or a colon.

continued >>

Quick Box 14.2

MLA Guidelines (continued) ■ ■ ■ ■ ■ ■

ARRANGEMENT OF ENTRIES

Alphabetize by author's last name. If no author is named, alphabetize by the title's first significant word (ignore *A*, *An*, or *The*).

AUTHORS' NAMES

Use first names and middle names or middle initials, if any, as given in the source. Don't reduce to initials any name that is given in full. For one author or the first-named author in multiauthor works, give the last name first. Use the word *and* with two or more authors. List multiple authors in the order given in the source. Use a comma between the first author's last and first names and after each complete author name except the last, which ends with a period: Fein, Ethel Andrea, Bert Griggs, and Delaware Rogash.

Include *Jr., Sr., II*, or *III* but no other titles or degrees before or after a name. For example, an entry for a work by Edward Meep III, MD, and Sir Richard Bolton would start like this: Meep, Edward, III, and Richard Bolton.

CAPITALIZATION OF TITLES

Capitalize all major words and the first and last words of all titles and subtitles. Don't capitalize ARTICLES (*a, an, the*), PREPOSITIONS, COORDINATING CONJUNCTIONS, or *to* in INFINITIVES in the middle of a title.

SPECIAL TREATMENT OF TITLES OF SOURCES

Use quotation marks around titles of shorter works (poems, short stories, essays, articles). Use italics for the titles of longer works (books, periodicals, plays).

When a book title includes the title of another work that is usually in italics (such as a novel, play, or long poem), the preferred MLA style is not to italicize the incorporated title: *Decoding* Jane Eyre.

If the incorporated title is usually enclosed in quotation marks (such as a short story or short poem), keep the quotation marks and italicize the complete title of the book: *Theme and Form in "I Shall Laugh Purely": A Brief Study*.

Drop *A, An*, or *The* as the first word of a periodical title.

PLACE OF PUBLICATION

If several cities are listed for the place of publication, give only the first. MLA doesn't require US state names. For an unfamiliar city outside the United States, include an abbreviated name of the country or Canadian province.

PUBLISHER

Use shortened names as long as they're clear: *Random* for *Random House*. For companies named for more than one person, name only the first: *Prentice* for *Prentice Hall*. For university presses, use the capital letters *U* and *P* (without periods): Oxford UP, U of Chicago P. If there is no publisher, use "N.p."

PUBLICATION MONTH ABBREVIATIONS

Abbreviate all publication months except *May, June*, and *July*. Use the first three letters followed by a period (*Dec., Feb.*) except for *Sept.*

continued >>

MLA
14D

Quick Box 14.2   MLA Guidelines (continued) ■ ■ ■ ■ ■ ■

PAGE RANGES

Give the page range—the starting page number and the ending page number, connected by a hyphen—of any paginated electronic source and any paginated print source that is part of a longer work (for example, a chapter in a book, an article in a journal). A range indicates that the cited work is on those pages and all pages in between. If that is not the case, use the style shown next for discontinuous pages. In either case, use numerals only, without the word *page* or *pages* or the abbreviation *p.* or *pp.*

Use the full second number through 99. Above that, use only the last two digits for the second number unless it would be unclear: 103–04 is clear, but 567–602 requires full numbers.

DISCONTINUOUS PAGES

When the source is interrupted by material that's not part of the source (for example, an article beginning on page 32 but continued on page 54), use the starting page number followed by a plus sign (+): 32+.

MEDIUM OF PUBLICATION

Include the medium of publication for each Works Cited entry. For example, every entry for a print source must include "Print" at the end, followed by a period. Supplementary bibliographic information like the original publication information for a work cited in translation, name of a book series, or the number of volumes in a set should follow the medium of publication. Every source from the World Wide Web must include *Web* at the end, followed by a period and the date of access. The medium of publication also needs to be included for broadcast sources (*Television*, *Radio*), sound recordings (*CD*, *Podcast*, *LP*, *Audiocassette*), as well as films, DVDs, live performances, musical scores, works of visual art, and so on.

ISSUE AND VOLUME NUMBERS FOR SCHOLARLY JOURNALS

Include both an issue and volume number for scholarly journals. This applies both to journals that are continuously paginated and those that are not.

URLs IN ELECTRONIC SOURCES

Entries for online citations should include the URL *only when the reader probably could not locate the source without it.* If the entry requires a URL, enclose the URL in angle brackets <like this>. Put the URL before the access date, and end it with a period. If your computer automatically creates a hyperlink when you type a URL, format the URL to look the same as the rest of the entry. If a URL must be divided between two lines, break the URL only after a slash and do not use a hyphen.

14E What are MLA examples for sources in a Works Cited list?

To find different types of citation models, use the decision-making flowchart shown in Figure 14.1. You can also use the directory of Works Cited citation models in Quick Box 14.3. We show almost 100 different citation models, but if you cannot find what you need in this section, check the MLA Web site.

Figure 14.1 Decision-making flowchart for finding the right MLA citation format.

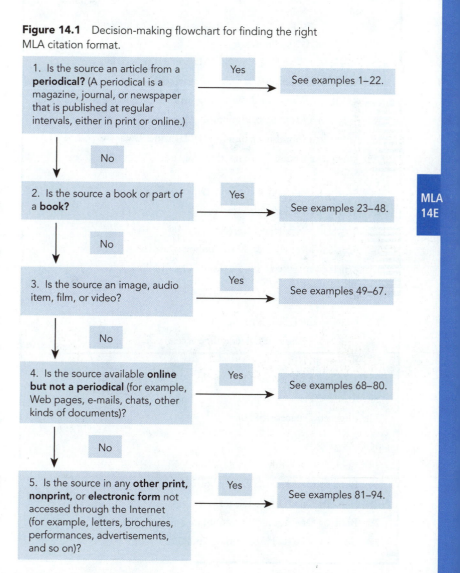

Quick Box 14.3

■ ■ ■ ■ ■ ■

MLA Works Cited List Directory

continued >>

Quick Box 14.3   Works Cited Directory (continued)   ■ ■ ■ ■ ■ ■

MLA
14E

continued >>

**MLA
14E**

continued >>

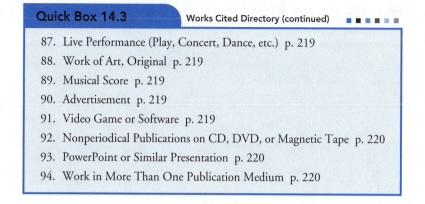

PERIODICALS

You can read periodical articles in four different formats. Some articles appear in all print and electronic versions; others are published in only one or two formats.

1. **Print.** Figure 14.2 shows how to cite a print article from a scholarly journal.

2. **Digital version in a database.** You most commonly access these sources through a DATABASE such as EBSCO or Academic Search Premier, which your library purchases.

3. **Digital version with direct online access.** Without going through a database, you access these sources directly on the Web, either by entering a specific URL or clicking on links provided by a search. Figure 14.3, p. 203, shows how to cite an article from a scholarly journal that was accessed in a database.

4. **Digital version on a digital reader.** Many devices allow you to access online content. These include e-readers like Kindle or Nook, tablet computers (like iPads), or smart phones (like Android).

1. Article in a Scholarly Journal: Print

Williams, Bronwyn T. "Seeking New Worlds: The Study of Writing beyond Our Classrooms." *College Composition and Communication* 62.1 (2010): 127–46. Print.

Provide both volume and issue number, if available.

2. Article in Scholarly Journal with a Print Version: Database

Williams, Bronwyn T. "Seeking New Worlds: The Study of Writing beyond Our Classrooms." *College Composition and Communication*. 62.1 (2010): 127–46. Proquest. Web. 24 Oct. 2013.

The final date (24 Oct. 2013) is the date you accessed the article on the Web.

MLA
14E

Figure 14.2 Print article from a scholarly journal, accessed in print.

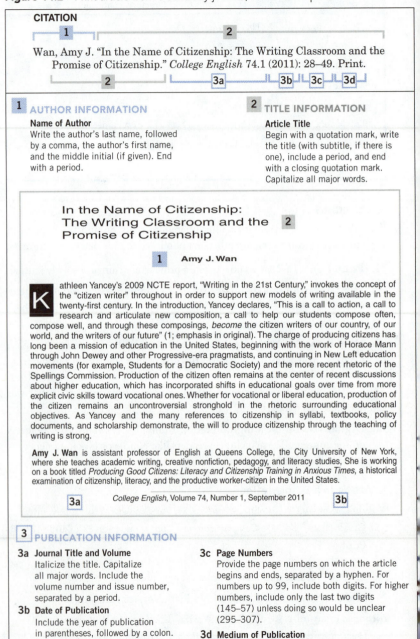

CITATION

1 **2**

Wan, Amy J. "In the Name of Citizenship: The Writing Classroom and the Promise of Citizenship." *College English* 74.1 (2011): 28–49. Print.

2 **3a** **3b** **3c** **3d**

1 AUTHOR INFORMATION

Name of Author
Write the author's last name, followed by a comma, the author's first name, and the middle initial (if given). End with a period.

2 TITLE INFORMATION

Article Title
Begin with a quotation mark, write the title (with subtitle, if there is one), include a period, and end with a closing quotation mark. Capitalize all major words.

> ## In the Name of Citizenship: The Writing Classroom and the **2** Promise of Citizenship
>
> **1** Amy J. Wan
>
> **K**athleen Yancey's 2009 NCTE report, "Writing in the 21st Century," invokes the concept of the "citizen writer" throughout in order to support new models of writing available in the twenty-first century. In the introduction, Yancey declares, "This is a call to action, a call to research and articulate new composition, a call to help our students compose often, compose well, and through these composings, *become* the citizen writers of our country, of our world, and the writers of our future" (1; emphasis in original). The charge of producing citizens has long been a mission of education in the United States, beginning with the work of Horace Mann through John Dewey and other Progressive-era pragmatists, and continuing in New Left education movements (for example, Students for a Democratic Society) and the more recent rhetoric of the Spellings Commission. Production of the citizen often remains at the center of recent discussions about higher education, which has incorporated shifts in educational goals over time from more explicit civic skills toward vocational ones. Whether for vocational or liberal education, production of the citizen remains an uncontroversial stronghold in the rhetoric surrounding educational objectives. As Yancey and the many references to citizenship in syllabi, textbooks, policy documents, and scholarship demonstrate, the will to produce citizenship through the teaching of writing is strong.
>
> **Amy J. Wan** is assistant professor of English at Queens College, the City University of New York, where she teaches academic writing, creative nonfiction, pedagogy, and literacy studies, She is working on a book titled *Producing Good Citizens: Literacy and Citizenship Training in Anxious Times*, a historical examination of citizenship, literacy, and the productive worker-citizen in the United States.
>
> **3a** *College English*, Volume 74, Number 1, September 2011 **3b**

3 PUBLICATION INFORMATION

3a Journal Title and Volume
Italicize the title. Capitalize all major words. Include the volume number and issue number, separated by a period.

3b Date of Publication
Include the year of publication in parentheses, followed by a colon.

3c Page Numbers
Provide the page numbers on which the article begins and ends, separated by a hyphen. For numbers up to 99, include both digits. For higher numbers, include only the last two digits (145–57) unless doing so would be unclear (295–307).

3d Medium of Publication
Print.

Figure 14.3 Article from a scholarly journal accessed in a database.

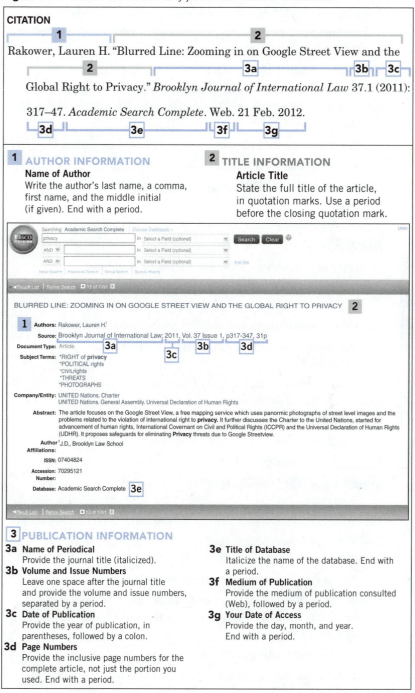

CITATION

Rakower, Lauren H. "Blurred Line: Zooming in on Google Street View and the Global Right to Privacy." *Brooklyn Journal of International Law* 37.1 (2011): 317–47. *Academic Search Complete*. Web. 21 Feb. 2012.

1 AUTHOR INFORMATION

Name of Author
Write the author's last name, a comma, first name, and the middle initial (if given). End with a period.

2 TITLE INFORMATION

Article Title
State the full title of the article, in quotation marks. Use a period before the closing quotation mark.

3 PUBLICATION INFORMATION

3a Name of Periodical
Provide the journal title (italicized).

3b Volume and Issue Numbers
Leave one space after the journal title and provide the volume and issue numbers, separated by a period.

3c Date of Publication
Provide the year of publication, in parentheses, followed by a colon.

3d Page Numbers
Provide the inclusive page numbers for the complete article, not just the portion you used. End with a period.

3e Title of Database
Italicize the name of the database. End with a period.

3f Medium of Publication
Provide the medium of publication consulted (Web), followed by a period.

3g Your Date of Access
Provide the day, month, and year. End with a period.

3. Article in a Scholarly Journal with a Print Version: Direct online access

Hoge, Charles W., et al. "Mild Traumatic Brain Injury in U.S. Soldiers
    Returning from Iraq." *New England Journal of Medicine* 358.5 (2008):
    453–63. Web. 10 Sept. 2008.

4. Article in a Scholarly Journal Published Only Online: Direct online access

Rutz, Paul X. "What a Painter of 'Historical Narrative' Can Tell Us about War
    Photography." *Kairos* 14.3 (2010). Web. 11 Nov. 2010.

Some periodicals appear only online and publish no print version.

5. Article in a Weekly or Biweekly Magazine: Print

Foroohar, Rana. "Why the World Isn't Getting Smaller." *Time* 27 June 2011: 20.
    Print.

If there is no author given, begin with the title of the article.

"The Price Is Wrong." *Economist* 2 Aug. 2003: 58–59. Print.

6. Article in a Weekly or Biweekly Magazine: Database

Foroohar, Rana. "Why the World Isn't Getting Smaller." *Time* 19 June 2011.
    Academic Search Complete. Web. 28 Aug. 2011.

7. Article in a Weekly or Biweekly Magazine: Direct online access

Foroohar, Rana. "Why the World Isn't Getting Smaller." *Time*. Time, 19 June
    2011. Web. 27 Aug. 2011.

The name of the Web site is italicized. The sponsor (owner) of the Web site
precedes the date of publication.

8. Article in a Monthly or Bimonthly Magazine: Print

Goetz, Thomas. "The Feedback Loop." *Wired* July 2011: 126–33. Print.

9. Article in a Monthly or Bimonthly Magazine: Database

Goetz, Thomas. "The Feedback Loop." *Wired* July 2011: 126–33. *ProQuest*.
    Web. 16 Sept. 2013.

10. Article in a Monthly or Bimonthly Magazine: Direct online access

Goetz, Thomas. "The Feedback Loop." *Wired*. Conde Nast, 19 June 2011. Web.
    16 Sept. 2013.

11. Article Published Only Online: Direct online access

Ramirez, Eddy. "Comparing American Students with Those in China and
    India." *U.S. News and World Report*. U.S. News and World Report, 30 Jan.
    2008. Web. 4 Mar. 2008.

12. Article in a Newspaper: Print

Hesse, Monica. "Love among the Ruins." *Washington Post* 24 Apr. 2011: F1+.
    Print.

Omit *A, An,* or *The* as the first word in a newspaper title. Give the day, month, and year of the issue (and the edition, if applicable). If sections are designated, give the section letter as well as the page number. If an article runs on non-consecutive pages, give the starting page number followed by a plus sign (for example, 1+ for an article that starts on page 1 and continues on a later page).

If no author is listed, begin with the title of the article.

"Prepping for Uranium Work." *Denver Post* 18 June 2011: B2. Print.

If the city of publication is not part of the newspaper's name, put it in square brackets after the name, not italicized.

13. Article in a Newspaper: Database

Hesse, Monica. "Falling in Love with St. Andrews, Scotland." *Washington Post*
　　24 Apr. 2011. *LexisNexis Academic.* Web. 3 Oct. 2013.

14. Article in a Newspaper: Direct online access

Hesse, Monica. "Falling in Love with St. Andrews, Scotland." *Washington Post.*
　　Washington Post, 22 Apr. 2011. Web. 3 Oct. 2013.

15. Article from a News Site Published Only Online: Direct online access

Katz, David. "What to Do about Flu? Get Vaccinated." *Huffington Post.*
　　Huffington Post, 28 Oct. 2010. Web. 25 May 2011.

16. Editorial

"Primary Considerations." Editorial. *Washington Post* 27 Jan. 2008: B6. Print.

If an author is listed, include her or his name before the title, then provide the title and information about the type of publication.

17. Letter to the Editor: Print

Goldstein, Lester. "Roach Coaches: The Upside." Letter. *Sierra* May/June 2011:
　　2. Print.

If there is no title, include just the type, as in example 18.

18. Letter to the Editor: Direct online access

Ennis, Heather B. Letter. *U.S. News and World Report.* U.S. News and World
　　Report, 20 Dec. 2007. Web. 22 Dec. 2007.

19. Review

Shenk, David. "Toolmaker, Brain Builder." Rev. of *Beyond Big Blue: Building
　　the Computer That Defeated the World Chess Champion,* by Feng-Hsiung
　　Hsu. *American Scholar* 72 (2003): 150–52. Print.

20. Article in a Collection of Reprinted Articles: Print

Brumberg, Abraham. "Russia after Perestroika." *New York Review of Books* 27
　　June 1991: 53–62. Rpt. in *Russian and Soviet History.* Ed. Alexander-Dallin.
　　Vol. 14. New York: Garland, 1992. 300–20. Print.

Textbooks used in college writing courses often collect previously printed articles.

Wallace, David Foster. "Consider the Lobster." *Gourmet* Aug. 2004: 50–55. Rpt. in *Creating Nonfiction: A Guide and Anthology*. By Becky Bradway and Doug Hesse. Boston: Bedford, 2009. 755–69. Print.

21. Abstract: Print

Marcus, Hazel R., and Shinobu Kitayamo. "Culture and the Self: Implications for Cognition, Emotion, and Motivation." *Psychological Review* 88 (1991): 224–53. Abstract. *Psychological Abstracts* 78 (1991): item 23878. Print.

For abstracts identified by item numbers rather than page numbers, use the word *item* before the item number.

22. Abstract: Database

Marcus, Hazel R., and Shinobu Kitayamo. "Culture and the Self: Implications for Cognition, Emotion, and Motivation." Abstract. *Psychological Abstracts* 78 (1991): item 23878. *PsycINFO*. Web. 10 Apr. 2004.

BOOKS

MLA
14E

You can read books in four different formats.

1. **Print.** Figure 14.4 shows how to cite a single-author print book.

2. **Digital version through an e-book.** E-books are electronic versions of books for digital readers like the Kindle, Nook, iPad, and so on.

3. **Digital version from a database.** Some books are available through library databases; in a sense, you're "checking out the books" online.

4. **Digital version through direct online access.** Versions of some older books, whose copyrights have expired because their authors died more than 70 years ago, are available directly on the Web. Portions of several more recent books are also available directly on the Web, through sites like Google Books. However, the section you might need for your research is frequently not available.

We provide examples of all formats in examples 23–26. The same principles apply to all books, so you can adapt these basic models as needed. We also note that there are audio versions of some books: recordings of an actor (or sometimes, the author) reading the book. We explain how to cite audio books in example 59.

23. Book by One Author: Print

Turkle, Sherry. *Alone Together: Why We Expect More from Technology and Less from Each Other*. New York: Basic, 2011. Print.

Figure 14.4   Single-author print book.

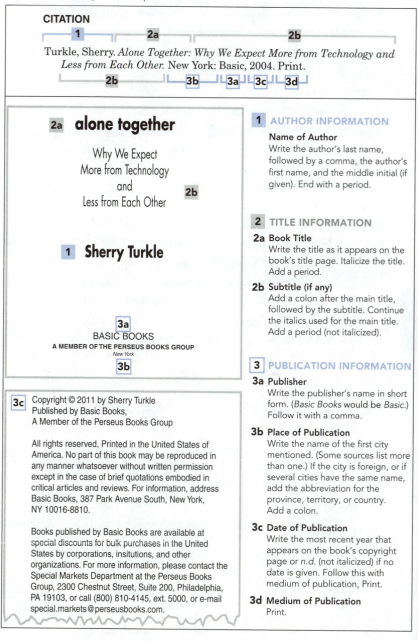

CITATION

1   2a   2b

Turkle, Sherry. *Alone Together: Why We Expect More from Technology and Less from Each Other.* New York: Basic, 2004. Print.

2b   3b   3a   3c   3d

2a alone together

Why We Expect
More from Technology
and
Less from Each Other   **2b**

1 Sherry Turkle

3a
BASIC BOOKS
A MEMBER OF THE PERSEUS BOOKS GROUP
New York
3b

3c Copyright © 2011 by Sherry Turkle
Published by Basic Books,
A Member of the Perseus Books Group

All rights reserved, Printed in the United States of America. No part of this book may be reproduced in any manner whatsoever without written permission except in the case of brief quotations embodied in critical articles and reviews. For information, address Basic Books, 387 Park Avenue South, New York, NY 10016-8810.

Books published by Basic Books are available at special discounts for bulk purchases in the United States by corporations, insitutions, and other organizations. For more information, please contact the Special Markets Department at the Perseus Books Group, 2300 Chestnut Street, Suite 200, Philadelphia, PA 19103, or call (800) 810-4145, ext. 5000, or e-mail special.markets@perseusbooks.com.

1 AUTHOR INFORMATION

Name of Author
Write the author's last name, followed by a comma, the author's first name, and the middle initial (if given). End with a period.

2 TITLE INFORMATION

2a Book Title
Write the title as it appears on the book's title page. Italicize the title. Add a period.

2b Subtitle (if any)
Add a colon after the main title, followed by the subtitle. Continue the italics used for the main title. Add a period (not italicized).

3 PUBLICATION INFORMATION

3a Publisher
Write the publisher's name in short form. (*Basic Books* would be *Basic*.) Follow it with a comma.

3b Place of Publication
Write the name of the first city mentioned. (Some sources list more than one.) If the city is foreign, or if several cities have the same name, add the abbreviation for the province, territory, or country. Add a colon.

3c Date of Publication
Write the most recent year that appears on the book's copyright page or *n.d.* (not italicized) if no date is given. Follow this with medium of publication, Print.

3d Medium of Publication
Print.

24. Book by One Author: E-Book

Turkle, Sherry. *Alone Together: Why We Expect More from Technology and Less from Each Other*. New York: Basic, 2011. Kindle file.

25. Book by One Author: Database

Turkle, Sherry. *Evocative Objects: Things We Think With*. Cambridge: MIT P, 2007. *Ebrary*. Web. 3 May 2013.

26. Book by One Author: Direct online access

Turkle, Sherry. *Alone Together: Why We Expect More from Technology and Less from Each Other*. New York: Basic, 2011. *Google Books*. Google, 2011. Web. 25 July 2011.

Chopin, Kate. *The Awakening*. 1899. *PBS Electronic Library*. PBS, 10 Dec. 1998. Web. 13 Nov. 2004.

27. Book by Two or Three Authors

Edin, Kathryn, and Maria Kefalas. *Promises I Can Keep: Why Poor Women Put Motherhood before Marriage*. Berkeley: U of California P, 2005. Print.

Lynam, John K., Cyrus G. Ndiritu, and Adiel N. Mbabu. *Transformation of Agricultural Research Systems in Africa: Lessons from Kenya*. East Lansing: Michigan State UP, 2004. Print.

MLA
14E

For these and the following citations, you can adapt the elements to examples 24–26. For e-books, adapt the model to example 24. For a book in a database, see example 25. For a book accessed directly online, see example 26.

28. Book by More Than Three Authors

Saul, Wendy, et al. *Beyond the Science Fair: Creating a Kids' Inquiry Conference*. Portsmouth: Heinemann, 2005. Print.

Give only the first author's name, followed by a comma and the phrase *et al.* (abbreviated from the Latin *et alii*, meaning "and others"), or list all names in full in the order in which they appear on the title page.

29. Two or More Works by the Same Author(s)

Jenkins, Henry. *Convergence Culture: Where Old and New Media Collide*. New York: New York UP, 2006. Print.

---. *Fans, Bloggers, and Gamers: Exploring Participatory Culture*. New York: New York UP, 2006. Print.

Give author name(s) in the first entry only. In the second and subsequent entries, use three hyphens and a period to stand for exactly the same name(s). Arrange the works in alphabetical (not chronological) order according to title.

30. Book by a Group or Corporate Author

American Psychological Association. *Publication Manual of the American Psychological Association*. 6th ed. Washington: APA, 2010. Print.

When a corporate author is also the publisher, use a shortened form of the corporate name at the publisher position.

31. Book with No Author Named

The Chicago Manual of Style. 16th ed. Chicago: U of Chicago P, 2010. Print.

If there is no author's name on the title page, begin the citation with the title. Alphabetize the entry according to the first significant word of the title (ignore *A*, *An*, or *The*).

32. Book with an Author and an Editor

Stowe, Harriet Beecher. *Uncle Tom's Cabin*. Ed. Elizabeth Ammons. New York: Norton, 2010. Print.

If your paper refers to the work of the book's author, put the author's name first. If your paper refers to the work of the editor, put the editor's name first.

Ammons, Elizabeth, ed. *Uncle Tom's Cabin*. By Harriet Beecher Stowe. New York: Norton, 2010. Print.

33. Translation

Nesbo, Jo. *The Leopard*. Trans. Don Bartlett. New York: Vintage, 2011.

34. Work in Several Volumes or Parts

Chrisley, Ronald, ed. *Artificial Intelligence: Critical Concepts*. Vol. 1. London: Routledge, 2000. Print. 4 vols.

If you are citing only one volume, put the volume number before the publication information. If you wish, you can give the total number of volumes at the end of the entry. MLA recommends using arabic numerals, even if the source uses roman numerals (*Vol. 6* rather than *Vol. VI*).

35. Anthology or Edited Book

Purdy, John L., and James Ruppert, eds. *Nothing but the Truth: An Anthology of Native American Literature*. Upper Saddle River: Prentice, 2001. Print.

Use this model if you are citing an entire anthology. In the example above, *ed.* stands for "editor," so use *eds.* when more than one editor is named.

36. One Selection from an Anthology or an Edited Book

Trujillo, Laura. "Balancing Act." *Border-Line Personalities: A New Generation of Latinas Dish on Sex, Sass, and Cultural Shifting*. Ed. Robyn Moreno and Michelle Herrera Mulligan. New York: Harper, 2004. 61–72. Print.

Teasdale, Sara. "Driftwood." *Flame and Shadow*. Ed. A. Light. N.p., 1920. *Project Gutenberg*. 1 July 1996. Web. 18 Aug. 2013.

Give the author and title of the selection first and then the full title of the anthology. Information about the editor starts with *Ed.* (for "Edited by"), so don't use *Eds.* when there is more than one editor. Give the name(s) of the editor(s) in normal order rather than reversing first and last names. Give the page range of the selection at the end.

MLA
14E

37. More Than One Selection from the Same Anthology or Edited Book

Bond, Ruskin. "The Night Train at Deoli." Chaudhuri 415–18.

Chaudhuri, Amit, ed. *The Vintage Book of Modern Indian Literature*. New York:

    Vintage, 2004. Print.

Vijayan, O.V. "The Rocks." Chaudhuri 291–96.

If you cite more than one selection from the same anthology, you can list the anthology as a separate entry with all of the publication information. Also list each selection from the anthology by author and title of the selection, but give only the name(s) of the editor(s) of the anthology and the page number(s) for each selection. Here, *ed.* stands for "editor," so it is correct to use *eds.* when more than one editor is named. List selections separately in alphabetical order by author's last name.

38. Article in a Reference Book

Burnbam, John C. "Freud, Sigmund." *The Encyclopedia of Psychiatry,*

    Psychology, and Psychoanalysis. Ed. Benjamin B. Wolman. New York:

    Holt, 1996. Print.

If the articles are alphabetically arranged, you don't need to give volume and page numbers.

    If no author is listed, begin with the title of the article.

MLA
14E

"Ireland." *The New Encyclopaedia Britannica: Macropaedia*. 15th ed. 2002.

    Print.

If you're citing a widely used reference work, don't give full publication information. Instead, give only the edition and year of publication.

39. Second or Later Edition

MLA Handbook for Writers of Research Papers. 7th ed. New York: MLA, 2009.

    Print.

If a book is not a first edition, the edition number is on the title page. Place the abbreviated information (*2nd ed., 3rd ed.*, etc.) between the title and the publication information. Give only the latest copyright date for the edition you are using.

40. Introduction, Preface, Foreword, or Afterword

Hesse, Doug. Foreword. *The End of Composition Studies*. By David W. Smit.

    Carbondale: Southern Illinois UP, 2004. ix–xiii. Print.

Give first the name of the writer of the part you're citing and then the name of the cited part, capitalized. After the book title, put *By* and the book author's full name, if different from the writer of the cited material. If the writer of the cited material is the same as the book author, use a separate entry only when there is also an editor or translator of the book. After the publication information, give inclusive page numbers for the cited part. When the introduction, preface, foreword, or afterword has a title, include it in the citation before the section name, as in the following example:

Fox-Genovese, Elizabeth. "Mothers and Daughters: The Ties That Bind."

Foreword. *Southern Mothers*. Ed. Nagueyalti Warren and Sally Wolff.

Baton Rouge: Louisiana State UP, 1999. iv–xviii. Print.

41. Unpublished Dissertation or Essay

Stuart, Gina Anne. "Exploring the Harry Potter Book Series: A Study of

Adolescent Reading Motivation." Diss. Utah State U, 2006. Print.

Treat published dissertations as books.

42. Reprint of an Older Book

Coover, Robert. *A Night at the Movies, Or, You Must Remember This*. 1987.

Champaign: Dalkey Archive, 2007.

Republishing information can be found on the copyright page.

43. Book in a Series or Scholarly Project

Ardell, Jean Hastings. *Breaking into Baseball: Women and the National

Pastime*. Carbondale: Southern Illinois UP, 2005. Print. Writing Baseball

Series.

44. Book with a Title within a Title

Lumiansky, Robert M., and Herschel Baker, eds. *Critical Approaches to Six

Major English Works: Beowulf through Paradise Lost*. Philadelphia:

U of Pennsylvania P, 1968. Print.

MLA also accepts a second style for embedded titles:

Lumiansky, Robert M., and Herschel Baker, eds. *Critical Approaches to Six

Major English Works: "Beowulf" through "Paradise Lost."* Philadelphia:

U of Pennsylvania P, 1968. Print.

45. Bible or Sacred Text

Bhagavad Gita. Trans. Juan Mascaro. Rev. ed. New York: Penguin, 2003. Print.

The Holy Bible: New International Version. New York: Harper, 1983. Print.

The Qur'an. Trans. M.A.S. Abdel Haleem. New York: Oxford UP, 2004. Print.

46. Government Publication with No Author

United States. Cong. Senate. Select Committee on Intelligence. *Report on the

U.S. Intelligence Community's Prewar Intelligence Assessment of Iraq*.

108th Cong., 1st sess. Washington: GPO, 2004. Print.

Start with the name of the government. Then name the government agency. (*GPO* stands for *Government Printing Office*.) Then include the title, any series information, the publication date, and the medium of publication.

47. Government Publication with Named Author

Wallace, David Rains. *Yellowstone: A Natural and Human History,*
Yellowstone National Park, Idaho, Montana, and Wyoming. US Interior
Dept. National Park Service. Official National Park Handbook 150.
Washington: GPO, 2001. Print.

MLA also permits an alternative format:

United States. Interior Dept. National Park Service. *Yellowstone: A Natural*
and Human History, Yellowstone National Park, Idaho, Montana, and
Wyoming. By David Rains Wallace. Official National Park Handbook 150.
Washington: GPO, 2001. Print.

48. Published Proceedings of a Conference

Rocha, Luis Mateus, et al., eds. *Artificial Life X: Proceedings of the Tenth*
International Conference on the Simulation and Synthesis of Living
Systems. 3–7 June 2006, Bloomington, IN. Cambridge: MIT P, 2006. Print.

IMAGES, AUDIO, FILM, AND VIDEO

49. Photograph, Painting, Drawing, Illustration, etc. (Original)

Mydans, Carl. *General Douglas MacArthur Landing at Luzon, 1945*. Gelatin
silver print. Soho Triad Fine Art Gallery, New York. 21 Oct.–28 Nov. 1999.

If the image has no title, provide a brief description.

50. Photograph, Painting, Drawing, Illustration, etc. in a Periodical: Print

Greene, Herb. *Grace Slick*. Photograph. *Rolling Stone* 30 Sept. 2004: 102. Print.

Include maker, title, and type as in example 49, but include publication information as for a print article.

51. Photograph, Painting, Drawing, Illustration, etc. in a Periodical: Direct online access

Morris, Christopher. *Man in Camouflage*. Photograph. *Atlantic*. The Atlantic
Monthly Group, July/Aug. 2011. Web. 5 Aug. 2013.

52. Photograph, Painting, Drawing, Illustration, etc. in a Book: Print

The World's Most Populous Countries. Illustration. *Maps of the Imagination:*
The Writer as Cartographer. By Peter Turchi. San Antonio: Trinity UP, 2004.
116–17. Print.

53. Photograph, Painting, Drawing, Illustration, etc.: Direct online access

Bourke-White, Margaret. *Fort Peck Dam, Montana*. 1936. Gelatin silver print.
Metropolitan Museum of Art. Web. 5 Aug. 2013.

54. Comic or Cartoon

Sutton, Ward. "Ryan's a Late Adopter." Cartoon. *New Yorker* 2 May 2011: 64.
Print.

55. Photo Essay: Direct online access

Nachtwey, James. "Crime in Middle America." *Time*. Time, 2 Dec. 2006. Web. 5
May 2007.

56. Image from a Social Networking Site

Gristellar, Ferdinand. *The Gateway Arch.* Photograph. *Ferdinand Gristellar.*
Facebook, 7 Aug. 2009. Web. 3 Sept. 2009.

57. Image from a Service or Distributor

World Perspectives. *Launching of the Space Shuttle* Columbia, *Florida, USA,*
1998. Photograph. Getty Images #AT3775-001. Web. 3 Mar. 2011.

In this example, the photographer was listed as "World Perspectives."

58. Map, Chart, or Other Graphic: Direct online access

"Hurricane Rita." Graphic. *New York Times Online.* New York Times, 24 Sept.
2005. Web. 24 Sept. 2005.

MLA
14E

59. Audio Book

Turkle, Sherry. *Alone Together: Why We Expect More from Technology and*
Less from Each Other. Narr. Laural Merlington. Tantor Media, 2011. CD.

60. Sound Recording: CD, DVD

Verdi, Giuseppe. *Requiem.* Chicago Symphony Orchestra and Chorus. Cond.
Ricardo Muti. CSO Resound, 2010. CD.

Put first the name most relevant to what you discuss in your paper (performer,
conductor, work performed). Include the recording's title, the medium for any
recording other than a CD (*LP, Audiocassette*), the name of the issuer, and the
year the work was issued.

61. Sound Recording: MP3

Radiohead. "Jigsaw Falling into Place." *In Rainbows.* Radiohead, 2007. MP3 file.

62. Sound Recording: Direct online access

Komunyakaa, Yusef. "My Father's Love Letters." Poets.org *Listening Booth.*
Academy of American Poets, 5 May 1993. Web. 19 Aug. 2013.

63. Podcast: Direct online access

Blumberg, Alex, and Adam Davidson. "The Giant Pool of Money." *This*
American Life. NPR, 9 May 2008. Web. 19 Oct. 2012.

A podcast is an audio recording that is posted online. Thus, the publication
medium is *Web.*

64. Film, Video, or DVD

It Happened One Night. Screenplay by Robert Riskin. Dir. and Prod. Frank
    Capra. Perf. Clark Gable and Claudette Colbert. 1934. Sony Pictures, 1999.
    DVD.

Give the title first, and include the director, the distributor, and the year.
For films that were subsequently released on tape or DVD, provide the
original release date of the movie *before* the type of medium. Other information (writer, producer, major actors) is optional but helpful. Put first
names first.

65. Video or Film: Direct online access

For video downloads, include the download date and the source.

It Happened One Night. Screenplay by Robert Riskin. Dir. and Prod. Frank
    Capra. Perf. Clark Gable and Claudette Colbert. 1934. *Netflix*. Web. 15
    Dec. 2011.

CNN. *Challenger Disaster Live on CNN*. *YouTube*. YouTube, 27 Jan. 2011. Web.
    4 Mar. 2011.

66. Broadcast Television or Radio Program

Include at least the title of the program (in italics), the network, the local station and its city, and the date of the broadcast.

*Not for Ourselves Alone: The Story of Elizabeth Cady Stanton and Susan
    B. Anthony*. By Ken Burns. Perf. Julie Harris, Ronnie Gilbert, and Sally
    Kellerman. Prod. Paul Barnes and Ken Burns. PBS. WNET, New York. 8
    Nov. 1999. Television.

The Madeleine Brand Show. SCPR. KPCC, Pasadena. 20 June 2011. Radio.

For a series, also supply the title of the specific episode (in quotation marks)
before the title of the program (italicized).

"The Bruce-Partington Plans." *Sherlock Holmes*. RMPBS. KRMA, Denver. 30
    June 2011. Television.

67. Television or Radio Program: Direct online access

"Bill Moyers." *The Daily Show*. Perf. Jon Stewart. Comedy Central. *Hulu.com*.
    Hulu, 1 June 2011. Web. 22 Sept. 2011.

"The Disappearing Incandescent Bulb." *The Madeleine Brand
    Show*. SCPR. KPCC, Pasadena. 20 June 2011. Web. 6 Oct. 2011.
    http://www.scpr.org/programs/madeleine-brand/2011/06/20/
    the-disappearing-incandescent-bulb.

Because this source may be difficult to find, the URL is listed.

OTHER INTERNET SOURCES

This section shows models for other online sources. For such sources, provide as much of the following information as you can.

1. The author's name, if given

2. In quotation marks, the title of a short work (Web page, brief document, essay, article, message, and so on); or italicized, the title of a book

3. Publication information for any print version, if it exists

4. The name of an editor, translator, or compiler, if any, with an abbreviation such as *Ed., Trans.,* or *Comp*. before the name

5. Publication information for the Web:

   a. The italicized title of the Internet site (scholarly project, database, online periodical, professional or personal Web site). If the site has no title, describe it: for example, Home page.

   b. The date of electronic publication or posting or the most recent update.

   c. The name of a sponsoring organization, if any.

   d. The medium of publication: Web.

   e. The date you accessed the material.

   f. The URL in angle brackets (< >), only when the reader probably could not locate the source without it. If you must break a URL at the end of a line, break only after a slash and do not use a hyphen.

MLA 14E

Figure 14.5 shows how to cite a page from a Web site.

68. Entire Web Site

WebdelSol.Com. Ed. Michael Neff. 2011. Web. 4 Aug. 2013.

69. Home Page (Organization or Company)

Association for the Advancement of Artificial Intelligence. AAAI, n.d. Web. 17 Oct. 2011.

70. Personal Home Page

Hesse, Doug. Home page. Web. 1 Nov. 2011. <http://portfolio.du.edu/dhesse>.

Provide the URL if the page might be difficult to find.

71. Page from a Web Site

"Protecting Whales from Dangerous Sonar." *National Resources Defense Council*. NRDC, 9 Nov. 2005. Web. 12 Dec. 2005.

"Ethical and Social Implications of AI for Society." *Association for the Advancement of Artificial Intelligence*. AAAI, 3 May 2012. Web. 19 May 2012.

Figure 14.5   Page from a Web site.

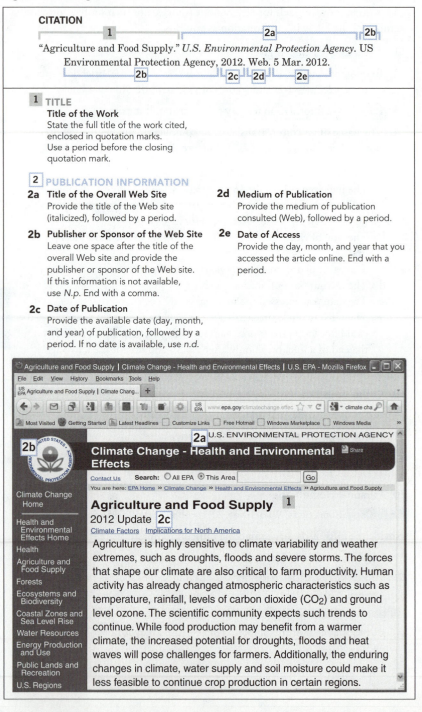

CITATION

"Agriculture and Food Supply." *U.S. Environmental Protection Agency.* US Environmental Protection Agency, 2012. Web. 5 Mar. 2012.

1 TITLE

Title of the Work
State the full title of the work cited, enclosed in quotation marks. Use a period before the closing quotation mark.

2 PUBLICATION INFORMATION

2a Title of the Overall Web Site
Provide the title of the Web site (italicized), followed by a period.

2b Publisher or Sponsor of the Web Site
Leave one space after the title of the overall Web site and provide the publisher or sponsor of the Web site. If this information is not available, use *N.p.* End with a comma.

2c Date of Publication
Provide the available date (day, month, and year) of publication, followed by a period. If no date is available, use *n.d.*

2d Medium of Publication
Provide the medium of publication consulted (Web), followed by a period.

2e Date of Access
Provide the day, month, and year that you accessed the article online. End with a period.

Provide as much information as you can, starting with the author, if available, and the title of the page, followed by the site information.

72. Academic Department Home Page

Writing. Dept. home page. Grand Valley State U. Web. 26 Feb. 2010.

73. Course Home Page

St. Germain, Sheryl. Myths and Fairytales: From *Inanna* to *Edward Scissorhands*. Course home page. Summer 2003. Dept. of English, Iowa State U. Web. 20 Feb. 2005.

74. Government or Institutional Web Site

Home Education and Private Tutoring. Pennsylvania Department of Education, 2005. Web. 5 Aug. 2013.

75. Online Discussion Posting

Firrantello, Larry. "Van Gogh on Prozac." Online posting. 23 May 2005. *Salon Table Talk*. Web. 7 June 2005.

Give the date of the posting and the name of the bulletin board, if any. Then give the publication medium, the access date and, in angle brackets, the URL if needed.

76. Chat or Real-Time Communication

Berzsenyi, Christyne. Online discussion of "Writing to Meet Your Match: Rhetoric, Perceptions, and Self-Presentation for Four Online Daters." *Computers and Writing Online*. AcadianaMoo, 13 May 2007. Web. 13 May 2013.

Glenn, Maria. Chat. *Laurence Smith*. Facebook, 9 Sept. 2010. Web. 9 Sept. 2010.

Give the name of the speaker or writer, a title for the event (if any), the Web page or forum, date, publication medium, access date, and URL if needed.

77. E-Mail Message

Martin, Tara. "Visit to Los Alamos." Message to David Sanz. 25 July 2010. E-mail.

78. Posting on a Blog

Phillips, Matthew. "Need to Go to the ER? Not Until the Game's Over." *Freakonomics*. Freakonomics, LLC, 15 June 2011. Web. 14 Aug. 2011.

79. Wiki

"NASCAR Sprint Cup Series." *NASCAR Wiki*. Wikia, 11 Jan. 2011. Web. 6 Apr. 2011.

80. Posting on Facebook or Twitter

Adler-Kassner, Linda. "Conversations toward Action." *Council of Writing Program Administrators*. Facebook, 5 Feb. 2010. Web. 6 May 2011.

Author. Title. Type of source. Publication information.

Adams, John Quincy (JQ Adams_MHS). "3|12|1812: Brancia called and read me
all the official Correspondence concerning the duels at Naples. An idle
day." 20 Mar. 2012, 2:09 p.m. Tweet.

Reproduce the entire tweet and the time you accessed it.

OTHER PRINT, NONPRINT, AND ELECTRONIC SOURCES

81. Published or Unpublished Letter

Irvin, William. Letter to Lesley Osburn. 7 Dec. 2011. MS.

Williams, William Carlos. Letter to his son. 13 Mar. 1935. *Letters of the Century:
America 1900–1999*. Ed. Lisa Grunwald and Stephen J. Adler. New York:
Dial, 1999: 225–26. Print.

Begin the entry with the author of the letter. Note the recipient, too. If the
letter is published in a periodical, a book, or online, follow the appropriate
citation format, shown here.

82. Microfiche Collection of Articles

Wenzell, Ron. "Businesses Prepare for a More Diverse Work Force." *St. Louis
Post Dispatch* 3 Feb. 1990: 17. Microform. *NewsBank: Employment* 27 (1990):
fiche 2, grid D12.

A microfiche is a transparent sheet of film (a *fiche*) with microscopic printing
that needs to be read through a special magnifier.

83. Report or Pamphlet

National Commission on Writing in America's Schools and Colleges. *The
Neglected "R": The Need for a Writing Revolution*. New York: College
Board, 2003. Print.

Use the format for books, to the extent possible, including whether you're
citing a print or digital version.

84. Legal Source

Brown v. Board of Educ. 347 US 483-96. Supreme Court of the US. 1954. Print.

Include the name of the case, the number of the case (preceded by *No.*), the
name of the court deciding the case, and the date of the decision. Legal sources
can frequently be accessed through a database:

Brown v. Board of Educ. 347 US 483-96. Supreme Court of the US. 1954.
LexisNexis Academic. Web. 25 Jan. 2013.

85. Interview

Friedman, Randi. Telephone interview. 30 Aug. 2013.

Winfrey, Oprah. "Ten Questions for Oprah Winfrey." By Richard Zoglin. *Time*
15 Dec. 2003: 8. Print.

MLA
14E

Pope, Carl. Interview by Amy Standen. *Salon.com*. Salon Media Group, 29 Apr.
2002. Web. 27 Jan. 2005.

Note the type of interview, for example "Telephone" or "Personal" (face-to-
face). For a published interview, give the name of the interviewed person first,
identify the source as an interview, and then give details as for any published
source: title; author (preceded by the word *By*); and publication details. Follow the citation format for a periodical, book, or Web source, as appropriate.

86. Lecture or Speech

Kennedy, John Fitzgerald. Greater Houston Ministerial Assn. Rice Hotel,
Houston. 12 Sept. 1960. Speech.

Katz, Jennifer. "Spiral Galaxies." Astronomy 1000. University of Denver,
Denver. 7 Feb. 2011. Lecture.

87. Live Performance (Play, Concert, Dance, etc.)

All My Sons. By Arthur Miller. Dir. Calvin McLean. Center for the Performing
Arts, Normal, IL. 27 Sept. 2005. Performance.

Nelson, Willie. Concert. Red Rocks Amphitheater, Denver. 22 June 2011.
Performance.

88. Work of Art, Original

Cassatt, Mary. *La Toilette*. 1890. Oil on canvas. Art Institute of Chicago.

Fourquet, Léon. *The Man with the Broken Nose*. 1865. Marble. Musée Rodin, Paris.

89. Musical Score

Schubert, Franz. *Unfinished Symphony*. 1822. Print.

Italicize any musical work that has a title, such as an opera, a ballet, or a named
symphony. Don't underline or put in quotation marks music identified only
by form, number, and key, as follows.

Schubert, Franz. Symphony no. 8 in B minor. 1822. Print.

To cite a published score, use the following format.

Schubert, Franz. *Symphony in B Minor (Unfinished)*. 1822. Ed. Martin Cusid.
New York: Norton, 1971. Print.

90. Advertisement

Southwest Airlines. Advertisement. ABC. 24 Aug. 2010. Television.

Canon Digital Cameras. Advertisement. *Time* 2 June 2003: 77. Print.

Samsung. Advertisement. *RollingStone*. Wenner Media, 8 Nov. 2005. Web. 11
Nov. 2005.

91. Video Game or Software

The Island: Castaway. N.p.: Awem Studio, 2010. Game.

"N.p." indicates that the place of publication is unknown.

92. Nonperiodical Publications on CD, DVD, or Magnetic Tape

Perl, Sondra. *Felt Sense: Guidelines for Composing*. Portsmouth: Boynton, 2004.
CD.

Citations for publications on DVD, CD-ROM, or other recording formats
follow guidelines for print publications, with two additions: list the publication medium (for example, *CD*), and give the vendor's name and date of issue.

93. PowerPoint or Similar Presentation

Delyser, Ariel. "Political Movements in the Philippines." University of Denver,
7 Feb. 2010. PowerPoint.

94. Work in More Than One Publication Medium

Shamoon, Linda, et al., eds. *Coming of Age: The Advanced Writing Curriculum*.
Coming of Age Course Descriptions. Portsmouth: Boynton, 2000. Print,
CD-ROM.

This book and CD-ROM come together. Each has its own title, but the publication information—Portsmouth: Boynton, 2000—applies to both.

14F What are MLA guidelines for content or bibliographic notes?

In MLA STYLE, footnotes or endnotes serve two specific purposes: (1) You can
use them for ideas and information that do not fit into your paper but are still
worth relating; and (2) you can use them for bibliographic information that
would intrude if you were to include it in your text. See 14G for advice about
formatting notes.

TEXT OF PAPER

Eudora Welty's literary biography, *One Writer's Beginnings*, shows us how
both the inner world of self and the outer world of family and place form a
writer's imagination.[1]

CONTENT NOTE—MLA

1. Welty, who valued her privacy, resisted investigation of her
life. However, at the age of seventy-four, she chose to present her own
autobiographical reflections in a series of lectures at Harvard University.

TEXT OF PAPER

Barbara Randolph believes that enthusiasm is contagious (65).[1] Many
psychologists have found that panic, fear, and rage spread more quickly
in crowds than positive emotions do, however.

BIBLIOGRAPHIC NOTE—MLA

1. Others who agree with Randolph include Thurman 21, 84, 155; Kelley 421–25; and Brookes 65–76.

14G What are MLA format guidelines for research papers?

Check whether your instructor has special instructions for the final draft of your research paper. If there are no special instructions, you can use the MLA STYLE guidelines here. The student paper in 14H was prepared according to MLA guidelines.

■ General formatting instructions—MLA

Use 8½-by-11-inch white paper. Double-space throughout. Use a one-inch margin on the left, right, top, and bottom. Don't justify the type.

Paragraph indents in the body of the paper and indents in Notes and Works Cited are ½ inch, or about five characters. The indent in Microsoft Word is a hanging indent of ½ inch for "first line." The indent for a set-off quotation (p. 226) is 1 inch, or about ten characters.

■ Order of parts—MLA

Use this order for the parts of your paper: body of the paper; endnotes, if any (headed "Notes," without quotation marks); Works Cited list; and attachments, if any (such as questionnaires, data sheets, or any other material your instructor tells you to include). Number all pages consecutively.

■ Name-and-page-number header for all pages—MLA

Use a header consisting of a name-and-page-number line on every page of your paper, including the first, unless your instructor requires otherwise. Most word-processing programs have an "insert header" or "view header" function that automatically places a header ½ inch from the top edge of the page. In the header, type your last name, then a one-character space, and then the page number. Align the header an inch from the right edge of the paper; in most word-processing programs, this is a "flush right" setting.

■ First page—MLA

Use a name-and-page number line. MLA doesn't require a cover page but understands that some instructors do, in which case you should follow your instructor's prescribed format.

If your instructor does not require a cover page, use a four-line heading at the top of the first page. Drop down 1 inch from the top of the page. Start each line at the left margin, and include the following information.

Your name (first line)

Your instructor's name (second line)

Your course name and section (third line)

The date you hand in your paper (fourth line)

On the line below this heading, center the title of your paper. Don't underline the title or enclose it in quotation marks. On the line below the title, start your paper.

❗ Capitalization Alerts: (1) Use a capital letter for the first word of your title and the first word of a subtitle, if you use one. Start every NOUN, PRO-NOUN, VERB, ADVERB, ADJECTIVE, and SUBORDINATING CONJUNCTION with a capital letter. Capitalize the last word of your title, no matter what part of speech it is. In a hyphenated compound word (two or more words used together to express one idea), capitalize every word that you would normally capitalize: Father-in-Law.

(2) Don't capitalize an article (*a, an, the*) unless one of the preceding capitalization rules applies to it. Don't capitalize any PREPOSITIONS, no matter how many letters they contain. Don't capitalize COORDINATING CONJUNCTIONS. Don't capitalize the word *to* used in an INFINITIVE. ●

■ Notes—MLA

If you use a note in your paper (p. 220), try to structure the sentence so that the note number falls at the end. The ideal place for a note number, which appears slightly raised above the line of words, is after the sentence-ending punctuation. Don't leave a space before the number. Word processing programs have commands for inserting "references" such as notes, and you'll want to choose endnotes rather than footnotes.

Your notes belong on a separate page after the last page of the body of your paper and before the Works Cited list. Center the word *Notes* at the top of the page, using the same 1-inch margin; don't underline it or enclose it in quotation marks.

Number the notes consecutively throughout the paper, except for notes accompanying tables or figures. Place table or figure notes below the table or illustration. Instead of note numbers, use raised lowercase letters: a, b, c.

■ Works Cited list—MLA

The Works Cited list starts on a new page that has the same name-and-page-number heading as the previous pages. One inch below the top edge of the page, center the words "Works Cited." Don't underline them or put them in quotation marks.

One double space after the Works Cited heading, start the first entry in your list at the left margin. If an entry takes more than one line, indent each subsequent line after the first by ½ inch. Use no extra spacing between entries.

14H   A student's MLA-style research paper

MLA style doesn't require an outline before a research paper. Nevertheless, many instructors want students to submit them. Most instructors prefer the standard traditional outline format that we discuss in 4G. Unless you're told otherwise, use that format.

Some instructors prefer what they consider a more contemporary outline format. Never use it unless it's explicitly assigned. It differs because it outlines the content of the INTRODUCTORY and CONCLUDING PARAGRAPHS, and full wording of the THESIS STATEMENT is placed in the outline of the introductory paragraph. We show an example of this type in the topic outline of Andrei Gurov's paper that follows.

MLA
14H

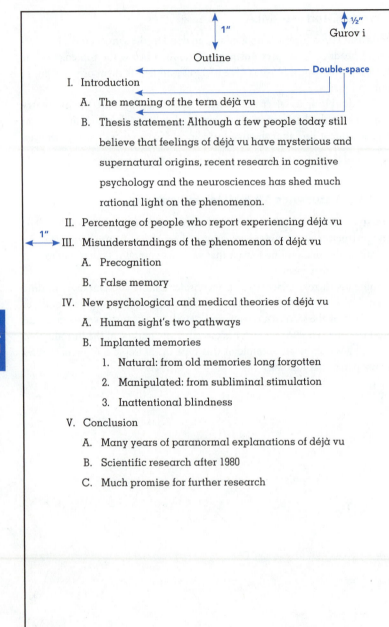

½″

Gurov i

1″

Outline

Double-space

I. Introduction

   A. The meaning of the term déjà vu

   B. Thesis statement: Although a few people today still believe that feelings of déjà vu have mysterious and supernatural origins, recent research in cognitive psychology and the neurosciences has shed much rational light on the phenomenon.

II. Percentage of people who report experiencing déjà vu

1″

III. Misunderstandings of the phenomenon of déjà vu

   A. Precognition

   B. False memory

IV. New psychological and medical theories of déjà vu

   A. Human sight's two pathways

   B. Implanted memories

      1. Natural: from old memories long forgotten

      2. Manipulated: from subliminal stimulation

      3. Inattentional blindness

V. Conclusion

   A. Many years of paranormal explanations of déjà vu

   B. Scientific research after 1980

   C. Much promise for further research

MLA
14H

1"

½"

Gurov 1

Andrei Gurov

Put identifying information in upper left corner.

Professor Ryan

Use ½-inch top margin, 1-inch bottom and side margins; double-space throughout.

English 101, Section A4

12 Dec. 2011

Déjà Vu: At Last a Subject for Serious Study

Center title.

"Brain hiccup" might be another name for *déjà vu*, French for "already seen." During a moment of déjà vu, a person relives an event that in reality is happening for the first time. The hiccup metaphor seems apt because each modern scientific explanation of the déjà vu phenomenon involves a doubled event, as this paper will demonstrate. However, such modern scientific work was long in coming. In his article "The Déjà Vu Illusion," today's leading researcher in the field, Alan S. Brown at Southern Methodist University, states that "for over 170 years, this most puzzling of memory illusions has intrigued scholars" but was hampered when "during the behaviorist era . . . the plethora of parapsychological and psychodynamic interpretations" multiplied rapidly (256). Thus, notions of the supernatural and magic halted the scientific study of déjà vu for almost two centuries. By the first quarter of the twentieth century, it began again slowly. Although a few people today still believe that feelings of déjà vu have mysterious or supernatural origins, recent research in cognitive psychology and the neurosciences has shed much rational light on the phenomenon.

Quotation marks around phrases show they appeared separately in the source.

The ellipsis indicates words omitted from a quotation.

MLA
14H

continued >>

(Proportions shown in this paper are adjusted to fit space limitations of this book. Follow actual dimensions discussed in this book along with your instructor's directions.)

Header has student's last name and page number.

Some people report never having experienced déjà vu, and the percentages vary for the number of people who report having lived through at least one episode of it. In 2004, Brown reports that of the subjects he has interviewed, an average of 66 percent say that they have had one or more déjà vu experiences during their lives (*Experience* 33). However, in early 2005 in "Strangely Familiar," Uwe Wolfradt reports that "various studies indicate that from 50 to 90 percent of the people [studied] can recall having had at least one such déjà vu incident in their lives."

This Web source has no page numbers or paragraph numbers.

Perhaps part of the reason for this variation in the range of percentages stems from a general misunderstanding of the phrase *déjà vu*, even by some of the earlier scientific researchers twenty or more years ago. Indeed, in today's society, people throw around the term *déjà vu* without much thought. For example, it is fairly common for someone to see or hear about an event and then say, "Wow. This is déjà vu. I had a dream that this exact same thing happened." However, dreaming about an event ahead of time is a different phenomenon known as *precognition*, which relates to the paranormal experience of extrasensory perception. To date, precognition has never been scientifically demonstrated. As Johnson explains about dreams, however,

Use block indent of 1-inch (about ten spaces) for a quotation longer than four typed lines.

> . . . there is usually very little "data," evidence, or documentation to confirm that a Precognition has taken place. If a person learns about some disaster and THEN [author's emphasis] tells people that he/she has foreseen it the day before, that may or may not be true, because there is usually not corroborative confirmation of what the person claims.

MLA 14H

continued >>

Gurov 3

Thus, precognition, a phenomenon talked about frequently but one that has never held up under scientific scrutiny, is definitely not the same as déjà vu.

False memory is another phenomenon mislabeled *déjà vu*. It happens when people are convinced that certain events took place in their lives, even though the events never happened. This occurs when people have strong memories of many unrelated occurrences that suddenly come together into a whole that's very close to the current experience. It seems like a déjà vu experience. This occurs from the

> converging elements of many different but related experiences. When this abstract representation, which has emerged strictly from the melding together of strongly associated elements, happens to correspond to the present experience, a déjà vu may be the outcome. (Brown, *Experience* 160)

To illustrate lab-induced false memory, Brown in *The Déjà Vu Experience* cites investigations in which subjects are shown lists of words related to sleep; however, the word *sleep* itself is not on the list. In recalling the list of words, most subjects insist that the word *sleep* was indeed on the list, which means that the memory of a word that was never there is false memory. This is exactly what happens when well-intentioned eyewitnesses believe they recall certain criminal acts even though, in fact, they never saw or experienced the events at all (159).

In the last twenty years especially, new theories have come to the fore as a result of rigorous work from psychological and medical points of view. In *Experience*, Brown surveys the literature and concludes that this relatively young field of investigation is dividing itself into four categories: (1) dual

Introductory phrase smoothly leads into direct quotation.

MLA 14H

Put only page number in parentheses when author is named in text.

continued >>

Gurov 4

processing, (2) memory, (3) neurological, and (4) attentional. This paper briefly discusses the first and second as each relates to the third. Next, I discuss the first as it relates to the second.

Brain-based studies of the human sense of sight are one heavily researched theory of déjà vu that has been partially explained in the last two decades. Such studies focus on the dual pathways by which the sight of an event reaches the brain (Glenn; Carey F1). For example, the left hemisphere processes information from the right eye and the right hemisphere processes information from the left eye. The brain is incapable of storing data with respect to time and is only able to "see" events in relation to others. Each eye interprets data separately, at the same precise time. According to research, the human brain can perceive two visual stimuli at one instant as long as they are "seen" less than 25 milliseconds apart. Since the human brain is capable of interpreting both signals within this time, when events are perceived normally, they are seen and recognized by the brain as one single event (Weiten 69, 97–99, 211).

Occasionally, however, the neurological impulses that carry data from each eye to the brain are delayed. As Johnson explains, the person might be fatigued or have had his or her attention seriously distracted (as when crossing the street at a dangerous intersection). As a result, one signal may reach the brain in under 25 milliseconds, while the other signal is slowed and reaches the brain slightly more than 25 milliseconds later. Even a few milliseconds' delay makes the second incoming signal arrive late—and, without fail, the brain interprets the stimuli as two separate events rather than one event. The person thus has the sensation of having seen the event before because the brain has recognized the milliseconds-later event as a memory.

MLA 14H

Put author and page number in parentheses when author is not named in the sentence.

Paragraph summarizes several pages of source material, as parenthetical citation shows.

continued >>

Implanted memories are another well-researched explanation for the déjà vu phenomenon. Examples of implanted memories originate in both the natural and the lab-induced experiences of people. For instance, perhaps a person walks into the kitchen of a new friend for the first time and, although the person has never been there before, the person feels certain that he or she has. With hypnosis and other techniques, researchers could uncover that the cupboards are almost exactly like those that the person had forgotten were in the kitchen of the person's grandparents' house and that the scent of baking apple pie is identical to the smell the person loved when walking into the grandparents' home during holidays (Carey F1). Colorado State University Professor Anne Cleary and her colleagues conducted an experiment in which students studied images of simple scenes and then were shown a second set of images. Some of the second set were made to resemble the original study images. Students tended to "remember" those scenes that had elements in common, even if they were not identical (1083).

Thomas McHugh, a researcher at MIT, believes he has even discovered the specific "memory circuit" in the brain that is the source of this kind of déjà vu (Lemonick). This circuit allows people to complete memories with just a single cue. For example, you can remember much about a football game you saw even if someone just mentions the two teams involved. Sometimes, however, the circuit "misfires," and it signals that a new memory is actually part of the pattern of an old one. Researchers Akira O'Connor, Colin Lever, and Chris Moulin claim that the false sensations of memory differ from those of familiarity. They call the former "déjà vécue," and

MLA
14H

continued >>

Gurov 6

note serious cases in which people live much of their life in this state. It remains to be seen whether their distinction will be confirmed.

Wolfradt describes a lab-induced experiment in which psychologist Larry L. Jacoby in 1989 manipulated a group of subjects so that he could implant a memory that would lead to a déjà vu experience for each of them. He arranged for his subjects to assemble in a room equipped with a screen in front. He flashed on the screen one word so quickly that no one was consciously aware they had seen the word. Jacoby was certain, however, that the visual centers of the brain of each subject had indeed "seen" the word. Later, when he flashed the word leaving it on the screen long enough for the subjects to consciously see it, everyone indicated they had seen the word somewhere before. All the subjects were firmly convinced that the first time they had seen the word, it absolutely was not on the screen at the front of the room they were in. Some became annoyed at being asked over and over. Since Jacoby's work, lab-induced memory research has become very popular in psychology. In fact, it has been given its own name: *priming*. Alan Brown and Elizabeth Marsh confirmed Jacoby's findings in three follow-up studies (38–41).

Inattention, or what some researchers call "inattentional blindness," is also an extensively researched explanation for the déjà vu experience. Sometimes people can see objects without any impediment right before them but still not process the objects because they're paying attention to something else (Brown, *Experience* 181). The distraction might be daydreaming, a sudden lowering of energy, or simply being drawn to another

continued >>

Gurov 7

object in the environment. As David Glenn explains in "The Tease of Memory":

> Imagine that you drive through an unfamiliar town but pay little attention because you're talking on a cellphone [sic]. If you then drive back down the same streets a few moments later, this time focusing on the landscape, you might be prone to experience déjà vu. During your second pass, the visual information is consciously processed in the hippocampus [of the brain] but feels falsely "old" because the images from your earlier drive still linger in your short term memory.

The busy lifestyle today would seem to lead to many distractions of perception and thus to frequent experiences of déjà vu; however, these are no more frequently reported than any other causes reported concerning déjà vu.

One compelling laboratory experiment studying inattention is described by Carey in "Déjà Vu: If It All Seems Familiar, There May Be a Reason." He recounts a test with many college students from Duke University in Durham, North Carolina. The students were asked to look at a group of photographs of the campus of Southern Methodist University in Dallas, Texas, that were flashed before them at a very quick speed. A small black or white cross was superimposed on each photograph, and the students were instructed to find the cross and focus on it (F6). Brown in *Experience* explains that the researchers assumed that the quick speed at which the photographs had been shown would result in no one's having noticed the background scenes. A week's time passed, and the same students were shown the pictures again, this

continued >>

MLA
14H

Gurov 8

time without the crosses. Almost all insisted that they had been to the college campus shown in the photos, which was physically impossible for that many students since they lived in Durham, North Carolina, and the college in the photographs was in Dallas, Texas (182–83). This means that the scenes in the photographs did indeed register in the visual memories of the students in spite of the quick speed and the distraction of looking only for the crosses.

Concluding paragraph summarizes paper.

The worlds of psychology and neurology have learned much since the age of paranormal interpretations of déjà vu experiences, starting around 1935. That is when rational science energetically began its disciplined investigations of brain-based origins of the déjà vu phenomenon. Concepts such as dual processing of sight, implanted memories, and inattentional blindness, among other theories, have gone far in opening the door to the possibilities of many more inventive theories to explain incidents of déjà vu. The leading researcher in the field today, Alan S. Brown, is among the strongest voices urging a vast expansion of investigations into this still relatively unexplored phenomenon. He is optimistic this will happen, given his whimsical remark to Carlin Flora of *Psychology Today*: "We are always fascinated when the brain goes haywire." Researchers conducting these studies might watch for the unsettling experiences of other investigators who "have had déjà vu about having déjà vu" (Phillips 29).

MLA
14H

continued >>

Gurov 9

Works Cited

Brown, Alan S. *The Déjà Vu Experience: Essays in Cognitive Psychology*. New York: Psychology, 2004. Print.

---. "The Déjà Vu Illusion." *Current Directions in Psychological Science* 13.6 (2004): 256–59. Print.

--- and Elizabeth J. Marsh. "Digging into Deja Vu: Recent Research on Possible Mechanisms." *The Psychology of Learning and Motivation: Advances in Research and Theory*. Ed. Brian H. Ross. Burlington: Academic, 2010, 33–62. *LexisNexis*. Web. 20 Nov. 2011.

Carey, Benedict. "Déjà Vu: If It All Seems Familiar, There May Be a Reason." *New York Times* 14 Sept. 2004: F1+. *LexisNexis*. Web. 11 Nov. 2011.

Cleary, Anne M., Anthony J. Ryals, and Jason S. Nomi. "Can Déjà Vu Result from Similarity to a Prior Experience? Support for the Similarity Hypothesis of Déjà Vu." *Psychonomic Bulletin & Review* 16.6 (2009): 1082–88. Web. 3 Dec. 2011.

Flora, Carlin. "Giving Déjà Vu Its Due." *Psychology Today* Mar.–Apr. 2005: 27. *Academic Search Premier*. Web. 7 Nov. 2011.

Glenn, David. "The Tease of Memory." *Chronicle of Higher Education* 23 July 2004: A12. Print.

Johnson, C. "A Theory on the Déjà Vu Phenomenon." *MB-soft.com*, 8 Dec. 2001. Web. 20 Nov. 2011.

Lemonick, Michael D. "Explaining Déjà Vu." *Time* 20 Aug. 2007. *Academic Search Premier*. Web. 5 Dec. 2011.

O'Connor, Akira R., Colin Lever, and Chris J.A. Moulin. "Novel Insights into False Recollection: A Model of Déjà Vécue." *Cognitive Neuropsychiatry* 15.1–3 (2010): 118–44. Web. 14 Nov. 2011.

Works Cited begins on a new page. Note that heading is centered.

Three hyphens indicate same author as entry above.

Double-space throughout.

MLA 14H

List sources in alphabetical order by last name.

continued >>

Gurov 10

Phillips, Helen. "Looks Familiar." *New Scientist* 201.2701 (2009):

28–31. Web. 20 Nov. 2011.

Weiten, Wayne. *Psychology: Themes and Variations*. Belmont:

Wadsworth, 2005. Print.

Wolfradt, Uwe. "Strangely Familiar." *Scientific American*

Mind 16.1 (2005): 32–37. *Academic Search Elite*. Web.

7 Nov. 2011.

15 APA-Style Documentation and Format

▪ ▪ ▪ ▪ ▪ ▪

Quick Points   You will learn to

➤ Cite sources in your writing using APA style in-text citations (see below).

➤ Cite sources at the end of your paper in a References list (see pp. 240–261).

➤ Format your paper according to APA guidelines (see pp. 262–273).

MyWritingLab™ Visit mywritinglab.com for more resources on APA-style documentation and format.

15A What is APA documentation style?

The American Psychological Association (APA) sponsors the **APA style**, a DOCUMENTATION system widely used in the social sciences. APA style has two equally important features that need to appear in research papers.

APA 15B

1. Within the body of your paper, use IN-TEXT CITATIONS, in parentheses, to acknowledge your SOURCES. Sections 15B and 15C explain the proper way to provide in-text citations.

2. At the end of the paper, provide a list of the sources you used—and only those sources. Title this list, which contains complete bibliographic information about each source, "References." Section 15E provides examples.

See 15G for a sample student paper in APA style.

15B What are APA in-text parenthetical citations?

APA style requires parenthetical in-text citations that identify a source by the author's name and the copyright year. If there is no author, use a shortened version of the title. In addition, APA style requires page numbers for DIRECT QUOTATIONS, but it recommends using them also for PARAPHRASES and SUMMARIES. Find out your instructor's preference to avoid any problems. Put page numbers in parentheses, using the abbreviation *p.* before a single page number and *pp.* when the material you're citing falls on more than one page. Separate the parts of a parenthetical citation with commas. End punctuation always follows the citation unless it's a long quotation set in block style.

If you refer to a work more than once in a paragraph, APA style recommends giving the author's name and the date at the first mention and then using only the name after that. However, if you're citing two or more works by the same author, include the date in each citation to identify which work you're citing. When two or more sources have the same last name, keep them clear by using both first and last names in the text or first initial(s) and last names in parentheses.

15C   What are APA examples for in-text citations?

This section shows how to cite various kinds of sources in the body of your paper. The directory in Quick Box 15.1 corresponds to the numbered examples in this section.

APA
15C

Quick Box 15.1   ■ ■ ■ ■ ■ ■

APA In-Text Citations Directory

1. Paraphrased or Summarized Source p. 236
2. Source of a Short Quotation p. 237
3. Source of a Long Quotation p. 237
4. One Author p. 237
5. Two Authors p. 237
6. Three, Four, or Five Authors p. 238
7. Six or More Authors p. 238
8. Author(s) with Two or More Works in the Same Year p. 238
9. Two or More Authors with the Same Last Name p. 238
10. Group or Corporate Author p. 239
11. Work Listed by Title p. 239
12. Two or More Sources in One Reference p. 239
13. Personal Communication, Including E-Mail and Other Nonretrievable Sources p. 239
14. Retrievable Online Sources p. 240
15. Sources with No Page Numbers p. 240
16. Source Lines for Graphics and Table Data p. 240

---

1. Paraphrased or Summarized Source

Modern technologies and social media tend to fragment individual identities (Conley, 2009).

Author name and date cited in parentheses.

Dalton Conley (2009) contends that modern technologies and social media fragment individual identities.

Author name cited in text; date cited in parentheses.

2. Source of a Short Quotation

Approaches adopted from business to treat students as consumers "do not necessarily yield improved outcomes in terms of student learning" (Arum & Roksa, 2011, p. 137).

Author names, date, and page reference cited in parentheses.

Arum & Roksa (2011) find that approaches adopted from business to treat students as consumers "do not necessarily yield improved outcomes in terms of student learning" (p. 137).

Author names cited in text, followed by the date cited in parentheses incorporated into the words introducing the quotation; page number in parentheses immediately following the quotation.

3. Source of a Long Quotation

When you use a quotation of forty or more words, set it off in block style indented ½ inch from the left margin. Don't use quotation marks. Place the parenthetical reference one space after the end punctuation of the quotation's last sentence.

APA
15C

> Although some have called for regulating online games, others see such actions as unwarranted:
>
> > Any activity when taken to excess can cause problems in a person's life, but it is unlikely that there would be legislation against, for example, people excessively reading or exercising. There is no argument that online gaming should be treated any differently. (Griffiths, 2010, pp. 38–39)

Author name, date, and page reference are cited in parentheses following the end punctuation.

4. One Author

One of his questions is, "What binds together a Mormon banker in Utah with his brother or other coreligionists in Illinois or Massachusetts?" (Coles, 1993, p. 2).

In a parenthetical reference in APA style, a comma and a space separate a name from a year and a year from a page reference.

5. Two Authors

Give both names in each citation.

One report describes 2,123 occurrences (Krait & Cooper, 2003).

The results that Krait and Cooper (2003) report would not support the conclusions Davis and Sherman (1999) draw in their review of the literature.

When you write a parenthetical in-text citation naming two (or more) authors, use an ampersand (&) between the final two names, but write out the word *and* for any reference in your own sentence.

6. Three, Four, or Five Authors

Use all the authors' last names in the first reference. In all subsequent references, use only the first author's last name followed by *et al.* (meaning "and others"). No period follows *et*, but one always follows *al.*

FIRST REFERENCE

In one study, only 30% of the survey population could name the most commonly spoken languages in five Middle Eastern countries (Ludwig, Rodriquez, Novak, & Ehlers, 2008).

SUBSEQUENT REFERENCE

Ludwig et al. (2008) found that most Americans could identify the language spoken in Saudi Arabia.

7. Six or More Authors

Name the first author followed by *et al.* in all in-text references, including the first.

These injuries can lead to an inability to perform athletically, in addition to initiating degenerative changes at the joint level (Mandelbaum et al., 2005).

8. Author(s) with Two or More Works in the Same Year

If you use more than one source written in the same year by the same author(s), alphabetize the works by title for the REFERENCES list, and assign letters in alphabetical order to each work: (2007a), (2007b), (2007c). Use the year–letter combination in parenthetical references. Note that a citation of two or more such works lists the year extensions in alphabetical order.

Most recently, Torrevillas (2007c) draws new conclusions from the results of eight experiments conducted with experienced readers (Torrevillas, 2007a, 2007b).

9. Two or More Authors with the Same Last Name

Include first initials for every in-text citation of authors who share a last name. Use the initials appearing in the References list. (In the second example, a parenthetical citation, the name order is alphabetical, as explained in item 12.)

R. A. Smith (2008) and C. Smith (1999) both confirm these results.

These results have been confirmed independently (C. Smith, 1999; R. A. Smith, 2008).

10. Group or Corporate Author

If you use a source in which the "author" is a corporation, agency, or group, an in-text reference gives that name as author. Use the full name in each citation, unless an abbreviated version of the name is likely to be familiar to your audience. In that case, use the full name and give its abbreviation at the first citation; then, use the abbreviation for subsequent citations.

> Although the space shuttle program has ended, other programs will continue to send Americans into space (National Aeronautics and Space Administration [NASA], 2011).

In subsequent citations, use the abbreviated form alone.

11. Work Listed by Title

If no author is named, use a shortened form of the title for in-text citations. Ignoring *A, An,* or *The,* make the first word the one by which you alphabetize the title in your References list. The following example refers to an article fully titled "Are You a Day or Night Person?"

> Scientists group people as "larks" or "owls" on the basis of whether individuals are more efficient in the morning or at night ("Are You," 1989).

12. Two or More Sources in One Reference

If more than one source has contributed to an idea or opinion in your paper, cite them alphabetically by author in one set of parentheses; separate each source of information with a semicolon.

> Conceptions of personal space vary among cultures (Morris, 1977; Worchel & Cooper, 1983).

13. Personal Communication, Including E-Mail and Other Nonretrievable Sources

Telephone calls, personal letters, interviews, and e-mail messages are "personal communications" that your readers can't access or retrieve. Acknowledge personal communications in parenthetical references, but never include them in your References list at the end of your paper.

> Recalling his first summer at camp, one person said, "The proximity of 12 other kids made me—an only child with older, quiet parents—frantic for eight weeks" (A. Weiss, personal communication, January 12, 2011).

14. Retrievable Online Sources

When you quote, paraphrase, or summarize an online source that is available to others, cite the author (if any) or title and the date as you would for a print source, and include the work in your References list.

> It is possible that similarity in personality is important in having a happy marriage (Luo & Clonen, 2005, p. 324).

15. Sources with No Page Numbers

If a source doesn't provide page numbers, use the paragraph number preceded by the abbreviation *para*. If there are no printed paragraph numbers, count down from the beginning of the document, or cite the closest subheading and count down paragraphs from that.

> (Daniels, 2010, para. 4)

> (Sanz, 2009, Introduction)

> (Herring, 2011)

16. Source Lines for Graphics and Table Data

If you use a graphic from another source or create a table using data from another source, provide a note at the bottom of the table or graphic, crediting the original author and the copyright holder. Here are examples of two source notes, one for a graphic using data from an article, the other for a graphic reprinted from a book.

GRAPHIC USING DATA FROM AN ARTICLE

Note. The data in columns 1 and 2 are from "Advance Organizers in Advisory Reports: Selective Reading, Recall, and Perception," by L. Lagerwerf et al., 2008, *Written Communication, 25*(1), p. 68. Copyright 2008 by Sage Publications.

GRAPHIC FROM A BOOK

Note. From *Academically Adrift: Limited Learning on College Campuses* (p. 97), by R. Arum and J. Roksa, 2011, Chicago: University of Chicago Press. Copyright 2011 by The University of Chicago.

15D   What are APA guidelines for a References list?

Include in the **References** list all the sources you quote, paraphrase, or summarize in your paper so that readers can find the same sources with reasonable effort. Never include in your References list any source that's not generally available to other people (see item 13 in 15C).

An APA References list needs to meet specific requirements in terms of its title, placement, contents and format, spacing, arrangement, type and order of elements included for each kind of entry, punctuation, capitalization, and so on. Quick Box 15.2 provides details.

Quick Box 15.2   ■ ■ ■ ■ ■ ■

Guidelines for an APA-style References list

TITLE
The title is "References," centered, without quotation marks, italics, or underlining.

PLACEMENT OF LIST
Start a new page numbered sequentially with the rest of the paper, immediately after the body of the paper.

CONTENTS AND FORMAT
Include all quoted, paraphrased, or summarized sources in your paper that are not personal communications; however, if your instructor tells you also to include all the references you have simply consulted, please do so. Start each entry on a new line, and double-space all lines. Use a *hanging indent* style: The first line of each entry begins flush left at the margin, and all other lines are indented ½ inch.

Wolfe, C. R. (2011). Argumentation across the curriculum. *Written Communication, 28,* 193–218.

SPACING AFTER PUNCTUATION
APA calls for one space after commas, periods, question marks, and colons. The exception is no space between "doi:" and the doi number. (See Quick Box 15.4.)

ARRANGEMENT OF ENTRIES
Alphabetize by the author's last name. If no author is named, alphabetize by the first significant word (ignore *A, An,* or *The*) in the title of the work.

AUTHORS' NAMES
Use last names, first initials, and middle initials, if any. Reverse the order for all authors' names, and use an ampersand (&) before the last author's name: Mills, J. F., & Holahan, R. H.

Give names in the order in which they appear on the work. Use a comma between each author's last name and first initial and after each complete name except the last. Use a period after the last author's name. When the author name is the same as the publisher, write "author" at the end of the citation.

continued >>

APA 15D

Quick Box 15.2   APA Guidelines (continued)   ■ ■ ■ ■ ■ ■

DATES

Date information follows the name information and is enclosed in parentheses. Place a period followed by one space after the closing parenthesis.

For books, articles in journals that have volume numbers, and many other print and nonprint sources, the year of publication or production is the date to use. For articles from most general-circulation magazines and newspapers, use the year followed by a comma and then the exact date that appears on the issue (month, month and day, or season, depending on the frequency of the publication). Capitalize any words in dates, and use no abbreviations.

CAPITALIZATION OF TITLES

For book, article, and chapter titles, capitalize the first word, the first word after a colon between a title and subtitle, and any proper nouns. For names of journals and proceedings of meetings, capitalize the first word; all NOUNS, VERBS, ADVERBS, and ADJECTIVES; and any other words four or more letters long.

SPECIAL TREATMENT OF TITLES OF SOURCES

Use no special treatment for titles of shorter works (poems, short stories, essays, articles, Web pages). Italicize titles of longer works (books, newspapers, journals, or Web sites). If an italic typeface is unavailable, underline the title and the end punctuation using one unbroken line.

Do not drop any words (such as *A*, *An*, or *The*) from the titles of periodicals such as newspapers, magazines, and journals.

ABBREVIATIONS OF MONTHS

Do not abbreviate the names of months in any context.

PAGE NUMBERS

Use all digits, omitting none. For references to books and newspapers only, use *p.* and *pp.* before page numbers. List all discontinuous pages, with numbers separated by commas: pp. 32, 44–45, 47–49, 53.

PUBLICATION INFORMATION

See 15E for how to cite articles from periodicals (both print or online), books (both print or digital), images and video, other Web sources, and miscellaneous sources.

15E What are APA examples for sources in a References list?

To find different types of citation models, use the decision-making flowchart shown in Figure 15.1. You can also use the directory of References citation models in Quick Box 15.3. We show more than 70 different citation models, but if you cannot find what you need in this section, check the APA Web site.

Figure 15.1   Decision-making flowchart for APA References citations.

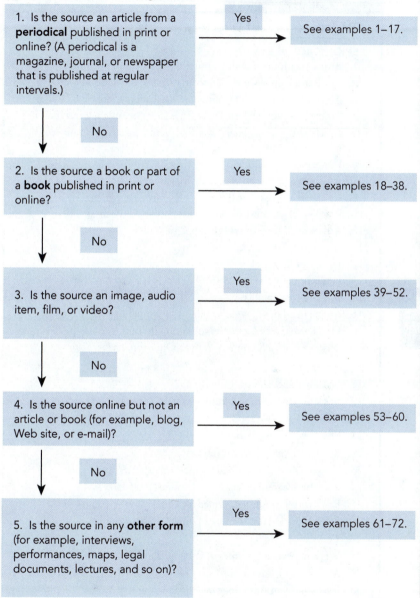

continued >>

APA 15E

Quick Box 15.3   References Directory (continued) ■ ■ ■ ■ ■ ■

APA
15E

continued >>

> ### Quick Box 15.3   References Directory (continued) ■ ■ ■ ■ ■ ■
>
> 70. Microfiche Collection of Articles p. 261
> 71. Musical Score p. 261
> 72. Nonperiodical Publications on CD, DVD, or Magnetic Tape p. 261

PERIODICALS—APA REFERENCES

Citations for periodical articles contain four major parts: author, date, title of article, and publication information (usually, the periodical title, volume number, page numbers, and sometimes a digital object identifier).

Quick Box 15.4 summarizes the basic entries for periodical articles. Variations on the basic entries follow the Quick Box.

> ### Quick Box 15.4   ■ ■ ■ ■ ■ ■
>
> ### Basic entries for periodical articles—APA
>
> #### 1. Articles with a DOI: Print or online
>
> A **DOI** (digital object identifier) is a numerical code sometimes assigned to journal articles. The DOI for an article will be the same even if the article appears in different versions, including print and online. (To see where you can find an article's DOI, refer to Figure 15.2.) If a source contains a numeric DOI, simply conclude the citation with the letters "doi" followed by a colon, then the number.
>
> AUTHOR   DATE   ARTICLE TITLE
>
> Agliata, A. K., Tantelff-Dunn, S., & Renk, K. (2007). Interpretation of
>
>   PUBLICATION INFORMATION
>
> teasing during early adolescence. *Journal of Clinical Psychology,*
>
>   DOI
>
> 63(1), 23–30. doi:10.1002/jclp.20302
>
> Recent sources may show the DOI in the form of a URL: http://dx.doi.org/xxxxx. If the source you are consulting uses this format, include the URL at the end of the citation:
>
> AUTHOR   DATE   ARTICLE TITLE
>
> McElroy, B. W., & Lubich, B. H. (2013). Predictors of course outcomes:
>
>   MAGAZINE TITLE
>
> Early indicators of delay in online classrooms. *Distance Education,*
>
> VOLUME
> NUMBER   ONLINE RETRIEVAL INFORMATION
>
> 34(1). http://dx.doi.org/10.1080/01587919.2013.770433
>
> continued >>

Quick Box 15.4   Periodical entries (continued)   ■ ■ ■ ■ ■ ■

2. Articles with no DOI: Print

For print articles without a DOI, use this format.

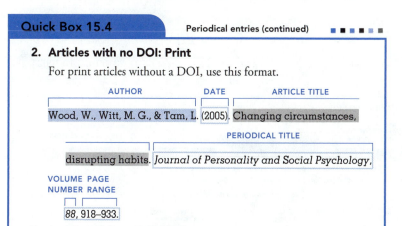

3. Articles with no DOI: Online

For online articles without a DOI, retrieval information begins with the words "Retrieved from," then the URL of the periodical's Web home page, and, occasionally, additional information. If you found the article through an online subscription database, do a Web search for the URL of the periodical's home page on the Web, and include the home page URL. If you can't find the periodical's Web home page, then name the database in your retrieval statement: Retrieved from Academic Search Premier database. (See citation 20.) If a URL must be divided between two or more lines, only break the address before slashes or punctuation marks.

Retrieval date: Include the date you retrieved the information only if the item does not have a publication date, is from an online reference book, or is likely to be changed in the future (such as a prepublication version of an article, a Web page, or a Wiki; see citation 58).

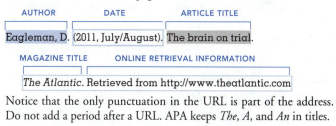

Notice that the only punctuation in the URL is part of the address. Do not add a period after a URL. APA keeps *The*, *A*, and *An* in titles.

APA 15E

1. Article in a Journal with Continuous Pagination: Print

Williams, B. T. (2010). Seeking new worlds: The study of writing beyond our classrooms. *College Composition and Communication, 62,* 127–146.

Continuous pagination means that page numbers in each issue of a volume begin where the page numbers in the previous issue left off. So, for example, if issue one stopped at page 125, issue two would start at page 126. Just give the volume number, italicized, after the journal title.

Figure 15.2 Journal article available (a) online and (b) in print, with a DOI.

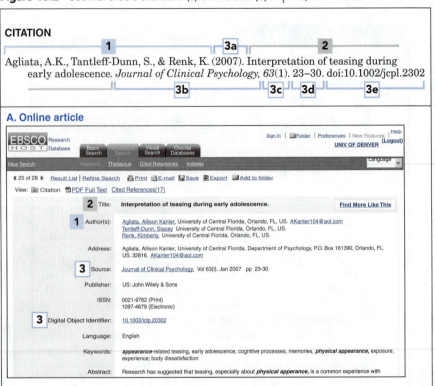

CITATION

1   3a   2

Agliata, A.K., Tantleff-Dunn, S., & Renk, K. (2007). Interpretation of teasing during early adolescence. *Journal of Clinical Psychology, 63*(1). 23–30. doi:10.1002/jcpl.2302

3b   3c   3d   3e

A. Online article

EBSCO HOST | Research Database

Sign In | Folder | Preferences | New Features; | Help
UNIV OF DENVER (Logout)

Basic Search | Search | Visual Search | Choose Databases

New Search   Keyword   Thesaurus   Cited References   Indexes   Language

◀ 25 of 28 ▶   Result List | Refine Search   🖶 Print   ✉ E-mail   💾 Save   📤 Export   Add to folder

View: 📖 Citation   📄 PDF Full Text   Cited References(17)

2 Title:	**Interpretation of teasing during early adolescence.**	**Find More Like This**
1 Author(s):	Agliata, Allison Kanler, University of Central Florida, Orlando, FL, US. AKanter104@aol.com Tentleff-Dunn, Stacey University of Central Florida, Orlando, FL, US. Renk, Kimberly, University of Central Florida, Orlando, FL, US.	
Address:	Agliata, Allison Kanter, University of Central Florida, Department of Psychology, P.O. Box 161390, Orlando, FL. US. 32816. AKanter104@aol.com	
3 Source:	Journal of Clinical Psychology, Vol 63(I), Jan 2007 pp 23-30	
Publisher:	US: John Willey & Sons	
ISSN:	0021-9762 (Print) 1097-4679 (Electronic)	
3 Digital Object Identifier:	10.1002/iclp.20302	
Language:	English	
Keywords:	*appearance*-related teasing, early adolescence, cognitive processes, memories, *physical appearance*, exposure, experience; body dissatisfaction	
Abstract:	Research has suggested that teasing, especially about *physical apperance*, is a common experience with	

1 AUTHOR INFORMATION

Name of Author
Write author's last name, comma, initials.
For two or more authors, separate with a comma
and use & before last author's name.

2 TITLE INFORMATION

Article Title
State the full title. Use capital letters for the
first word and proper nouns only.

2. Article in a Journal with Continuous Pagination: Online, with DOI

Gurung, R., & Vespia, K. (2007). Looking good, teaching well? Linking liking, looks, and learning. *Teaching of Psychology, 34*, 5–10. doi:10.1207 /s15328023top3401_2

3. Article in a Journal with Continuous Pagination: Online, no DOI

Pollard, R. (2002). Evidence of a reduced home field advantage when a team moves to a new stadium. *Journal of Sports Sciences, 20*, 969–974. Retrieved from http://www.tandf.co.uk/journals/rjsp

No retrieval date is included because the final version of the article is being referenced.

B. Print article

Interpretation of Teasing During Early Adolescence [2]

Allison Kanter Agliata, Stacey Tantleff-Dunn, [1]
and Kimberly Renk
University of Central Florida

Research has suggested that teasing, especially about physical appearance, is a common experience with negative consequences for adolescents. This study aimed to examine the cognitive processes of adolescents exposed to teasing. Students from two middle schools were assigned randomly to view videotaped vignettes of appearance-related teasing, competency teasing, or a control situation and completed questionnaires to assess their cognitive reactions and memories of the teasing. Results indicated that adolescent girls recalled appearance-related teasing more readily than competency teasing, adolescent girls with high body dissatisfaction recalled fewer positive appearance words, and participants exposed to competency teasing were

Correspondence concerning this article should be addressed to: Allison Kanter Agliata, University of Central Florida, Department of Psychology, P.O. Box 161390, Orlando, FL 32816; e-mail: AKanter104@aol.com

[3]

JOURNAL OF CLINICAL PSYCHOLOGY, Vol. 63(1), 23–30 (2007) © 2007 Wiley Periodicals, Inc.
Published online in Wiley InterScience (www.interscience.wiley.com). DOI: 0.1002/jclp.20302

WILEY InterScience®
DISCOVER SOMETHING GREAT

[3] **PUBLICATION INFORMATION**

3a Date
3b Journal title
3c Volume and issue number
3d Page range
3e DOI (Digital Object Identifier)

4. Article in a Journal That Pages Each Issue Separately: Print

Peters, B. (2011). Lessons about writing to learn from a university–high school partnership. *WPA: Writing Program Administration, 34*(2), 59–88.

Give the volume number, italicized, with the journal title, followed by the issue number in parentheses (not italicized), and the page number(s).

5. Article in a Journal That Pages Each Issue Separately: Online, with no DOI

Peters, B. (2011). Lessons about writing to learn from a university–high school partnership. *WPA: Writing Program Administration, 34*(2). Retrieved from http://wpacouncil.org/journal/index.html

6. In-press Article: Online

George, S. (in press). How accurately should we estimate the anatomical source of exhaled nitric oxide? *Journal of Applied Physiology*. doi:10.1152 / japplphysiol.00111.2008. Retrieved February 2008 from http://jap.physiology .org/papbyrecent.shtml

In press means that an article has been accepted for publication but has not yet been published in its final form. Therefore, there is no publication date, so although the article has a DOI, it also has a "retrieved from" statement that includes a date, in case anything changes.

7. Article in a Weekly or Biweekly Magazine: Print

Foroohar, R. (2011, June 27). Why the world isn't getting smaller. *Time*, 20.

Give the year, month, and date. If no author is listed, begin with the title of the article.

The price is wrong. (2003, August 2). *The Economist, 368*, 58–59.

8. Article in a Weekly or Biweekly Magazine: Online

Foroohar, R. (2011, June 27). Why the world isn't getting smaller. *Time*.
Retrieved from http://www.time.com/time/

9. Article in a Monthly or Bimonthly Periodical: Print

Goetz, T. (2011, July). The feedback loop. *Wired, 19*(7), 126–133.

Give the year and month(s). Insert the volume number, italicized with the periodical title. Put the issue number in parentheses; do not italicize it.

10. Article in a Newspaper: Print

Hesse, M. (2011, April 24). Love among the ruins. *The Washington Post*, p. F1.

Use the abbreviation *p*. (or *pp*. for more than one page) for newspapers. If no author is listed, begin with the title of the article.

Prepping for uranium work. (2011, June 18). *The Denver Post*, p. B2.

11. Article in a Newspaper: Online

Hesse, M. (2011, April 22). Falling in love with St. Andrews, Scotland. *The Washington Post*. Retrieved from http://www.washingtonpost.com/

Give the URL from the newspaper's Web site.

12. Unsigned Editorial

Editorial: Primary considerations. [Editorial]. (2008, January 27). *The Washington Post*, p. B6.

13. Letter to the Editor

Ennis, H. B. (2007, December 22). [Letter to the editor]. *U.S. News and World Report*. Retrieved from http://www.usnews.com

14. Book Review

Shenk, D. (2003, Spring). Toolmaker, brain builder. [Review of the book *Beyond Deep Blue: Building the computer that defeated the world chess champion* by Feng-Hsiung Hsu]. *The American Scholar, 72*, 150–152.

15. Article in a Looseleaf Collection of Reprinted Articles

Hayden, T. (2002). The age of robots. In E. Goldstein (Ed.), *Applied Science 2002. SIRS 2002*, Article 66. (Reprinted from *U.S. News & World Report*, pp. 44–50, 2001, April 23).

16. Online Magazine Content Not Found in Print Version

Shulman, M. (2008, January 3). 12 diseases that altered history. [Supplemental material]. *U.S. News & World Report*. Retrieved from http://health.usnews .com/

17. Abstract as a Secondary Source: Online

Walther, J. B., Van Der Heide, B., Kim, S., Westerman, D., & Tong, S. (2008). The role of friends' appearance and behavior on evaluations of individuals on Facebook: Are we known by the company we keep? *Human Communication Research 34*(1), 28–49. Abstract retrieved from PsycINFO database.

APA 15E

BOOKS—APA REFERENCES

Quick Box 15.5 summarizes the basic entry for books, both print and electronic. Variations on the basic entries follow. Where to locate a book's citation information is shown in Figure 15.3 (page 253).

Quick Box 15.5   ■ ■ ■ ■ ■ ■

Basic entries for books—APA

All citations for books have four main parts: author, date, title, and publication information. For traditional print books, publication information includes place of publication and the name of the publisher. For electronic versions of books, publication information also includes retrieval information.

PLACE OF PUBLICATION
For US publishers, give the city and state, using two-letter postal abbreviations listed in most dictionaries. For publishers in other countries, give city and country spelled out. However, if the state or country is part of the publisher's name, omit it after the name of the city.

continued >>

Quick Box 15.5   Book entries (continued) ■ ■ ■ ■ ■ ■

PUBLISHERS

Use a shortened version of the publisher's name except for an association, corporation, or university press. Drop *Co., Inc., Publishers*, and the like, but retain *Books* or *Press*.

AUTHOR   DATE   TITLE

Wood, G. S. (2011). *The idea of America: Reflections on the birth of the*

PUBLICATION INFORMATION

United States. New York, NY: Penguin Press.

RETRIEVAL INFORMATION FOR ELECTRONIC BOOKS

If a book has a DOI (Digital Object Identifier), include that number or URL after the title. Most electronic books do not have a DOI. When there is no DOI, use "Retrieved from" followed by the URL where you accessed the book.

18. Book by One Author: Print

Turkle, S. (2011). *Alone together: Why we expect more from technology and less from each other.* New York: Basic Books.

19. Book by One Author: Online

Turkle, S. (2007). *Evocative objects: Things we think with.* Retrieved from
    http://0-site.ebrary.com.bianca.penlib.du.edu/

Some books are increasingly available through library databases. APA does not include the name or location of the publisher in citations for online books.

20. Book by One Author: E-book or E-reader

Hertsgaard, M. (2011). *Hot: Living through the next fifty years on Earth.* [Kindle version]. Retrieved from http://www.amazon.com

The name of the version appears in brackets following the title, for example [Kindle version] or [Nook version]. "Retrieved from" precedes the URL of the site from which you downloaded the book.

21. Book by Two Authors

Edin, K., & Kefalas, M. (2005). *Promises I can keep: Why poor women put motherhood before marriage.* Berkeley: University of California Press.

Figure 15.3 Citation information for a print book—APA.

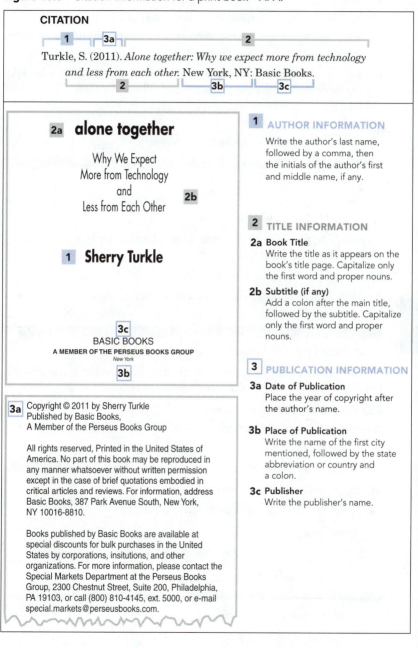

CITATION

1 **3a** **2**

Turkle, S. (2011). *Alone together: Why we expect more from technology and less from each other.* New York, NY: Basic Books.

2 **3b** **3c**

2a **alone together**

Why We Expect
More from Technology
and
Less from Each Other **2b**

1 **Sherry Turkle**

3c
BASIC BOOKS
A MEMBER OF THE PERSEUS BOOKS GROUP
New York
3b

3a Copyright © 2011 by Sherry Turkle
Published by Basic Books,
A Member of the Perseus Books Group

All rights reserved, Printed in the United States of America. No part of this book may be reproduced in any manner whatsoever without written permission except in the case of brief quotations embodied in critical articles and reviews. For information, address Basic Books, 387 Park Avenue South, New York, NY 10016-8810.

Books published by Basic Books are available at special discounts for bulk purchases in the United States by corporations, insitutions, and other organizations. For more information, please contact the Special Markets Department at the Perseus Books Group, 2300 Chestnut Street, Suite 200, Philadelphia, PA 19103, or call (800) 810-4145, ext. 5000, or e-mail special.markets@perseusbooks.com.

1 **AUTHOR INFORMATION**

Write the author's last name, followed by a comma, then the initials of the author's first and middle name, if any.

2 **TITLE INFORMATION**

2a Book Title
Write the title as it appears on the book's title page. Capitalize only the first word and proper nouns.

2b Subtitle (if any)
Add a colon after the main title, followed by the subtitle. Capitalize only the first word and proper nouns.

3 **PUBLICATION INFORMATION**

3a Date of Publication
Place the year of copyright after the author's name.

3b Place of Publication
Write the name of the first city mentioned, followed by the state abbreviation or country and a colon.

3c Publisher
Write the publisher's name.

22. Book by Three to Seven Authors

Lynam, J. K., Ndiritu, C. G., & Mbabu, A. N. (2004). *Transformation of agricultural research systems in Africa: Lessons from Kenya.* East Lansing: Michigan State University Press.

For a book by three to seven authors, include all the names. For a book by eight or more authors, use the first six names followed by three ellipsis points and then the last author's name: Smith, A., Jones, B., Ramos, C., Abrams, D., Sagan, E., Chin, F. . . . Havel, J.

23. Two or More Books by the Same Author(s)

Jenkins, H. (1992). *Textual poachers: Television fans and participatory culture.* New York, NY: Routledge.

Jenkins, H. (2006). *Convergence culture: Where old and new media collide.* New York, NY: New York University Press.

References by the same author are arranged chronologically, with the earlier date of publication listed first.

24. Book by a Group or Corporate Author

American Psychological Association. (2010). *Publication manual of the American Psychological Association* (6th ed.). Washington, DC: Author.

Boston Women's Health Collective. (1998). *Our bodies, ourselves for the new century.* New York: Simon & Schuster.

Cite the full name of the corporate author first. If the author is also the publisher, use the word *Author* as the name of the publisher.

25. Book with No Author Named

The Chicago manual of style (16th ed.). (2010). Chicago, IL: University of Chicago Press.

This would be alphabetized under *Chicago*, the first important word in the title.

26. Book with an Author and an Editor

Stowe, H. B. (2010). *Uncle Tom's cabin* (E. Ammons, Ed.). New York, NY: Norton.

27. Translation

Nesbo, J. (2011). *The leopard* (D. Bartlett, Trans.) New York, NY: Vintage.

28. Work in Several Volumes or Parts

Chrisley, R. (Ed.). (2000). *Artificial intelligence: Critical concepts* (Vols. 1–4). London, England: Routledge.

29. Anthology or Edited Book

Purdy, J. L., & Ruppert, J. (Eds.). (2001). *Nothing but the truth: An anthology of Native American literature.* Upper Saddle River, NJ: Prentice Hall.

APA
15E

30. Selection in an Anthology or an Edited Book

Trujillo, L. (2004). Balancing act. In R. Moreno & M. H. Mulligan (Eds.),
 Borderline personalities: A new generation of Latinas dish on sex, sass,
 and cultural shifting (pp. 61–72). New York, NY: HarperCollins.

To refer to an anthology, see example 29 or the Chaudhuri citation in example 31.

31. Selection in a Work Already Listed in References

Bond, R. (2004). The night train at Deoli. In A. Chaudhuri (Ed.), *The Vintage book*
 of modern Indian literature (pp. 415–418). New York, NY: Vintage Books.

Chaudhuri, A. (Ed.). (2004). *The Vintage book of modern Indian literature.* New
 York, NY: Vintage Books.

Provide full information for the already cited anthology (first example), along
with information about the individual selection. Put entries in alphabetical
order.

32. Second or Later Edition

Modern Language Association. (2009). *MLA handbook for writers of research*
 papers (7th ed.). New York, NY: Author.

Any edition number appears on the title page.

33. Introduction, Preface, Foreword, or Afterword

Hesse, D. (2004). Foreword. In D. Smit, *The end of composition studies* (pp. ix–xiii).
 Carbondale: Southern Illinois University Press.

If you're citing an introduction, preface, foreword, or afterword, give its
author's name first. After the year, give the name of the part cited. If the writer
of the material you're citing isn't the author of the book, use the word *In* and
the author's name before the title of the book.

34. Reprint of an Older Book

Coover, R. (2007). *A night at the movies, or, you must remember this.*
 Champaign: Dalkey Archive, 2007. (Original work published 1987)

35. Government Publication

U.S. Congress. House Subcommittee on Health and Environment of the
 Committee on Commerce. (1999). *The nursing home resident protection*
 amendments of 1999 (99-0266-P). Washington, DC: U.S. Government
 Printing Office.

36. Published Proceedings of a Conference

Rocha, L., Yaeger, L., Bedau, M., Floreano, D., Goldstone, R., & Vespignani, A.
 (Eds.). (2006, June). *Artificial Life X: Proceedings of the Tenth International*
 Conference on the Simulation and Synthesis of Living Systems.
 Bloomington, IN. Cambridge, MA: MIT Press.

APA
15E

37. Thesis or Dissertation

Stuart, G. A. (2006). *Exploring the Harry Potter book series: A study of adolescent reading motivation*. Retrieved from ProQuest Digital Dissertations. (AAT 3246355)

The number in parentheses at the end is the accession number.

38. Entry from Encyclopedia: Print or Online

Ireland. (2002). In *The new Encyclopædia Britannica: Macropaedia* (15th ed., Vol. 21, pp. 997–1018). Chicago, IL: Encyclopaedia Britannica.

Turing test. (2008). In *Encyclopædia Britannica*. Retrieved from http://www.britannica.com/bps/topic/609757/Turing-test

IMAGES, AUDIO, FILM, AND VIDEO

39. Photograph, Painting, Drawing, Illustration, etc.: Original

Cassatt, Mary. (1890). *La toilette*. [Painting]. Art Institute of Chicago.

Fourquet, Léon. (1865). *The man with the broken nose*. [Sculpture]. Paris, France: Musée Rodin.

Mydans, C. (1999, October 21–November 28). *General Douglas MacArthur landing at Luzon, 1945* [Photograph]. New York, NY: Soho Triad Fine Art Gallery.

This form is for original works appearing in a gallery, museum, private collection, etc. The date in the third example shows that the work appeared only for a brief period, in this case at the Soho Triad Fine Art Gallery.

40. Photograph, Painting, Drawing, Illustration, etc. in a Periodical

Greene, H. *Grace Slick*. (2004, September 30). [Photograph]. *Rolling Stone*, 102.

41. Photograph, Painting, Drawing, Illustration, etc. in a Book

The world's most populous countries. (2004). [Illustration]. In P. Turchi, *Maps of the imagination: The writer as cartographer* (pp. 116–117). San Antonio, TX: Trinity University Press.

Indicate the type of image in brackets following the title or, as in this example, the date.

42. Comic or Cartoon

Sutton, W. (2011, May 2). *Ryan's a late adopter*. [Cartoon]. *The New Yorker*, 87(11), 64.

43. Photo Essay

Nachtwey, J. (2006, December 2). *Crime in middle America*. [Photo essay]. *Time*. Retrieved from http://www.time.com

44. Image from a Social Networking Site

Gristellar, F. (2009, August 7). *The Gateway Arch*. [Photograph]. Retrieved from
https://www.facebook.com/qzprofile.php?id=7716zf92444

45. Map, Chart, or Other Graphic: Online

Hurricane Rita. (2005, September 24) [Graphic]. *New York Times
Online*. Retrieved from http://www.nytimes.com/packages/html
/national/20050923_RITA_GRAPHIC/index.html

46. Audio Book

Turkle, S. (2011). *Alone together: Why we expect more from technology and less
from each other*. [MP3-CD]. Old Saybrook, CT: Tantor Media.

47. Sound Recording

Verdi, G. (1874). Requiem. [Recorded by R. Muti (Conductor) and the Chicago
Symphony Orchestra and Chorus]. On *Requiem* [CD]. Chicago: CSO
Resound. (2010)

Winehouse, A. (2007). Rehab. On *Back to Black* [MP3]. Universal Republic
Records. Retrieved from http://amazon.com

48. Audio Podcast

Blumberg, A., & Davidson, D. (Producers). (2008, May 9). *The giant pool of
money*. [Audio podcast]. Retrieved from http://thisamericanlife.org

APA
15E

49. Film, Videotape, or DVD

Capra, F. (Director/Producer). (1934). *It happened one night* [Motion picture].
United States: Columbia Pictures.

Madden, J. (Director), Parfitt, D., Gigliotti, D., Weinstein, H., Zwick, E., &
Norman, M. (Producers). (2003). *Shakespeare in love* [DVD]. United States:
Miramax. (Original motion picture released 1998)

50. Video: Online

For video downloads, include the download date and the source.

Capra, F. (Director/Producer). (2010). *It happened one night* [Video file].
United States: Columbia Pictures. Retrieved from Netflix. (Original
motion picture released 1934)

Wesch, M. (2007, January 31). *Web 2.0 . . . the machine is us/ing us* [Video file].
Retrieved from http://www.youtube.com/watch?v=6gmP4nk0EOE

51. Broadcast Television or Radio Program

Burns, K. (Writer/Producer), & Barnes, P. (Producer). (1999, November 8). *Not for
ourselves alone: The story of Elizabeth Cady Stanton and Susan B. Anthony*
[Television broadcast]. New York, NY: Public Broadcasting Service.

52. Television or Radio Program: Online

Stewart, J. (Performer). (2011, June 1). Bill Moyers. *The Daily Show*. [Video file].
Retrieved from http://www.hulu.com

The disappearing incandescent bulb. (2011, June 20). *The Madeleine
Brand Show*. [Radio recording]. KPCC, Pasadena. Retrieved
from http://www.scpr.org/programs/madeleine-brand/2011/06/20
/the-disappearing-incandescent-bulb/

Give the name of the writer, director, or performer, if available; the date; the
title of the episode; the title of the program or series; the type of recording;
and retrieval information. Because the second source may be difficult to find,
the URL is listed.

OTHER ONLINE SOURCES

Because Web sites may change, the retrieval statement includes the date
retrieved as well as the URL. This example has no author.

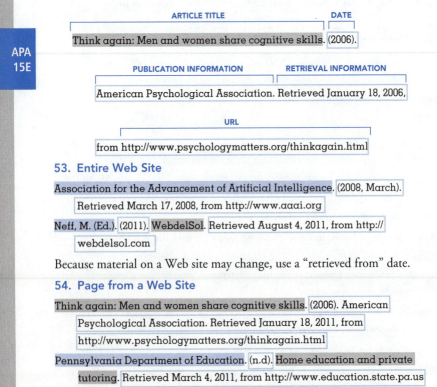

ARTICLE TITLE   DATE

Think again: Men and women share cognitive skills. (2006).

PUBLICATION INFORMATION   RETRIEVAL INFORMATION

American Psychological Association. Retrieved January 18, 2006,

URL

from http://www.psychologymatters.org/thinkagain.html

53. Entire Web Site

Association for the Advancement of Artificial Intelligence. (2008, March).
Retrieved March 17, 2008, from http://www.aaai.org

Neff, M. (Ed.). (2011). WebdelSol. Retrieved August 4, 2011, from http://
webdelsol.com

Because material on a Web site may change, use a "retrieved from" date.

54. Page from a Web Site

Think again: Men and women share cognitive skills. (2006). American
Psychological Association. Retrieved January 18, 2011, from
http://www.psychologymatters.org/thinkagain.html

Pennsylvania Department of Education. (n.d). Home education and private
tutoring. Retrieved March 4, 2011, from http://www.education.state.pa.us
/portal/server.pt/community/home_education_and_private_tutoring/20311

In the second example, "n.d." indicates there was no date given. The retrieval information, however, contains a date.

55. Real-Time Online Communication

Berzsenyi, C. (2007, May 13). Writing to meet your match: Rhetoric, perceptions, and self-presentation for four online daters. *Computers and Writing Online*. [Synchronous discussion]. Retrieved from http://acadianamoo.org

If a chat, discussion, or synchronous (meaning available as it is happening) online presentation can be retrieved by others, include it in your References list.

56. E-Mail Message

Because e-mails to individuals cannot be retrieved by others, they should not appear on the References list. Cite them in the body of your paper, as in this example:

> The wildfires threatened several of the laboratory facilities at Los Alamos (T. Martin, personal communication, June 20, 2011).

57. Posting on a Blog

Phillips, M. (2011, June 15). Need to go to the ER? Not until the game's over. [Web log post]. Retrieved from http://www.freakonomics.com/2011/06/15 /need-to-go-to-the-er-not-until-the-games-over/

58. Wiki

NASCAR Sprint Cup series. (2011). [Wiki]. Retrieved April 6, 2011, from http://nascarwiki.com

Machine learning. (n.d.) Retrieved January 5, 2008, from Artificial Intelligence Wiki: http://www.ifi.unizh.ch/ailab/aiwiki/aiw.cgi

N.d. means "no date." Because a Wiki can change by its very nature, always include a retrieval date.

59. Posting on Facebook

Adler-Kassner, L. (2011, May 6). Conversations toward action. [Facebook group]. Retrieved from Council of Writing Program Administrators at https://www.facebook.com/groups/106575940874

Include the citation in your References list only if it is retrievable by others. If it's not, cite it only in the body of your paper, as in example 56.

60. Message on an Online Forum, Discussion Group, or Electronic Mailing List

Firrantello, L. (2005, May 23). Van Gogh on Prozac. *Salon Table Talk*. [Online forum posting]. Retrieved February 15, 2009, from http://www.salon.com

Boyle, F. (2002, October 11). Psyche: Cemi field theory: The hard problem made easy [Discussion group posting]. Retrieved from news://sci.psychology .consciousness

Haswell, R. (2005, October 17). A new graphic/text interface. [Electronic mailing list message]. Retrieved May 20, 2011, from http://lists.asu.edu/archives /wpa-l.html

APA advises using *electronic mailing list*, as Listserv is the name of specific software.

OTHER SOURCES

61. Letters

Williams, W. C. (1935). [Letter to his son]. In L. Grunwald & S. J. Adler (Eds.), *Letters of the century: America 1900–1999* (pp. 225–226). New York, NY: Dial Press.

In the APA system, unpublished letters are considered personal communications inaccessible to general readers, so they do not appear in the References list. They are cited only in the body of the paper (see example 56). Letters that have been published or can be retrieved by others are cited as above.

62. Report, Pamphlet, or Brochure

National Commission on Writing in America's Schools and Colleges. (2003). *The neglected "R": The need for a writing revolution* (Report No. 2). New York, NY: College Board.

U.S. Department of Agriculture. (2007). *Organic foods and labels* [Brochure]. Retrieved December 8, 2008, from http://www.ams.usda.gov/nop /Consumers/brochure.html

63. Legal Source

Brown v. Board of Educ., 347 U.S. 483 (1954).

For Supreme Court cases, give the name of the case, volume number, source, page number, and date of the decision. For other courts, add the court with the date: (E.D. Wisc. 1985) for "Eastern District of Wisconsin."

64. Advertisement

Swim at home. (2005). [Advertisement]. *The American Scholar 74*(2), 2.

Nikon D7000. (2010, November). [Advertisement]. Retrieved December 12, 2010, from http://rollingstone.com

65. Computer Software or Video Game

The Island: Castaway. (2010). [Video game]. N.p.: Awem Studio.

"N.p." indicates that the place of publication is unknown.

Guitar hero III: Legends of rock. (2007). [Video game]. Santa Monica, CA:
Activision.

Provide an author name, if available. Standard software (Microsoft Word) and program languages (C++) don't need to be given in the References list.

66. Presentation Slides or Images

Alaska Conservation Solutions. (2006). *Montana global warming* [PowerPoint
slides]. Retrieved from http://www.alaskaconservationsolutions.com/acs
/presentations.html

67. Interview

In APA style, a personal interview is not included in the References list. Cite the interview in the text as a personal communication.

Randi Friedman (personal communication, June 30, 2010) endorses this view.

If the interview is published or can be retrieved by others, cite it as an article.

68. Lecture, Speech, or Address

Kennedy, J. F. (1960, September 12). Speech to the Greater Houston Ministerial
Association, Rice Hotel, Houston, TX.

APA
15E

69. Live Performance

Miller, A. (Author), & McLean, C. (Director). (2005, September 27). *All my sons*
[Theatrical performance]. Center for the Performing Arts, Normal, IL.

Nelson, W. (2011, June 22). *Country Throwdown Tour* [Concert]. Red Rocks
Amphitheater, Denver, CO.

70. Microfiche Collection of Articles

Wenzell, R. (1990, February 3). Businesses prepare for a more diverse work
force [Microform]. *St. Louis Post Dispatch*, p. 17. NewsBank: Employment 27,
fiche 2, grid D12.

A microfiche is a transparent sheet of film (a *fiche*) with microscopic printing that needs to be read through a special magnifier. Each fiche holds several pages, with each page designated by a grid position. A long document may appear on more than one fiche.

71. Musical Score

Schubert, F. (1971). *Symphony in B Minor (Unfinished)*. M. Cusid (Ed.). [Musical
score]. New York, NY: Norton. (Original work composed 1822)

72. Nonperiodical Publications on CD, DVD, or Magnetic Tape

Perl, S. (2004). *Felt Sense: Guidelines for Composing*. [CD]. Portsmouth, NH:
Boynton.

15F What are APA format guidelines for research papers?

Ask whether your instructor has instructions for preparing a final draft. If not, you can use the APA guidelines here. For an illustration of these guidelines, see the student paper in 15G.

■ General instructions—APA

Print on 8½-by-11-inch white paper and double space. Set at least a 1-inch margin on the left, and leave no less than 1 inch on the right and at the bottom.

Indent the first line of all paragraphs ½ inch, except in an abstract, the first line of which isn't indented. Do not justify the right margin. Indent footnotes ½ inch.

■ Order of parts—APA

Number all pages consecutively. Use this order for the parts of your paper:

1. Title page
2. Abstract (if required)
3. Body of the paper
4. References
5. Footnotes, if any
6. Appendixes, if any (questionnaires, data sheets, or other material your instructor asks you to include)

■ Title-and-page-number line (running head) for all pages—APA

Use a title-and-page-number line on all pages of your paper. Place it ½ inch from the top edge of the paper, typing the title (use a shortened version if necessary). Place the page number 1 inch from the right edge of the paper. Ask whether your instructor wants you to include your last name in the running head. The "header" tool on a word processing program will help you create the title-and-page-number line easily. See the sample student paper on page 264.

■ Title page—APA

Use a separate title page. Include your running head. Center your complete title horizontally and place it in the top half of the page. (Don't italicize, underline, or enclose your title in quotation marks.) On the next line, center your name, and below that center the course title and section, your professor's name, and the date. See the sample student paper on page 264.

❶ **Alerts:** (1) Use the guidelines here for capitalizing the title of your own paper and for capitalizing titles you mention in the body of your paper, but not in the REFERENCES list; see Quick Box 15.2.

(2) Use a capital letter for the first word of your title and for the first word of a subtitle, if any. Start every NOUN, PRONOUN, VERB, ADVERB, and ADJECTIVE with a capital letter. Capitalize each main word in a hyphenated compound word (two or more words used together to express one idea): *Father-in-Law, Self-Consciousness.*

(3) Do not capitalize ARTICLES (*a, an, the*) unless one of the other capitalization rules applies to them. Do not capitalize PREPOSITIONS and CONJUNCTIONS unless they're four or more letters long. Do not capitalize the word *to* used in an INFINITIVE. ●

■ Abstract—APA

An abstract is a summary of your paper in 150 to 250 words. Type the abstract on a separate page, using the numeral 2 in the title-and-page-number line. Center the word *Abstract* 1 inch from the top of the paper. Do not italicize or underline it or enclose it in quotation marks. Double-space below this title, and then start your abstract, double-spacing it. Do not indent the first line.

■ Set-off quotations—APA

Set off (display in block style) quotations of forty words or more. See 15C for a detailed explanation and example.

■ References list—APA

Start a new page for your References list immediately after the end of the body of your paper. One inch from the top of the paper, center the word *References*. Don't italicize, underline, or put it in quotation marks. Double-space below it. Start the first line of each entry at the left margin, and indent any subsequent lines five spaces or ½ inch from the left margin. Use this hanging indent style unless your instructor prefers a different one. Double-space within each entry and between entries.

■ Notes—APA

Put any notes on a separate page after the last page of your References list. Center the word *Footnotes* one inch from the top of the paper. Do not italicize or underline it or put it in quotation marks.

On the next line, indent ½ inch and begin the note. Raise the note number slightly (you can use the superscript feature in your word processing program), and then start the words of your note, leaving no space after the number. If the note is more than one typed line, do not indent any line after the first. Double-space throughout.

APA
15F

15G   A student's APA-style research paper

Leslie Palm wrote the following paper in response to an assignment that asked students to research how gender was portrayed in a specific circumstance.

½″

Header on each page: shortened title + page number

Running head: WOMEN IN VIDEO GAMES   1

1″

First page is title page.

Center the title, your name, course, instructor, and date in the top half of the page. Use double spacing.

The Troubling Roles of Women in Video Games

Leslie Palm

Sociology 200

Professor K. Thetard

May 9, 2011

APA 15G

½″

WOMEN IN VIDEO GAMES   2

1″   1″

Abstract

Double-space

Place your abstract, if required, on the second page.

Despite the fact that 40% of video game players are women, female characters and players are treated in ways that are problematic. Video games often portray unrealistic physical characteristics of female characters, exaggerating certain body features. Many games portray women either as vulnerable "damsels in distress" or as sexually aggressive. Women game players often experience stereotyping or harassment. Recent games are changing the way they present female characters.

1″

continued >>

WOMEN IN VIDEO GAMES   3

The Troubling Roles of Women in Video Games

Lady Reagan Cousland the First jogs across a virtual pastoral landscape with a two-handed battleax strapped across her shoulders. She is the Player Character in a play through of *Dragon Age: Origins*, a 2009 single-player role-play game, and she is trying to progress through the main quest. However, other characters taunt her. "I have never seen a woman Grey Warden before," says one skeptically. Lady rolls her eyes before sharply answering, "That's because women are too smart to join."

"So what does that make you?" asks the interrupter.

"Insane," she replies.

This exchange exemplifies how women have frequently been portrayed and treated in videogames for over two decades. Gaming has long been inaccurately considered an activity pursued almost solely by reclusive males caricatured as "pale loners crouched in the dark among Mountain Dew bottles and pizza boxes" (Wong, 2010). Game producers have mostly catered to this stereotypical player, with discouraging results. Despite evidence that large numbers of women play video games, and despite some important changes, women game characters continue to be physically objectified, represented either as passive or sexually aggressive, and even harassed.

According to data from the Entertainment Software Association (2011), 67% of American households own a video game console of some variety—and 40% of all players are women. In fact, "Women over 18 years of age are one of the industry's fastest growing demographics, [representing] a greater portion of the game-playing population (33 percent) than boys age 17 or younger (20 percent)" (Entertainment

APA 15G

Begin the body of your paper on page 2 if you have no abstract, on page 3 if you do.

Introductory paragraphs create interest.

Paragraph 2 provides background information.

Thesis statement gives paper's focus.

Paragraph 3 gives data.

Brackets show the writer added language.

continued >>

WOMEN IN VIDEO GAMES   4

Software Association, 2011). And yet, studies show that both male and female gamers believe games to be a "particularly masculine pursuit" (Selwyn, 2007, p. 533).

Physical Characteristics of Female Characters

The most obvious gender stereotyping in many games comes from the nature of the characters' bodies or avatars. A 2007 content analysis of images of video game characters from top-selling American gaming magazines showed that male characters (83%) are more likely than female characters (62%) to be portrayed as aggressive; however, female characters are more likely to be sexualized (60 vs 1%) and scantily clad (39 vs 1%) (Dill & Thill, 2007, p. 851–864). Even female characters that are considered strong or dominant in personality (such as Morrigan in *Dragon Age: Origins* or Sheva in *Resident Evil 5*) routinely dress in tops that are essentially strips of fabric and skin-tight leather pants. In fact, the reward for beating *Resident Evil 5* is that you get to dress the avatar Sheva in a leopard-print bikini.

In *Gender Inclusive Game Design*, S. G. Ray (2003) outlined the physical traits seen between male and female avatars: females are characterized by "exaggerated sexual features such as large breasts set high on their torso, large buttocks, and a waist smaller than her head" (pp. 102–104). Dickerman, Christensen, and Kerl-McClain (2008) found similar qualities. Analyzing characters in 60 video games, Downs and Smith (2010) found that women were more likely to be "hypersexualized" than men, depicted with unrealistic body proportions, inappropriate clothing, and other qualities (p. 728).

Even nonhuman females receive this treatment. Game designer J. Rubenstein (2007) questions why females of

APA 15G

Citation with page number for direct quotation.

First heading.

Paragraph 4 starts to develop the first main point.

Paragraph 5 summarizes research related to the first main point.

Author and date are included in sentence, so only page numbers are in parentheses.

Paragraph 6 extends the first main point.

continued >>

WOMEN IN VIDEO GAMES   5

nonhuman races in the popular game *World of Warcraft* are so much smaller and more feminine than their male counterparts. Of one species she notes, "The male is massive: tall with unnaturally large muscles and equally large hooves. . . . It would not be unreasonable to expect the female of the species to be similar." Apparently in *World of Warcraft's* earliest designs, the genders were far more similar; however, when screened to a pool of test gamers, complaints that the females were "ugly" resulted in their being changed to their current form. One scholar notes, "Since gamers and the like have been used to video representations of scantily-clad females and steroid-enhanced males," it is understandable that they would design nonhuman races in a similar way (Bates, 2005, p. 13).

Gender and Character Behavior

The personalities of the characters also demonstrate the gender bias in many games. Dietz's 1998 study of 33 games found that most did not portray women at all. Even ten years later, 86% of game characters were male (Downs & Smith, 2010). Only five of the games in Dietz's study portrayed women as heroes or action characters. The second most common portrayal in this study was as "victim or as the proverbial 'Damsel in Distress'" (Dietz, 1998, pp. 434–435). Examples of vulnerable women stretch from the 1980s to today, from Princess Peach (Nintendo's *Mario*) and Princess Zelda (Nintendo's *The Legend of Zelda*) to Alice Wake (Remedy Entertainment's *Alan Wake*), Ashley Graham (Capcom's *Resident Evil 4*), and Alex Roivas (Nintendo's *Eternal Darkness: Sanity's Requiem*). The helpless woman, simply put, is a video game staple, as college students overwhelmingly recognized in one study (Ogletree & Drake, 2007).

If the source had page numbers, a page reference would appear in parentheses.

Direct quotation embedded in a sentence.

Second heading.

APA 15G

Topic sentence states second main point.

The in-text citation for Downs & Smith refers to a source by two authors.

No page number because examples are names of video games.

continued >>

WOMEN IN VIDEO GAMES   6

Paragraph 8 introduces a slightly different aspect of the second main point.

A different staple role gaining popularity is that of the aggressive but sexy woman who will seduce you at night and then shoot you in the morning. Bayonetta, Jill Valentine (in *Resident Evil 3* and *Resident Evil 5*) and, of course, Lara Croft of the *Tomb Raider* series are all examples of this archetype. There is some debate as to whether these examples are evidence of new female power and liberation or simply a new form of exploitation. Dill and Thill (2007) argue that an aggressive female is not necessarily a liberated one and that "many of these images of aggressive female video game characters glamorize and sexualize aggression." Eugene Provenzo agrees, pointing out the contradiction between "the seeming empowerment of women, while at the same time . . . they're really being exploited in terms of how they're shown, graphically" (as cited in Huntemann, 2000).

Ellipses dots mean words were dropped from the quotation.

APA 15G

Paragraph 9 provides a specific example.

Lara Croft is perhaps the epitome of the energetic, aggressive character as an over-exaggerated sexual object. Lead graphic artist Gard went through five designs before arriving at her final appearance, and he began with the desire to counter stereotypical female characters, which he describes as "either a bimbo or a dominatrix" (as cited in Yang, 2007). Gard's inspirations included Swedish pop artist Neneh Cherry and comic book character Tank Girl, both feminist icons. Croft's original incarnation was as the South American woman Lara Cruz. Gard disavows accusations of sexism in the design, and insists that the character's iconic breasts were a programming accident that the rest of the team fought to keep (McLaughlin, 2008).

Third heading.

The Treatment of Women Gamers

Topic sentence of paragraph 10 explains third main point.

Video game culture reinforces negative gender roles for female players. Many multiplayer games encourage players

continued >>

WOMEN IN VIDEO GAMES   7

to use headsets and microphones, a gender-revealing practice
that is intended for easy strategizing. However, it often leads to
sexual harassment and lewd commentary that also carries over
to message boards, comments sections, and internet forums.
Technology blogger Kathy Sierra was forced to abandon her
website after multiple misogynistic comments and e-mails.
Ailin Graef, who has made millions in the 3D chat-platform
Second Life, was "swarmed by flying pink penises" during an
interview in that virtual world (McCabe, 2008).

Specific examples illustrate the point.

   A study by psychologists at Nottingham Trent University
in England determined that 70% of female players in massively
multiplayer online games chose to "construct male characters
when given the option," presumably in an attempt to avoid
such actions as female posters on gaming message boards
being asked to post pictures of their breasts or "get the f*** off"
(McCabe, 2008). Women gamers are considered so rare (which
is surprising, given that they makes up 40% of players) that
it's a common occurrence for male gamers to respond with a
degree of shock any time a female shows up in a game—even
if that shock is complimentary or respectful. Sarah Rutledge, a
25-year-old female med student, said of her gaming on *World of
Warcraft*,

Paragraph 11: more about treatment of women players.

> On the one hand, you get a lot of help and attention from
> guys playing the game, which can be helpful. You get
> invitations to join groups. But it's clear this has less to do
> with my ability than the fact I'm that curious creature: a
> woman. (personal communication, April 29, 2011)

Because this source was a personal interview and is not retrievable by others, student cites it only in the text, not in her References.

One team of researchers found significant differences between
men and women game players in gaining positive effects from
gaming. They found males more likely than females to

Explains different treatments of men and women matter.

continued >>

develop leadership, teamwork, and communicative skills, and they suggest this demonstrates games' biases toward males (Thirunarayanon, Vilchez, Abreau, Ledesma, & Lopez, 2010, p. 324).

Gradual Changes in Gender Roles and Gaming

In recent years, gender roles have somewhat shifted. Often role-playing games permit the user to choose various characteristics of the Player Character, including making her female. Aside from appearance and responses from Non-Player Characters, the gender rarely affects a character's actual skills or attributes. More games have been released with females as the sole protagonists, including *Silent Hill 3* (Heather Mason), *No One Lives Forever* (Cate Archer), *Mirror's Edge* (Faith), and *Heavenly Sword* (Nariko). Jade, the protagonist of *Beyond Good and Evil* (released in 2003), has been praised for being strong and confident without being overtly sexualized. So have characters like Alyx Vance (co-protagonist of 2004's *Half-Life 2*) and Chell (protagonist of *Portal*, 2007, and *Portal 2*, 2011).

Chell in particular was heralded as a massive step forward in gender dynamics. People were surprised that "as the player, you're never even aware that you're a woman until you catch a glimpse of yourself in the third person" (iVirtua, 2007). In this way, Chell echoes the "original" feminist character Samus Aran of Nintendo's 1986 *Metroid*; one only discovers that Aran is female when she removes her bulky robot-armor during the ending scene, after twenty-plus hours of gameplay. *Portal*, despite being an indie game produced by students as their thesis, became a hit, was wildly acclaimed by critics, and won multiple awards.

These developments don't satisfy all fans. Some argue that a more all-inclusive focus actually threatens the quality of

---

Fourth heading.

Topic sentence in paragraph 12 explains the fourth (and final) main point.

APA
15G

Paragraph 13 provides more detail about an example mentioned in the previous paragraph.

Paragraph 14 explains some fans' responses.

continued >>

experience for stereotypically straight male gamers. Bioware, a Canada-based gaming company, came under fire during the releases of two major titles for featuring romance and dialogue options that cater not only to women, but to gays and lesbians. The release of *Dragon Age 2* in 2011 caused an uproar on its own message boards for allowing romantic options to be bisexual. One fan, "Bastal" (2011), protested that

> the overwhelming majority of RPG gamers are indeed straight and male. . . . That's not to say there isn't a significant number of women who play Dragon Age and that BioWare should forego the option of playing as a woman altogether, but there should have been much more focus on making sure us male gamers were happy.

He and others then go on to propose a mode, which, if activated, would force male companions to flirt only with female PCs, and vice versa. However, such views disturb game creators like Gaider (2010), who argued that people like Bastal are

> so used to being catered to that they see the lack of catering as an imbalance. . . . The person who says that the only way to please them is to restrict options for others is, if you ask me, the one who deserves it least.

"If we just continue to cater to existing (male) players, we're never going to grow," says Beth Llewellyn, senior director of corporate communications for Nintendo (as cited in Kerwick, 2007). Video game companies have begun producing a new generation of games that give women the opportunity to grab a laser gun or broadsword and duke it out in billion-dollar franchises like *Halo*, *Fallout*, *Mass Effect*, *World of Warcraft*,

Quotations over 40 words in block style, no quotation marks.

APA 15G

If online sources: no page numbers.

Concluding paragraph.

Key quotation begins the concluding paragraph based on idea in previous paragraph.

continued >>

and *Guild Wars*. However, depicting women more accurately and favorably in games reaches a goal more important than mere entertainment. "Video-simulated interfaces" are being used to train people for various professions (Terlecki et al., 2010, p. 30), and it is crucial that these environments are suitable for all. The promising news is that while there is still extensive gender stereotyping (in both the gaming and the real world), game makers are taking giant strides—in both boots and heels.

Sentence helps answer the "so what?" question.

Because there are more than 6 authors for this citation, student uses the first author and "et al."

APA
15G

continued >>

References

Bastal. (2011, March 22). Bioware neglected their main
    demographic: the straight male gamer [Online
    discussion posting]. Retrieved from http://social.bioware
    .com/forum/1/topic/304/index/6661775&lf=8 (Topic 304,
    Msg. 1)

Bates, M. (2005). *Implicit identity theory in the rhetoric of
    the massively multiplayer online role-playing game
    (MMORPG)* (Doctoral Dissertation, Pennsylvania State
    University.) Available from ProQuest Dissertations and
    Theses database. (AAT 3172955)

Dickerman, C., Christensen, J., & Kerl-McClain, S. B. (2008). Big
    breasts and bad guys: Depictions of gender and race in
    video games. *Journal of Creativity in Mental Health, 3*(1),
    20–29. doi:10.1080/15401380801995076

Dietz, T. L. (1998). An examination of violence and gender role
    portrayals in video games: Implications for gender
    socialization and aggressive behavior. *Sex Roles, 38,*
    433–435.

Dill, K. E., & Thill, K. P. (2007, October 17). Video game characters
    and the socialization of gender roles: Young people's
    perceptions mirror sexist media depictions. *Sex Roles, 57,*
    861–864.

Downs, E., & Smith, S. L. (2010). Keeping abreast of hypersexuality:
    A video game character content analysis. *Sex Roles, 62,*
    721–733. doi:10:1007/s11199-009-9637-1

Dragon Age: Origins. (2009). [Video game]. Edmonton, Canada:
    Bioware Studios.

Begin References on a new page, with hanging indent.

Dissertation from a database, with accession number.

APA
15G

Journal article in print.

Note online digital object identifier (doi).

Video game.

continued >>

APA
15G

Report available online. Because the author is the same as the publisher, the publisher is listed as "Author."

Entertainment Software Association. (2011). *Essential facts about the computer and video game industry 2010: Sales, demographic and usage data.* Washington, DC: Author. Retrieved from http://www.theesa.com/

Comment in an online discussion.

Gaider, D. (2011, April 2). Re: Bioware neglected their main demographic. [Online forum comment]. Retrieved May 3, 2011, from http://social.bioware.com/forum/1/topic/304 /index/6661775&lf=8 (Topic 304, Msg. 2)

Huntemann, N. (Producer & Director). (2000). *Game over: Gender, race & violence in video games.* [Video file]. USA: Media Education Foundation. Retrieved from

Online video.

http://www.mediaed.org/

iVirtua Editorial Team. (2007, December 9). Portal is a feminist masterpiece. London, England: iVirtua Media Group. Retrieved from http://www.ivirtuaforums.com/portal-is-a-feminist-masterpiece-great-read-media-studies-t14-61

Kerwick, M. (2007, May 13). Video games now starring strong female characters. *The Record.* Retrieved from http://www.popmatters.com/female-characters

Newspaper article available online.

McCabe, J. (2008, March 6). Sexual harassment is rife online: No wonder women swap gender. *The Guardian,* p. G2. Retrieved from http://www.guardian.co.uk/

McLaughlin, R. (2008). The history of Tomb Raider. IGN Entertainment, Inc. Retrieved from http://m.ign.com /articles/856183

Ogletree, S. M., & Drake, R. (2007). College students' video game participation and perceptions: Gender differences and implications. *Sex Roles, 56,* 537–542. doi:10.1007 /s11199-007-9193-5

continued >>

WOMEN IN VIDEO GAMES   13

Ray, S. G. (2003). *Gender inclusive game design: Expanding the*   **Book.**
    market. Hingham, MA: Charles River Media.

Rubenstein, J. (2007, May 26). Idealizing fantasy bodies. *Iris*
    Gaming Network. Retrieved from http://theirisnetwork.org/

Selwyn, N. (2007). Hi-tech = Guy-tech? An exploration of
    undergraduate students' gendered perceptions of
    information and communication technologies. *Sex*
    Roles, 56, 525–536. doi:10.1007/s11199-007-9191-7

Terlecki, M., Brown, J., Harner-Steciw, L., Irvin-Hannum, J.,
    Marchetto-Ryan, N., Ruhl, L., & Wiggins, J. (2011). Sex
    differences and similarities in video game experience,
    preferences, and self-efficacy: Implications for the
    gaming industry. *Current Psychology, 30*, 22–33.
    doi:10.1007/s12144-010-9095-5

Thirunarayanon, M. O., Vilchez, M., Abreu, L., Ledesma, C.,
    & Lopez, S. (2010). A survey of video game players in a
    public, urban research university. *Educational Media*
    International, 47, 311–327. doi:10.1080/09523987-2010.535338

Wong, D. (2010, May 24). Five reasons it's still not cool to admit
    you're a gamer. *Cracked*. Retrieved April 20, 2011, from
    http://www.cracked.com/article_18571

Yang, R. (2007). The man behind Lara. [Interview]. *GameDaily*.
    Retrieved from http://gamedaily.com/articles/features
    /the-man-behind-lara

APA
15G

Part 5
Grammar, Style, Punctuation, and Mechanics

16 Parts of Speech and Parts of Sentences

■ ■ ■ ■ ■ ■

Quick Points   You will learn to

➤ Identify the parts of speech (pp. 278–286).
➤ Identify the parts of sentences (pp. 286–294).

MyWritingLab™   Visit mywritinglab.com for more resources on parts of speech and parts of sentences.

PARTS OF SPEECH

To identify a word's part of speech, see how the word functions in the sentence. Sometimes the same word functions differently in sentences.

● We ate **fish**.

   Fish is a NOUN.* It represents a thing.

● We **fish** on weekends.

   Fish is a VERB. It represents an action.

16A   What is a noun?

A **noun** names a person, place, thing, or idea: *student, college, textbook, education*. Quick Box 16.1 lists types of nouns.

ESOL Tips: (1) Speakers of languages other than English find it helpful to know whether nouns are count nouns or noncount nouns. We cover this topic in Chapter 42.

(2) Nouns often appear with words that tell how much, how many, whose, which one, and similar information. These words include ARTICLES (*a, an, the*), ADJECTIVES, and other DETERMINERS, which we discuss in Chapters 42–43.

(3) Words with the SUFFIXES (word endings) *-ance, -ence, -ment, -ness*, and *-ty* are usually nouns. We discuss the spelling of suffixes in 29B. ●

---

*Words printed in SMALL CAPITAL LETTERS are discussed elsewhere in the text and are defined in the Terms Glossary at the back of the book.

Quick Box 16.1

■ ■ ■ ■ ■ ■

Types of nouns

PROPER	names of specific people, places, or things (first letter is always capitalized)	*Will Smith, Paris, Buick*
COMMON	general things, places, or people	*singer, city, car*
CONCRETE	things experienced through the senses: sight, hearing, taste, smell, and touch	*landscape, pizza, thunder*
ABSTRACT	qualities, states, or ideas	*freedom, shyness*
COLLECTIVE	groups	*family, team*
NONCOUNT	"uncountable" things	*beef, dirt*
COUNT	countable items (singular or plural)	*lake (lakes), minute (minutes)*

Note: Some nouns are more than one type. *Love* is both common and abstract.

16B What is a pronoun?

A **pronoun** replaces or refers to a noun. The words a pronoun replaces are its **antecedents** (see 19A). Quick Box 16.2 (p. 280) lists types of pronouns.

- **Sonya** is an architect.   [noun]
- **She** is an architect.   [pronoun]
- The interior designer needs to consult **her**.

  The pronoun *her* refers to its antecedents, *Sonya* in the first sentence and *she* in the second.

🌐 **ESOL Tip:** Pronouns and nouns are covered in Chapters 42, 43, 45, and 46. ●

16C

16C What is a verb?

Verbs are of two types: main verbs and AUXILIARY VERBS (Ch. 47). **Main verbs** express action, occurrence, or state of being (see Chs. 17 and 47).

- You **danced**.
- The audience **grew** silent.
- Your dancing **was** awesome.

Quick Box 16.2

Types of pronouns

PERSONAL *I, you, they, her, its, ours,* and others	refers to people or things	I saw **her** take a book to **them**.
RELATIVE *who, which, that*	introduces certain NOUN CLAUSES and ADJECTIVE CLAUSES	The book **that** I lost was valuable.
INTERROGATIVE *who, whose, what, which,* and others	introduces a question	**Who** called?
DEMONSTRATIVE *this, these, that, those*	points out the antecedent	Whose books are **these**?
REFLEXIVE, INTENSIVE *myself, themselves,* and other *-self* or *-selves* words	refers to or intensifies the antecedent	They claim to support **themselves**. I **myself** doubt it.
RECIPROCAL *each other, one another*	refers to individual parts of a plural antecedent	We respect **each other**.
INDEFINITE *all, anyone, each,* and others	refers to nonspecific persons or things	**Everyone** is welcome here.

16D

⏺ **Alert:** When you're not sure if a word is a verb, try putting it into a different TENSE. If the sentence still makes sense, the word is a verb. (For help with verb tenses, see 17E.)

NO   He is a **changed** person. He is a **will change** person.

YES   The store **changed** owners. The store **will change** owners. ⏺

Chapters 17 and 47 cover verbs in more detail.

16D   What is a verbal?

Verbals are verb forms that function as nouns, adjectives, or ADVERBS. Quick Box 16.3 lists types of verbals.

Quick Box 16.3

Types of verbals and functions they perform

INFINITIVE *to* + SIMPLE FORM of verb	1. NOUN: represents an action, state, or condition	**To eat** soon is our goal.
	2. ADJECTIVE or ADVERB: describes or modifies	Still, we have nothing **to eat**.
PAST PARTICIPLE *-ed* form of REGULAR VERB or equivalent for IRREGULAR VERB	ADJECTIVE: describes or modifies	**Boiled, filtered** water is usually safe to drink.
PRESENT PARTICIPLE *-ing* form of verb	1. ADJECTIVE: describes or modifies	**Running** water may not be safe.
	2. NOUN: represents an action, state, or condition*	**Drinking** contaminated water is dangerous.

*A present participle functioning as a noun is called a GERUND.

ESOL Tips: The word *to* has several functions, as discussed in Chapters 45–47. (1) As part of the INFINITIVE *to eat*, the word *to* modifies (limits) the PRONOUN *nothing*.

- He has nothing **to eat**.

(2) *To* can be part of a MODAL AUXILIARY VERB, such as *have to*, which means "must" (see 47B).

- He **has to eat** something.

(3) *To* is also a preposition that must be followed by a noun, pronoun, or gerund OBJECT—in this example, the word *eating* (see 46A).

- He is **accustomed to eating** at noon. ●

16E   What is an adjective?

Adjectives modify—describe or limit—nouns, pronouns, and word groups that function as nouns.

- I saw a **green** and **leafy** tree.

  Green and *leafy* modify the noun *tree*.

16E

Descriptive adjectives, such as *green* and *leafy*, can show levels of intensity: *green, greener, greenest; leafy, more leafy, most leafy* (20D). **Proper adjectives** emerge from PROPER NOUNS: *American, Victorian*. In addition, words with these suffixes (word endings) are usually adjectives: *-ful, -ish, -less*, and *-like*. (For more about suffixes, see 29B.)

Determiners, sometimes called *limiting adjectives* because they "limit" nouns, tell whether a noun is general (**a** *tree*) or specific (**the** *tree*). Determiners also tell which one (**this** *tree*), how many (**twelve** *trees*), whose (**our** *tree*), and similar information. Quick Box 16.4 lists types of determiners.

Quick Box 16.4 ■ ■ ■ ■ ■ ■

Types of determiners

ARTICLES *a, an, the*	**A** reporter working on **an** assignment is using **the** telephone.
DEMONSTRATIVE *this, these, that, those*	**Those** students rent **that** house.
INDEFINITE *any, each, few*, and others	**Few** films today have complex plots.
INTERROGATIVE *what, which, whose*	**What** answer did you give?
NUMERICAL *one, first, two, second*, and others	The **fifth** question was tricky.
POSSESSIVE *my, your, their*, and others	**My** dog is older than **your** cat.
RELATIVE *what, which, whose, whatever*, and others	He is the instructor **whose** course I enjoyed.

ESOL Tip: To provide more help for multilingual writers, we discuss articles extensively in Chapter 43. ●

16F   What is an adverb?

An **adverb** modifies—describes or limits—verbs, adjectives, other adverbs, and CLAUSES.

- Chefs plan meals **carefully**.

  Carefully modifies the verb *plan*.

- Vegetables provide **very** important vitamins.

  Very modifies the adjective *important*.

- Those french fries are **too** heavily salted.

  Too modifies the adverb *heavily*.

- **Fortunately**, people realize that salt can do harm.

  Fortunately modifies the entire sentence.

Descriptive adverbs show levels of intensity, often by adding *more* (or *less*) and *most* (or *least*): *more happily, least clearly*. Many descriptive adverbs are formed by adding *-ly* to adjectives: *sadly, loudly, normally*. Some adverbs don't end in *-ly: very, always, not*, and *well* are some. Some *-ly* words look like adverbs but are really adjectives: *brotherly, lovely*. (For more on adverbs, see Chapter 20.)

Relative adverbs begin adjective clauses with words like *where, why*, and *when*.

Conjunctive adverbs modify by creating logical connections to express relationships as shown in Quick Box 16.5.

Quick Box 16.5

Conjunctive adverbs and relationships they express

Relationship	Adverbs
ADDITION	*also, furthermore, moreover, besides*
CONTRAST	*however, still, nevertheless, conversely, nonetheless, instead, otherwise*
COMPARISON	*similarly, likewise*
RESULT OR SUMMARY	*therefore, thus, consequently, accordingly, hence, then*
TIME	*next, then, meanwhile, finally, subsequently*
EMPHASIS	*indeed, certainly*

16G

16G What is a preposition?

Prepositions are common words that show relationships: *The professor walked **into** the classroom **before** the students.* Some common prepositions are *on, in, at, by, for, during, after, over*, and *above*.

Prepositions combine with other words to form PREPOSITIONAL PHRASES. These phrases often express relationships in time or space: *in April, at home*.

⬤ **ESOL Tip:** Prepositions play an important role in PHRASAL VERBS, which multilingual writers need to study closely. We discuss them in Chapter 45. ⬤

16H   What is a conjunction?

A **conjunction** connects words, phrases, or clauses. **Coordinating conjunctions**, which express the types of relationships listed in Quick Box 16.6, join two or more grammatically equivalent structures.

- We hike **and** camp every summer.

  And joins two verbs.

- I love the outdoors, **but** my family does not.

  But joins two INDEPENDENT CLAUSES.

Quick Box 16.6

■ ■ ■ ■ ■ ■

Coordinating conjunctions and relationships they express

Relationship	Coordinating Conjunction
ADDITION	*and*
CONTRAST	*but, yet*
REASON OR CAUSE	*for*
RESULT OR EFFECT	*so*
CHOICE	*or*
NEGATIVE CHOICE	*nor*

Correlative conjunctions function in pairs. They include *both . . . and, either . . . or, neither . . . nor, not only . . . but (also),* and *whether . . . or.*

- **Not only** students **but also** businesspeople should study a second language.

Subordinating conjunctions introduce DEPENDENT CLAUSES. They show that dependent clauses are less important than the independent clauses.

- **Because** it snowed, the school superintendent canceled all classes.

  The important part is that the superintendent canceled classes.

Quick Box 16.7 shows the various relationships subordinating conjunctions express.

Quick Box 16.7

Subordinating conjunctions and relationships they express

Relationship	Subordinating Conjunction
TIME	*after, before, once, since, until, when, whenever, while*
REASON OR CAUSE	*as, because, since*
RESULT OR EFFECT	*in order that, so, so that, that*
CONDITION	*if, even if, provided that, unless*
CONTRAST	*although, even though, though, whereas*
LOCATION	*where, wherever*
CHOICE	*rather than, than, whether*

16I What is an interjection?

An **interjection** expresses surprise or strong emotion. When it stands alone, punctuate an interjection with an exclamation point: *Hooray!* As part of a sentence, set off an interjection with a comma or commas: *Hooray, you got the promotion.* Use interjections sparingly, if at all, in ACADEMIC WRITING.

● **EXERCISE 16-1** Identify the part of speech of each numbered and under-lined word. Choose from noun, pronoun, verb, adjective, adverb, preposition, coordinating conjunction, correlative conjunction, and subordinating conjunction. For help, consult 16B through 16I.

The Mason-Dixon line primarily¹ marks the boundary² between Pennsylvania and Maryland. It was surveyed in the eighteenth³ century by Charles Mason and Jeremiah Dixon, who had previously⁴ worked together on a scientific⁵ expedition to South Africa.

In 1760, the Calverts of Maryland and the Penns of Pennsylvania hired⁶ Mason and Dixon to settle a boundary⁷ dispute between their parcels of⁸ land. Mason and Dixon marked⁹ their line every five¹⁰ miles using stones¹¹ shipped from England, which are called crownstones. These markers were decorated with two coats-of-arms and can still be found scattered throughout¹² this part of the country.

<u>Even though</u> Mason <u>and</u> Dixon were British, <u>they</u> had very different backgrounds. Mason was the son of a baker and trained in astronomy. Dixon was a Quaker, and <u>he</u> specialized in surveying.

The line they drew in America eventually <u>became</u> a <u>symbolic</u> division <u>between</u> free states and slave states <u>until</u> the end of the Civil War. <u>Because of</u> the line's importance, <u>it</u> has been the focus of <u>both</u> literature <u>and</u> music, such as the <u>song</u> "Sailing to Philadelphia" by Mark Knopfler. ●

PARTS OF SENTENCES

16J   What are subjects and predicates?

A sentence consists of two basic parts: a **subject** and a **predicate**.

A **simple subject** is the word (or words) that acts, is described, or is acted on: *The **telephone** rang*. A **complete subject** is the subject and all its MODIFIERS: ***The red telephone** rang*.

The **simple predicate** consists of the verb: *The telephone **rang***. The **complete predicate** is the verb and all its modifiers: *The telephone **rang loudly***. Quick Box 16.8 explains three subject and predicate sentence patterns.

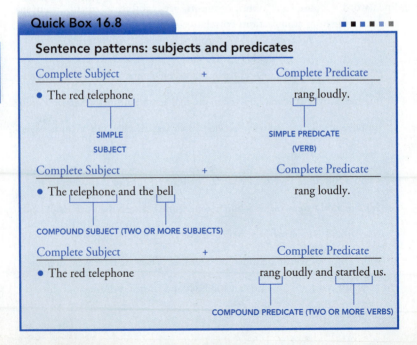

Quick Box 16.8

Sentence patterns: subjects and predicates

Complete Subject	+	Complete Predicate
● The red telephone		rang loudly.

SIMPLE SUBJECT — SIMPLE PREDICATE (VERB)

Complete Subject	+	Complete Predicate
● The telephone and the bell		rang loudly.

COMPOUND SUBJECT (TWO OR MORE SUBJECTS)

Complete Subject	+	Complete Predicate
● The red telephone		rang loudly and startled us.

COMPOUND PREDICATE (TWO OR MORE VERBS)

🌐 **ESOL Tip:** Never add a PERSONAL PRONOUN to repeat a stated SUBJECT.

NO   My grandfather **he** lived to be eighty-seven.

YES   My grandfather lived to be eighty-seven. ●

16K   What are direct and indirect objects?

A **direct object** completes the meaning of TRANSITIVE VERBS. To find a direct object, ask *whom?* or *what?* about the verb: *Keisha bought* [what?] ***a sweater***. To find an **indirect object**, ask *to whom?* or *for whom?* after the verb: *Keisha bought* [for whom?] ***me*** *a sweater*. Quick Box 16.9 illustrates direct and indirect objects.

Quick Box 16.9   ■ ■ ■ ■ ■ ■

Sentence patterns: direct and indirect objects

Complete Subject	+	Complete Predicate

● The doctor   offered advice.
                                     VERB   **DIRECT OBJECT**

Complete Subject	+	Complete Predicate

● The doctor   offered the lawyer advice.
               VERB   **INDIRECT**   **DIRECT**
                             OBJECT   **OBJECT**

Complete Subject	+	Complete Predicate

● The doctor   offered advice to the lawyer.
               VERB   **DIRECT**   **INDIRECT**
                       OBJECT   **OBJECT**

16K

🌐 **ESOL Tips:** (1) In sentences with indirect objects that follow the word *to* or *for*, always put the direct object before the indirect object.

NO   Will you please give **to** John this letter?

YES   Will you please give this letter **to** John?

(2) When a pronoun works as an indirect object, some verbs that go with the pronoun require *to* or *for* before the pronoun.

NO   Please explain **me** the rule.

YES   Please explain the rule **to me**.

(3) Even if a verb doesn't require *to* before an indirect object, you may use *to* if you wish. If you do use *to*, put the direct object before the indirect object.

> **NO**   Please give **to me** that book.
>
> **YES**   Please give that book **to me**.

(4) When both the direct object and the indirect object are pronouns, put the direct object first, and use *to* with the indirect object.

> **NO**   He gave **me it**.
>
> **YES**   He gave **it to me**. ●

16L   What are complements, modifiers, and appositives?

■ Recognizing complements

A **complement** renames or describes a subject or an object in the predicate of a sentence. A **subject complement** is a noun, a pronoun, or an adjective after a LINKING VERB. An **object complement** is a noun or an adjective after a DIRECT OBJECT. We illustrate both complements in Quick Box 16.10.

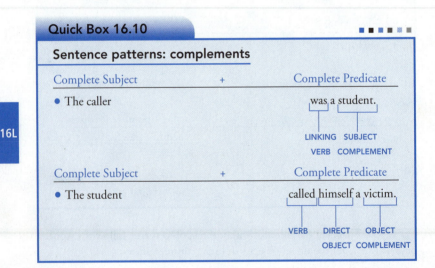

Quick Box 16.10   ■ ■ ■ ■ ■ ■

Sentence patterns: complements

Complete Subject	+	Complete Predicate
● The caller		was a student.

LINKING   SUBJECT
VERB   COMPLEMENT

Complete Subject	+	Complete Predicate
● The student		called himself a victim.

VERB   DIRECT   OBJECT
OBJECT   COMPLEMENT

■ Recognizing modifiers

A **modifier** is a word or words that function as an adjective or adverb.

● The **large red** telephone rang **loudly**.

> The adjectives *large* and *red* modify the noun *telephone;* the adverb *loudly* modifies the verb *rang*.

- The person **on the telephone** was **extremely** upset.

  The prepositional phrase *on the telephone* modifies the noun *person;* the adverb *extremely* modifies the adjective *upset.*

- **Because the lawyer's voice was calm**, the caller felt reassured.

  Because the lawyer's voice was calm is a single ADVERB CLAUSE; it modifies the independent clause *the caller felt reassured.*

■ Recognizing appositives

An **appositive** renames the noun or pronoun that comes before it.

- The student's story, **a tale of broken promises**, was complicated.

  A tale of broken promises is an appositive that renames the noun *story.*

- The lawyer consulted an expert, **her law professor**.

  Her law professor is an appositive that renames the noun *expert.*

  For details about commas with appositives, see 30F.

16M What is a phrase?

A **phrase** is a group of related words not containing both a subject and a predicate. A phrase can never stand alone as a sentence.

A **noun phrase** functions as a noun.

- **The modern population census** started in the seventeenth century.

  A **verb phrase** functions as a verb.

- Two military censuses **are mentioned** in the Bible.

  A **prepositional phrase**, which starts with a PREPOSITION and contains a noun or pronoun, functions as a modifier.

- William the Conqueror conducted a census **of landowners in 1086**.

  Two prepositional phrases come in a row, beginning with *of* and *in.*

  An **absolute phrase** is a noun phrase that modifies the entire sentence.

- **Censuses being the fashion**, Quebec and Nova Scotia took sixteen counts between 1665 and 1754.

  A **verbal phrase** is a word group that contains a VERBAL.

- In 1624, Virginia began **to count** its citizens in a census.

  The INFINITIVE PHRASE functions as a direct object.

- **Going from door to door**, census takers interview millions of people.

  The participial phrase functions as an adjective modifying *census takers.*

- **Going from door to door** takes many hours.

The gerund phrase functions as the subject.

Although both gerund phrases and participial phrases use the *-ing* form of a verb, a **gerund phrase** functions only as a *noun*, whereas a **present-tense participial phrase** functions only as a *modifier*.

● **EXERCISE 16-2**   Combine each set of sentences into a single sentence by converting one sentence into a phrase—a noun phrase, a verb phrase, prepositional phrase, absolute phrase, verbal phrase, or gerund phrase. You can omit, add, or change words. Identify which type of phrase you created.

EXAMPLE

The key grip is an important person in the making of a film. The key grip is the chief rigging technician on the movie set.

Serving as the chief rigging technician on a movie set, the key grip is an important person in the making of a film. (verbal phrase)

1. The key grip is the head of the grip department. Grips provide support to the camera department.
2. Grips work with such camera equipment as tripods, dollies, and cranes. Grips have to set up this equipment in a variety of settings during the making of a feature film.
3. Grips are also responsible for safety on the movie set. They have to watch over potentially dangerous equipment like ladders, stands, and scaffolds.
4. The "best boy grip" is the assistant to the key grip. The "best boy electric" is the assistant to the gaffer, who is the head electrician.
5. Electricians handle all of the lights on a movie set. Grips are in charge of all of the nonelectrical equipment related to light.
6. Sometimes grips are needed to reduce sunlight. They can do this by installing black fabric over windows and other openings.
7. The use of grips dates back to circuses and vaudeville. Early grips held on to hand-cranked cameras to reduce movement. ●

16N   What is a clause?

A **clause** is a group of words that contains both a subject and a predicate.

■ Recognizing independent clauses

An **independent** or **main clause** can be a sentence, as in Quick Box 16.11.

16N

Quick Box 16.11

Sentence patterns: independent clauses

Complete Subject	+	Complete Predicate
• The telephone		rang.

■ Recognizing dependent clauses

A **dependent** or a **subordinate clause** contains both a subject and a predicate, but it cannot stand alone as a sentence (see Quick Box 16.12).

Dependent clauses that start with *subordinating conjunctions* are called **adverb clauses**. They function as adverbs, usually answering one of these questions about the independent clause: *How? Why? When? Under what circumstances?*

- **If the bond issue passes**, the city will install sewers.

  The adverb clause modifies the verb *will install*, explaining under what circumstances.

- They are drawing up plans **as quickly as they can**.

  The adverb clause modifies the verb *are drawing up*, explaining how.

- The homeowners rejoice **because flooding will be controlled**.

  The adverb clause modifies the independent clause, explaining why.

❶ Alert: When an adverb clause comes before its independent clause, the clauses are usually separated by a comma (see 30B). ●

16N

Adjective clauses that are dependent clauses start with **relative pronouns** (*who, whom, which, whose,* and *that*) or occasionally with RELATIVE ADVERBS such as *when* or *where*. They modify a subject, object, or complement.

- The car **that Jack bought** is practical.

  The adjective clause describes the noun *car*.

- The day **when I can buy my own car** is getting closer.

  The adjective clause modifies the noun *day*.

- Politicians **who make promises** get voters' attention.

  The adjective clause *who make promises* modifies the noun *politicians*, which is the antecedent of *who*.

Quick Box 16.12 illustrates adverb and adjective clauses.

Quick Box 16.12

Sentence patterns: dependent clauses

ADVERB CLAUSE

Dependent Clause	+	Independent Clause

• **Although** the hour was late, the telephone rang.

SUBORDINATING   COMPLETE   COMPLETE   COMPLETE   COMPLETE
CONJUNCTION   SUBJECT   PREDICATE   SUBJECT   PREDICATE

ADJECTIVE CLAUSE

First Part of Independent Clause	+	Dependent Clause	+	Second Part of Independent Clause

• The red telephone, **which** belonged to me, rang loudly.

COMPLETE   RELATIVE   COMPLETE
SUBJECT   PRONOUN   PREDICATE

Noun clauses are subjects, objects, or complements. They usually begin with *that, who,* or *which,* but they can also start with *whoever, whichever, when, where, whether, why, what,* or *how.*

- **What politicians promise** is not always dependable.
- Often voters do not know **the truth**.
- Often voters do not know **that the truth is being manipulated**.

Alert: A noun clause functioning as a subject takes a *singular* verb: *What most politicians need **is** new careers. How we vote **matters.*** ●

160   What are sentence types?

A **sentence** can be simple, compound, complex, or compound-complex.

- A **simple sentence** is composed of a single independent clause.

  - Charlie Chaplin was born in London on April 16, 1889.
  - As a mime, he was famous for his character the Little Tramp.

160

- A **compound sentence** is composed of two or more independent clauses joined by a comma and a COORDINATING CONJUNCTION or just a semicolon.

  - Chaplin's father died early, and his mother spent time in mental hospitals.
  - Many people enjoy Chaplin's films; they laugh at his characters.

- A **complex sentence** consists of one independent clause along with one or more dependent clauses. (Dependent clauses are boldfaced.)

  - **When Chaplin performed with a troupe that was touring the United States**, he was hired by Mack Sennett, **who owned the Keystone Comedies**.

- A **compound-complex sentence** joins a compound sentence with a complex sentence. (The dependent clause is boldfaced.)

  - **When studios could no longer afford him**, Chaplin cofounded United Artists, and then he was able to produce and distribute his own films.

● **EXERCISE 16-3**   Use subordinate conjunctions and relative pronouns from the following list to combine each pair of sentences. You may use words more than once, but try to use as many different ones as possible. Some sentence pairs may be combined in several ways. Create at least one elliptical construction.

since	which	if	after	when	as
although	so that	unless	because	even though	that

EXAMPLE

Bluegrass music is associated with the American South. It has roots in Irish and Scottish folk music.

Even though it has roots in Irish and Scottish folk music, bluegrass is associated with the American South.

1. Certain aspects of jazz seem to have influenced bluegrass. It involves players of an instrumental ensemble improvising around a standard melody.
2. However, the instruments used in jazz are very different than those played in bluegrass. This style of music usually uses a banjo, fiddle, mandolin, and dobro.
3. The singing in bluegrass involves tight harmonies and a tenor lead singer. People who listen closely to the vocal arrangements can hear this.
4. Bill Monroe, the founder of bluegrass, added banjo player Earl Scruggs to his band, the Blue Grass Boys. This allowed him to produce a fuller sound.
5. The Blue Grass Boys went into the studio in 1945 to record some songs for Columbia Records. They hit the charts with "Kentucky Waltz" and "Footprints in the Snow."
6. They began touring America with their own large circus tent. They then became one of the most popular acts in country music.
7. Lester Flatt and Earl Scruggs left Bill Monroe's band. They formed their own group called the Foggy Mountain Boys.

8. A famous Flatt & Scruggs song is considered one of the most popular and difficult to play on the banjo. This song is called "Foggy Mountain Breakdown."
9. Most banjo players cannot play "Foggy Mountain Breakdown" at the same speed that Earl Scruggs plays it. Very skilled players can.
10. Bluegrass must continue to attract new and young fans. Otherwise, it will fade into obscurity. ●

17 Verbs

Quick Points   You will learn to

➤ Explain the functions and forms of verbs (pp. 294–299).
➤ Use verb tenses to express time (pp. 299–302).

MyWritingLab™   Visit mywritinglab.com for more resources on verbs.

17A   How do verbs function?

A **verb** expresses an action (*Many people **overeat** on Thanksgiving*), an occurrence (*Mother's Day **fell** early this year*), or a state of being (*Memorial Day **is** tomorrow*). Verbs also convey other information.

PERSON	First person (the speaker: *I dance*), second person (the one spoken to: *you dance*), or third person (the one spoken about: *the pop star dances*).
NUMBER	Singular (one) or plural (more than one).
TENSE	Past (*we **danced***), present (*we **dance***), or future (*we **will dance***); see 17E.
MOOD	Moods are indicative (*we dance*), imperative (commands and polite requests: *Dance*), or subjunctive (speculation, wishes: *if we were dancing*); see 17F.
VOICE	Active voice or passive voice; see 17G.

Types of verbs vary as listed in Quick Box 17.1.

Quick Box 17.1

Types of verbs

MAIN VERB	The word in a PREDICATE that says something about the SUBJECT: *She **danced** for the group.*
AUXILIARY VERB	A verb that combines with a main verb to convey information about TENSE, MOOD, or VOICE (see 17C). The verbs *be, do,* and *have* can be auxiliary verbs or main verbs. The verbs *can, could, may, might, should, would, must,* and others are MODAL AUXILIARY VERBS (see Ch. 47). They add shades of meaning such as ability or possibility to verbs: *She **might dance** again.*
LINKING VERB	A verb that links a subject to a **complement**, a word or words that rename or describe the subject: *She **was** happy dancing. Be* is the most common linking verb; sometimes sense verbs (*smell, taste*) or verbs of perception (*seem, feel*) function as linking verbs. (For a sentence pattern with a linking verb, see Quick Box 16.10.)
TRANSITIVE VERB	A verb followed by a DIRECT OBJECT that completes the verb's message: *They **sent** her a fan letter.* (For sentence patterns with objects, see Quick Box 16.9.)
INTRANSITIVE VERB	A verb that does not require a direct object: *Yesterday she **danced**.*

17B What are the forms of main verbs?

The **simple form** expresses an action, occurrence, or state of being in the present (*I laugh*) or, with an AUXILIARY VERB, in the future (*I will laugh*).

The **past-tense form** represents an action, occurrence, or state completed in the past (*I laughed*). Regular verbs add *-ed* or *-d* to the simple form. Irregular verbs vary as listed in Quick Box 17.2.

The **past participle** uses the same form as the past tense for regular verbs. Irregular verbs vary (see Quick Box 17.2). To function as a verb, a past participle must combine with one or more auxiliary verbs: *I have laughed*. Used alone, past participles function as ADJECTIVES: *crumbled cookies*.

The **present participle** is formed by adding *-ing* to the simple form (*laughing*). To function as a verb, a present participle must combine with one or more auxiliary verbs (*I was laughing*). Used alone, present participles function as NOUNS (*Laughing is healthy*) or as adjectives (*my laughing friends*).

Quick Box 17.2

Common irregular verbs

Simple Form	Past Tense	Past Participle
awake	awoke *or* awaked	awaked *or* awoken
be	was, were	been
become	became	become
begin	began	begun
break	broke	broken
bring	brought	brought
build	built	built
buy	bought	bought
catch	caught	caught
choose	chose	chosen
cost	cost	cost
deal	dealt	dealt
dive	dived *or* dove	dived
do	did	done
drink	drank	drunk
drive	drove	driven
eat	ate	eaten
fall	fell	fallen
fight	fought	fought
find	found	found
freeze	froze	frozen
get	got	got *or* gotten
give	gave	given
go	went	gone
grow	grew	grown
have	had	had
hear	heard	heard
keep	kept	kept
know	knew	known
lay	laid	laid
lead	led	led
lie	lay	lain

17B

continued >>

Quick Box 17.2 — Common irregular verbs (continued) ▪ ▪ ▪ ▪ ▪ ▪

Simple Form	Past Tense	Past Participle
lose	lost	lost
make	made	made
read	read	read
ring	rang	rung
run	ran	run
say	said	said
see	saw	seen
send	sent	sent
sing	sang	sung
sink	sank	sunk
sit	sat	sat
sleep	slept	slept
speak	spoke	spoken
stand	stood	stood
steal	stole	stolen
swim	swam	swum
take	took	taken
teach	taught	taught
throw	threw	thrown
wear	wore	worn
write	wrote	written

17B

■ Using regular verbs

Regular verbs form the past tense and past participle by adding *-ed* or *-d* to the simple form: *enter, entered; fix, fixed; smile, smiled.*

■ Using irregular verbs

More than two hundred English verbs are *irregular*, meaning that they form their past tense and past participle in unusual ways. Memorizing the most common **irregular verbs**, listed in Quick Box 17.2, can save you time.

■ Using the -s form of verbs

The *-s* form of a verb is used only in the third-person singular of the present tense. The *-s* ending attaches to the simple form (*laugh, laughs; teach, teaches*).

❶ Alert: Only the verbs *be* and *have* have irregular forms for the third-person singular of the present tense: *is* and *has*. They are the standard third-person singular forms to use in EDITED AMERICAN ENGLISH.

NO   Jasper be studying hard because he have to win a scholarship.

YES   Jasper **is** studying hard because he **has** to win a scholarship. ●

17C   What are auxiliary verbs?

Auxiliary verbs, also called **helping verbs**, combine with MAIN VERBS to make VERB PHRASES.

AUXILIARY   MAIN
  VERB   VERB

● I **am   shopping** for new shoes.

VERB PHRASE

● Clothing prices **have** [auxiliary verb] **soared** [main verb] recently.
  Have soared is a verb phrase.

● Leather shoes **can** [auxiliary verb] **be** [main verb] expensive.
  Can be is a verb phrase.

Modal auxiliary verbs include *can, could, may, might, must, shall, should, will, would*, and others. Modals communicate meanings of ability, permission, obligation, advisability, necessity, or possibility.

🌐 ESOL Tip: Modal auxiliary verbs can challenge multilingual writers, so we discuss them in detail in Chapter 47. ●

The three frequently used auxiliary verbs *be, do*, and *have* vary widely in form.

FORMS OF *BE, DO*, AND *HAVE*

	Be	Do	Have
SIMPLE FORM	be	do	have
PAST TENSE	was, were	did	had
PAST PARTICIPLE	been	done	had
-S FORM	is	does	has
PRESENT PARTICIPLE	being	doing	having

🌐 **ESOL Tips:** (1) Write with edited American English forms of *be*.

- The gym **is** a busy place. [meaning "it is always that way"]

- The gym **is filling** with young athletes. [meaning "it is happening right now"]

(2) If you use an auxiliary verb with a main verb, the auxiliary verb (not the main verb) often changes to an *-s* form to agree with a third-person singular subject.

- **Does** the gym **close** [*not* closes] at midnight? ●

17D Should I use *lie* or *lay*?

Many people confuse the forms of the irregular verbs *lie* ("to recline") and *lay* ("to place something down"). *Lie* is intransitive, so a direct object can *never* follow it. *Lay* is transitive, so a direct object *must* follow it.

	Lie	Lay
SIMPLE FORM	lie	lay
PAST TENSE	lay	laid
PAST PARTICIPLE	lain	laid
-S FORM	lies	lays
PRESENT PARTICIPLE	lying	laying

- The hikers are ~~laying~~ *lying* down to rest.
- Yesterday, the hikers ~~laid~~ *lay* down to rest.
- The hikers took off their gear and ~~lay~~ *laid* it on the rocks.

17E What are verb tenses?

The **tenses** of a verb express time. To do this, main verbs change form and combine with auxiliary verbs. **Simple tenses** divide time into the past, the present, and the future. **Progressive forms** show ongoing actions or conditions.

SIMPLE TENSES

		Progressive Forms
PRESENT	I talk.	I am talking.
PAST	I talked.	I was talking.
FUTURE	I will talk.	I will be talking.

17E

PERFECT TENSES

		Progressive Forms
PRESENT PERFECT	I have talked.	I have been talking.
PAST PERFECT	I had talked.	I had been talking.
FUTURE PERFECT	I will have talked.	I will have been talking.

■ Using the simple present tense

The simple **present tense** describes (1) what is happening now, (2) what is true at the moment, (3) what is generally or consistently true, or (4) what event will take place at a fixed time in the future.

- The tourists **are** on vacation.
- They **enjoy** the sunshine.
- Ocean voyages **make** them seasick.
- Their ship **departs** at midnight.

❗ Alert: Use the present tense to discuss action in literature.

- In *Romeo and Juliet*, Juliet's father **wants** Juliet to marry Paris.
- Shakespeare's play **depicts** the tragedy of ill-fated love. ●

ESOL Tip: In a dependent clause that begins with *if, when, before, after, until,* or *as soon as,* use the simple present in that clause; use *will* with the verb in the INDEPENDENT CLAUSE.

NO   After they **will arrive**, the meeting **will begin**.

YES   After they **arrive**, the meeting **will** begin. ●

■ Using tense sequence accurately

The sequence of verb tenses communicates different time relationships. Accurate sequence becomes an issue only when your sentence contains both an independent clause and a dependent clause. Quick Box 17.3 shows how the **tense sequence** communicates when something is happening, has happened, or will happen.

Quick Box 17.3

■ ■ ■ ■ ■ ■

Sequence of verb tenses with independent and dependent clauses

Tense in the Independent Clause	Tense to Use in the Dependent Clause
PRESENT	Use *present tense* to show same-time action: ● I **avoid** shellfish because I *am allergic* to it. Use *past tense* to show earlier action: ● I **am sure** that I *deposited* the check. Use *present perfect tense* to show (1) a period of time extending from some point in the past to the present or (2) an indefinite time in the past: ● They **say** that they *have lived* in Canada since 1979. ● I **believe** that I *have seen* this movie before. Use *future tense* for action to come: ● The book **is** open because I *will be reading* it later.
PAST	Use *past perfect tense* to show earlier action: ● The sprinter **knew** that she *had broken* the record. Use *present tense* to state a general truth: ● Columbus **determined** that the world *is* round.
PRESENT PERFECT OR PAST PERFECT	Use *past tense:* ● The bread **has become** moldy since I *purchased* it. ● Sugar prices **had** already **declined** when artificial sweeteners first *appeared*.
FUTURE	Use *present tense* to show action happening at the same time: ● You **will be** rich if you *win* the prize. Use *past tense* to show earlier action: ● You **will have** a good chance of winning if you *remembered* to send in your entry form.

17E

continued >>

Quick Box 17.3 — Sequence of tenses (continued) ■ ■ ■ ■ ■ ■

FUTURE   Use *present perfect tense* to show future action occurring sooner than the action of the verb in the independent clause:

- The river **will flood** again next year unless we ***have built*** a better dam by then.

FUTURE PERFECT   Use *present tense* or *past perfect tense*:

- Dr. Chang **will have delivered** five thousand babies by the time she ***retires***.
- Dr. Chang **will have delivered** five thousand babies by the time she ***has retired***.

● **EXERCISE 17-1**   Underline the correct verb in each pair of parentheses that best suits the sequence of tenses. Be ready to explain your choices. For help, consult 17E.

EXAMPLE

When he (is, was) seven years old, Yo-Yo Ma, possibly the world's greatest living cellist, (moves, moved) to the United States with his family.

1. Yo-Yo Ma, who (had been born, was born) in France to Chinese parents, (lived, lives) in Boston, Massachusetts, today and (toured, tours) as one of the world's greatest cellists.
2. Years from now, after Mr. Ma has given his last concert, music lovers still (treasure, will treasure) his many fine recordings.
3. Mr. Ma's older sister, Dr. Yeou-Cheng Ma, was nearly the person with the concert career. She had been training to become a concert violinist when her brother's musical genius (began, had begun) to be noticed.
4. Even though Dr. Ma eventually (becomes, became) a physician, she still (had been playing, plays) the violin.
5. The family interest in music (continues, was continuing), for Mr. Ma's children (take, had taken) piano lessons.
6. Although most people today (knew, know) Mr. Ma as a brilliant cellist, he (was making, has made) films as well.
7. One year, while he (had been traveling, was traveling) in the Kalahari Desert, he (films, filmed) dances of southern Africa's bush people.
8. Mr. Ma first (becomes, became) interested in the Kalahari people when he (had studied, studied) anthropology as an undergraduate at Harvard University.
9. When he shows visitors around Boston now, Mr. Ma has been known to point out the Harvard University library where, he claims, he (fell asleep, was falling asleep) in the stacks when he (had been, was) a student.
10. Indicating another building, Mr. Ma admits that in one of its classrooms he almost (failed, had failed) German. ●

17E

17F What are indicative, imperative, and subjunctive moods?

Mood conveys an attitude toward the action in a sentence. The **indicative mood** expresses statements about real things (*The door* **opened**) or highly likely ones (*She* **seemed** *lost*). Questions about real events and facts are also expressed in the indicative (**Do** *you* **need** *help?*).

The **imperative mood** expresses commands and direct requests (*Please* **shut** *the door.* **Watch out!**). If the subject is omitted in an imperative sentence, the subject is understood to be *you*.

The **subjunctive mood** expresses conditions that are not literally true or do not currently exist, such as wishes, recommendations, demands, indirect requests, and speculations: *If I* **were** *you, I* **would** *ask for directions.*

■ Using the subjunctive with *if, as if, as though,* and *unless* clauses

Many CLAUSES introduced by *if, as if, as though,* and *unless* require the subjunctive, but some don't. Use the subjunctive only when such clauses describe a speculation or condition contrary to fact.

INDICATIVE	If she **leaves** late, I **will drive** her to the party.
	This is a fact, not speculation.
SUBJUNCTIVE	If she **were** [*not* was] **going to leave** late, I **would drive** her to the party.
SUBJUNCTIVE	If it **were** [*not* was] sunny, people **would go out**.

■ Using the subjunctive in *that* clauses

When *that* clauses express wishes, indirect requests, recommendations, and demands, use the subjunctive.

- I wish **that** this party **were** [*not* was] scheduled for tomorrow.
- I requested **that** the birthday cake **be ready** [*not* is ready] at noon.

17G What is "voice" in verbs?

Voice indicates how the subject relates to the action of the verb. In the **active voice**, the subject performs the action. In the **passive voice**, the subject is acted upon.

ACTIVE	**Svetlana considers** clams a delicacy.
	The subject, *Svetlana*, performs the action.
PASSIVE	**Clams are considered** a delicacy by Svetlana.
	The subject, *clams*, is acted on by Svetlana.

The active voice—which is usually more direct, concise, and dramatic than the passive voice—emphasizes the doer of an action. The passive voice, however, is appropriate when who or what did the action is unknown or unimportant.

- The lock **was broken** sometime last night.

  The doer of the action is unknown.

- The formula **was discovered** years ago.

  The doer of the action is unimportant.

🌐 **ESOL Tip:** The passive voice works only with TRANSITIVE VERBS. Many English verbs are not transitive, so if you're not certain, check a dictionary. ●

Do not use the passive voice to make your writing seem "lofty."

NO   An experiment **was conducted by me** to demonstrate the existence of carbon.

This is pointless passive that is trying to sound lofty.

YES   I **conducted** an experiment to demonstrate the existence of carbon.

● **EXERCISE 17-2**   First, determine which sentences are in the active voice and which the passive voice. Second, rewrite each sentence in the other voice, and then decide which voice better suits the meaning. Be ready to explain your choice.

EXAMPLE

When Alfred Nobel wrote his last will in 1895, he created the Nobel Prizes. (*active; change to passive*)

The Nobel Prizes were created by Alfred Nobel, when he wrote his last will in 1895.

1. An enormous fortune was earned by Nobel when he invented dynamite in the 1860s.
2. An avid inventor, Nobel held over 300 patents.
3. *Nemesis,* a four-act play, was written by Nobel shortly before his death.
4. Beginning in 1901, the Nobel Prizes have honored people who work in physics, literature, chemistry, and world peace.
5. The list of categories for the Nobel Prize does not include mathematics. ●

17G

18 Subject–Verb Agreement

Quick Points   You will learn to

➤ Match subjects and verbs in person and number.

MyWritingLab™ Visit mywritinglab.com for more resources on subject–verb agreement.

18A What is subject–verb agreement?

Subject–verb agreement means that SUBJECTS and their VERBS match in **number** (singular or plural) and **person** (see 17A). **Singular** subjects require singular verbs, **plural** subjects require plural verbs, and third-person singular subjects require the *-s* form of present-tense verbs and AUXILIARIES.

The examples in Quick Box 18.1 show how the *-s* ending works in most cases.

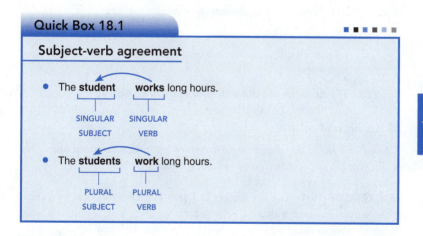

Quick Box 18.1

Subject-verb agreement

- The **student**   **works** long hours.

  SINGULAR   SINGULAR
  SUBJECT   VERB

- The **students**   **work** long hours.

  PLURAL   PLURAL
  SUBJECT VERB

ESOL Tip: Although some spoken versions of English don't observe rules of agreement, for ACADEMIC WRITING, you'll want to observe these rules. ●

18B Can I ignore words between a subject and its verb?

For subject–verb agreement, you can ignore words between a subject and verb.

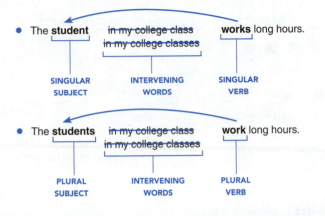

- The **student** ~~in my college class~~ / ~~in my college classes~~ **works** long hours.

  SINGULAR SUBJECT — INTERVENING WORDS — SINGULAR VERB

- The **students** ~~in my college class~~ / ~~in my college classes~~ **work** long hours.

  PLURAL SUBJECT — INTERVENING WORDS — PLURAL VERB

NO   The **winners** in the state competition **goes** to the national finals.

Winners is the subject, so the verb must agree with it. *In the state competition* is a PREPOSITIONAL PHRASE that comes before the verb, and it does not alter subject–verb agreement.

YES   The **winners** in the state competition **go** to the national finals.

To locate the subject of a sentence, first eliminate any PREPOSITIONAL PHRASES. What remains usually makes the subject stand out.

NO   The **moon**, as well as the stars, **are** visible in the night sky.

Moon is the subject, so the verb needs to agree with it. *Are* does not agree with *moon*.

YES   The **moon**, as well as the stars, **is** visible in the night sky.

18B ■ Using *one of the*

The subject *one of the* takes a singular verb to agree with the word *one*. (This is not true of the construction *one of the . . . **who**;* see 18G.)

● **EXERCISE 18-1**   Use the subject and verb in each set to write two complete sentences—one with a singular subject and one with a plural subject. Keep all verbs in the present tense. For help, consult 18A and 18B.

EXAMPLE

bird, sing

SINGULAR SUBJECT: When a *bird sings*, you will know spring is here.

PLURAL SUBJECT: When *birds sing*, you will know spring is here.

1. chair, rock
2. leaf, fall
3. river, flow

4. clock, tick
5. singer, sing
6. girl, laugh
7. hand, grab
8. loaf, rise ●

18C How do verbs work when subjects are connected by *and*?

Subject joined by *and* are plural and require a plural verb.

● **The student and the instructor**   **work** long hours.

      COMPOUND SUBJECT (USES *AND*)   **PLURAL VERB**

● **The Cascade Diner and Joe's Diner have** [*not* has] fried catfish today.

However, use a singular verb for subjects joined by *and* that refer to a single person or thing.

● **Spaghetti and meatballs is** [*not* are] the special tomorrow.

■ Using *each* and *every*

Each and *every* are singular PRONOUNS and always require singular verbs.

● **Each** human hand and foot **leaves** a distinctive print.
● **Every** human hand and foot **leaves** a distinctive print.

18D How do verbs work when subjects are connected by *or*?

18D

When *or*, *nor*, or *but* join subjects, the verb agrees only with the subject nearest it.

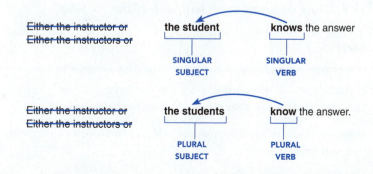

~~Either the instructor or~~
~~Either the instructors or~~   **the student**   **knows** the answer

       SINGULAR SUBJECT   **SINGULAR VERB**

~~Either the instructor or~~
~~Either the instructors or~~   **the students**   **know** the answer.

       PLURAL SUBJECT   **PLURAL VERB**

18E   How do verbs work with indefinite pronouns?

Indefinite pronouns refer to nonspecific people or things. They are usually singular, so they usually take singular verbs.

COMMON INDEFINITE PRONOUNS

another	each	everything	nothing
anybody	either	neither	somebody
anyone	every	nobody	someone
anything	everyone	no one	something

- **Neither** of these directions **seems** [*not* seem] simple.
- **Everything** about these roads **is** [*not* are] dangerous.
- **Each** of the roads **has** [*not* have] to be resurfaced.

A few indefinite pronouns—*none, some, more, most, any*, and *all*—can be either singular or plural, depending on the meaning of the sentence.

- **Some** of our streams **are** polluted; **some** pollution **is** reversible, but **all** pollution **is** a threat to the balance of nature.

  The first *some* refers to the plural *streams*, so the plural verb *are* agrees with it; the second *some* and *all* refer to the singular word *pollution*, so the singular verb *is* agrees with them.

18F   How do verbs work with *who, which*, and *that*?

When *who, which*, or *that* is the subject of a CLAUSE, the verb agrees with the noun or pronoun to which *who, which*, or *that* refers (its ANTECEDENT).

- Each of us **who are** graduating knows our distinguished director well.
- David Pappas is the student **who assists** our director.
- It is David **who is** introducing her.

18G   How do verbs work with *one of the . . . who*?

Use a plural verb following the phrases *one of the . . . who, one of the . . . that,* and *one of the . . . which.*

- Here is **one of the books that are** [*not* is] recommended.
- Its author is **one of the experts who are** [*not* is] addressing us today.
- Music file sharing is **one of the topics which are** [*not* is] featured.

However, always follow the phrase *the only one of the* with a singular verb to agree with *the only one.*

- He is **the only one of the authors who is** [*not* are] speaking today.
- Music file sharing is **the only one of the topics which is** [*not* are] featured today.

18H How do verbs work in other complicated types of subject–verb agreement?

■ Finding the subject in inverted word order

Inverted word order (*In walked the mayor*) reverses the order of subject and verb but has no effect on subject–verb agreement. In statements and questions (which are often inverted), verbs and subjects agree.

- Across the street **stand** [*not* stands] many **protestors**.
- **Are they** serious about their demands?

■ Finding the subject with an expletive

It and *there* form **expletives** when they introduce a verb that precedes its subject. The expletive *it* requires a singular verb; after the expletive *there*, subjects and verbs agree.

- **It is** astronomers who study the planets.
- There **are** nine **planets** in our solar system.
- There **is** probably no **life** on eight of them.

■ Agreeing with the subject, not the subject complement

A verb agrees with its subject, not the SUBJECT COMPLEMENT, the NOUN or ADJECTIVE that follows a **linking verb**.

NO	The worst **part** of owning a car **are** the bills.
	The verb *are* agrees with the subject complement *bills*.
YES	The worst **part** of owning a car **is** the bills.
	Now singular *part* agrees with singular *is*.
YES	**Bills are** the worst part of owning a car.
	The sentence is rewritten to make the plural noun *bills* the subject, so the plural verb *are* is correct.

■ Making verbs agree with collective nouns

A **collective noun** names a group of people or things, such as *family, group, audience, class*, or *number*. When the group acts as one unit, use a singular verb. When the members of the group act individually, use a plural verb.

18H

- The senior **class has** [*not* have] 793 people in it.

  Here, *class* operates as one unit, so the singular verb *has* agrees with it.

- The senior **class were** [*not* was] **fitted** for their graduation robes today.

  Here, *class* means the people in the class acting as individual members within the group, so the plural verb phrase *were fitted* agrees with it.

🛈 **Alert:** Notice that the pronouns also agree with the nouns to which they refer (*it* agrees with *class, their* agrees with *class*). ●

■ Making verbs agree with subjects that specify amounts

Use a singular verb with a subject that specifies an amount of money, time, weight, or distance considered as one unit.

- **Ninety cents is** the current bus fare.
- **Two miles passes** quickly for a serious jogger.

In contrast, when a subject refers to units of measurement, each of which is considered individually rather than as a unit, use a plural verb.

- **Eighteen inches are** marked off on that ruler.
- **Fifty percent** of these peaches **are** rotten.

■ Making verbs agree with singular subjects in plural form

A few subjects look plural, particularly those naming fields of study (*statistics, mathematics, economics, physics*). These take singular verbs when they mean the field of study, but they are plural when they refer to items of data. Some other subjects (*news, measles, gallows*) look plural but are always singular.

18H

- **Statistics is** an especially demanding major.
- **Statistics show** that a recession is inevitable.
- This **news is** making voters nervous.

Some other nouns that end in *-s* may be singular or plural, as shown by their meaning in the sentence.

- Six new television **series are** beginning this week.
- A **series** of setbacks **has** plagued their debut.
- One **means** to fame **is** producing a successful television show.
- *Jersey Shore*'s **means** to high ratings **include** sex appeal and shocking behavior.

■ Using singular verbs with titles, terms, and plural words representing a single unit

The title of a work or a series of words used as a term is a single unit. Therefore, use a singular verb, even when the title or term contains plural words.

- *Cats* **was** [*not* were] a popular musical.
- **"Protective reaction strikes" is** a euphemism for bombing.

    The entire expression *"protective reaction strikes"* acts as a single unit; it therefore calls for the singular verb *is*.

    Used alone, the word *states* is always plural. However, the name *United States* refers to a single country, so it takes a singular verb.

- **The United States has** [*not* have] a large television industry.

● **EXERCISE 18-2**   This exercise covers all rules for subject–verb agreement (see 18A through 18H). Supply the correct form of the verb in parentheses.

EXAMPLE

Recent research suggests that high levels of social status (to bring) <u>bring</u> high levels of stress.

1. Most people (to believe) _____ that poor people obviously suffer considerably more from stress than do very wealthy people.
2. They understand that meeting basic needs like food and shelter (to generate) _____ huge amounts of stress.
3. A steady income and a large saving account clearly (to reduce) _____ stress levels and (to have) _____ mental and physical health benefits.
4. However, these benefits (to be) _____ true only to a certain point.
5. Research by sociologist Scott Schieman shows that people at the highest levels of society actually (to have) _____ high levels of stress.
6. There (to be) _____ many possible reasons for this effect.
7. One reason (to suggest) _____ that success makes people who are driven to succeed work even harder, creating a vicious cycle for them.
8. Another reason, which (to view) _____ an apparent perk of high status as an actual disadvantage, (to say) _____ that having authority over others (to result) _____ in people continually getting involved in conflict.
9. Statistics (to show) _____ that young professionals who (to be) _____ used to technological interruptions in demanding work settings may deal with stress better than older ones.
10. Even if it brings high stress, most of us (to prefer) _____ having high status over having low. ●

18H

Pronouns: Agreement, Reference, and Case

Quick Points   You will learn to

➤ Match pronouns with their antecedents (pp. 312–315).

➤ Use pronouns with clear reference (pp. 315–318).

➤ Use the proper pronoun case (pp. 318–323).

MyWritingLab™ Visit mywritinglab.com for more resources on pronouns.

PRONOUN–ANTECEDENT AGREEMENT

19A   What is pronoun–antecedent agreement?

Pronoun–antecedent agreement means that a PRONOUN must match the grammatical form of the word or words it refers to (the pronoun's ANTECEDENT). For example, if an antecedent is third-person singular, the pronoun that refers to it needs to be third-person singular, too (see Quick Box 19.1).

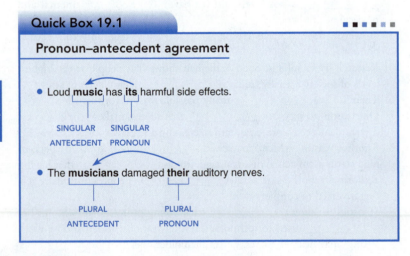

Quick Box 19.1

Pronoun–antecedent agreement

- Loud **music** has **its** harmful side effects.

  SINGULAR   SINGULAR
  ANTECEDENT   PRONOUN

- The **musicians** damaged **their** auditory nerves.

  PLURAL   PLURAL
  ANTECEDENT   PRONOUN

19B   How do pronouns work when *and* connects antecedents?

Two or more antecedents joined by *and* require a plural pronoun, even if each antecedent is itself singular.

- **Chris and Pat** homeschool **their** children.

One exception occurs when *each* or *every* comes before singular NOUNS joined by *and*. In such cases, a singular pronoun is correct.

- **Every car and truck** that comes through the border station has **its** [*not* their] contents inspected.

  Each car and truck is separate.

Another exception occurs when singular nouns joined by *and* refer to a single person or thing. In such cases, a singular pronoun is correct.

- Our **guide and translator** told us to watch out for traffic as **she** [*not* they] helped us off the tour bus.

  The guide is the same person as the translator.

19C How do pronouns work when *or* connects antecedents?

Some antecedents are joined by the word *or* or *nor*. In addition, CORRELATIVE CONJUNCTIONS such as *either . . . or* and *not only . . . but (also)* can join antecedents. These antecedents can mix masculine and feminine as well as SINGULAR and PLURAL. However, for the purposes of agreement, ignore everything before the final antecedent.

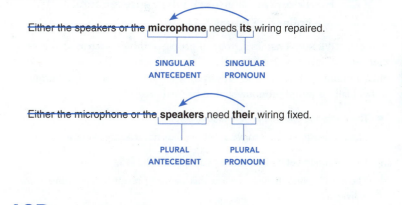

19D How do pronouns work when their antecedents are indefinite pronouns?

INDEFINITE PRONOUNS point to no particular person, thing, or idea (see 18E). They are generic and take on meanings according to the sentence they're in.

Indefinite pronouns are usually singular: ***Anyone*** *who knows the answer should raise **his or her** hand*. Some indefinite pronouns can be either singular or plural (*none, some, more, most, any, all*), depending on the meaning of the sentence.

- **None** fear that **they** will fail.

  All in the group expect to pass; the plural pronoun *they* shows this meaning.

- **None** fears that **he or she** will fail.

  No one expects to fail; the singular pronouns *he or she* show this meaning.

The pronouns *each* and *every* are singular, no matter what words follow.

- Each of the students handed in ~~their~~ final term paper.

his or her

- Every student in my classes is studying ~~their~~ hardest.

his or her

Be especially careful about agreement when you use the words *this* (singular) and *these* (plural): ***This** kind of hard work has **its** advantages. **These** kinds of difficult jobs have **their** advantages.*

> **❗ Alert:** The expression *he or she* operates as a single unit and therefore calls for a singular antecedent. Generally, however, try to avoid this awkward expression by switching to plural forms. ●

19E   How do pronouns work when antecedents are collective nouns?

A COLLECTIVE NOUN names a group of people or things, such as *family, group, audience, class,* or *number* (see 18H). When the group acts as one unit, a singular pronoun can refer to it. However, when the members of the group act individually, a plural pronoun should be used.

- The **audience** cheered as **it** rose to applaud.

  The singular pronoun *it* conveys that the audience is acting as one unit.

- The **audience** put on **their** coats and walked to the exits.

  The plural pronoun *their* conveys that audience members are acting as many individuals.

● **EXERCISE 19-1**   Underline the correct pronoun in parentheses. For help, consult 19A through 19E.

EXAMPLE

Many wonder where inventors like Benjamin Franklin get (his or her, <u>their</u>) creative energy.

1. Many so-called Founding Fathers are famous for one or two of (his, his or her, their) accomplishments, but anyone who knows (his, her, his or her, their) history knows that Franklin is known for many things, including (his, her, his or her, their) inventions.

2. The armonica is not one of his well-known inventions, but (its, their) design is ingenious.

3. Also called the glass harmonica, the armonica required a person to place (himself, herself, himself or herself) in front of the instrument and to rotate (its, their) glass bowls.

4. The lightning rod and the Franklin stove established his reputation as an inventor, but (it, they) remained in the public domain because Franklin refused to secure patents for his inventions.

5. An inventor like Franklin does not limit (his, her, his or her, their) imagination to one field of science.

6. (He, She, He or she, They) can instead pursue many questions and the challenges (they, it) pose.

7. All scientists who study electricity should know that Ben Franklin provided the names (he, she, he or she, they) still use today for positive and negative electrons.

8. Franklin also named the Gulf Stream and mapped (their, its) current.

9. Franklin formed the first public lending library in America, which allowed people to borrow (its, their) books and read them at (his, her, his or her, their) leisure.

10. His public service record also includes the reform of the postal system and the establishment of The Academy and College of Philadelphia, which later merged (their, its) students with those of the State of Pennsylvania to become the University of Pennsylvania. ●

19F

PRONOUN REFERENCE

19F How can I avoid unclear pronoun reference?

In sentences that contain more than one logical antecedent, meaning can get muddled.

UNCLEAR PRONOUN REFERENCE	In 1911, Roald Amundsen reached the South Pole just thirty-five days before Robert F. Scott arrived. **He** [*Amundsen or Scott?*] had told people that he was going to sail north to the Arctic, but then **he** [*Amundsen or Scott?*] turned south for the Antarctic.
REVISED	In 1911, Roald Amundsen discovered the South Pole just thirty-five days before Robert F. Scott arrived. Amundsen had told people that he was going to sail north to the Arctic, but then he turned south for the Antarctic.

In addition, when too much material comes between a pronoun and its antecedent, readers often lose track of the meaning.

● Alfred Wegener, a German meteorologist and professor of geophysics at the University of Graz, was the first to suggest that all the continents on earth were originally part of one large landmass. According to his theory, the supercontinent broke up long ago and the fragments drifted apart. Slowly, these fragments formed the pattern of landmasses and oceans that we know today. Although they do so slowly over centuries, the landmasses are continuing to move. ~~He~~ named this supercontinent Pangaea.

Wegener

Wegener, the antecedent of *he*, may be too distant for readers. Remember to keep your pronouns and antecedents close.

19G   How do pronouns work with *it, that, this,* and *which*?

Too often writers use the words *it, that, this,* and *which* carelessly, making it difficult for readers to understand what's being referred to.

NO   Comets usually fly by the earth at 100,000 mph, whereas asteroids sometimes collide with the earth. **This** interests scientists.

This could refer to the speed of comets, comets flying by the earth, or asteroids colliding with the earth.

YES   Comets usually fly by the earth at 100,000 mph, whereas asteroids sometimes collide with the earth. **This difference** interests scientists.

In ACADEMIC WRITING, avoid imprecise statements such as "It said on the news . . ." or "In Washington, they say . . ."

NO   In California, **they say** that no one feels a minor earthquake.

Who are *they?*

YES   **Residents of California say** that no one feels a minor earthquake.

19H   When do I use *you* for direct address?

Reserve *you* for **direct address**, writing that speaks directly to the reader. Avoid using *you* in generalizations referring to people, situations, or occurrences.

NO   Prison uprisings often happen when you allow overcrowding.

The reader did not allow the overcrowding.

YES   Prison uprisings often happen when prisons are overcrowded.

19I   When do I use *who, which,* and *that*?

Who refers to people and animals mentioned by name.

- **Theodore Roosevelt, who** served as the twenty-sixth US president, inspired the creation of the stuffed animal called the teddy bear.

- **Lassie, who** was known for her intelligence and courage, was actually played by a series of male collies.

Which and *that* refer to animals, things, and sometimes anonymous or collective groups of people. Quick Box 19.2 shows how to choose *that* or *which*. (For help in using commas with *that* and *which*, see 30F.)

Quick Box 19.2

Choosing between *that* and *which*

In informal writing, you can use either *that* or *which* in a restrictive clause (a clause that is essential to the sentence's meaning), as long as you do so consistently in each piece of writing. However, in academic writing, your instructor and peers usually expect you to use *that*.

- The zoos **that most children like** display newborn and baby animals.

  The clause *that most children like* is essential to the meaning of the sentence; if you remove it, the meaning changes substantially.

  Use *which* in a NONRESTRICTIVE CLAUSE (a clause that isn't essential to the sentence's meaning).

- Zoos, **which most children like**, attract more visitors if they display newborn and baby animals.

  The clause *which most children like* is not essential to the meaning of the sentence; if you remove it, the meaning of the sentence doesn't change substantially.

19I

● **EXERCISE 19-2**   Revise so that each pronoun refers clearly to its antecedent. Either replace pronouns with nouns or restructure the material to clarify pronoun reference. For help, consult 19F through 19I.

EXAMPLE

People who return to work after years away from the corporate world often discover that business practices have changed. They may find fiercer competition in the workplace, but they may also discover that they are more flexible than before.

HERE IS ONE POSSIBLE REVISION: *People who return to work after years away from the corporate world often discover that business practices have changed. Those people may find fiercer competition in the workplace, but they may also discover that business practices are more flexible than before.*

Most companies used to frown on employees who became involved in office romances. They often considered them to be using company time for their own enjoyment. Now, however, managers realize that happy employees are productive employees. With more women than ever before in the workforce and with people working longer hours, they have begun to see that male and female employees want and need to socialize. They are also dropping their opposition to having married couples on the payroll. They no longer automatically believe that they will bring family matters into the workplace or stick up for each other at the company's expense.

One departmental manager had doubts when a systems analyst for research named Laura announced that she had become engaged to Peter, who worked as a technician in the same department. She told her that either one or the other might have to transfer out of the research department. After listening to her plea that they be allowed to work together on a trial basis, the manager reconsidered. She decided to give Laura and Peter a chance to prove that their relationship would not affect their work. The decision paid off. They demonstrated that they could work as an effective research team, right through their engagement and subsequent marriage. Two years later, when Laura was promoted to assistant manager for product development and after he asked to move also, she enthusiastically recommended that Peter follow Laura to her new department. ●

PRONOUN CASE

19J   What is pronoun case?

Case shows the relationship (subject, object, possession) of nouns and pronouns to other words in a sentence. Pronouns use different forms in different cases (subjective, objective, possessive). Nouns change form only in the possessive case. (For use of the apostrophe in the possessive, see Chapter 33.)

19K   What are personal pronouns?

Personal pronouns refer to persons or things. Quick Box 19.3 shows the case forms of personal pronouns (subjective, objective, and possessive) in both the singular and the plural.

Most questions about pronoun case concern *who/whom* and *whoever/whomever*. For a full discussion, see 19P.

19L   How can I select the correct case?

When you're unsure whether to use the SUBJECTIVE CASE or the OBJECTIVE CASE, try the three-step test shown in Quick Box 19.4.

> **Quick Box 19.3**   ■ ■ ■ ■ ■ ■
>
> ### Case forms of personal pronouns
>
> | | **Subjective** | **Objective** | **Possessive** |
> |---|---|---|---|
> | **SINGULAR** | I, you, he, she, it | me, you, him, her, it | mine, yours, his, hers, its |
> | **PLURAL** | we, you, they | us, you, them | ours, yours, theirs |

19M Which case is correct when *and* connects pronouns?

When *and* connects more than one noun, one pronoun, or a noun and a pronoun, it forms a **compound subject** or a compound object. Compounding doesn't affect pronoun case—use the same case for all the pronouns.

> **COMPOUND PRONOUN SUBJECT**   **He and I** saw the solar eclipse.
>
> **COMPOUND PRONOUN OBJECT**   That eclipse astonished **him and me**.

Whenever you're unsure of whether to use pronouns in the subjective or objective case, use the QA case test in Quick Box 19.4 to get the answer.

- **She and I** [*not* Her and me, She and me, *or* Her and I] work as a team.
- He trained **her and me** [*not* she and I, her and I, *or* she and me] well.

> **Quick Box 19.4**   ■ ■ ■ ■ ■ ■
>
> ### Using the "QA case test"
>
> These examples use pronouns. The test also works with nouns.
>
> **Step 1** Write the sentence twice, once using the subjective case and once using the objective case. Then cross out enough words to isolate the element you're questioning.
>
> ~~Janet and~~ me learned about the moon.
>
> ~~Janet and~~ I learned about the moon.
>
> **Step 2** Omit the crossed-out words and read both sentences aloud to see which one sounds right.
>
> Me learned about the moon.   [No, this doesn't sound right.]
>
> I learned about the moon.   [This sounds right.]
>
> **Step 3** Select the correct version and restore what you crossed out.
>
> Janet and I learned about the moon.

19M

❶ Alert: As objects of PREPOSITIONS, PRONOUNS are in the objective case.

> **NO**   Mrs. Parks gave an assignment to Sam and I.

> **YES**   Mrs. Parks gave an assignment to **Sam and me**.

> **NO**   Mrs. Parks divided the work between **he and I**.

> **YES**   Mrs. Parks divided the work between **him and me**. ●

19N   How can I match case in appositives?

Match an APPOSITIVE to the same case as the word or words it renames. If you're uncertain which case to use, see the QA case test in Quick Box 19.4 to help you determine the answer.

- **We** [*not* Us] tennis players practice hard.

    The subjective pronoun *we* renames the subject *tennis players*.

- The winners, **she and I** [*not* her and me], advanced to the finals.

    The subjective pronouns *she and I* rename the subject *winners*.

- The coach trains **us** [*not* we] tennis players to practice hard.

    The objective pronoun *us* renames the object *tennis players*.

- The crowd cheered the winners, **her and me** [*not* she and I].

    The objective pronouns *her and me* rename the object *winners*.

19O   How does the subjective case work after linking verbs?

A pronoun that comes after a LINKING VERB either renames the SUBJECT or shows possession. In such cases, always use a pronoun in the subjective case.

- The contest winner was **I** [*not* me].

    I renames the subject, which is the noun *contest winner*, so the subjective-case *I* is correct.

- The prize was **mine**.

    Mine shows possession, so the possessive-case *mine* is correct.

19P   When do I use *who, whoever, whom,* and *whomever*?

The pronouns *who* and *whoever* are in the subjective case. The pronouns *whom* and *whomever* are in the objective case.

Whenever you're unsure of whether to use the subjective-case *who* and *whoever* or the objective-case *whom* and *whomever*, use a variation of the QA case test in Quick Box 19.4. For *who* and *whoever*, substitute *he, she,* or *they.* For *whom* and *whomever*, substitute *him, her,* or *them.*

- **Who/Whom** is coming to your party?

  He/She is coming to your party, so *who* is correct.

- Will you let **whoever/whomever** into the house?

  You will let *him/her* into the house, so *whomever* is correct.

In sentences with more than one CLAUSE, isolate the clause with the pronoun (shown in **boldface**), and apply the test.

- Give the package to **whoever/whomever is at the door**.

  He is at the door, so *whoever* is correct.

- Invite those guests **who/whom you can trust**.

  You believe you can trust *them*, so *whom* is correct.

- I will invite **whoever/whomever I wish to come**.

  I wish *them* to come, so *whomever* is correct.

- I will invite **whoever/whomever pleases me**.

  He pleases me, so *whoever* is correct.

- I will not invite strangers **who/whom show up at the house**.

  They show up at the house, so *who* is correct.

- Don't Twitter people **who/whom I did not invite**.

  I did not invite *them*, so *whom* is correct.

- If uninvited guests arrive, I will tell the police **who/whom they are**.

  They are *they* (not *them*), so *who* is correct.

Remember that *who* and *whoever* can function only as SUBJECTS or SUBJECT COMPLEMENTS in clauses. If the person(s) you refer to perform some action or are linked to a subject, *who/whoever* is correct.

19Q What case do I use after *than* and *as*?

When a pronoun follows *than* or *as*, choose its case according to the meaning you want to convey. These two sentences convey very different messages.

SENTENCE 1   My sister loved that dog more than **me**.

SENTENCE 2   My sister loved that dog more than **I**.

19Q

Sentence 1 means "My sister loved that dog more than she loved me" because the pronoun *me* is in the objective case. Sentence 2 means "My sister loved that dog more than I loved it" because the pronoun *I* is in the subjective case.

To make sure that your sentences using *than* or *as* deliver the message you intend, mentally fill in the implied words.

19R   What case do I use with infinitives and *-ing* words?

When you use INFINITIVES, make sure that your pronouns are in the objective case. This rule holds whether the pronoun is the subject or the object of the infinitive.

- Our tennis coach expects **me *to serve***.

  Me is the subject of the infinitive *to serve*.

- Our tennis coach expects him ***to beat* me**.

  Me is the object of the infinitive *to beat*.

With *-ing* words, the POSSESSIVE CASE can change a sentence's meaning entirely. For example, the following two sentences convey very different messages simply because of the change in case of the noun *man*. The same distinction applies to both nouns and pronouns.

SENTENCE 1   The detective noticed the **man** staggering.

> *Man* is in the objective case.

SENTENCE 2   The detective noticed the **man's** staggering.

> *Man's* is in the possessive case.

Sentence 1 means that the detective noticed the *man*. In contrast, sentence 2 means that the detective noticed the *staggering*. The same differences exist for the following two sentences, which use pronouns.

SENTENCE 3   The detective noticed **him** staggering.

SENTENCE 4   The detective noticed **his** staggering.

19S   What case do I use for *-self* pronouns?

Pronouns that end in *-self* (singular) or *-selves* (plural) usually refer to the subject of the sentence. They have a limited number of case forms.

FIRST PERSON   myself; ourselves

SECOND PERSON   yourself; yourselves

THIRD PERSON   himself, herself, itself; themselves

-Self pronouns are called **reflexive pronouns** when they refer to the subject. They cannot be subjects.

- She freed **herself** from a difficult situation.
- They allowed **themselves** another break from work.
- He is not **himself** today.
- Their new business can't possibly pay for **itself**.

Never use a reflexive pronoun in place of a subject or an object.

> **NO** The detective and **myself** had a long talk. He wanted my partner and **myself** to help him.
>
> The reflexive pronoun *myself* does not refer to the subject; it is the subject.

> **YES** The detective and **I** had a long talk. He wanted my partner and **me** to help him.

-Self pronouns are called **intensive pronouns** when they provide emphasis by intensifying the meaning of a nearby word: *The detective felt that his **career itself** was at risk.*

● **EXERCISE 19-3** Underline the correct pronoun of each pair in parentheses. For help, consult 19J through 19S.

EXAMPLE

Ricky Jay holds the world's record for card throwing; no one can throw a playing card faster than (he/him).

(1) Many magicians agree that no one is better at sleight-of-hand magic than (he/him). (2) Younger magicians often say that Ricky Jay influenced (their/them) to become professional performers. (3) In addition to (him/his) being a respected sleight-of-hand artist, Jay is also a scholar and historian. (4) His interest in strange performers led (him/he) to write *Learned Pigs and Fireproof Women*, which discusses unusual acts and begins with (him/his) explaining their appeal to audiences. (5) Jay's acting career has involved (his/him) performing in several different movies and TV shows. (6) In the James Bond film *Tomorrow Never Dies*, few could have played a villain as well as (he/him). (7) Other roles include (him/his) narrating the introduction to the movie *Magnolia*. (8) Overall, few performers have had such as varied and interesting career as (him/he). ●

19S

20 Adjectives and Adverbs

Quick Points   You will learn to

➤ Distinguish between adjectives and adverbs (pp. 324–325).

➤ Use adjectives and adverbs properly (pp. 325–329).

MyWritingLab™   Visit mywritinglab.com for more resources on adjectives and adverbs.

20A   What are the differences between adjectives and adverbs?

Both **adjectives** and **adverbs** are MODIFIERS. Modifiers describe other words. Adjectives and adverbs, however, modify very different parts of speech.

WHAT ADJECTIVES MODIFY

NOUNS	The *busy* **lawyer** rested.
PRONOUNS	**She** felt *tired*.

WHAT ADVERBS MODIFY

VERBS	The lawyer **spoke** *quickly*.
ADVERBS	The lawyer spoke *very* quickly.
ADJECTIVES	The lawyer was *extremely* busy.
INDEPENDENT CLAUSES	*Undoubtedly*, the lawyer needed a rest.

Many adverbs end in *-ly* (*run **swiftly***), but some do not (*run **often***). Also, some adjectives end in *-ly* (***friendly*** *dog*). Therefore, never depend entirely on an *-ly* ending to identify a word as an adverb.

20B   What's wrong with double negatives?

A **double negative** is nonstandard. STANDARD ENGLISH requires only one negative (for example, *no, not, never, none, nothing*, or *hardly*) in a sentence.

NO   The union members did **not** have **no** money in the reserve fund.

Two negatives, *not* and *no*, are used in the same sentence, contrary to the rules of standard English.

YES The union members did **not** have **any** money in the reserve fund.

Only one negative, *not*, is in this sentence.

YES The union members had **no** money in the reserve fund.

20C Do adjectives or adverbs come after linking verbs?

LINKING VERBS use adjectives as COMPLEMENTS. ACTION VERBS use adverbs.

● Anne **looks** *happy*.

Here *looks* functions as a linking verb, so the adjective *happy* is correct.

● Anne **looks** *happily* at the sunset.

Here *looks* functions as an action verb, so the adverb *happily* is correct.

■ Using *bad* and *badly*

Never substitute *badly* (adverb) for *bad* (adjective) after linking verbs such as *feel, smell,* and *taste*.

NO The student **felt** *badly*, so he went home.

Here *felt* links the adverb *badly* to *student*, a noun subject.

YES The student **felt** *bad*, so he went home.

Here *felt* links the adjective *bad* to *student*, a noun subject.

■ Using *good* and *well*

Good is always an adjective. *Well* is an adjective only when it is referring to health; otherwise, *well* is an adverb.

● You look **well**.

This means "You look to be in fine health." *Well* functions as an adjective.

● You write **well**.

This means "You write skillfully." *Well* functions as an adverb.

20C

● **EXERCISE 20-1** Underline the correct uses of adjectives and adverbs by selecting one of the choices in parentheses.

EXAMPLE

The Concert for Bangladesh (famous, <u>famously</u>) occurred on August 1st, 1971, and included two (<u>large</u>, largely) shows performed (energetic, <u>energetically</u>) at Madison Square Garden.

1. The concert did a (good, well) job raising awareness of the refugees who were treated (bad, badly) during the Bangladesh Liberation War and who also suffered (great, greatly) from a massive cyclone that hit the area in 1970.

2. The (high, highly) anticipated concert included several (famous, famously) musicians, who played (good, well) for the audience.

3. Members of the audience didn't (ever, never) expect to see George Harrison, who had not performed since the Beatles broke up, but he looked (happily, happy) as he played some of his (great, greatly) songs.

4. Another (notable, notably) important appearance was that of Bob Dylan, who appeared (rare, rarely) in public in the early 1970s, but he neither disappointed (nor, or) frustrated the crowd when he took the stage.

5. Many people consider this (massively, massive) show to be one of the first benefit concerts that are now more (common, commonly), and its roster of rock stars (easy, easily) makes it an important event. ●

20D What are correct comparative and superlative forms?

When adjectives and adverbs show comparisons, most forms are regular.

■ Regular forms of adjectives and adverbs

In the **comparative**, used to compare two items, regular adjectives and adverbs add either an *-er* ending or the word *more* or *less*. In the **superlative**, used to compare three items or more, regular forms add either an *-est* ending or the word *most* or *least*.

Positive [1]	Comparative [2]	Superlative [3+]
green	greener	greenest
early	earlier	earliest
selfish	less selfish	least selfish
beautiful	more beautiful	most beautiful

[1]   That tree is **green**.

[2]   That tree is **greener** than this tree.

[3+]   That tree is the **greenest** tree on the block.

The number of syllables in the adjective or adverb usually determines whether you use *-er* or *more* (comparative) or *-est* or *most* (superlative).

- Add *-er* and *-est* to one-syllable adjectives and adverbs: *large, larger, largest* (adjective); *far, farther, farthest* (adverb).
- Use *more* and *most* for adverbs with two or more syllables: for example, *easily, more easily, most easily.*
- Use either the *-er* and *-est* endings or *more* and *most* for two-syllable adjectives. The only way to know which forms are correct is to check the dictionary. The forms vary greatly.
- Add *more* and *most* to adjectives and adverbs with three or more syllables: *protective, more protective* [*not* "protectiver"], *most protective* [*not* "protectivest"].

❶ Alert: Never use *more* or *most* together with the *-er* or *-est* ending. For example, *more louder* and *most soonest* are incorrect forms. ●

■ Irregular forms of adjectives and adverbs

Few adjectives and adverbs are irregular in the comparative and superlative.

Positive [1]	Comparative [2]	Superlative [3+]
good [adjective]	better	best
well [adverb]	better	best
well [adjective]		
bad [adjective]	worse	worst
badly [adverb]	worse	worst
many	more	most
much	more	most
some	more	most
little	less	least

[1]   The Millers had **little** trouble finding jobs.
[2]   The Millers had **less** trouble finding jobs than the Smiths did.
[3+] The Millers had the **least** trouble finding jobs of everyone.

❶ Alert: Use *less* to refer to NONCOUNT NOUNS and *fewer* to refer to numbers and COUNT NOUNS: *They consumed **fewer calories** by using **less sugar**.* ●

20D

20E   Why do I avoid using too many nouns as modifiers?

Nouns sometimes modify other nouns: *truck driver, train track, security system.* Usually, these combinations don't trouble readers. However, when you string together too many nouns in a row as modifiers, you challenge readers to distinguish nouns that are modifying from nouns that are being modified. You can revise such sentences in several ways.

SENTENCE REWRITTEN

NO   The traffic accident vehicle description form instructions are clear.

YES   The form for descriptions of vehicles in traffic accidents has clear instructions.

NOUN REVISED TO POSSESSIVE CASE

NO   Some students might take the **US Navy engineering training examination**.

YES   Some students might take the **US Navy's examination** for **engineering training**.

NOUN REVISED TO PREPOSITIONAL PHRASE

NO   Our **student adviser training program** has won merit awards.

YES   Our **training program for student advisers** has won merit awards.

This revision also requires the plural *advisers*. Plural nouns are generally changed to singular when used as modifiers.

ESOL Tips: (1) Never add *-s* to an adjective, even when it modifies a plural noun.

NO   The instructor taught us **hards lessons**.

YES   The instructor taught us **hard lessons**.

(2) Never put an adverb between a VERB and a DIRECT OBJECT.

NO   He drank **quietly** the cola.

YES   He **quietly** drank the cola.

YES   He drank the cola **quietly**. ●

● **EXERCISE 20-2**   Underline the better choice in parentheses. For help, consult this entire chapter.

EXAMPLE

Alexis, a huge and powerful six-year-old Siberian tiger, (curious, <u>curiously</u>) explores her new zoo home together with five other tigers.

1. The new tiger home at the world-famous Bronx Zoo is a (special, specially) designed habitat, planted with (dense, denser) undergrowth so that it (close, closely) imitates the tigers' natural wilderness.

2. Like tigers in the wild, the six tigers in this habitat, which (more, many) experts consider the (more authentic, most authentic) of all artificial tiger environments in the world, will face some of the physical challenges and sensory experiences that keep them happy and (healthy, healthier).

3. Research shows that tigers feel (bad, badly) and fail to thrive in zoos without enrichment features placed in (good, well) locations to inspire tigers to stalk (stealthy, stealthily) through underbrush, loll (lazy, lazily) on heated rocks, or tug (vigorous, vigorously) on massive pull toys.

4. Wildlife zoologists think that the new Tiger Mountain exhibit will also serve zoo visitors (good, well) by allowing them to observe and admire the amazing strength, agility, and intelligence of a (rapid, rapidly) dwindling species.

5. Today, (fewer, less) than 5,000 Siberian tigers remain in the wild, which makes it imperative for zoos to raise people's awareness of the (great, greatest) need to prevent the extinction of these big cats that are considered among the (more, most) powerful, beautiful animals in the world.●

21 Sentence Fragments

■ ■ ■ ■ ■ ■

21A

Quick Points   You will learn to

➤ Identify sentence fragments (pp. 329–331).
➤ Correct sentence fragments (pp. 331–334).
➤ Use intentional sentence fragments when appropriate (p. 334).

MyWritingLab™   Visit mywritinglab.com for more resources on sentence fragments.

21A   How can I recognize sentence fragments?

A **sentence fragment** is a written error because it looks like a sentence but isn't one. Even though it starts with a capital letter and ends with a period, it's not a sentence. If you avoid the four types of sentence fragments listed in Quick Box 21.1, your sentences will be complete.

Quick Box 21.1

■ ■ ■ ■ ■ ■

How to recognize four types of sentence fragments

1. If a word group starts with a SUBORDINATING CONJUNCTION, such as *when*, without being joined to a complete sentence, it's a sentence fragment (see 21B).

    FRAGMENT **When winter comes early**.

    CORRECT **When winter comes early**, ice often traps whales in the Arctic Ocean.

    CORRECT Winter comes early.

2. If a word group includes no VERB and ends with a period, it's a sentence fragment.

    FRAGMENT **Whales in the Arctic Ocean**.

    CORRECT Whales **live** in the Arctic Ocean.

    Note that a VERBAL (the ones ending in *-ing* or *-ed*) is not a verb unless it teams up with an AUXILIARY VERB, such as *is* or *are* (see 21C). Verbals beginning with *to*, called INFINITIVES, remain as verbals. Auxiliary verbs have no effect on them.

    FRAGMENT **Whales living in the Arctic Ocean**.

    CORRECT Whales **are living** in the Arctic Ocean.

3. If a word group lacks a SUBJECT and ends with a period, it's a sentence fragment (see 21D).

    FRAGMENT **Were trapped by the solid ice**.

    CORRECT The whales **were trapped by the solid ice**.

4. If a word group is the second half of a COMPOUND PREDICATE and stands alone ending in a period, it's a sentence fragment. Compound predicates always start with one of the seven COORDINATING CONJUNCTIONS (*and, but, so, yet, for, or, nor;* see 21E).

    FRAGMENT The whales panicked in the confines of the ice. **And thrashed about, bumping into each other**.

    CORRECT The whales panicked in the confines of the ice **and thrashed about, bumping into each other**.

21A

● **EXERCISE 21-1** Identify each word group as either a complete sentence or a fragment. If the word group is a sentence, circle its number. If it's a fragment, tell why it's incomplete. For help, see Quick Box 21.1.

EXAMPLE

Although having a five-year-old Twinkie might not seem desirable.

[Fragment. Starts with a subordinating conjunction (although) and lacks an independent clause to complete the thought.]

1. Because scientists are working on making foods "indestructible."
2. New preservation technologies responsible for bread puddings that can last four years.
3. Success with current experiments might mean people having to buy groceries only once a month.
4. That people on limited budgets won't have to throw away as much food.
5. Solves three challenges in making food last longer: controlling moisture, exposure to air, and bacteria and molds.
6. "Super sandwiches" packaged with chemicals that absorb oxygen can last three to five years.
7. To control bacteria, sterilizing food in a pouch subjected to pressures of 87,000 pounds per square inch.
8. Because of their tough protein fibers, meat products stand up particularly well to new preserving techniques.
9. Although victims of disasters like earthquakes, floods, and fires benefit from foods that can be stockpiled.
10. Stores with less need of refrigeration. ●

21B How can I correct a fragment that starts with a subordinating word?

First, you want to become entirely familiar with the list of SUBORDINATING CONJUNCTIONS (complete list appears in section 16H). If a word group starts with a subordinating conjunction without being joined to a complete sentence, it's a sentence fragment.

FRAGMENT Because the ship had to cut through the ice.

CORRECT **Because the ship had to cut through the ice**, the rescue effort took time.

The sentence fragment starts with the subordinating conjunction *because* and ends in a period, so it's a word group, not a complete sentence. Attaching the fragment to the start of an added complete sentence corrects the error.

CORRECT The rescue effort took time **because the ship had to cut through the ice**.

Attaching the fragment to the end of an added complete sentence corrects the error.

> **CORRECT**   **The ship had to cut through the ice**.
>
> Dropping the subordinating conjunction *because* from the fragment corrects the error.

Unless they start a question, the subordinating words *who* or *which* create a special type of sentence fragment.

> **FRAGMENT**   **Who feared the whales would die without enough space for air**.
>
> **CORRECT**   The ship's noisy motor worried the crew, **who feared the whales would die without enough space for air**.
>
> Attaching the *who* sentence fragment at the end of the complete sentence, where it makes sense, corrects the error.

> **FRAGMENT**   **Which sent booming sound waves through the water**.
>
> **CORRECT**   The ship's noisy motor, **which sent booming sound waves through the water**, worried the crew.
>
> Placing the *which* fragment in the middle of the complete sentence, where it makes sense, corrects the error.

> **CORRECT**   The ship's noisy motor, **which sent booming sound waves through the water**, worried the crew, **who feared the whales would die without enough space for air**.
>
> Combining both the *who* and *which* sentence fragments with the complete sentence creates a richly textured message.

21C   How can I correct a fragment that lacks a verb?

If a word group includes no VERB and ends with a period, it's a sentence fragment. In looking for a verb, don't mistake a verbal for a complete verb. Verbals ending in *-ing* or *-ed* become verbs only when teamed up with an AUXILIARY VERB. Verbals beginning with *to*, called INFINITIVES, remain as verbals; auxiliary verbs have no effect on them.

> **FRAGMENT**   The sailors **debating** whether **to play** classical music over the ship's sound system.
>
> **CORRECT**   The sailors **were debating** whether **to play** classical music over the ship's sound system.
>
> Adding the auxiliary verb *were* to *debating* creates a complete verb, which corrects the error. *To play* doesn't change.

An APPOSITIVE is a descriptive word group that lacks a verb, so it can't stand alone as a sentence. An appositive needs to be placed within a sentence immediately next to what it describes.

> **FRAGMENT**   **An enormously powerful icebreaker**. The ship arrived to free the whales.

CORRECT | **An enormously powerful icebreaker**, the ship arrived to free the whales.

CORRECT | The ship, **an enormously powerful icebreaker**, arrived to free the whales.

The appositive placed immediately next to "the ship" within the sentence corrects the error.

If a TRANSITIONAL EXPRESSION (complete list in Quick Box 5.3) starts a word group that lacks a verb, it's a sentence fragment.

FRAGMENT | **Such as Bach's sonatas for flute**.

CORRECT | The ship's crew chose Bach's sonatas for flute.

CORRECT | The crew wanted to play high-pitched music, **such as Bach's sonatas for flute**.

The sentence fragment revised into a complete sentence or attached to a nearby sentence corrects the error.

21D   How can I correct a fragment that lacks a subject?

If a word group lacks a SUBJECT and ends with a period, it's a sentence fragment.

FRAGMENT | **Had heard recordings of the high-pitched calls whales make**.

CORRECT | Some crew members **had heard recordings of the high-pitched calls whale make**.

Inserting the subject *Some crew members* at the start of the fragment corrects the error.

21E

21E   How can I correct a fragment that's a part of a compound predicate?

Many types of COMPOUND PREDICATES occur in sentences. One type contains two or more verbs connected by a COORDINATING CONJUNCTION (*and, but, for, or, nor, yet, so*). When a compound predicate isn't attached to the end of its companion sentence, it is a sentence fragment.

FRAGMENT | With a flute concerto playing loudly on its speakers, the ship finally reached the whales. **And led them to freedom**.

CORRECT | With a flute concerto playing loudly on its speakers, the ship finally reached the whales **and led them to freedom**.

Joining the compound predicate to the end of the complete sentence corrects the error.

> **CORRECT** With a flute concerto playing loudly on its speakers, the ship finally reached the whales. **The ship led them to freedom**.
>
> Dropping *and* and inserting a subject, "the ship," corrects the error.

● **EXERCISE 21-2** Revise this paragraph to eliminate all sentence fragments. In some cases, you can combine word groups to create complete sentences; in other cases, you must supply missing elements to revise word groups. Some sentences may not require revision. In your final version, check not only the individual sentences but also the clarity of the whole paragraph. Refer to 21A through 21E for help.

(1) The English games cricket and rounders. (2) Are the forerunners of the American game baseball. (3) Which became popular in America in the nineteenth century. (4) According to the *New York Morning News*, in an article from 1845. (5) Members of the New York Knickerbockers Club played the first reported baseball game. (6) Taking place at Elysian Fields in Hoboken, New Jersey. (7) Creating one of baseball's first teams, and writing "20 Original Rules of Baseball." (8) Alexander Cartwright is often called the Father of Baseball. (9) By scholars and historians of the game. (10) His new rules, which became known as Knickerbocker Rules. (11) Changed baseball in a number of ways. (12) Such as giving each batter three strikes and each inning three outs. (13) The first game, therefore. (14) That used the Knickerbocker Rules was played on June 19, 1846, in New Jersey. (15) Acting as umpire for this game. (16) Cartwright charged six-cent fines for swearing. (17) The Knickerbockers lost this game by 22 points to a team. (18) That was known as "The New York Nine." ●

21F What are intentional fragments?

Professional writers sometimes intentionally use sentence fragments for emphasis and effect. Today, such fragments are not unusual in popular magazines and in written advertisements. A writer's ability to judge the difference between acceptable and unacceptable sentence fragments comes from much experience writing as well as exposure to the works of skilled writers. Some instructors consider a sentence fragment an error in ACADEMIC WRITING. Other teachers occasionally accept well-placed intentional fragments after a student has shown the consistent ability to write well-constructed complete sentences. Therefore, if you'd like to use a fragment for emphasis and effect, we advise that you either inquire about your teacher's stance ahead of time or write a footnote in your essay that says you're using a sentence fragment intentionally for effect.

22 Comma Splices and Run-On Sentences

■ ■ ■ ■ ■ ■

Quick Points You will learn to

➤ Identify comma splices and run-on sentences (p. 335).
➤ Correct comma splices and run-on sentences (pp. 335–338).

MyWritingLab™ Visit mywritinglab.com for more resources on comma splices and run-on sentences.

22A What are comma splices and run-on sentences?

Comma splices and run-on sentences are errors that incorrectly join two INDE-PENDENT CLAUSES. A **comma splice** is created when only a comma separates independent clauses. A **run-on sentence** is created when no punctuation at all separates independent clauses (see Quick Box 22.1).

> **COMMA SPLICE** The storm **intensified, it** turned toward land.

> **RUN-ON SENTENCE** The storm **intensified it** turned toward land.

🛈 **Alert:** Occasionally, experienced writers use a comma to join short, con-trasting independent clauses: *Mosquitoes do not **bite, they** stab*. Your teacher may consider this punctuation an error, so check before you use it. ●

22B How can I correct comma splices and run-on sentences?

To correct comma splices and run-on sentences, you can use punctuation or a coordinating conjunction, or you can revise one of the two incorrectly joined sentences into a DEPENDENT CLAUSE.

■ Using punctuation

You can use a period or a semicolon to separate independent clauses in a comma splice or run-on sentence.

> **COMMA SPLICE** A shark's skeleton is all **cartilage, the shark** does not have a bone in its body.

> **RUN-ON SENTENCE** A shark's skeleton is all **cartilage the shark** does not have a bone in its body.

> **CORRECT** A shark's skeleton is all **cartilage. The shark** does not have a bone in its body.

335

Quick Box 22.1

How to identify and correct comma splices and run-on sentences

1. Watch out for a second independent clause that starts with a PERSONAL PRONOUN.

COMMA SPLICE	Thomas Edison was a productive **inventor, he held** more than 1,300 American and foreign patents.
RUN-ON SENTENCE	Thomas Edison was a productive **inventor he held** more than 1,300 American and foreign patents.
CORRECT	Thomas Edison was a productive **inventor. He held** more than 1,300 American and foreign patents.

2. Watch out for a CONJUNCTIVE ADVERB that joins two sentences.

COMMA SPLICE	Thomas Edison was a brilliant **scientist, however**, he spent only three months in school.
RUN-ON SENTENCE	Thomas Edison was a brilliant **scientist however**, he spent only three months in school.
CORRECT	Thomas Edison was a brilliant **scientist; however**, he spent only three months in school.

3. Watch out for a TRANSITIONAL EXPRESSION that joins two sentences.

COMMA SPLICE	Thomas Edison invented the **microphone, in addition, he created** a superior storage battery.
RUN-ON SENTENCE	Thomas Edison invented the **microphone in addition, he created** a superior storage battery.
CORRECT	Thomas Edison invented the **microphone. In addition, he created** a superior storage battery.

4. Watch out when a second independent clause explains or gives an example of the information in the first independent clause.

COMMA SPLICE	Edison created **many inventions**, his best known include the phonograph and the incandescent lamp.
RUN-ON SENTENCE	Edison created **many inventions** his best known include the phonograph and the incandescent lamp.
CORRECT	Edison created many **inventions**. His best known include the phonograph and the incandescent lamp.

22B

■ Using a coordinating conjunction

If the ideas in your independent clauses relate closely in meaning and are grammatically equivalent, you can connect them with a comma followed by a coordinating conjunction (*and, but, for, or, nor, yet, so*).

COMMA SPLICE	Every living creature sends a weak electrical charge in **water,** a shark can detect these signals.
RUN-ON SENTENCE	Every living creature sends a weak electrical charge in **water** a shark can detect these signals.
CORRECT	Every living creature sends a weak electrical charge in **water,** *and* a shark can detect these signals.

■ Revising an independent clause into a dependent clause

If one of two independent clauses expresses information that can be logically subordinated to the other independent clause, start it with a subordinating word and join it correctly to the independent clause.

COMMA SPLICE	Costa Rica's Cocos Island harbors more sharks than anywhere else on **earth, it is** paradise to underwater filmmakers.
RUN-ON SENTENCE	Costa Rica's Cocos Island harbors more sharks than anywhere else on **earth it is** paradise to underwater filmmakers.
CORRECT	*Because* Costa Rica's Cocos Island harbors more sharks than anywhere else on **earth, it is** paradise to underwater filmmakers.
	Because makes the first clause dependent.

COMMA SPLICE	Some sharks have large, triangular **teeth, these** teeth can tear flesh.
RUN-ON SENTENCE	Some sharks have large, triangular **teeth these** teeth can tear flesh.
CORRECT	Some sharks have large, triangular **teeth** *that* can tear flesh.
	That makes the second clause dependent.

When a conjunctive adverb (such as *however, therefore, also, next, then, thus, furthermore,* or *nevertheless*) or a transitional expression (such as *for example* or *for instance*) falls between spliced or run-on independent clauses, you need to use a period or a semicolon to correct the error.

COMMA SPLICE	Some sharks cannot **bite, for example**, the whale shark filters plants through its tiny mouth.
RUN-ON SENTENCE	Some sharks cannot **bite for example**, the whale shark filters plants through its tiny mouth.

22B

CORRECT   Some sharks cannot **bite. For example**, the whale shark filters plants through its tiny mouth.

CORRECT   Some sharks cannot **bite; for example**, the whale shark filters plants through its tiny mouth.

● **EXERCISE 22-1**   Identify and then revise the comma splices and run-on sentences. Circle the numbers of correct sentences.

EXAMPLE

COMMA SPLICE   Basketball was invented in 1891, today, it is one of the world's most popular sports.

RUN-ON SENTENCE   Basketball was invented in 1891 today, it is one of the world's most popular sports.

CORRECT   Basketball was invented in 1891; today, it is one of the world's most popular sports.

1. James Naismith, a physical education professor at what is known today as Springfield College, needed an indoor sport for his students to play on rainy days, he invented basketball.

2. At first, he didn't use a net he used a peach basket.

3. Dribbling, the act of bouncing the ball between passes and shots, did not become common in basketball until much later, originally, players merely carried the ball.

4. Backboards were also not introduced until later, this kept fans from being able to interfere with the action.

5. Without balls made specifically for the sport, early basketball players had to use soccer balls in the 1950s, Tony Hinkle introduced the now famous orange balls that are easier for players and spectators to see.

6. The first official basketball game was played in 1892 in Albany, New York, only one point was scored.

7. Founded in 1946, the National Basketball Association (NBA) began with the help of owners of ice hockey arenas, many consider the game between the Toronto Huskies and the New York Knickerbockers in 1946 as the first official NBA game.

8. Although a three-point rule was first used in 1933, the NBA did not officially add the rule until 1979, the year that Larry Bird and Magic Johnson began playing professionally.

9. On March 2nd, 1962, in Hershey, Pennsylvania, Wilt Chamberlain, playing for the Philadelphia Warriors, scored a record 100 points in one game his average for the season was 50.4 points per game.

10. Now a worldwide sport, basketball debuted in the Olympics in 1936, the United States defeated Canada in a game played outdoors. ●

22B

Problems with Sentence Shifts

■ ■ ■ ■ ■ ■

Quick Points You will learn to

➤ Write sentences that have consistent grammatical forms.

MyWritingLab™ Visit mywritinglab.com for more resources on problems with sentence shifts.

Shifts are mismatched grammatical forms that cloud your meaning and baffle your readers. To avoid writing sentence shifts, be consistent in using the grammatical forms covered in 23A–23D.

23A How can I be consistent in person and number?

Person indicates who or what performs or receives action. FIRST PERSON (*I, we*) is the writer or speaker; SECOND PERSON (*you*) is someone written or spoken to; THIRD PERSON (*he, she it, they*) is someone or something written or spoken about. Unintended shifts in person blur your meaning.

NO I enjoy reading financial forecasts, but **you** wonder which are accurate.

First person *I* shifts unnecessarily to second person *you*.

YES I enjoy reading financial forecasts, but **I** wonder which are accurate.

🛈 **Alert:** All NOUNS and many PRONOUNS are always in third person. ●

23A

Number refers to SINGULAR (one) or PLURAL (more than one). Don't mix singular and plural unless your meaning calls for it.

NO Because **people** are living longer, **an employee** now retires later.

The plural *people* shifts to the singular *employee*.

YES Because **people** are living longer, **employees** now retire later.

🛈 **Alerts:** (1) Watch for shifts from nouns to the second-person pronoun *you*.

● By the year 2020, **most people** will live longer, and ~~you~~ will have to work longer, too.
^{they}

339

(2) Watch for shifts between singular and plural in the third person.

- The longer ~~a person stays~~ _{people stay} in the workforce, the more competition they will face from younger job seekers. ●

23B How can I be consistent in subject and voice?

A needless shift in SUBJECT can cause your writing to lose its emphasis.

NO   I **realize** the dangers of sugary, high-fat foods, but **donuts are often** my breakfast.

The subject needlessly shifts from *I* to *donuts.*

YES   I **realize** the dangers of sugary, high-fat foods, but **I often eat donuts** for breakfast.

VOICE tells whether the subject acts (ACTIVE VOICE) or is acted upon (PASSIVE VOICE). In addition, shifts in voice also necessitate shifts in subject.

NO   The officers **confronted** me, and I **was accused** of the crime.

The sentence shifts from active voice *confronted* to passive voice *was accused.*

YES   The officers **confronted** me and **accused** me of a crime.

YES   I **was confronted** by the officers and **accused** of a crime.

23C How can I be consistent in mood?

MOOD tells what the writer wishes to convey in a verb: a statement or question (INDICATIVE MOOD), a command or request (IMPERATIVE MOOD), a condition or supposition (SUBJUNCTIVE MOOD). Shifts in mood perplex your readers.

NO   Students **should bring** identification to the exam, and **don't be** late.

The verb switches from the indicative *should bring* to the imperative *don't be.*

YES   Students **should bring** identification to the exam and **arrive** on time.

YES   **Bring** your identification to the exam and **be** on time.

23D How can I be consistent in verb tense?

To be consistent in verb tense, remain in the same tense unless a shift is necessary to show time passing (see Quick Box 17.3).

NO   She **stared** at the exam and **wonders** about her grade in this class.

The verb tense shifts from past tense *stared* to present tense *wonders.*

YES   She **stared** at the exam and **wondered** about her grade in this class.

YES   She **stares** at the exam and **wonders** about her grade.

23E   How can I be consistent in direct and indirect discourse?

Direct discourse repeats someone's words exactly, with quotation marks enclosing them. **Indirect discourse** reports, rather than repeats exactly, someone's words without using quotation marks. Shifts between these two disrupt the smoothness of your sentence.

NO   She asked me was I going out.

> This sentence shifts from indirect to direct discourse. Direct discourse requires quotation marks and changes in language.

YES   She asked me whether I was going out.

YES   She asked me, "Are you going out?"

23F   What happens in sentences with mixed parts?

A sentence with mixed parts starts in one direction but confusingly goes off in a different direction. To revise such errors, think through exactly what you want to say.

■ Avoiding mixed clauses

In a sentence containing a DEPENDENT CLAUSE and an INDEPENDENT CLAUSE, the clauses are clear when they carry meaning in one direction, not two directions.

NO   When we lost first prize motivated us to train harder.

> The second part of the sentence, *motivated us to train harder,* has no subject.

YES   When we lost first prize, we became motivated to train harder.

YES   Losing first prize motivated us to train harder.

■ Avoiding mixed constructions

If a group of words contains a PHRASE and only part of an independent clause, it forms a **mixed construction** that makes no sense.

NO   By tweeting her fans creates much excitement.

> This sentence opens with the phrase *by tweeting her fans,* then moves to the verb *creates.*

YES   Tweeting her fans creates much excitement.

Dropping the preposition *by* focuses the sentence's meaning.

YES   Tweeting her fans, she creates much excitement.

The subject *she* and the verb *creates* are logically and grammatically related.

■ Avoiding faulty predication

Faulty predication results when the subject and PREDICATE of a sentence don't make sense together. You can avoid the error by revising either part.

NO   The purpose of television was invented to entertain.

The subject of the sentence, *purpose,* doesn't make sense with the predicate *was invented to entertain.*

YES   **Television** was invented to entertain.

YES   The purpose of television **was to entertain**.

23G   How do elliptical constructions and comparisons work?

An **elliptical construction** deliberately leaves out one or more words that appear earlier in a sentence. An elliptical sentence is correct only when it omits exactly the same words as have been used previously in the same sentence.

- In 1920s Chicago, cornetist Manuel Perez ~~was leading~~ *led* one outstanding jazz group, Tommy and Jimmy Dorsey another.

  The singular verb *was leading* cannot take the place of *were leading* in the second part of the sentence. *Led* works because it goes with both the singular *Perez* and the plural *Tommy and Jimmy Dorsey.*

- The period of the big jazz dance bands began *in* and lasted through World War II.

  Began needs to be followed by *in*, because *through* doesn't work after both *began* and *lasted*.

In writing a comparison, you can omit words as long as the reader can clearly tell what the missing words are.

- High achievers make better business executives *than low achievers do*.

  Better implies a comparison, but none is stated, so the revision corrects the problem.

- Most stockholders value high achievers more than *they value* risk takers.

  The revised sentence states clearly who values whom. Another revision, *Most stockholders value high achievers more than risk takers do*, changes the meaning.

● A risk taker's ability to manage long-term growth is very different. *from that of a high achiever*

Different from what? When the comparison expresses both items, it succeeds.

⚠ **Alert:** When you write *as much as*, *as . . . as . . . than* (for example, *as tall as*, *if not taller than*), and similar comparisons, be sure to state the second *as*.

● High achievers value success as much, if not more than, high salary. ● *as*

● **EXERCISE 23-1**   Revise these sentences to correct elliptical constructions, to complete comparisons, or to insert any missing words.

1. Champagne is a kind of sparkling wine grown in Champagne region France.
2. To be considered champagne, a sparkling wine must meet several conditions described French law.
3. The location of the vineyard is one requirement, and type of grapes another.
4. Most champagne producers agree that the Chardonnay and Pinot Noir grapes make champagne taste better.
5. When owners celebrate the launch of a new ship, they use bottles of champagne more often. ●

24 Misplaced Modifiers
■ ■ ■ ■ ■ ■

Quick Points   You will learn to

➤ Place modifiers carefully so that your intended meaning is clear.

MyWritingLab™   Visit mywritinglab.com for more resources on misplaced modifiers.

A MODIFIER is a word, PHRASE, or CLAUSE that describes or limits other words, phrases, or clauses. When you write, place modifiers carefully so that your intended meaning is clear.

24A   How can I correct misplaced modifiers?

The correct placement for a modifier is almost always next to the word that it modifies. If you misplace the modifier, the sentence becomes confusing.

> **MISPLACED**   Nicholas Cugnot built the first self-propelled vehicle,
> **MODIFIER**   determined to travel without horses.
>
> > Because the modifier *determined to travel without horses* is positioned next to *vehicle*, the sentence says the *vehicle* was determined to travel without horses, not Nicholas Cugnot.
>
> **CORRECT**   Determined to travel without horses, Nicholas Cugnot built the first self-propelled vehicle.

Carefully place ADVERBS such as *only, just, almost, hardly, scarcely*, and *simply* to say precisely what you mean. For example, notice how various positions of *only* influence the meaning of the sentence *Professional coaches say that high salaries motivate players.*

- **Only** professional coaches say that high salaries motivate players.

  No one else says that.

- Professional coaches **only** say that high salaries motivate players.

  The coaches don't believe it.

- Professional coaches say that **only** high salaries motivate players.

  The coaches think nothing else works.

- Professional coaches say that high salaries motivate **only** players.

  No one else is motivated by high salaries.

24B   How can I correct squinting modifiers?

A misplaced **squinting modifier** can modify both the words before it and after it. The writer needs to put the modifier near the word it modifies to communicate the meaning clearly.

> **NO**   Witnesses claimed **furiously** the driver bolted from the scene.
>
> > Which happened furiously: *witnesses claimed* or *the driver bolted*?
>
> **YES**   Witnesses claimed the driver bolted **furiously** from the scene.

24C   How can I correct split infinitives?

A misplaced **split infinitive** occurs when words separate *to* from the verb that completes the infinitive. I want *to boldly design.* Often, the effect is awkward.

NO   The student tried **to in some way pacify** his instructor.

In some way is misplaced because it splits *to pacify*.

YES   The student tried **to pacify** his instructor in some way.

YES   In some way, the student tried **to pacify** his instructor.

24D   How can I keep modifiers from disrupting a sentence?

Avoid writing complex descriptive phrases or clauses that separate the SUBJECT and VERB of a sentence. Such modifiers make a sentence overly complicated, disturbing its smooth flow.

- ~~The invention of the automobile,~~ *If* if we consider the complete history of people working independently in different countries, should probably be credited to *the invention of the automobile* Nicholas Cugnot in 1769.

Also, interrupting a VERB PHRASE with modifiers disturbs sentence flow. Follow the general rule to put modifiers next to the word they modify.

- Karl Benz has ~~by most automobile historians~~ *by most automobile historians* been given credit for the invention of the automobile.

● **EXERCISE 24-1**   Revise these ten sentences to correct misplaced modifiers, split infinitives, and other splits. If a sentence is correct, circle its number. For help, consult 24A through 24D.

EXAMPLE

The city of Deadwood is known for its many notorious residents **made popular by** a TV show including Wild Bill Hickok and Calamity Jane.

Made popular by a TV show, the city of Deadwood is known for its many notorious residents, including Wild Bill Hickok and Calamity Jane.

1. Deadwood, because of its location near the Deadwood Gulch and the Black Hills of South Dakota, was named for the dead trees found in that canyon.
2. The city's founding, during a gold rush that attracted a quarter of a million miners to the area, was in 1876.
3. The main source of revenue for the city was gambling, which was outlawed in 1905 but reinstated in 1989.
4. Today, tourists who visit Deadwood often gamble and enjoy the historical reenactments of the town's famous events.

24D

5. Deadwood nearly was the home to a dozen of famous characters from the Old West.

6. Serving as the sheriff of Hays City and Abilene, Wild Bill Hickok worked to with an iron fist tame the lawless towns of the frontier.

7. Hickok moved to Deadwood after he without much success performed in a Wild West show.

8. During a poker game at Nuttall & Mann's saloon, Jack McCall shot for unknown reasons Wild Bill.

9. The cards Hickok was holding included a pair of black aces, a pair of black eights, and an unknown fifth card now known as the dead man's hand.

10. The legends of Deadwood and Wild Bill in the stories of fiction writers and TV shows continue to grow. ●

24E   How can I correct dangling modifiers?

A **dangling modifier** is an introductory phrase that hangs (or dangles) help-lessly because the NOUN it modifies isn't the intended subject. Introductory phrases attach their meaning to the first noun after the phrase—the sentence's subject. If some other word falls in that position, the result is confusing.

> **NO**   **Approaching the island, a mountainous rock wall** was terrifying.
>
> This sentence suggests that the mountainous wall was approaching the island.
>
> **YES**   Approaching the island, **we** saw a foreboding mountainous wall.
>
> **YES**   As we approached the island, **we** saw a frightening mountainous wall.
>
> Both revised sentences include the subject *we*.

> **NO**   To ease our fears, our ship swerved around the island.
>
> This sentence suggests that our ship eased our fears.
>
> **YES**   To ease our fears, the pilot steered our ship around the island.

● **EXERCISE 24-2**   Using each list of words and phrases, create all the possi-ble logical sentences. Insert commas as needed. Explain differences in meaning among the alternatives you create. For help, consult 24A through 24E.

EXAMPLE

exchange students

learned to speak French

while in Paris

last summer

A. Last summer,/exchange students/learned to speak French/while in Paris.

B. While in Paris,/exchange students/learned to speak French/last summer.

C. Exchange students/learned to speak French/while in Paris/last summer.

D. Exchange students/learned to speak French/last summer/while in Paris.

1. chicken soup
    according to folklore
    helps
    cure colds

2. tadpoles
    instinctively
    swim
    toward
    their genetic relatives

3. the young driver
    while driving
    in the snow
    skidded carelessly

4. climbed
    the limber teenager
    a tall palm tree
    to pick a ripe coconut
    quickly

5. and cause mini-avalanches
    ski patrollers
    set explosives
    often
    to prevent
    big avalanches ●

25

25 Conciseness
■ ■ ■ ■ ■ ■

Quick Points   You will learn to

➤ Write concisely.

MyWritingLab™   Visit mywritinglab.com for more resources on conciseness.

Conciseness is desirable because it makes writing direct. **Wordiness** uses empty, unnecessary words and PHRASES that contribute nothing to meaning.

25A How can I write concisely?

You can write concisely by deleting all words not necessary for delivering your message clearly. Get rid of the unneeded words listed in Quick Box 25.1 and similar expressions.

25B How can I avoid redundant writing?

Redundant writing is undesirably repetitious writing that duplicates a message that has already been stated. Unlike intentional repetition, which can create powerful rhythms, redundant writing is sloppy and burdensome to readers.

- ~~People who are~~ anesthetized ~~for surgery~~ can remain semiconscious during sur- gery but nevertheless feel no pain.

  Surgery is used twice unnecessarily. The word *anesthetized* carries the concept of surgery. The revision is not redundant.

- The cell phone was red ~~in color~~ and rectangular ~~in shape~~.

  Red includes the concept of color; *rectangular* includes shape.

- Concise writing in college is a ~~required~~ necessity.

  The concept *necessity* includes the concept *required*.

● **EXERCISE 25-1**   Revise this paragraph in two steps. First, underline all words that interfere with conciseness. Second, revise each sentence to make it more concise. (You'll need to drop words and replace or rearrange others.)

25A

EXAMPLE

Because of the fact that a new building in Dubai was recently declared the "Tallest Building in the World," some people have a tendency to wonder how such a title is granted.

1. Because <u>of the fact that</u> a new building in Dubai was recently declared the "Tallest Building in the World," some people <u>have a tendency to</u> wonder who grants such a title.

2. Because a new building in Dubai was recently declared the "Tallest Building in the World," some wonder who grants such a title.

1. Tall buildings that exist are measured by a group known as The Council on Tall Buildings and Urban Habitat.
2. This group, as a matter of fact, was founded in 1969 and is responsible for determining which building is the tallest.

Quick Box 25.1

Deleting unneeded words

Empty Words	Wordy Examples Revised
as a matter of fact, the fact of the matter	~~As a matter of fact,~~ ^M many marriages end in divorce.
at the present time	The bill is being debated ^{now} ~~at the present time~~.
because of the fact that, in light of the fact that, due to the fact that	Because ~~of the fact that~~ a special exhibit is scheduled, the museum is open late.
factor	The project's final cost was ~~an~~ essential ~~factor~~ to consider.
that exists	The crime rate ~~that exists~~ is unacceptable.
for the purpose of	A work crew arrived ^{to} ~~for the purpose of~~ fixing the pothole.
in a very real sense	~~In a very real sense,~~ ^D drainage problems persist.
in the case of	~~In the case of~~ ^T the proposed tax ^{angered} residents ~~were angry~~.
in the event that	~~In the event that~~ ^{If} you are late, I will buy our tickets.
it seems that	~~It seems that~~ ^T the union struck over wages.
manner	The hikers looked at the snake ~~in a fearful~~ ^{fearfully} ~~manner~~.
nature	The review was ~~of a~~ markedly sarcastic ~~nature~~.
the point that I am trying to make	~~The point that I am trying to make is that~~ ^N news reporters often invade people's privacy.
what I mean to say	~~What I mean to say is that~~ I expect a bonus.
type of, kind of	Gordon took a relaxing ~~type of~~ vacation.

25B

3. Due to the fact that buildings serve many purposes, it seems that there is debate on which buildings deserve consideration.
4. I am trying to make the point that The Council on Tall Buildings and Urban Habitat must distinguish between buildings and towers.
5. To be considered, a building has to be the kind of structure that has usable floor area.
6. In the event that a structure has no usable floor area, it is designated a tower.
7. Height is determined by means of measuring from the lowest pedestrian entrance to the highest point of the building.
8. There are debates that exist over the definitions used by the Council on Tall Buildings.
9. For example, in the event that a building has not opened yet, it cannot be considered.
10. Another debate and matter of controversy is whether a building's antenna is an essential factor in determining its height. ●

25C How can I avoid wordy sentence structures?

Expletive constructions and the passive voice frequently cause wordiness.

■ Avoiding expletive constructions

An **expletive construction** places *it* or *there* and a form of *be* before the subject of the sentence. To make such sentences more concise, revise them to eliminate the expletive.

                                 S   *need*

● ~~It is necessary for~~ students to fill out both registration forms.

                                        T   *offers three majors*

● ~~There are three majors offered by~~ the computer science department.

■ Using the passive voice appropriately

The PASSIVE VOICE is generally less lively and concise than the ACTIVE VOICE (see 17G). Unless your meaning calls for the passive voice, write in the active voice.

PASSIVE	Volunteer work **was done by me** for extra credit.
	Here the passive voice is unnecessary. The writer, who is doing the action of volunteer work, needs to be the subject of this sentence.
ACTIVE	**I did** volunteer work for extra credit.
ACTIVE	**Volunteer work earned me** extra credit.
	Here, *Volunteer work*, the subject, performs the action *earned*.

25D   How can combining sentence elements help me be concise?

Sometimes you can combine sentences to save words. Look at two sentences at a time to see if words in one sentence can be included in another.

- ~~The Titanic was discovered~~ seventy-three years after being sunk by an iceberg.
  t   Titanic
  ~~The liner~~ was located under the water by a team of French and American scientists.

Sometimes you can shorten longer structures to a phrase or a word.

- The *Titanic*, ~~which was~~ a huge ocean liner, sank in 1911.

- The scientists who discovered the *Titanic* held a memorial service
  dead
  for the passengers and crew members ~~who had died.~~
  T   luxury
  ~~Loaded with luxuries,~~ the liner was thought to be unsinkable.

25E   How do action verbs improve conciseness?

Action verbs are strong verbs. Weak verbs, especially forms of *be* and *have*, usually lead to wordy sentences.

> **WEAK VERB**   The plan before the city council **has to do with** tax rebates.
> **STRONG VERB**   The plan before the city council **proposes** tax rebates.

Alert: Revise phrase patterns such as *be aware of* and *be capable of* to make them more concise. Often action verbs have greater impact than these wordy phrases. Here are some examples: I *envy* [not *am envious of*] your self-confidence. We *support* [not *are supportive of*] your cause. ●

25E

When you revise to use strong VERBS, turn nouns that end with *-ance*, *-ment*, and *-tion* into verbs to write more concisely.

> **NO**   The **accumulation** of old newspapers went on for seven years.
>
> **YES**   The old newspapers **accumulated** for seven years.

● **EXERCISE 25-2**   Combine each set of sentences to eliminate wordy constructions.

EXAMPLE

Original: The Brooklyn Bridge was completed in 1883. It is one of the oldest suspension bridges in the United States

Revised: Completed in 1883, the Brooklyn Bridge is one of the oldest suspension bridges in the United States

1. The Brooklyn Bridge spans the East River. It connects Manhattan and Brooklyn. The span of the bridge is 1,595 feet.
2. When the Brooklyn Bridge opened, it was the longest suspension bridge in the world. It was the longest suspension bridge until 1903. In 1903, the Williamsburg Bridge became the longest suspension bridge in the world.
3. The original designer of the bridge was John Augustus Roebling. He was a German immigrant. He injured his foot then died from an infection. Before he died, he turned over control of construction to his son. His son's name was Washington Roebling.
4. Emily Warren Roebling supervised most of the building of the Brooklyn Bridge. Her husband, Washington Roebling, was unable to oversee construction. He had to stop working after suffering an illness.
5. Emily Warren Roebling spent fourteen years helping her husband oversee the building of the bridge. Her husband was sick. She had to learn important things. She learned about stress analysis, cable construction, and catenary curves.
6. The bridge opened in May of 1883. Its opening was attended by several thousand people. The current president, Chester A. Arthur, attended the opening. ●

26

Coordination and Subordination

■ ■ ■ ■ ■ ■

Quick Points   You will learn to

➤ Use coordination and subordination so that your intended meaning is clear.

MyWritingLab™   Visit mywritinglab.com for more resources on coordination and subordination.

Coordination and *subordination* are two ways of arranging ideas to communicate relationships. Many experienced writers use both to convey meaning and achieve variety in their writing styles.

TWO IDEAS	The sky grew cloudy. The wind howled.
COORDINATION	The sky grew cloudy, **and** the wind howled.
	Here, the *sky* and *wind* get equal emphasis.
SUBORDINATION 1	**As** the sky grew cloudy, the wind howled.
	Here, the *wind* is the main focus.
SUBORDINATION 2	**As** the wind howled, the sky grew cloudy.
	Here, the *sky* is the main focus.

26A   How does coordination show that ideas are equivalent?

Coordination is an arrangement of ideas of approximately equal importance. A COMPOUND SENTENCE joins independent clauses either by a semicolon or by a comma (30C) and a COORDINATING CONJUNCTION (*and, but, for, or, nor, yet, so*).

- The sky turned brighter, **and** the wind calmed down.
- The sky turned brighter; the wind calmed down.

26B   How can I avoid problems with coordination?

First, be sure to join logically related and equivalent ideas with a coordinating conjunction.

NO   Computers came into common use in the 1970s, and they sometimes make costly errors.

Computers came into common use in the 1970s, and they sometimes
make costly errors.

The ideas aren't logically connected, so they can't be coordinated.

YES   Computers came into common use in the 1970s, and now they are indispensable business tools.

Second, be sure not to bundle more than two or three ideas together with coordinating conjunctions (*and, but, for, or, nor, yet, so*).

NO   Dinosaurs could have disappeared for many reasons, **and** one theory holds that the climate suddenly became cold, **and** another suggests that a sudden shower of meteors and asteroids hit the earth, **so** the impact created a huge dust cloud that caused a false winter. The winter lasted for years, **and** the dinosaurs died.

YES   Dinosaurs could have disappeared for many reasons. One theory holds that the climate suddenly became cold, **and** another suggests that a sudden shower of meteors and asteroids hit the earth. The impact created a huge dust cloud that caused a false winter. The winter lasted for years, killing the dinosaurs.

● **EXERCISE 26-1**   Revise these sentences to eliminate illogical or overused coordination. If you think a sentence needs no revision, explain why.

EXAMPLE

The ratel is an animal often called a "honey badger," and it's actually more closely related to a weasel than a badger.

The ratel is an animal often called a "honey badger," **but** it's actually more closely related to a weasel than a badger.

1. The honey badger is a difficult opponent for predators, and it has thick, loose skin that protects it from injury, and it is able to fight fiercely with its strong claws.
2. Honey badgers are known to be fearless fighters, but they can often survive bites from venomous snakes.
3. They are skilled at digging their own burrows, but these holes usually only have one passage and are not very large.
4. Primarily carnivorous, honey badgers hunt rodents, snakes, and even tortoises, so at times they also eat vegetables, roots, and berries.
5. Honey badgers are difficult to kill and are expert burrowers, but they are a common nuisance to farmers and ranchers. ●

26C   How does subordination work to express nonequivalent ideas?

Subordination is an arrangement of ideas of unequal importance within a sentence. Effective subordination places the more important idea in an INDEPENDENT CLAUSE and the less important, subordinate idea in a DEPENDENT CLAUSE. Let your own meaning decide which of your ideas is most important, and subordinate other ideas to it.

> **NO**   In 1888, two cowboys had to fight a dangerous Colorado snowstorm. They were looking for cattle. They came to a canyon. They saw outlines of buildings through the snow. Survival then seemed certain.
>
> The sentences are disconnected because no idea is emphasized.

> **YES**   In 1888, two cowboys had to fight a dangerous Colorado snowstorm **while** they were looking for cattle. **When** they came to a canyon, they saw outlines of buildings through the snow. Survival then seemed certain.
>
> The two underlined independent clauses get the emphasis; the other clauses are now dependent clauses.

To subordinate successfully, use a SUBORDINATING CONJUNCTION to start the clause. Subordinating conjunctions (see Quick Box 26.1) start ADVERB CLAUSES. RELATIVE PRONOUNS, such as *who, which,* and *that* (see 16B), and RELATIVE ADVERBS, such as *where, why,* and *when* (see 16F), start ADJECTIVE CLAUSES.

26C

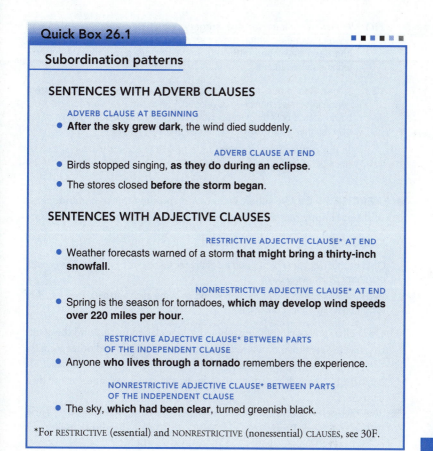

Quick Box 26.1

Subordination patterns

SENTENCES WITH ADVERB CLAUSES

ADVERB CLAUSE AT BEGINNING
- **After the sky grew dark**, the wind died suddenly.

ADVERB CLAUSE AT END
- Birds stopped singing, **as they do during an eclipse**.

- The stores closed **before the storm began**.

SENTENCES WITH ADJECTIVE CLAUSES

RESTRICTIVE ADJECTIVE CLAUSE* AT END
- Weather forecasts warned of a storm **that might bring a thirty-inch snowfall**.

NONRESTRICTIVE ADJECTIVE CLAUSE* AT END
- Spring is the season for tornadoes, **which may develop wind speeds over 220 miles per hour**.

RESTRICTIVE ADJECTIVE CLAUSE* BETWEEN PARTS OF THE INDEPENDENT CLAUSE
- Anyone **who lives through a tornado** remembers the experience.

NONRESTRICTIVE ADJECTIVE CLAUSE* BETWEEN PARTS OF THE INDEPENDENT CLAUSE
- The sky, **which had been clear**, turned greenish black.

*For RESTRICTIVE (essential) and NONRESTRICTIVE (nonessential) CLAUSES, see 30F.

26D

26D   How can I avoid problems with subordination?

First, be sure your subordinating conjunctions communicate a logical relationship between your clauses. (For the relationships subordinating conjunctions express, see Quick Box 16.7.)

NO   **Because** he was injured in the sixth inning, he remained in the game.

Because is illogical here; it says that his injury caused him to remain.

YES   **Although** he was injured in the sixth inning, he remained in the game.

Although is logical here; it says that he remained despite his injury.

Second, be sure not to overuse subordination. Your readers lose track of your message because you crowd too many ideas together.

NO A new technique for eye surgery, **which** is supposed to correct nearsightedness, **which** previously could be corrected only by glasses, has been developed, **although** many doctors disapprove of the new technique **because** it can create unstable vision.

YES A new technique for eye surgery, which is supposed to correct nearsightedness, has been developed. Previously, nearsightedness could be corrected only by glasses. However, many doctors disapprove of the new technique because it can create unstable vision.

In this revision, one long sentence is broken into three sentences, making the relationships among ideas clearer.

● **EXERCISE 26-2** Use subordination and coordination to combine these sets of short, choppy sentences. For help, consult all sections of this chapter.

EXAMPLE

Owls cannot digest the bones and fur of the mice and birds they eat. They cough up a furry pellet every day.

Because owls cannot digest the bones and fur of the mice and birds they *eat, they* cough up a furry pellet every day.

1. Owl pellets are a rich teaching tool in biology classrooms around the country. The pellets provide an alternative to dissecting frogs and other animals.
2. Inside the pellet are the remains of the owl's nightly meal. They include beautifully cleaned hummingbird skulls, rat skeletons, and lots of bird feathers.
3. The owl-pellet market has been cornered by companies in New York, California, and Washington. These companies distribute pellets to thousands of biology classrooms all over the world.
4. Company workers scour barns and the ground under trees where owls nest to pick up the pellets. The pellets sell for $1 each.
5. The owl-pellet business may have a short future. The rural areas of the United States are vanishing. Old barns are being bulldozed. All the barns are torn down. The owls will be gone, too. ●

26D

27

Sentence Style

■ ■ ■ ■ ■ ■

Quick Points   You will learn to

➤ Use parallel structures to give rhythm and grace to your writing (pp. 357–359).

➤ Use a variety of sentence patterns to give interest to your writing (pp. 359–360).

My**Writing**Lab™ Visit mywritinglab.com for more resources on sentence style.

27A   What is parallelism?

When words, PHRASES, or CLAUSES within a sentence grammatically match, the result is **parallelism**. Parallelism serves to emphasize information or ideas. Also, balance and rhythm in parallel structures add style and grace to your writing.

PARALLEL WORDS	Recommended exercise includes **running**, **swimming**, and **cycling**.
PARALLEL PHRASES	Exercise helps people **maintain healthy bodies** and **handle mental pressures**.
PARALLEL CLAUSES	Many people exercise **because they want to look healthy, because they need to increase stamina**, and **because they hope to live longer**.

27B   How can I avoid faulty parallelism?

You can avoid faulty parallelism by checking that you always use the same grammatical form for words, phrases, or clauses.

NO	The strikers had tried **shouting**, **threats**, and **pleading**.	
	The list incorrectly mixes *-ing* forms and a plural.	
YES	The strikers had tried **shouting**, **threatening**, and **pleading**.	
	The three words are all in *-ing* form.	
YES	The strikers had tried **shouts**, **threats**, and **pleas**.	
	The three words are all plural nouns.	

27B

NO   The strikers **read** the offer, **were discussing** it, and the unanimous **decision was to reject** it.

Two verbs mix forms; the third switches to the PASSIVE VOICE.

YES   The strikers **read, discussed**, and **rejected** the offer.

All three verbs are in the past tense.

27C   How should I use parallelism with conjunctions?

Items joined with COORDINATING CONJUNCTIONS (*and, but, for, or, nor, yet, so*) deliver their message clearly and concisely when written in parallel form.

- You can cook a chicken by **roasting**, **grilling**, or **broiling** it.

Similarly, use parallel forms when you link sentence elements with COR-RELATIVE CONJUNCTIONS (such as *either . . . or* and *not only . . . but also*).

- **Either** you attend classes **or** you fail the course.

27D   How does parallelism strengthen my message?

Parallelism—which calls for deliberate but controlled repetition of word forms, word groups, and sounds—creates a rhythm that intensifies a sentence's message.

> You can fool some of the people all of the time and all of the people some of the time, but you cannot fool all of the people all of the time.
> —Abraham Lincoln

Another parallel structure that intensifies ideas is the balanced sentence. **Balanced sentences** consist of two short, contrasting independent clauses.

> **By night**, the litter and desperation disappeared as the city's glittering lights came on; **by day**, the filth and despair reappeared as the sun rose.
> —Jennifer Kirk, student

● **EXERCISE 27-1**   Revise these sentences by putting appropriate information in parallel structures. For help, consult sections 27A through 27D.

EXAMPLE

Difficult bosses affect not only their employees' performances but their private lives are affected as well.

Difficult bosses affect not only their employees' performances *but their private lives as well*.

1. According to the psychologist Harry Levinson, the five main types of bad boss are the workaholic, the kind of person you would describe as bullying, a person who communicates badly, the jellyfish type, and someone who insists on perfection.
2. As a way of getting ahead, to keep their self-respect, and for survival purposes, wise employees handle problem bosses with a variety of strategies.
3. To cope with a bad-tempered employer, workers can both stand up for themselves and reasoning with a bullying boss.
4. Often, bad bosses communicate poorly or fail to calculate the impact of their personality on others; being a careful listener and sensitivity to others' responses are qualities that good bosses possess.
5. Employees who take the trouble to understand what makes their bosses tick, engage in some self-analysis, and staying flexible are better prepared to cope with a difficult job environment than suffering in silence like some employees. ●

27E   What is sentence variety?

Writers use sentence variety when they vary the length and structure of their sentences in relation to each other.

■ Revising strings of short sentences

Sometimes several short sentences in a row create impact. Be careful, however, to avoid strings of short sentences that don't intensify your ideas; they tend to make reading dull.

NO   There is a problem. It is widely known as sick-building syndrome. It comes from indoor air pollution. It causes the suffering of office workers. They have trouble breathing. The workers develop rashes that are painful. Their heads ache badly. Their eyes burn.

YES   Widely known as sick-building syndrome, indoor air pollution causes office workers to suffer. They have trouble breathing. They have painful rashes. Their heads ache. Their eyes burn.

Here a long sentence introduces the interaction of indoor air pollution and its victims. Then a series of short sentences emphasizes each problem the victims suffer. The revision also reduces forty-two words to twenty-seven.

■ Revising for a mix of sentence lengths

You can emphasize one idea by expressing that idea in a sentence noticeably different in length or structure from sentences surrounding it. The "yes" example just shown illustrates the graceful impact of one long sentence

27E

among shorter ones. Here's an example of one short sentence among longer ones.

> Today is one of those excellent January partly cloudies in which light chooses an unexpected landscape to trick out in gilt, and then shadow sweeps it away. **You know you are alive**. You take huge steps, trying to feel the planet's roundness arc between your feet.
>
> —Annie Dillard, *Pilgrim at Tinker Creek*

27F   How does a sentence's subject affect emphasis?

Because the SUBJECT establishes the sentence's focus, always choose for the sentence's subject what you want to emphasize. Notice how changing the subject (and VERB, as needed) in the following sentences affects each sentence's meaning and emphasis.

- **Our study** showed that 25 percent of college freshmen gain weight.

  Focus is on the study.

- **College freshmen** gain weight 25 percent of the time, our study shows.

  Focus is on the freshmen.

- **Weight gain** hits 25 percent of college freshmen, our study shows.

  Focus is on the weight gain.

- **Twenty-five percent** of college freshmen gain weight, our study shows.

  Focus is on the percentage.

27F

27G   How does adding modifiers affect writing style?

You can add richness, variety, and focus to your writing with MODIFIERS.

BASIC SENTENCE	The river rose.
ADJECTIVE	The **swollen** river rose.
ADVERB	The river rose **dangerously**.
PREPOSITIONAL PHRASE	**In April**, the river rose **above its banks**.
PARTICIPIAL PHRASE	**Swelled by melting snow**, the river rose, **flooding the farmland**.
ABSOLUTE PHRASE	**Trees swirling away in the current**, the river rose.
ADVERB CLAUSE	**Because the snows had been heavy that winter**, the river rose.
ADJECTIVE CLAUSE	The river, **which runs through vital farmland**, rose.

● **EXERCISE 27-2**   Expand each sentence by adding each kind of modifier illustrated in section 27G.

1. We bought a house.
2. The roof leaked.
3. I remodeled the kitchen.
4. Neighbors brought food.
5. Everyone enjoyed the barbeque. ●

27H   How does inverting standard word order affect emphasis?

Standard word order, common in English sentences, places the subject before the verb: *The mayor* [subject] *walked* [verb] *into the room*.

When used sparingly, **inverted word order**, which places the verb before the subject, produces emphasis.

STANDARD	The mayor walked into the room.
INVERTED	Into the room walked the mayor.

28 Word Choice

■ ■ ■ ■ ■ ■

28

Quick Points   You will learn to

➤ Choose words according to your audience and purpose (pp. 362–367).
➤ Use a dictionary and a thesaurus (p. 362).
➤ Use gender-neutral language (pp. 364–365).
➤ Use figurative language to enrich your writing (pp. 367–368).
➤ Increase your vocabulary (p. 367).

MyWritingLab™   Visit mywritinglab.com for more resources on word choice.

28A   What is word choice?

Word choice is also known as **diction**. Using appropriate diction means that as college writers you choose your words carefully for their precise meaning. Also, you don't repeat bland, vague words such as *nice* and *interesting* but instead use accurate **synonyms**, which are words that have the same or nearly the same meaning, such as *pleasant*, *friendly*, *agreeable*, and *amiable* for *nice*.

28B   What tools do I need for college-level word choice?

Every writer needs tools that help with word definitions and alternatives. We urge you not to rely on the information included in word-processing software: synonyms (words with similar meanings) often have drastically different meanings, so if you randomly pick one, you can be mightily embarrassed. For example, for an alternative to *deep* in "they dug a *deep* hole," one popular word-processing program's synonyms include *profound*, which refers to thoughts, feelings, and insights. Imagine if you wrote, "They dug a *profound* hole"!

■ A dictionary

Almost all online dictionaries are free; for clear, accurate definitions, including extensive lists of synonyms and some antonyms (opposites), try the Dictionary or Merriam-Webster Web sites. The most unusual online dictionary is Onelook, which searches a multitude of different dictionaries for your word and lists a link to the definition in each; among its features is the "wildcard," to help you with spelling by asking for the first few letters of a word you don't know how to spell and then "guessing" many choices for the word. Smartphone dictionary apps are usually free, but many come with ads; you can upgrade to ad-free apps for a price.

28A

■ A thesaurus

A thesaurus is a collection of synonyms and antonyms. The Thesaurus Web site is free online; however, a Google search will usually turn up more results. Many smartphone thesaurus apps are free, but unless you upgrade for a fee, ads will be plentiful. For a print thesaurus, go to a bookstore that carries paperback and hardback versions; to select one, look up a word you use often and see how useful the synonyms are.

28C   What word concepts do I need to know?

Word concepts refer to the principles that operate behind word meanings.

■ Denotation and connotation

Denotation is the explicit, exact meaning of words, which you can always find in dictionaries. In contrast, **connotation** is the implied, suggested meaning of words. These concepts are important when you want to use a synonym for a word. Always check a dictionary for the exact meaning of the synonyms because differences in meaning can be subtle but important. (For example, *profound*, which relates to thinking and feeling, isn't a good synonym for *deep*, which refers to distance from top to bottom or front to back.)

● **EXERCISE 28-1** Look at each list of words and divide the words among three headings: "Positive" (good connotations); "Negative" (bad connotations); and "Neutral" (no connotations). If you think that a word belongs under more than one heading, you can assign it more than once, but be ready to explain your thinking. For help, consult a good dictionary.

EXAMPLE

assertive, pushy, firm, forceful, confident
Positive: assertive, confident; *Negative:* pushy, forceful; *Neutral:* firm

1. old, decrepit, elderly, mature, over the hill, venerable, veteran, antique, experienced
2. resting, inactive, unproductive, downtime, recess, quietude, standstill, vacation, interval
3. smart, know-it-all, brilliant, eggheaded, brainy, sharp, ingenious, keen, clever, intelligent
4. weird, unique, peculiar, strange, eccentric, inscrutable, kooky, singular, one-of-a-kind, distinctive
5. smell, aroma, stench, fragrance, scent, whiff, bouquet, odor ●

28C

■ General versus specific words

General words belong to a category, such as *cars*, and abstract ideas, such as *justice*. Specific words fit within a general category, such as *Honda* and *Jeep* in the general category of *cars*. Abstract words can become more specific when combined with NOUNS (the *fight* for *justice*) and verbs (*bring* to *justice*). The more you use specific words in your writing or conversation, the more effective you are in delivering your message. To see the impact of specific words, imagine how the following example would lose its clarity and impact with only general words.

GENERAL   SPECIFIC   SPECIFIC   SPECIFIC
- My **car**, a **220-horsepower Maxi Armo**, accelerates **from 0 to 50**

    SPECIFIC   SPECIFIC   SPECIFIC
miles per hour in **6 seconds** but gets only **18 miles per gallon**.

        SPECIFIC   GENERAL
In contrast, the **Gavin Motors' Bobcat** gets **very good** gas mileage,

    SPECIFIC   GENERAL   SPECIFIC   SPECIFIC
about **35 mpg** in **highway driving** and **30 mpg** in **stop-and-go traffic**.

● **EXERCISE 28-2** Revise this paragraph by providing specific words and phrases to explain and enliven the ideas presented here in general and abstract language. You may revise the sentences to accommodate your changes.

> A while ago, I visited a nice restaurant. It was located in a good neighborhood, and it was easy to find. The inside of the restaurant was pretty. There were a lot of decorations, which gave it character. The menu was creative and interesting. The food was delivered quickly, and the service was friendly. I enjoyed eating the meal. The appetizers were delicious and refreshing. The price of the meal was reasonable considering how much food I ordered. ●

■ **Gender-neutral language**

Gender-neutral language, also called *nonsexist language*, does not draw unnecessary attention to a person's gender. **Gender** classifies nouns and some pronouns as masculine, feminine, common, or neuter. Only a few words in English (such as *man, woman, he, her, princess, uncle*) have gender-specific meanings, all based on actual physical identity. When you write, use gender-neutral language. For example, use *police officer* instead of *policeman*, *representative* instead of *congressman*, and *salesperson* instead of *salesgirl*. Also, avoid the use of masculine PRONOUNS in sentences where gender is unknown or irrelevant. Also don't assume that nurses and homemakers are female (calling them *she*) and physicians and engineers are male (calling them *he*).

Use *he or she* (or *him or her*) to refer to singular nouns. Overuse of these phrases is awkward. Use plural nouns and *they* or *them* when possible. Follow the guidelines in Quick Box 28.1.

28C

● **EXERCISE 28-3** Revise these sentences to use gender-neutral language. For help, consult 28C.

1. Dogs were one of the first animals to be domesticated by mankind.
2. Traditionally, certain breeds of dogs have helped men in their work.
3. On their long shifts, firemen often kept Dalmatians as mascots and companions, whereas policemen preferred highly intelligent and easily trained German shepherds.

Quick Box 28.1

■ ■ ■ ■ ■ ■

Using gender-neutral language

Avoid using masculine pronouns to refer to both men and women.

- Use a pair of pronouns or use plurals.
  - S s they have
  - A successful doctor knows that ~~he has~~ to work hard.

- Omit gender-specific pronouns.
  - to
  - Everyone hopes ~~that he will~~ win the scholarship.

- Avoid stereotyping jobs and roles by gender.
  supervisor [*not* foreman]
  businessperson, business executive [*not* businessman]
  poet, actor [*not* poetess, actress]

- Avoid expressions that exclude one sex.
  person [*not* man]
  humanity, people [*not* mankind]
  the average person [*not* the common man]
  superstitions [*not* old wives' tales]

- Avoid demeaning and patronizing labels.
  nurse [*not* male nurse]
  professional, executive, manager [*not* career girl]
  My assistant will help you [*not* My girl will help you]

28D

4. Another breed, the Newfoundland, accompanied many fishermen on their ocean voyages, and the Newfoundland has been credited with rescuing many a man overboard.
5. Breeds known as hunting dogs have served as the helpers and companions of sportsmen. ●

28D What word choices are suitable for college-level writing?

■ Using appropriate language

Appropriate language matches your word choice to your AUDIENCE and PURPOSE. Obscene, profane words, for example, don't belong in ACADEMIC WRITING. Similarly, save scientific **jargon** for specialist readers familiar with the terms.

■ Being aware of levels of formality

Choose the **level of formality**—formal, semiformal, or informal—appropriate to your audience and your purpose. Informal language works in a friendly e-mail but not in a business e-mail. Formal language suits speeches at ceremonial occasions or at official events. Semiformal writing uses standard vocabulary (for example, someone is *angry*, not *mad*) and conventional sentence structure. Levels of formality are discussed more fully in 4I.

■ Using edited American English

Edited American English conforms to established rules of grammar, sentence structure, punctuation, and spelling. Use edited American English for college writing. That is the form of written language we use in this handbook. It's also the form you read in most well-respected newspapers such as the *New York Times* and the *San Francisco Chronicle*.

■ Avoiding clichés

A **cliché** is a worn-out expression that lacks freshness because of overuse: *lap of luxury, burned the midnight oil.* Some clichés are *similes* (comparisons using *like* or *as*) that have become corny, such as *gentle as a lamb.*

■ Avoiding slanted language

Slanted language attempts to bias readers with words containing emotionally charged connotations. Referring to a group of protestors as a *wild mob* shows the writer is over-emotional, while using *concerned citizens* makes the writer more reasonable.

■ Avoiding pretentious language

Pretentious language draws attention to itself with big, unusual words and overly complex sentence structures. Such overblown language obscures your message and damages your credibility with your readers.

> **NO** The **raison d'être** for my **matriculation** at this **institution of higher learning** is the **acquisition** of an education.
>
> **YES** My reason for being in college is to get an education.

■ Avoiding colloquialisms and regionalisms

Colloquial language is characteristic of casual conversation and informal writing: *The student flunked* [instead of *failed*] *chemistry.* **Regional language** (also called *dialect*) is specific to a particular geographic area: *They have nary a cent.*

Colloquial and regional language are not substandard or illiterate, but they're inappropriate for academic writing unless used for explicit contexts.

■ Avoiding euphemisms

Euphemisms attempt to avoid unpleasant truths by substituting "tactful" words for more direct, perhaps harsh-sounding words. When the truth is "Our leader tells many lies," you don't want to be overly indirect by writing "Our leader has a wonderfully vivid imagination." Of course, a euphemism is expected in certain social situations, such as when offering condolences; you use *passed away* instead of *died*.

● **EXERCISE 28-4** Revise these examples of pretentious language and euphemisms. For help, consult 28D.

1. Allow me to express my humble gratitude to you two benefactors for your generous pledge of indispensable support on behalf of the activities of our Bay City's youngsters.
2. No lateral transfer applications will be processed before an employee's six-month probation period terminates.
3. She gave up the ghost shortly after her husband kicked the bucket.
4. Creating nouns in positions meant for verbs is to utter ostentatious verbalizations that will lead inexorably to further obfuscations of meaning.
5. After his operation, he would list to port when he stood up and list to starboard when he sat down. ●

28E How does figurative language enrich my word choice?

Figurative language, also called *figures of speech*, is the use of words not in their literal sense but rather by suggesting an image that gives additional depth to word meanings. The list below names types of figurative language, most of which work well in writing, but some you need to avoid.

■ Effective figurative language

Analogy compares similar traits shared by dissimilar things. You can develop an analogy in one, several, or many sentences.

● A **cheetah sprinting across the dry plains** after its prey, the **base runner dashed** for home plate, cleats kicking up dust.

Irony uses words to suggest the opposite of their usual sense.

● Told that a minor repair to her home would cost $2,000 and take two weeks, she said, "**Oh, how nice!**"

Metaphor compares otherwise dissimilar things. A metaphor doesn't use the word *like* or *as* to make a comparison.

- Rush-hour **traffic** in the city **bled out through major arteries** to the suburbs.

Personification involves assigning a human trait to something not human.

- The **book begged** to be read.

Simile compares dissimilar things using the word *like* or *as*.

- Langston Hughes observes that a deferred dream dries up "**like a raisin in the sun**."

Understatement emphasizes by using deliberate restraint.

- **It only begins to feel warm** when the temperature reaches 105 degrees.

■ Ineffective figurative language

Avoid **mixed metaphors**, the combining of two or more inconsistent images in one sentence or expression. In the following example, a train ride is not stormy or destructive.

- The violence of the hurricane reminded me of a train ride.

Overstatement (also called **hyperbole**) exaggerates to emphasize.

- If this paper is late, **the professor will kill me**.

28F   How can I increase my vocabulary power?

As a writer, the more words you know, the more power you have to express your ideas effectively. All people have an **active vocabulary**, words that come to mind easily. Everyone also has a **passive vocabulary**, words people don't use actively yet recognize and understand. To increase your vocabulary, move words you already know passively into your active vocabulary. Also, select unfamiliar words as you read them and create a file of them to study and use. Listen closely to speakers who know the language well. Jot down words new to you, look them up, and use them.

To efficiently study new vocabulary words, select eight to ten words to study each week and write each meaning on an index card, in a notebook, or on a computer list. Then set aside time each day to study your selected words. (Carry your cards, notebook, or computer printout to study in spare moments.) You might try **mnemonics**—memory-jogging techniques—to help you memorize words. (For example, *desert*, spelled with one *s*, is filled with *sand*; in contrast, *dessert*, spelled with two *s*'s, could stand for *strawberry shortcake*.)

28F

29 Spelling

■ ■ ■ ■ ■ ■

Quick Points   You will learn to

➤ Use spelling rules to improve your spelling.
➤ Distinguish between homonyms and other easily confused words (pp. 371–374).

MyWritingLab™ Visit mywritinglab.com for more resources on spelling.

Fine writers aren't always good spellers. They check their spelling while EDITING their work. How do you look a word up in a dictionary when you can't spell it? If you know the first few letters, find them and then browse for the word. The online dictionary Onelook has a feature called "wild cards" to help you. Try a thesaurus to look up an easier-to-spell synonym. We offer a few common spelling rules and a list of homonyms (see 29D) to help you tell them apart.

29A   How are plurals spelled?

29A

- **Adding -s or -es:** Plurals of most words are formed by adding -s, including words that end in "hard" *ch* (sounding like *k*): *leg, legs; shoe, shoes; stomach, stomachs*. Words ending in *s, sh, x, z,* or "soft" *ch* (as in *beach*) add -es to form the plural: *lenses, wishes, taxes, coaches*.

- **Words ending in *o*:** Add -s if the *o* is preceded by a vowel: *radio, radios; cameo, cameos*. Add -es if the *o* is preceded by a consonant: *potato, potatoes*. A few words can be made plural either way: *cargo, volcano, tornado, zero*.

- **Words ending in *f* or *fe*:** Some *f* and *fe* words are made plural by adding -s: *belief, beliefs*. Others require changing *f* or *fe* to *ves*: *life, lives; leaf, leaves*. For words ending in *ff* or *ffe*, simply add -s: *staff, staffs; giraffe, giraffes*.

- **Compound words:** For most compound words, add -s or -es at the end of the last word: *checkbooks, player-coaches*. Sometimes, the first word is plural: *sister-in-law, sisters-in-law; attorney general, attorneys general*. (For guidelines on hyphens and compound words, see Quick Box 37.2.)

- **Internal changes and endings other than -s:** A few words change internally or add endings other than -s as plurals: *foot, feet; man, men; mouse, mice; crisis, crises; child, children*.

- **Foreign words:** Many Latin words ending in *um* become plural by changing *um* to *a: curriculum, curricula; datum, data; medium, media; stratum, strata.* Latin words that end in *us* often change to *i* in plural: *alumnus, alumni; syllabus, syllabi.* Greek words that end in *on* usually form the plural by changing *on* to *a: criterion, criteria; phenomenon, phenomena.*

- **One-form words:** Some words have the same form in both the singular and the plural: *deer, elk, fish, quail.*

29B How are suffixes spelled?

A SUFFIX is an ending added to a word to change the word's meaning or its grammatical function. For example, adding the suffix *-able* to the verb *depend* creates the adjective *dependable.*

- **Words ending in *y*:** If the letter before the final *y* is a consonant, change the *y* to *i* and add the suffix: *fry, fried.* If, however, the suffix begins with an *i*, keep the *y: fry, frying.* If the letter before the *y* is a vowel, keep the final *y: employ, employed, employing.* These rules do not apply to irregular verbs (see Quick Box 17.2).

- **Words ending in *e*:** Drop a final *e* when the suffix begins with a vowel unless this would cause confusion: *be + ing* does not become *bing,* but *require, requiring; like, liking.* Keep the final *e* when the suffix begins with a consonant: *require, requirement; like, likely.* Exceptions include *argument, judgment,* and *truly.*

- **Words that double a final letter:** If the final letter is a consonant, double it only if it passes all three of these tests: (1) Its last two letters are a vowel followed by a consonant. (2) It has one syllable or is accented on the last syllable. (3) The suffix begins with a vowel: *drop, dropped; begin, beginning; forget, forgettable.*

- **Words ending in *cede, ceed*, or *sede*:** Only one word in the English language ends in *sede: supersede.* Three words end in *ceed: exceed, proceed, succeed.* All other words with endings that sound like "seed" end in *cede: concede, intercede, precede.*

- **Adding *-ally* and *-ly*:** The suffixes *-ally* and *-ly* turn ADJECTIVES into ADVERBS. For all words ending in *ic* except *public,* add *-ally: logically, statistically.* Otherwise, add *-ly: quickly, sharply.*

29C What is the *ie, ei* rule?

The old rhyme for *ie* and *ei* is usually true: *I* before *e* [believe, field, grief] except after *c* [ceiling, conceit]; or when sounded like "ay" as in *neighbor* and *weigh* [eight, vein].

29B

You'll want to memorize (sorry!) these exceptions: For *ie*, conscience, financier, science, species. For *ei*, either, neither, leisure, seize, counterfeit, foreign, forfeit, sleight (as in *sleight of hand*), weird.

29D How are commonly confused words and homonyms spelled?

English is rich with **homonyms**—words that sound alike but have different meanings and spellings: *hear, here; to, too, two; elicit, illicit; accept, except*. See Quick Box 29.1 (pages 372–374) to distinguish these and other commonly confused words.

29E What else leads to spelling errors?

"Swallowed pronunciation," which occurs when speakers blur word endings, often leads to spelling errors: *use* for *used; suppose* for *supposed*. Mispronunciation may also cause misspellings in phrases like *all right* (not *alright*), *a lot* (not *alot*) and *should've* (not *should of*).

● **EXERCISE 29-1**   Circle the correct homonym or commonly confused word of each group in parentheses.

If (your, you're) an adult in 2014, (its, it's) three times more likely that you will live alone than you would (have, of) if you'd been an adult in 1950. (Know, No) longer is getting married (right, write, rite) out of high school or college considered a normal (right, write, rite) of passage. In the (passed, past), the (sight, cite, site) of a thirty-year-old living by him- or herself would have been (seen, scene) (by, buy, bye) many as (quite, quiet) disturbing. Even recently, the book *The Lonely American* (raised, razed) the concern that (maybe, may be) living alone would (lead, led) to (later, latter) depression. However, (to, two, too) (choose, chose) to live alone is no longer viewed as a (rode, road) to unhappiness. In fact, evidence shows that people who live alone tend to compensate by being socially active. (Weather, Whether) you feel lonely is less a matter of your circumstances (then, than) a matter of your activities. Sociologist Eric Klinenberg conveys the (sense, since) that (excepting, accepting) (whose, who's) happy simply on the basis of (their, there) living arrangements is (altogether, all together) a (waste, waist) of time. ●

29E

Quick Box 29.1

Homonyms and other commonly confused words

ALL READY	fully prepared
ALREADY	by this time
ALL TOGETHER	all in one place
ALTOGETHER	thoroughly
ASCENT	the act of rising or climbing
ASSENT	consent [NOUN, VERB]
BARE	nude, unadorned
BEAR	carry [VERB]; an animal [NOUN]
BUY	purchase
BY	next to, through the agency of
CAPITAL	major city; money
CAPITOL	government building
COUNCIL	governing body
COUNSEL	advice [NOUN]; advise [VERB]
DESERT	abandon [VERB]; dry, usually sandy area [NOUN]
DESSERT	final, sweet course in a meal
DEVICE	a plan; an implement
DEVISE	create
DIE	lose life (dying) [VERB]; one of a pair of dice [NOUN]
DYE	change the color of something (dyeing)
DOMINANT	commanding, controlling
DOMINATE	control
EMINENT	prominent
IMMANENT	living within; inherent
IMMINENT	about to happen
ENSURE	guarantee, protect
INSURE	buy or give insurance
FORMALLY	conventionally, with ceremony
FORMERLY	previously
FORTH	forward
FOURTH	number four in a series

29E

continued >>

Quick Box 29.1
Homonyms (continued)   ■ ■ ■ ■ ■ ■

GORILLA	animal in the ape family
GUERRILLA	soldier conducting surprise attacks
HOLE	opening
WHOLE	complete [ADJECTIVE]; an entire thing [NOUN]
ITS	POSSESSIVE form of *it*
IT'S	CONTRACTION for *it is*
LEAD	heavy metal substance [NOUN]; guide [VERB]
LED	PAST TENSE of *lead*
LIGHTENING	making lighter
LIGHTNING	storm-related electricity
LOOSE	unbound, not tightly fastened
LOSE	misplace
MAY BE	might be [VERB]
MAYBE	perhaps [ADVERB]
PASSED	PAST TENSE of *pass*
PAST	at an earlier time
PATIENCE	forbearance
PATIENTS	people under medical care
PLAIN	simple, unadorned [ADJECTIVE]; area of level land [NOUN]
PLANE	shave wood [VERB]; aircraft [NOUN]
PRECEDE	come before
PROCEED	continue
PRESENCE	being at hand; attendance at a place or in something
PRESENTS	gifts
PRINCIPAL	foremost [ADJECTIVE]; school head [NOUN]
PRINCIPLE	moral conviction, basic truth
RAIN	water that falls to earth [NOUN]; fall like rain [VERB]
REIGN	rule
REIN	strap to guide or control an animal [NOUN]; guide or control [VERB]
RESPECTFULLY	with respect
RESPECTIVELY	in that order

29E

continued >>

Quick Box 29.1   Homonyms (continued) ■ ■ ■ ■ ■ ■

RIGHT	correct; opposite of *left*
RITE	ritual
WRITE	put words on paper
SCENE	place of an action; segment of a play
SEEN	viewed
SENSE	perception, understanding
SINCE	from that time; because
STATIONARY	standing still
STATIONERY	writing paper
THAN	in comparison with; besides
THEN	at that time; next; therefore
THEIR	POSSESSIVE form of *they*
THERE	in that place
THEY'RE	CONTRACTION for *they are*
TO	toward
TOO	also; excessively
TWO	number following *one*
WEATHER	climatic conditions
WHETHER	if
WERE	PAST TENSE of *be*
WHERE	in which place
WHICH	one of a group
WITCH	female sorcerer
WHO'S	CONTRACTION for *who is*
WHOSE	POSSESSIVE form of *who*
YORE	long past
YOUR	POSSESSIVE form of *you*
YOU'RE	CONTRACTION for *you are*

29E

30 Commas

■ ■ ■ ■ ■

Quick Points   You will learn to

➤ Use commas correctly.

MyWritingLab™   Visit mywritinglab.com for more resources on commas.

30A   When do I use commas?

The comma separates sentence parts for greater clarity. Use commas as listed in Quick Box 30.1 (pages 376–377). For more about each rule in the chart, go to the chapter section given in parentheses.

30B   How do I use a comma to set off introductory words?

When introductory words come before an INDEPENDENT CLAUSE, usually place a comma after the introductory material unless it is very short.

- **When the topic is dieting,** many people say sugar craving is their worst problem.

  An introductory DEPENDENT CLAUSE (in bold) is followed by a comma.

- **Between 1544 and 1689,** sugar refineries appeared in New York.

  An introductory PREPOSITIONAL PHRASE is followed by a comma.

- **Beginning in infancy,** we develop lifelong tastes for sweet foods.

  An introductory PARTICIPIAL PHRASE is followed by a comma.

- **Sweets being a temptation for many adults,** candy sells well.

  An introductory ABSOLUTE PHRASE is followed by a comma.

- **For example,** fructose comes from fruit, but it is still sugar.

  An introductory TRANSITIONAL EXPRESSION is followed by a comma.

- **Nevertheless,** many people think fructose is not harmful.

  An introductory CONJUNCTIVE ADVERB is followed by a comma.

30B

Quick Box 30.1

When to use commas

COMMAS AFTER INTRODUCTORY ELEMENTS (see 30B)

- **Although most postcards cost only a quarter**, one recently sold for thousands of dollars.

- **On postcard racks**, several designs are usually available.

- **For example**, animals are timeless favorites for postcards.

- **However**, most postcards show local landmarks.

COMMAS WITH COORDINATING CONJUNCTIONS LINKING INDEPENDENT CLAUSES (see 30C)

- Postcards are ideal for brief greetings, **and** they are sometimes miniature works of art.

COMMAS WITH ITEMS IN SERIES (see 30D)

- **Places**, **paintings**, **and people** appear on postcards.

- The illustrations on postcards—**places**, **paintings**, **people**, **animals**—are chosen for their wide appeal.

COMMAS WITH COORDINATING ADJECTIVES (see 30E)

- Some postcards feature **breathtaking**, **dramatic** scenes.

NO COMMAS WITH CUMULATIVE ADJECTIVES (see 30E)

- Other postcards feature **famous historical** scenes.

COMMAS WITH NONRESTRICTIVE ELEMENTS (see 30F)

- **Four years after the first postcard appeared**, the US government began to issue prestamped postcards.

- The Golden Age of postcards, **which lasted from about 1900 to 1929**, yielded many especially valuable cards.

- Collectors attend postcard shows, **which are similar to baseball card shows**.

NO COMMAS WITH RESTRICTIVE ELEMENTS (see 30F)

- Collectors **who attend these shows** may specialize in a particular kind of postcard.

continued >>

30B

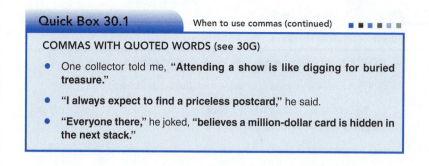

Quick Box 30.1   When to use commas (continued)   ■ ■ ■ ■ ■ ■

COMMAS WITH QUOTED WORDS (see 30G)

- One collector told me, **"Attending a show is like digging for buried treasure."**

- **"I always expect to find a priceless postcard,"** he said.

- **"Everyone there,"** he joked, **"believes a million-dollar card is hidden in the next stack."**

■ Exception

When an introductory element is short, some writers omit the comma. However, in ACADEMIC WRITING, you'll never be wrong if you use the comma.

> **YES**   In 1992, the Americans with Disabilities Act was passed.   [preferred]
>
> **YES**   In 1992 the Americans with Disabilities Act was passed.

30C How do I use a comma before a coordinating conjunction?

When you link independent clauses, place a comma before a COORDINATING CONJUNCTION (*and, but, for, or, nor, yet, so*).

- The sky turned black**, and** the wind blew fiercely.

  A comma and *and* link two independent clauses.

- The sky began to brighten**, but** the wind continued blowing strongly.

  A comma and *but* link two independent clauses.

- Soon high winds would start**, or** snow would begin.

When commas are already part of one or both independent clauses, use a semicolon to link them.

- With temperatures below freezing, the snow did not melt**; and** people, gazing at the white landscape, wondered when they would see grass again.

  Each of the two independent clauses contains one or more commas. Therefore, a semicolon with *and* does the linking of the independent clauses.

30C

❗ Alerts: (1) Never put a comma *after* a coordinating conjunction that joins independent clauses.

NO   A house is renovated in two weeks **but,** an apartment takes a week.

YES   A house is renovated in two weeks**,** **but** an apartment takes a week.

(2) Never use a comma when a coordinating conjunction links only two words, phrases, or dependent clauses.

NO   Habitat for Humanity depends on volunteer **labor, and donations** for its construction projects.

YES   Habitat for Humanity depends on volunteer **labor and donations** for its construction projects.

(3) Never use a comma between independent clauses unless you also use a coordinating conjunction. (If you make this error, you create a COMMA SPLICE.)

NO   Five inches of snow fell in two **hours, driving** was hazardous.

YES   Five inches of snow fell in two **hours, and driving** was hazardous. ●

● **EXERCISE 30-1**   Combine each pair of sentences using the coordinating conjunction shown in parentheses. Rearrange words when necessary.

EXAMPLE

Esperanto is a language invented by L. L. Zamenhof in 1887. It is now the most widely spoken artificial language. (and)

Esperanto is a language invented by L. L. Zamenhof in 1887, and it is now the most widely spoken artificial language.

30C

1. Zamenhof believed that his invention would foster world peace. He believed that if people spoke a common language wars would cease. (for)
2. No country recognizes Esperanto as an official language. It is spoken by many people in at least 115 countries. (but)
3. Published in Warsaw, the first book of Esperanto grammar appeared in 1887. The first world congress of Esperanto speakers was held in France in 1905. (and)
4. Before World War II, Hitler denounced Esperanto. Its creator was Jewish. (for)
5. Stalin also attacked Esperanto and would not grant it official status. He would not allow its use in the Soviet Union. (nor) ●

30D How do I use commas with a series?

A *series*, which always calls for commas, consists of three or more elements with the same grammatical form.

WORDS	The earliest clothing fabrics were made from natural fibers such as **cotton, silk, linen,** and **wool**.
PHRASES	Fabrics today are made **from natural fibers, from synthetic fibers, and from natural and synthetic fiber blends**.
CLAUSES	**Natural fibers are durable as well as absorbent, synthetic fibers resist wrinkling as well as fading,** and **blends of the two fibers offer the advantages of both**.

Although some professional writers omit the comma before a final coordinating conjunction in a series, most instructors prefer that you use that comma. The comma helps readers understand the sentence.

Items in a series often appear as numbered or lettered lists within a sentence. In such cases, use commas or semicolons exactly as you would if the numbers or letters were not there.

- Three synthetic fibers predominate in clothing manufacturing: **(1) rayon, (2) polyester,** and **(3) acrylic**.
- Three popular fabrics for blouses are **(a) cotton, a natural fiber; (b) rayon, a synthetic fiber;** and **(c) ramie, a natural fiber**.

❶ Alerts: (1) Never use a comma before the first item or after the last item in a series, unless another rule makes it necessary.

NO	We used, **red, white,** and **blue** ribbons for the Fourth of July.
NO	We used **red, white**, and **blue,** ribbons for the Fourth of July.
YES	We used **red, white,** and **blue** ribbons for the Fourth of July.

(2) Never use a comma when only two items are linked by a coordinating conjunction.

NO	Everyone enjoyed **the parade,** and **the concert**.
YES	Everyone enjoyed **the parade** and **the concert**. ●

30E When do I use a comma between adjectives?

Use a comma between **coordinating adjectives** (adjectives that carry equal weight when modifying a noun) unless a coordinating conjunction (such as *and* or *but*) already links them.

In contrast, never use a comma between **cumulative adjectives**, which do not carry equal weight in modifying a noun. The role of cumulative adjectives is to build up—accumulate—meaning as they move toward the noun.

To determine whether adjectives are carrying equal weight in a sentence, use the tests in Quick Box 30.2.

Quick Box 30.2

■ ■ ■ ■ ■ ■

Tests for coordinating and cumulative adjectives

If the answer to either of the following questions is yes, the adjectives are coordinating and need commas.

1. Can the order of the adjectives be changed without changing the sentence's meaning or creating nonsense?

   - The **large, restless, noisy** crowd wanted the concert to start.

     The order of adjectives can be changed (*noisy, restless, large*) and the sentence still makes sense, so these are *coordinating adjectives that need commas*.

   - The concert featured **several familiar backup** singers.

     Several familiar backup cannot be changed to *backup familiar several* and make sense, so these are *cumulative adjectives, which do not need commas*.

2. Can *and* be inserted between the adjectives without changing the meaning or creating nonsense?

   - The **large, restless, noisy** crowd wanted the concert to start.
     ^*and*   ^*and*

     Inserting *and* does not change the meaning of the sentence. Therefore, the adjectives are *coordinating and the commas are correct*.

   - The concert featured **several familiar backup** singers.
     ^*and*   ^*and*

     Inserting *and* creates nonsense. Therefore, the adjectives are *cumulative adjectives and do not need commas*.

30F How do commas work with nonrestrictive and restrictive elements?

A **restrictive element** pinpoints, narrows, or restricts the meaning of its ANTE-CEDENT to a particular person or class: *Don't eat tomatoes **that are canned***. A **nonrestrictive element** describes but does not pinpoint, narrow, or restrict the meaning of its antecedent: *Berries, **which sweeten your breakfast**, are highly nutritious*.

Use commas to separate nonrestrictive elements from the rest of a sentence. Do not use commas to separate restrictive elements from their antecedents. Simply stated:

- Restrictive element—do not use commas.
- Nonrestrictive element—use commas.

NO   Someone, **named Princess,** canceled the concert.

Named Princess narrows who *someone* is to Princess; it is restrictive. Commas are unnecessary.

YES   Someone **named Princess** canceled the concert.

A restrictive, pinpointing element requires no comma.

NO   Princess **who writes all her material** is suing her promoter.

Who writes all her material is descriptive and does not pinpoint Princess; it is nonrestrictive. Commas are required.

YES   Princess, **who writes all her material,** is suing her promoter.

A nonrestrictive element needs to be set off by commas.

NO   Princess started playing on a piano, **that was out of tune**.

That was out of tune is restrictive because it identifies the piano. No comma is necessary.

YES   Princess started playing on a piano **that was out of tune**.

A restrictive, pinpointing clause requires no comma.

NO   **A prolific artist** Princess is on her way to fame and fortune.

A prolific artist is a descriptive, nonrestrictive element, so it requires a comma.

YES   **A prolific artist,** Princess is on her way to fame and fortune.

A nonrestrictive element requires a comma.

30F

● **EXERCISE 30-2**   Using your knowledge of restrictive and nonrestrictive elements, insert commas as needed. If a sentence is correct, explain why. For help, consult 30F.

EXAMPLE

During the summer when butterflies are most active gardeners can attract them by planting the right flowers.

During the summer, when butterflies are most active, gardeners can attract them by planting the right flowers.

1. In spring as birds and bees look for water and food certain plants and trees provide those needs and thus attract the greatest number of airborne visitors.
2. Gardeners who learn to attract birds may find they have fewer problems with insects and other unwelcome pests.
3. During suburban sprawl when cities eat up more and more land birds have to adapt by putting their nests in buildings.
4. Birds are attracted to pines and evergreens where they can find food and shelter.
5. Hungry birds who are not picky will enjoy a feeder stocked with black oil sunflower seeds.
6. Birds also need to eat insects which provide a higher protein content than seeds.
7. Some common plants such as butterfly weed and lantana are ideal for attracting butterflies.
8. Because they have the nectar that butterflies want these plants enhance any butterfly garden.
9. As butterflies pass by a garden looking for bright colors and strong fragrances they will notice flowers planted in large clumps.
10. Gardens that are favorable to birds and butterflies will also invite honeybees and other pollinators. ●

30G How do I use commas with quoted words?

Use a comma to set off quoted words from explanations in the sentence.

- The poet William Blake wrote, "Love seeketh not itself to please."
- "I love you," Mary told John, "but I cannot marry you."
- "My love is a fever," declared William Shakespeare.

However, when you use *that* to introduce a quotation, never use a comma whether you write a DIRECT QUOTATION or an INDIRECT QUOTATION.

> **NO** Mary claims, that "our passion is strong."

> **NO** Mary claims that, "our passion is strong."

> **YES** Mary claims that "our passion is strong."

❶ Alert: When the quoted words end with an exclamation point or a question mark, retain that original punctuation, even if explanatory words follow.

QUOTED WORDS	*"O Romeo! Romeo!"*
NO	"O Romeo! Romeo**!,**" whispered Juliet from her window.
NO	"O Romeo! Romeo**,**" whispered Juliet from her window.
YES	"O Romeo! Romeo**!**" whispered Juliet from her window. ●

30H   What other word groups do I set off with commas?

Additional word groups that call for a comma to set them off include transitional expressions, conjunctive adverbs, asides, contrasts, words addressed directly to a reader or listener, and **tag questions** (such as *isn't it?* or *don't you think?*).

TRANSITIONAL EXPRESSIONS

- **For example,** California is a major food producer.
- California, **for example,** is a major food producer.
- California is a major food producer, **for example**.

CONJUNCTIVE ADVERBS

- **However,** the Midwest is the world's breadbasket.
- The Midwest, **however,** is the world's breadbasket.
- The Midwest is the world's breadbasket, **however**.

ASIDES

- Most large growers, **I imagine,** hope to export food.
- Most large growers hope to export food, **I imagine**.

CONTRASTS

- Food, **not technology,** tops the list of US exports.

WORDS ADDRESSED DIRECTLY TO READER

- **All you computer majors,** perhaps the future lies in soybeans rather than software.
- Perhaps the future, **all you computer majors,** lies in soybeans rather than software.
- Perhaps the future lies in soybeans rather than software, **all you computer majors**.

TAG QUESTIONS

- You know, **don't you,** what tag questions are**?**
- You know what tag questions are, **don't you?**

30H

301   How do I use commas in dates, names, places, addresses, letter format, and numbers?

■ Punctuating dates

Use a comma between the day and the year. In addition, use a comma between a day of the week and the month.

- July 20, 1969
- Sunday, July 20, 1969

When you use month-day-year order for dates, use a comma after the day and the year.

- Everyone watched television on July 20, 1969, to see the moon landing.

When you use day-month-year order for dates, never use commas.

- Everyone watched television on 20 July 1969 to see the moon landing.

Never use a comma between only a month and year, only a month and day, or only a season and year.

- The major news story in July 1969 was the moon landing; news coverage was especially heavy on July 21. Many older people will always remember summer 1969.

■ Punctuating names, places, and addresses

When an abbreviated academic degree (*MD, PhD*) comes after a name, use a comma between the name and the title (see 40B). When a sentence continues after a name and title, also use a comma after the title.

- Rosa Gonzales, MD, was the principal witness for the defense.

However, don't place a comma before or after *Jr., Sr., II*, or *2nd* (40C).

- Ron Gonzales Jr. was the defendant.

Use a comma between the last and first names in an inverted name.

- Troyka, David

Use a comma between a city and state. When a sentence continues after a city and state, also use a comma after the state.

- Philadelphia, Pennsylvania, is home to the Liberty Bell.

When a sentence includes a complete address, use a comma to separate all of the items in the address except the ZIP code (see 40E). The ZIP code follows the state after a space and no comma.

- I wrote to Mr. Hugh Lern, 10-01 Rule Road, Classgate, NJ 07632, for the instruction manual.

■ Punctuating letter openings and closings

Use a comma after the opening of an informal letter or e-mail. Use a colon after the opening of a formal letter.

- Dear Betty,
- Dear Ms. Renshaw:

After the closing of a formal or informal letter, use a comma.

- Sincerely yours,
- Love,

■ Punctuating numbers

In numbers more than four digits long, put a comma after every three digits, counting from the right.

- 150,567,066
- 72,867

In four-digit numbers, a comma is optional for money, distance, amounts, and most other measurements. Be consistent in each piece of writing.

- $1776 $1,776
- 1776 miles   1,776 miles
- 1776 potatoes 1,776 potatoes

Use a comma to separate the act and scene numbers in plays. In addition, use a comma to separate a page reference in any SOURCE from a line reference.

- act ii, scene iv [or act 2, scene 4]
- page 120, line 6

30J   How can a comma prevent a misreading?

Use a comma to clarify the meaning of a sentence, even if no other rule calls for one.

NO   People who can practice many hours a day.

YES   People who can, practice many hours a day.

● **EXERCISE 30-3**   Insert commas to prevent misreading.

EXAMPLE

NO   Of all the parts of the human body teeth tend to last the longest.

YES   Of all the parts of the human body, teeth tend to last the longest.

30J

1. Humans like some other animals have two sets of teeth over a lifetime.
2. Sharks known for having deadly bites develop several sets of teeth throughout their lives.
3. Adult humans typically have 32 teeth 12 more than they had as children.
4. For children eruptions of teeth, also called teething, can be painful.
5. People who brush their teeth develop healthy gums and mouths. ●

30K How can I avoid other comma errors?

In explaining comma rules in this chapter so far, we've covered the errors associated with those rules. Here are a few helpful tips for using commas.

1. Never put a comma in a number in an address or in a page reference.

    ● 11263 Dean Drive   ● see page 1338

2. Never put a comma in years expressed in four figures. If the year is expressed in five or more figures, use a comma. If you list years in a sentence, separate them with a comma.

    ● 1995, 2002   ● 25,000 BCE

3. Never put a comma after *such as*.

    NO The Wright brothers were fascinated by other vehicles, **such as,** bicycles and gliders.

    YES The Wright brothers were fascinated by other vehicles, such as bicycles and gliders.

4. Never put a comma before *than* in a comparison.

    NO The 1903 airplane sustained its flight longer, **than** any other engine-powered aircraft had.

    YES The 1903 airplane sustained its flight longer **than** any other engine-powered aircraft had.

5. Never put a comma before an opening parenthesis. When a comma is required, put it *after* the closing parenthesis.

    NO Because aviation enthralls many of us, **(especially children)** a popular spot to visit is Kitty Hawk's flight museum.

    YES Because aviation enthralls many of us **(especially children),** a popular spot to visit is Kitty Hawk's flight museum.

6. Never put a comma after a PREPOSITION.

    NO People expected more damage **from,** the high winds.

    YES People expected more damage **from** the high winds.

7. Never put a comma after a SUBORDINATING CONJUNCTION.

NO   **Although,** winds exceeded fifty miles an hour, little damage occurred.

YES   **Although** winds exceeded fifty miles an hour, little damage occurred.

8. Never put a comma between a SUBJECT and its VERB. (A pair of commas, however, is acceptable.)

NO   Orville and Wilbur Wright, made their first successful airplane flights in 1903.

YES   Orville and Wilbur Wright made their first successful airplane flights in 1903.

YES   Orville and Wilbur Wright, on a beach in North Carolina, made their first successful airplane flights in 1903.

9. Never put a comma between a verb and its OBJECT.

NO   These inventors tackled, the problems of powered flight.

YES   These inventors tackled the problems of powered flight.

10. Never put a comma between a verb and its COMPLEMENT.

NO   Flying has become, an important industry and a popular hobby.

YES   Flying has become an important industry and a popular hobby.

● **EXERCISE 30-4**   Some commas have been deliberately misused in these sentences. Delete misused commas. If a sentence is correct, explain why.

EXAMPLE

NO   Alchemy was an important philosophical and scientific tradition, that led to the development of chemistry and medicine.

YES   Alchemy was an important philosophical and scientific tradition that led to the development of chemistry and medicine.

1. One of the goals of alchemy was the development, of the philosopher's stone.
2. In addition to turning base metals into gold, the philosopher's stone, was supposed to grant immortality or eternal youth.
3. According to other legends, the philosopher's stone also, cured illnesses, revived dead plants, and created clones.
4. The fantastic claims about the philosopher's stone and mentions of it in historical writings, can be traced as far back as the fourth century.
5. Because, alchemists were attempting to turn metals into gold, they developed some laboratory techniques that are still used in chemistry.

30K

6. Alchemy also helped develop important ideas, that are used in modern medicine, such as the dangers of heavy metal poisoning.
7. Robert Boyle, considered to be a founder of modern chemistry, began his work, as an alchemist.
8. The famous, important, scientist Isaac Newton wrote more about his work in alchemy than he did about optics or physics.
9. The origins of European alchemy, date back to ancient Greece and Egypt.
10. Unlike modern science, alchemy also relied upon, religion, mythology, ancient wisdom, and the occult. ●

31 Semicolons

Quick Points   You will learn to

➤ Use semicolons correctly.

MyWritingLab™   Visit mywritinglab.com for more resources on semicolons.

31A When can I use a semicolon instead of a period between independent clauses?

You can choose whether to use a semicolon to replace a period, but do so only between two closely related INDEPENDENT CLAUSES; using a semicolon creates one sentence.

> **NO**   After she walked out the door; I never saw her again.
>
> *After she walked out the door* is not an independent clause; a comma should be used.
>
> **YES**   She walked out the door; I never saw her again.
>
> **YES**   She walked out the door; later, I never saw her again.
>
> The semicolon separates the two closely related independent clauses. In the second example, a CONJUNCTIVE ADVERB (*later, then*) introduces the second independent clause.

31B   When do I need to use a semicolon to replace a comma?

A semicolon replaces a comma when you use a COORDINATING CONJUNCTION to link independent clauses that already contain commas.

- Because Death Valley is the hottest place in North America, some people think that no animals live there; **but** visitors, especially, are amazed to see many tiny and a few larger animals emerge at night, when the temperatures drop, to find food.

In addition, when individual items in a series (see 30D) contain commas, use a semicolon instead of a comma to separate the items.

- The animals in Death Valley include **spiders**, such as black widows and tarantulas; **snakes**, such as coral snakes and sidewinders; and **small mammals**, such as kangaroo rats, which can convert seeds into water, and trade rats, which nest around cactus.

 Alert: Use a colon, never a semicolon, to introduce a list of items.

NO   Predators live in Death Valley; spiders, snakes, and some mammals.

YES   Predators live in Death Valley: spiders, snakes, and some mammals. ●

● **EXERCISE 31-1**   Combine each set of sentences into one sentence so that it contains two independent clauses. Use a semicolon correctly between the two clauses. You may add, omit, revise, and rearrange words. Try to use all the patterns in this chapter, and explain the reasoning behind your decisions. More than one revision may be correct. For help, consult all sections of this chapter.

EXAMPLE

Although not as well known as Thomas Edison, the inventor Nikola Tesla was a revolutionary and important scientist. One biographer calls him "the man who invented the twentieth century."

Although not as well known as Thomas Edison, the inventor Nikola Tesla was a revolutionary scientist; one biographer calls him "the man who invented the twentieth century."

1. Tesla was born in what is now Croatia and studied at the Technical University at Graz, Austria. He excelled in physics, mechanical engineering, and electrical engineering.
2. Tesla's accomplishments include inventing alternating current. He also contributed to the fields of robotics, computer science, and wireless technology. And he helped increase knowledge of nuclear physics, ballistics, and electromagnetism.
3. The Italian inventor Guglielmo Marconi and Tesla both claimed to have invented the radio. However, the US Supreme Court, in 1943, upheld Tesla's radio patent and officially credited him as the device's inventor.

31B

4. In 1901, Tesla began construction of a tower that he claimed would create a global network of wireless communication and be able to control the weather. Unfortunately, Tesla soon lost funding and never finished the project.

5. At his lab in Colorado Springs, he was able to produce artificial lightning. This scene was vividly portrayed in the 2006 film *The Prestige*. ●

32 Colons

■ ■ ■ ■ ■ ■

Quick Points   You will learn to

➤ Use colons correctly.

MyWritingLab™   Visit mywritinglab.com for more resources on colons.

32A   How do I use a colon with a list, an appositive, or a quotation?

Use a colon after an INDEPENDENT CLAUSE to introduce a list, an APPOSITIVE, or a QUOTATION. Some lead-in words, such as *the following* and *as follows*, are followed by a colon. Other lead-ins (*such as, like,* and *including*) aren't.

LISTED ITEMS

● The students demanded the following: an expanded menu in the cafeteria, improved janitorial services, and more up-to-date textbooks.

APPOSITIVE

● Museums in New York and Florida own the best-known works from Louis Tiffany's studio: those wonderful stained-glass windows.

Stained-glass windows is an appositive that renames *best-known works*.

QUOTATION

● The little boy in *E.T.* did say something neat: "How do you explain school to a higher intelligence?"

—George F. Will, "Well, I Don't Love You, E.T."

❶ Alert: If an incomplete sentence introduces a DIRECT QUOTATION, use a comma, not a colon (see 30G). ●

32B   When can I use a colon between sentences?

When one sentence introduces the next, you can use a colon between the two.

● I'll say it again: Snakes are lovable.

❶ Alerts: (1) Never use a colon when a DIRECT OBJECT consists of a series or list of items.

NO   We bought: eggs, milk, cheese, and bread.

YES   We bought eggs, milk, cheese, and bread.

(2) Never separate a DEPENDENT CLAUSE from an independent clause with a colon. Use a comma instead.

NO   After the drought ended: water restrictions were lifted.

YES   After the drought ended, water restrictions were lifted.

(3) Capitalizing the word after a colon is optional. Simply be consistent. ●

32C   What conventional formats call for colons?

BETWEEN TITLE AND SUBTITLE

● *Literature: An Introduction to Critical Reading*

BETWEEN HOURS AND MINUTES AND MINUTES AND SECONDS

● The runner passed the halfway point at 1:23:02.

BETWEEN NUMBERS IN RATIOS

● a proportion of 7:1   ● a 3:5 ratio

AFTER WORDS IN MEMO HEADINGS

● To: Dean Kristen Joy

● From: Professor Daniel Black

● Re: Student work-study program

AFTER FORMAL LETTER OPENINGS

● Dear Ms. Carter:

32C

BETWEEN BIBLE CHAPTERS AND VERSES

- Psalm 23:1–3

! **Alert:** In MLA STYLE, a period comes between chapter and verse in Bible references: *Ps. 23.1–3*. See Ch. 14 for other MLA rules. ●

● **EXERCISE 32-1**   Insert colons where needed and delete any not needed. If a sentence is correct, explain why.

EXAMPLE

NO   After months of work, Carlos was finally ready to mail his college applications to the following schools, Valley College, East California University, and Blakeville College.

YES   After months of work, Carlos was finally ready to mail his college applications to the following schools: Valley College, East California University, and Blakeville College.

1. To prepare for the application process, Carlos read the book *Expanding Your Options, A Guide to Writing a Successful College Application*.
2. Date March 2, 2012
   To Office of Admissions
   To whom it may concern
3. Since the post office closed at 530, Carlos had to rush to meet the application deadline.
4. To represent himself effectively, Carlos wrote his application letter about his many successes, such as: his high grade point average, his work as the high school newspaper editor, and his community service.
5. After his application was completed and in the mail: he started to look forward to hearing back from the colleges.
6. He decided not to worry when he remembered the words of his favorite Bible quote from Matthew 6, 34.
7. He also remembered the encouraging words from his guidance counselor: "Don't worry, Carlos. Something will work out for you."
8. He hoped that he would be accepted to his first choice, Valley College.
9. Valley College was his first choice because it offered: beautiful scenery, a diverse student body, and a small teacher-student ratio.
10. However: Valley College is very selective and admits only a small percentage of applicants. ●

32C

33 Apostrophes

Quick Points You will learn to

➤ Use apostrophes correctly.

MyWritingLab™ Visit mywritinglab.com for more resources on apostrophes.

33A How do I use an apostrophe to show that a noun is possessive?

The **possessive case** shows possession or ownership (*the writer's pen*) or other relationships (*the writer's parent*). To indicate possession in NOUNS, you can choose to use -'s (*the instructor's comments*), which calls for an apostrophe; or a PHRASE beginning with *of* (*the comments of the instructor*), which doesn't call for an apostrophe. Here are some applications of this general rule.

1. Add -'s to nouns not ending in *s*.

    - She felt a **parent's** joy.

    - We care about our **children's** education.

2. Add -'s to singular nouns ending in *s*.

    - The **business's** system for handling complaints is inefficient.

    - Lee **Jones's** car insurance is expensive.

3. Add only an apostrophe to plural nouns ending in *s*.

    - The two **boys'** eyewitness statements helped solve the crime.

    - The **workers'** contracts permit three **months'** maternity leave.

4. Add -'s to the last word in compound words and phrases.

    - His **mother-in-law's** company makes scuba gear.

5. Add -'s to each noun in individual possession.

    - **Avery's and Jimmy's** houses are next to each other.

6. Add -'s to only the last noun in joint or group possession.

    - **Lindsey and Ryan's** house has a screened porch.

33A

393

⚠ **Alerts:** (1) Never use an apostrophe at the end of a nonpossessive noun ending in *s*.

NO   The circus' has dropped all its animal acts.

YES   The circus has dropped all its animal acts.

(2) Never use an apostrophe with a nonpossessive plural noun.

NO   **Team's** of doctors are researching the effects of cholesterol.

Teams is a plural noun that ends in *s*, but the sentence expresses no possession.

YES   **Teams** of doctors are researching the effects of cholesterol. ●

33B   How do I use an apostrophe to show that an indefinite pronoun is possessive?

INDEFINITE PRONOUNS refer to general or nonspecific persons or things: *someone, somebody, anyone, anything, no one, else.* (For a complete list of types of pronouns, see Quick Box 16.2, p. 280.) To indicate possession in an indefinite pronoun, add *-'s*.

● I need **someone's** help to prepare for the test.

● Are **anyone else's** directions more accurate than mine are?

When one indefinite pronoun follows another (*anyone else*), the second one takes the possessive *-'s*.

33C   Do I ever use an apostrophe with *hers, his, its, ours, yours,* and *theirs*?

Never use an apostrophe with **possessive pronouns:** *hers, his, its, ours, yours,* and *theirs*. As possessive pronouns, they already carry possessive meaning.

NO   Because cholesterol has been widely publicized, **it's** role in heart disease is well known.

YES   Because cholesterol has been widely publicized, **its** role in heart disease is well known.

⚠ **Alert:** Never confuse *its*, the possessive pronoun, with the contraction *it's*, which stands for *it is*. A similar confusion arises between *you're* and *your*, *who's* and *whose*, and *they're* and *their*. ●

33D   Do I ever add an apostrophe to a verb that ends in -s?

Never add an apostrophe to a VERB that ends in *s*.

NO   Exercise **play's** a key role in longevity.

YES   Exercise **plays** a key role in longevity.

33E   How do I use apostrophes in contractions?

In **contractions**, an apostrophe indicates that one or more letters have been omitted from a word or a term: *can't, don't, I'm, isn't, it's, let's, they're, wasn't, weren't, we've, who's, won't, you're.*

- **It's** [*not* Its] still snowing.

! Alert: Many college instructors believe that contractions aren't appropriate in ACADEMIC WRITING. Indeed, the seventh edition of the *MLA Handbook* says they are "rarely acceptable in research papers" (74). ●

33F   Do I use an apostrophe with letters, numerals, symbols, and terms?

Use an apostrophe before the *s* to form the plurals of single letters, numbers written as figures, symbols, and words used as terms.

LETTERS	Printing **w's** is hard for some first graders.
NUMBERS IN FIGURES	The address includes six **2's**.
SYMBOLS	The use of **#'s** is now common on Twitter.
WORDS USED AS TERMS	All the **for's** were misspelled *four*.

33F

! Alert: When you use letters as letters or words as words, you can choose to underline them or put them in italics, or enclose them in quotation marks (see 34E). Whatever you choose, be consistent in each piece of writing. ●

● **EXERCISE 33-1**   Rewrite these sentences to insert *'s* or an apostrophe alone to make the words in parentheses show possession. (Delete the parentheses.) For help, consult this chapter.

EXAMPLE

All boxes, cans, and bottles on a (supermarket) shelves are designed to appeal to (people) emotions.

All boxes, cans, and bottles on a *supermarket's* shelves are designed to appeal to *people's* emotions.

1. A (product) manufacturer designs packaging to appeal to (consumers) emotions through color and design.

2. Marketing specialists know that (people) beliefs about a (product) quality are influenced by their emotional response to the design of its package.

3. Circles and ovals appearing on a (box) design supposedly increase a (product user) feelings of comfort, while bold patterns and colors attract a (shopper) attention.

4. Using both circles and bold designs in (Arm & Hammer) and (Tide) packaging produces both effects in consumers.

5. (Heinz) ketchup bottle and (Coca-Cola) famous logo achieve the same effects by combining a bright color with an old-fashioned, "comfortable" design.

6. Often, a (company) marketing consultants will custom design products to appeal to the supposedly "typical" (adult female) emotions or to (adult males), (children), or (teenagers) feelings.

7. One of the (marketing business) leading consultants, Stan Gross, tests (consumers) emotional reactions to (companies) products and their packages by asking consumers to associate products with well-known personalities.

8. Thus, (test takers) responses to (Gross) questions might reveal that a particular brand of laundry detergent has (Russell Crowe) toughness, (Oprah Winfrey) determination, or (someone else) sparkling personality.

9. Manufacturing (companies) products are not the only ones relying on (Gross) and other corporate (image makers) advice.

10. (Sports teams) owners also use marketing specialists to design their (teams) images, as anyone who has seen the angry bull logo of the Chicago Bulls basketball team will agree. ●

Quick Points   You will learn to

➤ Use quotation marks correctly.

MyWritingLab™ Visit mywritinglab.com for more resources on quotation marks.

34A   How do I use quotation marks with short direct quotations?

Quotation marks are most often used to enclose a **direct quotation**—a speaker or writer's exact words. Use quotation marks to enclose short direct quotations, which in MLA style means a quotation of fewer than four typed lines of prose or three typed lines of poetry.

- Remarked director Fritz Lang of his masterpiece *Siegfried*, "Nothing in this film is accidental" (228).

For MLA in-text citation style with quotations, see Chapter 14; for APA style, see Chapter 15.

■ Using double quotation marks (" ")

Use double quotation marks to enclose a short quotation.

- Edward T. Hall explains the practicality of close conversational distances: **"If you are interested in something, your pupils dilate; if I say something you don't like, they tend to contract"** (47). Some cultures prefer arm's length for all but the most intimate conversations.

- As W. H. Auden wittily defined personal space, **"Some thirty inches from my nose / The frontier of my person goes"** (539).

■ Using single quotation marks (' ')

Use single quotation marks in short quotations only to replace any double quotation marks that appear in the original source.

ORIGINAL SOURCE

He has also said that he does not wish to be the arbiter for what is or is not an **"official"** intelligence.

—Thomas Hoerr, "The Naturalistic Intelligence," p. 24

34A

EXAMPLE FROM A RESEARCH PAPER

As Thomas Hoerr reports, Gardner "does not wish to be the arbiter for what is or is not an 'official' intelligence" (24).

⚠ **Alerts:** (1) Use a slash to signal a break between lines of poetry. (2) Capitalize and punctuate poetry you quote exactly as in the original. ●

34B   How do I use quotation marks with long direct quotations?

In MLA style, a **long quotation** runs five or more lines of prose or more than three lines of poetry. A long quotation starts on a new line and is indented, or *displayed*, as a whole block of words, 1 inch from the left margin in MLA style (see Ch. 14).

Because a block indentation signifies quoted material, don't use quotation marks to enclose block quotations. If, however, words in the original are in quotation marks, punctuate exactly as in the original. The following passage demonstrates such usage.

As Desmond Morris explains, personal space varies among cultures:

> When you are talking to someone in the street or in any open space, reach out with your arm and see where the nearest point on his body comes. If you hail from western Europe, you will find that he is at roughly fingertip distance from you. In other words, as you reach out, your fingertips will just about make contact with his shoulder. If you come from eastern Europe, you will find you are standing at "wrist distance." If you come from the Mediterranean region you will find that you are much closer to your companion. (23)

⚠ **Alert:** In MLA style, at the end of a long quotation, place the page number or the author's name and the page number (only if you don't mention the author's name in the sentence that leads into the quotation) in parentheses. Put the period that ends the sentence before the parentheses, never after them. ●

34C   How do I use quotation marks to indicate spoken words?

Spoken words are called DIRECT DISCOURSE. Use quotation marks when you quote direct discourse or write dialogue. Start a new paragraph—that is, indent the first line—each time the speaker changes.

"I don't know how you can see to drive," she said.
"Maybe you should put on your glasses."
"Putting on my glasses would help you to see?"
"Not me; you," Macon said. "You're focused on the windshield instead of the road."

—Ann Tyler, *The Accidental Tourist*

If the same speaker's words continue for more than one paragraph, use opening quotation marks only at the start of each paragraph. Use closing quotation marks only when you come to the final paragraph of that speaker's dialogue.

Alert: Never enclose INDIRECT DISCOURSE (see 23E) in quotation marks.

● The mayor said that he was tired.

This indirect discourse needs no quotation marks. As a direct quotation, this sentence would read *The mayor said, "I am tired."* ●

● **EXERCISE 34-1**   Decide whether each sentence that follows is direct or indirect discourse and then rewrite each sentence in the other form. Make any changes needed for grammatical correctness. With direct discourse, put the speaker's words wherever you think they belong in the sentence.

EXAMPLE

Dr. Sanchez explained to Mary that washing her hands in an important part of hygiene.

Dr. Sanchez explained, "Washing your hands is an important part of hygiene."

1. Mary asked, "If my hands aren't dirty, why is it so important to wash them?"
2. Dr. Sanchez replied that many diseases are spread because of inadequately washed and infected hands.
3. The Centers for Disease Control, explained Dr. Sanchez, argues that hand washing may seem trivial but it is a vital part of public health.
4. Mary asked, "Is it ok to use alcohol-based hand sanitizers instead of soap and water?"
5. Dr. Sanchez replied that soap and clean water are best, but a sanitizer with at least 60% alcohol is also very effective. ●

34D

34D   How do I use quotation marks with titles?

Use quotation marks around the titles of short published works: poems, short stories, essays, articles from periodicals, song titles, and individual episodes of a television or radio series. Use italics (or underlining) for longer works. See Chapter 39 for more on italics.

34E How do I use quotation marks to indicate terms, language translations, and irony?

You can choose either quotation marks or italics (or underlining) to indicate words that are technical terms; words in another language; translated words; and words meant ironically. Simply be consistent in your choice.

TECHNICAL TERM
"Plagiarism"—the unacknowledged use of another person's words or ideas—is a serious offense. Plagiarism by students can result in expulsion.

Once the term has been introduced, it needs no further quotation marks.

TRANSLATED WORDS
My grandfather usually ended arguments with an old saying: *de gustibus non disputandum est* ("there is no arguing about tastes").

IRONIC WORD
The tax "reform" is actually a tax increase.

34F When are quotation marks wrong?

Never use quotation marks around CLICHÉS, **slang**, or other language that is inappropriate in ACADEMIC WRITING. Use appropriate, alternative wording.

NO They "eat like birds" in public and "stuff their faces" in private.

YES They nibble in public and gorge themselves in private.

Never enclose a word in quotation marks merely to call attention to it.

NO Remember, the "customer" matters to your business.

YES Remember, the customer matters to your business.

Never enclose indirect discourse in quotation marks.

NO The College Code of Conduct points out that "plagiarism can result in expulsion."

The original words are "Grounds for expulsion include plagiarism." Here, the quotation is indirect, so quotation marks are wrong.

YES The College Code of Conduct points out that plagiarism can result in expulsion.

Never use quotation marks around the title of your own paper, unless your title includes another title of a short work (see Quick Box 39.1, on pp. 421–422).

NO "The Elderly in Nursing Homes: A Case Study"

YES The Elderly in Nursing Homes: A Case Study

NO   Sentence Structure in Emerson's Essay Self-Reliance

YES   Sentence Structure in Emerson's Essay "Self-Reliance"

34G How do I use quotation marks with other punctuation?

1. Put commas and periods inside closing quotation marks.

   - After we read Poe's poem "The Raven," we sought out his other works.
   - Edward T. Hall coined the word **"proxemics."**

2. Put colons and semicolons *outside* closing quotation marks.

   - We try to discover **"how close is too close"**: We do not want to invade others' personal space.
   - The sign read **"Dead Man's Hill"**; we knew we were in San Francisco.

3. Put question marks, exclamation points, and dashes outside quotation marks unless they are part of the original quotation.

   - **"Did I Hear You Call My Name?"** was the winning song.
   - They shouted, **"We won the lottery!"**

If a question mark, an exclamation point, or a dash punctuates words not enclosed in quotation marks, put it outside the closing quotation mark.

   - Have you read Nikki Giovanni's poem **"Knoxville, Tennessee"**?
   - Edward T. Hall's coined word **"proxemics"**—a term based on the noun **"proximity"**—can now be found in dictionaries.

● **EXERCISE 34-2**   Correct any errors in the use of quotation marks and other punctuation with quotation marks. If you think a sentence is correct, explain why.

1. Mark Twain's observation "—Facts are stubborn things, but statistics are more pliable.—" is an interesting critique of news media.
2. Twain valued travel and said that it "liberates the vandal." He argues that you cannot become: "bigoted, opinionated, stubborn, narrow-minded" if you travel. Someone who refuses to travel is, "stuck in one place" and thinks that "God made the world" for his "comfort and satisfaction."
3. In a poem called Genius, Mark Twain says that: Genius, like gold and precious stones / is chiefly prized because of its rarity.
4. Was it Shakespeare or Twain who wrote, "The course of true love never did run smooth?"
5. In a speech offering advice to young people, Twain said, "Be respectful to your superiors, if you have any". ●

34G

35 Periods, Question Marks, and Exclamation Points

Quick Points You will learn to

➤ Use periods, question marks, and exclamation points correctly.

MyWritingLab™ Visit mywritinglab.com for more resources on periods, question marks, and exclamation points.

35A When should I use a period?

A period is used after a statement, a mild command, or an **indirect question**, which reports a question that someone asks. (For help with periods in abbreviations, see Chapter 40.)

STATEMENT	Mountain climbers enjoy the outdoors.
MILD COMMAND	Pack warm clothes for the climb.
INDIRECT QUESTION	I asked if they wanted to climb Mount Ross.

35B When should I use a question mark?

A question mark is used after a **direct question** (which asks a question outright), a directly quoted question (which needs quotation marks), a series of questions, or a polite request. Use a question mark after each question in a series, whether or not you choose to capitalize the first word.

DIRECT QUESTION	Have you ever climbed a mountain?
DIRECTLY QUOTED QUESTION	I asked, "Do you want to climb Mount Everest?"
SERIES OF QUESTIONS WITH CAPITALS	The mountain climbers debated what to do: Turn back? Move on? Rest?
SERIES OF QUESTIONS WITH LOWERCASE	The mountain climbers debated what to do: turn back? move on? rest?

To end a polite request, you can choose a question mark or a period.

● Would you please send me the report.

This version emphasizes the politeness more than the request.

● Would you please send me the report?

This version emphasizes the request more than the politeness.

To convey IRONY or sarcasm, depend on words, not a question mark in parentheses, to communicate your message.

NO   Having altitude sickness is a **pleasant (?)** experience.

YES   Having altitude sickness is **as pleasant as having a terrible case of the flu**.

35C   When should I use an exclamation point?

An exclamation point is used after a strong command (*Look out!*); an emphatic declaration (*Those cars are going to crash!*); or an INTERJECTION, a word that conveys surprise or other emotion (*Oh! I'm terrified of heights!*). In ACADEMIC WRITING, reserve exclamation points for dialogue. Use words with sufficient impact for forceful messages.

NO   Each day in Nepal, we tried to see Mount Everest. Each day we failed! The summit remained shrouded! Clouds defeated us!

YES   Each day in Nepal, we tried to see Mount Everest. Each day we failed. The summit remained shrouded. Clouds defeated us!

To convey amazement or sarcasm, use precise words, not an exclamation point in parentheses.

NO   At 29,035 feet **(!)**, Everest is the world's highest mountain.

YES   Everest, the world's highest mountain, **soars** at 29,035 feet.

● **EXERCISE 35-1**   Insert needed periods, question marks, and exclamation points. For help, consult all sections of this chapter.

35C

Weather experts refer to a rise in surface temperature of the Pacific Ocean as El Niño, but La Niña refers to a drop in ocean temperature What effects can these changes cause In the spring of 1998, the cold water of La Niña surfaced quickly and produced chaotic and destructive weather In the American Northeast, rainfall amounts for June were three times above normal But no one expected the strangest consequence: snow in June Can you imagine waking up on an early summer morning in New England to snow Throughout the summer, most New England states failed to experience a single heat wave, which requires more than three days of 90 degree weather During that winter, the Great Lakes experienced record warmth, but California suffered from disastrously cold air A citrus freeze caused $600 million of damage That's more than half a billion dollars. ●

36 Other Punctuation Marks

Quick Points You will learn to

➤ Use dashes, parentheses, brackets, and ellipses correctly.

MyWritingLab™ Visit mywritinglab.com for more resources on other punctuation marks.

36A When should I use a dash?

The dash, typed as two unspaced hyphens, injects a thought within a sentence—in the middle or at the end—for special emphasis or commentary. You can set off EXAMPLES, DEFINITIONS, APPOSITIVES, contrasts, and asides with dashes.

> Two of the strongest animals in the jungle are vegetarians—the elephant and the gorilla. [examples]
> —Dick Gregory, *The Shadow That Scares Me*

> Although the emphasis at the school was mainly language—speaking, reading, writing—the lessons always began with an exercise in politeness. [definition]
> —Jade Snow Wong, *Fifth Chinese Daughter*

> The caretakers—the helpers, nurturers, teachers, mothers—are still systematically devalued. [appositive]
> —Ellen Goodman, "Just Woman's Work"

> Tampering with time brought most of the house tumbling down, and it was this that made Einstein's work so important—and controversial. [contrast]
> —Banesh Hoffman, "My Friend, Albert Einstein"

> I live on an income well below the poverty line—although it does not seem like poverty when the redbud and dogwood are in bloom together—and when I travel I have to be careful about expenses. [aside]
> —Sue Hubbell, *Beekeeper*

❶ Alerts: (1) If the words within a pair of dashes are a complete sentence and call for a question mark or an exclamation point, place such punctuation *before* the second dash:

- *A first love—do you remember?—stays in the memory forever.*

(2) Never use commas, semicolons, or periods next to dashes. Revise your writing to avoid these types of double punctuation. ●

36B   When should I use parentheses?

Like dashes (see 36A), parentheses let you interrupt a sentence's structure to add information. Parentheses tend to de-emphasize whatever they enclose; dashes tend to call attention to whatever they set off.

■ Using parentheses to add information

Parentheses can enclose the same kind of material that dashes can, such as explanations, definitions, examples, contrasts, and asides.

> In division (also known as partition), a subject commonly thought of as a single unit is reduced to its separate parts. [definition]
>
> —David Skwire, *Writing with a Thesis*

> Though other cities (Dresden, for instance) had been utterly destroyed in World War II, never before had a single weapon been responsible for such destruction. [example]
>
> —Lawrence Behrens and Leonard J. Rosen,
> *Writing and Reading Across the Curriculum*

> The sheer decibel level of the noise around us is not enough to make us cranky, irritable, or aggressive. (It can, however, affect our mental and physical health, which is another matter.) [aside]
>
> —Carol Tavris, *Anger: The Misunderstood Emotion*

■ Using parentheses to enclose numbers or letters

Conventional uses for parentheses include enclosing numbers or letters of listed items: *The topics to be discussed are (1) membership, (2) fund-raising, and (3) networking.* Another conventional use occurs in business writing when parentheses sometimes enclose a number written as a figure immediately after its spelled-out version: *We shipped **fifteen (15)** cartons yesterday.*

■ Using parentheses with other punctuation

A parenthetical complete sentence inserted within the body of another sentence does not start with a capital letter or end with a period. (It would, however, end with a question mark or exclamation point if one is required.) A complete parenthetical sentence standing alone follows regular rules of punctuation, as the previous sentence highlights.

> **NO**   If you decide to join us (We hope you do.), bring your dog also.
>
> **YES**   If you decide to join us (we hope you do), bring your dog also.

YES   If you decide to join us, bring your dog also. (We hope you do.)

YES   Your dog (isn't Rex his name?) will delight all my other guests.

As in the preceding examples, place a required comma outside your closing parenthesis unless you're using commas to set off a numbered list.

36C   When should I use brackets?

Use brackets to feature an insert, such as an additional word or a brief definition, added by you to material that you are quoting.

ORIGINAL SOURCE

For a variety of reasons, the system attempts to maintain stability and resist temporal change.

— Peter Bonner, "Travel Rhythms," *Sky Magazine*, p. 72

SOURCE IN A QUOTATION

In "Travel Rhythms," Bonner explains that **"maintain[ing]** stability and **resist[ing]** temporal change" are natural goals for human beings.

Brackets are used to fit the quotation's wording into the rest of the sentence structure.

ORIGINAL SOURCE

In the future, a trip to the doctor may well involve an evaluation of such environmental components of our health.

— Winifred Gallagher, *The Power of Place*, p. 19

SOURCE IN A QUOTATION

Gallagher points out that a doctor visit may soon include "an evaluation of such environmental components **[the air we breathe and water we drink]** of our health."

Brackets indicate words inserted by the writer, not the original author, Gallagher.

🛈 **Alert:** Use the bracketed term [*sic*] when you've found an error in something you're quoting—perhaps a wrong date or an error of fact. Adding [*sic*] tells the reader, "It is this way in the original." In MLA STYLE, use regular (roman) type, not italics or underlining, for sic. When this term falls within a sentence, use brackets around it, but use parentheses when the term falls at the end of a sentence, and place punctuation after them. In APA STYLE, italicize the term *sic* between roman brackets. ●

36D   When should I use ellipsis points?

Use **ellipsis points** (or ellipses) to indicate you've intentionally omitted words—even a sentence or more—from the source you're quoting.

■ Using ellipses in prose quotations

Use three spaced periods (. . .) to show where you have omitted a portion of the quoted material. If ellipsis points appear in the original source, include them. Never split ellipsis points between the end of a line and the beginning of the next.

ORIGINAL SOURCE

For over a century, twins have been used to study how genes make people what they are. Because they share precisely the same genes but live in different surroundings under different influences, identical twins reared apart are helping science sort out which qualities of body and mind are shaped by our genes and which by upbringing. Researchers needn't worry about running out of subjects: according to the Twins Foundation, there are approximately 4.5 million twin individuals in the United States alone, and about 70,000 more are born each year.

—Sharon Begley, "Twins," p. 84

MLA STYLE

According to Begley, "identical twins reared apart are helping science sort out which qualities of body and mind are shaped by our genes and which by upbringing" (84).

Ellipses are unnecessary; quotation has been worked into a sentence.

Begley says, "Because they share precisely the same genes . . . identical twins reared apart are helping science sort out which qualities of body and mind are shaped by our genes and which by upbringing" (84).

Ellipses show that the writer has omitted words from the middle of the quoted sentence or a longer passage.

Begley says, "Because they share precisely the same genes but live in different surroundings under different influences, identical twins reared apart are helping science . . . " (84).

Ellipses show that the writer has omitted words from the end of the quoted sentence or a longer passage.

36D

Begley says, "For over a century, twins have been used to study how genes make people what they are.... Researchers needn't worry about running out of subjects" (84).

Ellipses points between sentences show that one or more sentences have been omitted from the quoted material.

APA STYLE

Begley says, "Because they share precisely the same genes ..., identical twins reared apart are helping science sort out which qualities of body and mind are shaped by our genes and which by upbringing" (p. 84).

Ellipses show that the writer has omitted words from the middle of the quoted sentence.

Begley says, "Identical twins reared apart are helping science sort out which qualities of body and mind are shaped by our genes and which by upbringing" (p. 84).

Omission of words from the beginning of the quoted sentence doesn't require use of ellipses. Also, APA style permits a writer to change a lowercase letter at the start of a quotation to a capital letter.

Begley says, "Because they share precisely the same genes but live in different surroundings under different influences, identical twins reared apart are helping science" (p. 84).

APA style does not require ellipses to show that words have been omitted from the end of the quoted sentence.

Begley says, "For over a century, twins have been used to study how genes make people what they are. ... Researchers needn't worry about running out of subjects" (p. 84).

Ellipsis points between sentences show that one or more sentences have been omitted from the quoted material.

■ Using ellipses in quotations from poetry

Omission of words within a line of poetry is indicated with ellipsis points exactly as for prose. Omission of an entire line or more of poetry is indicated with a row of spaced periods in MLA style.

ORIGINAL SOURCE

Fear no more the heat o' the sun
Nor the furious winter's rages;

36D

Though thy worldly task has done,
Home art gone, and ta'en thy wages;
Golden lads and girls all must,
As chimney-sweepers, come to dust.

—William Shakespeare, *Cymbeline*

MLA STYLE

Ultimately, however, as Shakespeare reminds us, "Golden lads and girls all must / . . . come to dust."

Short poetry quotation with a few words omitted

Fear no more the heat o' the sun
Nor the furious winter's rages;

. . . .

Golden lads and girls all must

. . . come to dust.

Long poetry quotation with lines and words omitted

APA STYLE

Ultimately, however, as Shakespeare reminds us, "Golden lads and girls all must . . . come to dust."

Short poetry quotation with a few words omitted

Fear no more the heat o' the sun
Nor the furious winter's rages; . . .
Golden lads and girls all must
. . . come to dust.

Long poetry quotation with lines and words omitted

36E

36E When should I use a slash?

When quoting three or fewer lines of poetry, use a slash to divide one line from the next. Leave a space on each side of the slash.

> Consider the beginning of Anne Sexton's poem "Words": "Be careful of words, / even the miraculous ones."

To type numerical fractions (2/3, 1/16) or mixed numbers (12 1/2, 3 1/8), use a slash to separate the numerator from the denominator, leaving no space before or after the slash.

Revise a sentence to avoid word combinations like *and/or* when writing in the humanities. Where the use of word combinations is acceptable, separate the two words with a slash, leaving no space before or after it.

● **EXERCISE 36-1**   Supply needed dashes, parentheses, brackets, ellipsis points, and slashes. If a sentence is correct as written, circle its number. In some sentences, when you can use either dashes or parentheses, explain your choice.

EXAMPLE

There have been several famous entertainers Hedy Lamarr, Skunk Baxter, Brian May who are also accomplished scientists.

There have been several famous entertainers—Hedy Lamarr, Skunk Baxter, Brian May—who are also accomplished scientists.

1. Brian May is famous for being the guitar player for the rock band Queen one of my favorite bands of all time, but he also has a Ph.D. in astrophysics.
2. Besides being the guitarist, he also wrote one of Queen's biggest hits ("We Will Rock You" (1977)).
3. May wrote the lyrics for this famous rock anthem that includes the two lines, "Gonna take on the world some day, You got blood on your face."
4. After May earned his Ph.D. in astrophysics in 2008, another astronomer joked, "I don't know any scientists who look as much like Isaac Neuton (sic) as you do."
5. Of all the early Hollywood actresses, Lana Turner, Judy Garland, Ava Gardner, Hedy Lamarr may have been one of the most famous.
6. But Lamarr also invented a frequency-hopping system that is still used in the following modern devices: 1 wireless telephones 2 Bluetooth technology and 3 Wi-Fi networks.
7. Skunk Baxter is a guitar player known for his work with Steely Dan, "Rikki Don't Lose That Number" and "Reeling in the Years," and The Doobie Brothers, "Takin' It to the Street" and "What a Fool Believes."
8. In describing his decision to make a career change, Baxter said, "After we the band The Doobie Brothers had been together for so many years, many of the members diverged to their own musical directions."
9. Having some connections in the military, his next-door neighbor was a missile designer, Baxter began experimenting with new designs for data-compression algorithms.
10. This long-haired rock star—can you imagine?—was even granted high-level government security clearance by the US Department of Defense. ●

● **EXERCISE 36-2**   Follow the directions for each item. For help, consult all sections of this chapter.

EXAMPLE

Write a sentence that uses dashes and includes a definition.

I like to study Romance languages—languages derived from Latin.

1. Write a sentence that contains a numbered list.
2. Write a sentence that uses parentheses to set off a definition.
3. Quote a passage from the poem below that omits an entire line.
4. Write a sentence that quotes two lines from the poem below, and use a slash to separate the two lines.
5. Quote any part of the poem below and uses ellipsis points to omit word(s) from the poem.

> Little Lamb, who made thee?
>   Dost thou know who made thee?
> Gave thee life, and bid thee feed
> By the stream and o'er the mead;
> Gave thee clothing of delight,
> Softest clothing, woolly, bright;
> Gave thee such a tender voice,
> Making all the vales rejoice?
>   Little Lamb, who made thee?
>   Dost thou know who made thee?
>   —William Blake ●

37

37 Hyphens
■ ■ ■ ■ ■ ■

Quick Points   You will learn to

➤ Use hyphens correctly.

MyWritingLab™   Visit mywritinglab.com for more resources on hyphens.

37A When should I hyphenate at the end of a line?

Always set the default on your word processing program to avoid hyphenation. In handwritten reports, keep in mind the following procedures: (1) Wherever possible, avoid dividing words with hyphens at the end of a line; (2) If a division is necessary, divide longer words by syllable and between consonants if possible (*omit-ting, ful-ness, sep-arate*); (3) Never divide for one or two letters or for any one-syllable words (like *wealth* or *screamed*).

37B When should I hyphenate prefixes and suffixes?

Prefixes and **suffixes** are syllables attached to words—prefixes at the beginning and suffixes at the end. A few prefixes and suffixes call for hyphens, but most don't (see Quick Box 37.1).

Quick Box 37.1 ■ ■ ■ ■ ■ ■

Hyphenating prefixes and suffixes

Use hyphens after the prefixes *all-, ex-,* and *self-*.

> all-inclusive, self-reliant

Never use a hyphen when *self* is a root word onto which a suffix is attached.

> selfishness, selfless, selfhood

Use a hyphen to avoid a distracting string of repeated letters.

> anti-intellectual, bell-like

Use a hyphen between a prefix and the first word of a compound word.

> anti-gun control

Use a hyphen to prevent confusion in meaning or pronunciation.

> re-dress ("dress again"), un-ionize ("remove the ions")
>
> redress ("set right"), unionize ("form a union")

Use a hyphen when two or more prefixes apply to one root word.

> pre- and postwar eras

Use a hyphen before the suffix *-elect*.

> president-elect

Use a hyphen when a prefix comes before a number or before a word that starts with a capital letter.

> post-1950, pro-American

37A

37C   When should I hyphenate compound words?

You can write a **compound word**—two or more words combined to express one concept—in one of three ways: as separate words (*night shift*), as hyphenated words (*tractor-trailer*), or as one word (*handbook*). Follow the rules in Quick Box 37.2.

Quick Box 37.2   ▪ ▪ ▪ ▪ ▪ ▪

Hyphenating compound words

Use a hyphen for most compound modifiers that precede the noun. Never use a hyphen for compound modifiers *after* the noun.

> well-researched report; two-inch clearance [before the noun]

> report is well researched; clearance of two inches [after the noun]

Use a hyphen between compound nouns joining two units within a measure.

> light-year, kilowatt-hour, foot-pound

Never use a hyphen when a compound modifier starts with an adverb ending in *ly*.

> happily married couple

Use a hyphen for most compound modifiers in the comparative (*-er*) or superlative (*-est*) form. Never use a hyphen when the compound modifier includes *more/most* or *less/least*.

> better-fitting shoe, best-known work

> more significant factor, least welcome guest

Never use a hyphen when a compound modifier is a foreign phrase.

> post hoc fallacies

Never use a hyphen with a possessive compound modifier.

> a full week's work, eight hours' pay

37D

37D   When should I hyphenate spelled-out numbers?

For help in deciding when to use numerals and when to spell out numbers, see Chapter 41. Quick Box 37.3, p. 414, shows how to hyphenate spelled-out numbers.

Quick Box 37.3

Hyphenating spelled-out numbers

- Use a hyphen between two-word numbers from twenty-one through ninety-nine.

  thirty-five, two hundred thirty-five

- Use a hyphen in a compound modifier formed from a number and a word.

  fifty-minute class [also 50-minute class]

  three-to-one odds [also 3-to-1 odds]

- Use a hyphen between the numerator and the denominator of a two-word fraction.

  one-half, two-fifths, seven-tenths

Alert: Use figures for fractions that require more than two words in their spelled-out form. If you do spell out a fraction in three or more words, use a hyphen between words in the numerator or the denominator; use a space (but no hyphen) to separate the numerator from the denominator.

- 2/100 *or* two one-hundredths

- 33/10,000 *or* thirty-three ten-thousandths

37D

● **EXERCISE 37-1** Provide the correct form of the words in parentheses, according to the hyphenation rules in this chapter. Explain your reasoning for each.

1. The tiger is (all powerful) _____ in the cat family.
2. (Comparison and contrast) _____ studies of tigers and lions show that the tiger is the (more agile) _____ and powerful.
3. Male tigers and lions look similar except for their hair length: Tigers have (ultra short) _____ hair and male lions have (extra long) _____ hair in their manes.
4. The tiger's body is a (boldly striped) _____ orange, with a white (under body) _____.
5. The Bengal tiger, the largest of the family, is aggressive and (self confident) _____.

6. In India, where the Bengal tiger is called a (village destroyer) _____, it goes (in to) _____ villages to hunt for food.

7. Entire villages have been temporarily abandoned by (terror stricken) _____ people who have seen a Bengal tiger nearby.

8. Villagers seek to protect their homes by destroying tigers with traps, (spring loaded) _____ guns, and (poisoned arrows) _____.

9. Bengal tigers are also called (cattle killers) _____, although they attack domestic animals only when they cannot find wild ones.

10. Many people who do not live near a zoo get to see tigers only in (animal shows) _____, although (pro animal) _____ activists try to prevent tigers from being used this way. ●

38 Capitals

■ ■ ■ ■ ■ ■

Quick Points   You will learn to

➤ Use capitals correctly.

38A

MyWritingLab™ Visit mywritinglab.com for more resources on capitals.

38A When should I capitalize a "first" word?

Capitalize the first word in a sentence.

● Four inches of snow fell last night.

When a complete sentence follows a colon, choose consistently either a capital or lowercase letter in each piece of writing. If what follows your colon is not a complete sentence, don't capitalize the first word.

YES   The question remains: What will the jury decide?

YES   The question remains: what will the jury decide?

NO   The jury is considering all the evidence: Motive, means, opportunity.

YES   The jury is considering all the evidence: motive, means, opportunity.

If a series of questions imply, but are not themselves, complete sentences, you can choose capitals or not. Simply be consistent in each piece of writing.

● Whose rights does voter fraud deny? Mine? Yours? Or everyone's?

● Whose rights does voter fraud deny? mine? yours? or everyone's?

When a sentence itemizes other sentences, capitalize and punctuate the items as complete sentences.

● The bank robbers made demands: (1) They wanted money. (2) They wanted hostages. (3) They wanted transportation.

When the items are not complete sentences, use commas between them unless the items contain commas. When they do, use semicolons between items. Use the word *and* before the last item if there are three or more nonsentence items.

● The bank robbers made demands: (1) money, (2) hostages, and (3) transportation.

A complete sentence enclosed in parentheses may stand alone or fall within another sentence. If it stands alone, capitalize the first word and use an appropriate ending punctuation (a period, a question mark, or an exclamation point). If it falls within a sentence, don't capitalize the first word. Use ending punctuation *only* if your sentence in parentheses ends with a question mark or an exclamation point, not with a period.

I didn't know till years later that they called it the Cuban Missile Crisis. But I remember Castro. (We called him Castor Oil and were awed by his beard—beards were rare in those days.) We might not have worried so much (what would the Communists want with our small New Hampshire town?) except that we lived 10 miles from an air base.

—Joyce Maynard, *An 18-Year-Old Looks Back on Life*

38B   How should I capitalize quotations?

Capitalize the first word in a prose QUOTATION.

● Encouraging students to study in other countries, Mrs. Velez says, "You will absorb a good accent with the food."

When you interrupt quoted words, never capitalize the continued part of the quoted words.

- "You will absorb a good accent," says Mrs. Velez, "with the food."

If the quoted words form part of your own sentence, never capitalize the first quoted word unless it is a PROPER NOUN. Phrases such as *writes **that***, *thinks **that***, and *says **that*** usually signal this kind of quotation.

- Mrs. Velez believes that "you will absorb a good accent with the food" if you study in another country.

When you quote poetry in your writing, use capital and lowercase letters exactly as they appear in the original SOURCE. (If you need help using quotation marks, see Chapter 34.)

38C   When should I capitalize nouns and adjectives?

Capitalize **proper nouns** (*Mexico, Arthur*) and **proper adjectives** (*a Mexican diplomat, the Arthurian legend*). Capitalize certain **common nouns** when you add specific names or titles to them: For example, *We visit a **lake** every summer. This summer we went to **Lake Seminole***. See Quick Box 38.1.

❗ **Alerts:** (1) Never capitalize DETERMINERS and other words just because they accompany proper nouns or proper adjectives: *Here is a Canadian penny* [not *A Canadian penny* or *a Canadian Penny*].

(2) Be aware that some proper nouns and proper adjectives become so common that they lose their capital letters: *french fries, italics, pasteurized.* ●

Quick Box 38.1   ■ ■ ■ ■ ■ ■   38C

Capitalization guide

	Capitals	**Lowercase Letters**
NAMES	Mother Teresa [also when used as names: Mother, Dad, Mom, Pa]	my mother [relationship]
	Doc Holliday	the doctor [role]
TITLES	President Truman	the president
	Democrat [party member]	democrat [believer in democracy]
	Representative Harold Ford	the congressional representative
	Senator Edward M. Kennedy	the senator
	Queen Elizabeth II	the queen

continued >>

Quick Box 38.1 Capitalization guide (continued) ■ ■ ■ ■ ■ ■

	Capitals	Lowercase Letters
GROUPS OF PEOPLE	Caucasian [race]	white, black [*also* White, Black]
	Korean [nationality]	
	Jew, Buddhist [religious affiliation]	
	Hispanic [ethnic group]	
ORGANIZATIONS	Congress	legislative branch of the US government
	Ohio State Supreme Court	state supreme court
	the Republican Party	the party
	National Gypsum Company	the company
	American Medical Association	professional group
	Sigma Chi	fraternity
	Alcoholics Anonymous	self-help group
PLACES	Los Angeles	the city
	the South [region]	turn south [direction]
	the West Coast	the states along the western seaboard
	Main Street	the street
	Atlantic Ocean	the ocean
	the Black Hills	the hills
BUILDINGS	the Capitol [in Washington, DC]	the state capitol
	Central High School	a high school
	Highland Hospital	a hospital
SCIENTIFIC	Earth [as a planet]	the earth in the garden
	the Milky Way	the galaxy, the moon, the sun
	Streptococcus aureus	a streptococcal infection
	Gresham's law	the theory of relativity
LANGUAGES	Spanish, French, Chinese	foreign languages
SCHOOL COURSES	Chemistry 342	a chemistry course
	English 111	my English class
	Introduction to Photography	a photography class
NAMES OF SPECIFIC THINGS	the *Boston Globe*	the newspaper
	Time	the magazine
	Purdue University	the university
	Heinz ketchup	ketchup
SEASONS		spring, winter, autumn

continued >>

38C

Quick Box 38.1   Capitalization guide (continued) ■ ■ ■ ■ ■

	Capitals	**Lowercase Letters**
HOLIDAYS	Halloween, New Year's Day	
HISTORICAL EVENTS AND DOCUMENTS	World War II the Roaring Twenties the Great Depression the Paleozoic the Reformation the Bill of Rights	the war a decade a depression an era, an age the eighteenth century fifth-century manuscripts
RELIGIOUS TERMS	God Buddhism the Torah, the Koran, the Bible	a god, a goddess a religion
LETTER PARTS	Dear Ms. Kupperman: Sincerely, Yours truly,	
TITLES OF PUBLISHED AND RELEASED WORKS	"The Lottery" *A History of the United States to 1877* *Jazz on Ice*	[Capitalize the first letter of the first and last words and all other words except ARTICLES, short PREPOSITIONS, and COORDINATING CONJUNCTIONS.]
ACRONYMS AND INITIALISMS	NATO, FBI, AFL-CIO, UCLA, DNA, CD	
COMPUTER TERMS	Microsoft Word, WordPerfect Netscape Navigator World Wide Web, the Web Web site, Web page the Internet	computer software a browser a home page, a link a computer network
PROPER ADJECTIVES	Victorian Midwestern Indo-European	biblical transatlantic alpine

38C

● **EXERCISE 38-1**   Add capital letters as needed. See 38A through 38C for help.

1. The state of california is best known as the golden state, but other nicknames include the land of milk and honey, the el dorado state, and the grape state.

2. Most people think of san Francisco as northern california, but the city of Eureka, from the greek word meaning "I have found it," is 280 miles north of san Francisco, and the state line is another 90 miles north of eureka.

3. South of san Francisco on the california coast is santa Barbara, which hosts the annual Dickens Universe, a weeklong series of studies and celebrations of the famous writer charles dickens.

4. The highest point in the contiguous United States is mt. Whitney at 14,495 feet high, and the lowest place in the contiguous United States is bad Water in death valley at 282 feet below sea level, both located in california.

5. Having approximately 500,000 detectable seismic tremors per year, california rocks, literally.

6. Because the tehema county fairgrounds are located in red bluff, california hosts the largest three-day rodeo in the united States.

7. Numerous songs have been written about california, including "california girls" by the beach boys and the theme of the tv show *the beverly hillbillies*.

8. san Bernardino county with almost three million acres is the largest county in the united states.

9. Hollywood and movie stars are what many people associate california with, and well they might because two of California's governors, ronald reagan and arnold schwarzenegger, were actors before they became governors.

10. When told all these fantastic facts about california, a stereotypical valley girl would respond, "whatever." ●

39

39 Italics (Underlining)

■ ■ ■ ■ ■ ■

Quick Points   You will learn to

➤ Use italics (underlining) correctly.

MyWritingLab™   Visit mywritinglab.com for more resources on italics (underlining).

Most printed material is set in roman type. Type that slants to the right is called *italic type*. Italics and underlining mean the same thing. MLA style requires italics, not underlining, in all documents (see Chapter 14).

ITALIC TYPE	*Great Expectations*
HANDWRITTEN AND UNDERLINED	Great Expectations

39A   How do I choose between italics and quotation marks?

Generally, use italics for titles of long works or works that contain subsections. Use quotation marks for titles of shorter works or titles of subsections within a larger work. Consult Quick Box 39.1 for specifics.

Quick Box 39.1

■ ■ ■ ■ ■

Italics, quotation marks, or nothing

	Italicize	Quotations Marks or Nothing
TITLES	*The Bell Jar* [a novel]	title of student essay
	Death of a Salesman [a play]	act 3
	Collected Works of O. Henry [a book]	"The Last Leaf" [a story in the book]
	Simon & Schuster Handbook for Writers [a book]	"Verbs" [a chapter in the book]
	The Prose Reader [a collection of essays]	"Putting in a Good Word for Guilt" [title of an essay]
	The Iliad [a book-length poem]	"Nothing Gold Can Stay" [a short poem]
	Almost Famous [a film]	
	the *Los Angeles Times** [a newspaper]	"Supreme Court Judge Steps Down" [a headline]
	Scientific American [a magazine]	"The Molecules of Life" [an article in a magazine]
	Aida [an opera]	
	Symphonie Fantastique [a long musical work]	Concerto in B-flat Minor [a musical work identified by form, number, and key]
	The Twilight Zone [a television series]	"Terror at 30,000 Feet" [an episode of the television series]
	The Best of Bob Dylan [an album or CD]	"Mr. Tambourine Man" [one cut on an album or CD]

*Even if *The* is part of the title printed on a newspaper, don't capitalize it and don't italicize it in the body of your paper. In MLA-style documentation, omit the word *The* entirely. In APA-style documentation, retain *The* as part of the title.

continued >>

39A

Quick Box 39.1

Italics guide (continued) ■ ■ ■ ■ ■

	Italicize	Quotations Marks or Nothing
	the USS *Intrepid* [a ship] *Voyager 2* [specific aircraft, spacecraft, satellites]	aircraft carrier [a class of ship] Boeing 787 [names shared by classes of aircraft, spacecraft, or satellites]
OTHER WORDS	*semper fidelis* [words in a language other than English] What does *our* imply? [a word referred to as such] the *ABC*s; confusing *3*'s and *8*'s [letters and numerals referred to as such]	burrito, chutzpah [widely understood non-English words]

39B When should I use italics for emphasis?

Use italics sparingly for emphasis. Instead, use language for emphasis.

- The pain from my injury was *totally severe*.

- The pain from my injury was so severe that I could not breathe.

   That I could not breathe emphasizes with words, not with italics.

● **EXERCISE 39-1**   Edit these sentences for correct use of italics (or underlining), quotation marks, and capitals.

1. While waiting for my Dentist to call my name, I flipped through a copy of a magazine called "Entertainment Digest."

2. I enjoyed reading the Magazine because it included several interesting articles: Movie reviews, recipes, and tips for Spring cleaning.

3. I read a review of the movie "Night comes calling," which I learned is an adaptation of english writer Hugo Barrington's short story *Adventures in the Fog*.

4. I asked the Receptionist if I could keep the magazine because a few of the articles might help me in my Spanish and Economics classes.

5. For example, there was an article on a composer who wrote an Opera about *The Spanish Civil War*. ●

40

Abbreviations

■ ■ ■ ■ ■ ■

Quick Points   You will learn to

➤ Use abbreviations correctly.

MyWritingLab™ Visit mywritinglab.com for more resources on abbreviations.

The guidelines in this chapter apply to writing in the humanities. Guidelines in other disciplines vary. For disciplines outside the humanities, check your college dictionary for capitalization, spacing, and use of periods.

🔔 **Alerts:** (1) Place only one period after a sentence that ends with an abbreviated word: *At the picnic, we hosted Mr. John Janes Jr.*

(2) Place a question mark or an exclamation point after the abbreviation's period at the end: *Do we have paper plates, plastic forks, etc.?*●

40A   What abbreviations can I use with times and amounts?

With exact times, use abbreviations (*a.m.* or *A.M.* and *p.m.* or *P.M.*), including the periods. Consistently choose capital or lowercase letters for these.

- 7:15 a.m.
- 7:15 A.M.
- 3:47 p.m.
- 3:47 P.M.

Use capital letters without periods for abbreviations for eras.

BC (meaning *before Christ*)—place after the year number: *1200 BC.*

BCE (meaning *before the Common Era*), which is a more inclusionary, contemporary form—place after the year: *1200 BCE.*

AD (Latin for *anno Domini*, which means *in the year of the Lord*)—place before the year: *AD 977.*

CE (meaning *Common Era*), a more contemporary form—place after the year: *1507 CE.*

In tables, you can abbreviate amounts and measurements (such as *in., mi., cm, km, gal., ml, lb., kg*) when you use them with exact numbers. You can also abbreviate days and months (*Mon., Jan., Aug.*).

Use the symbol *$* with exact amounts of money expressed in numerals or numerals and words.

- $4.95
- $34 million

As a rule, let common sense and clarity guide your use of symbols. If measurements like temperatures appear only once or twice in your paper, spell them out: *sixty degrees Fahrenheit, minus seven degrees Celsius.* If your work uses temperatures throughout, use numbers and symbols: 60°F, –7°C.

40B   How should I use abbreviations with people's names?

Use *Mr., Mrs., Ms.,* and *Dr.* with either full names or last names only.

- Dr. Anna Freud
- Dr. Freud
- Mr. Daljit Singh
- Mr. Singh

When you follow a person's name with the abbreviation of a professional or academic degree, use no periods. Also, never use in the same context both a title of address before a name and an abbreviated degree after a name.

NO   Dr. Jill Sih, **MD**

YES   Jill Sih, **MD**

YES   **Dr.** Jill Sih

Follow the official military title abbreviations for each branch of the US armed forces (you can find the most up-to-date ones on the Internet). Today these abbreviations are almost always in all capital letters, and they use no periods.

- **ADM**   admiral
- **CPO**   chief petty officer
- **CO**   Commanding officer
- **COL**   colonel
- **ENS**   ensign
- **GEN**   general

40C   How do I use *Jr., Sr., II, III, 2nd,* and *3rd*?

Indications of birth order apply only to males, not to females, as below:

1. End only the birth order indicators *Jr.* and *Sr.* with a period.

2. Never use a comma before or after *Jr.* or *Sr.* unless another rule calls for one.

- Under the pseudonym James Tiptree **Jr.**, Alice B. Sheldon wrote outstanding science fiction.

   A comma is correct here because *Jr.* ends an introductory phrase.

- The James Tiptree **Jr**. Memorial Award honors Alice B. Sheldon.

  No comma appears after *Jr.* because no other rule calls for one.

- Douglas Young **III** is a physical therapist.

  Neither a period nor a comma is required.

- Douglas Young **III**, a physical therapist, specializes in geriatrics.

  Commas are necessary to set off the appositive, *a physical therapist*.

- Douglas Young **III, PT, MA**

  Use commas between multiple titles.

3. Never use a birth-order abbreviation with a last name only: not *Syms Jr.* If you add initials to the last name, however, you can use it: *I. J. Syms Jr.*

40D   When can I abbreviate names of countries, organizations, and government agencies?

Spell out the names of countries as a sign of respect. You can abbreviate *United States* without a period only as an adjective (*the **US** Constitution*). Never abbreviate *United States* as a noun (*Constitution of the **United States***).

When you refer to an organization, spell the full name the first time you use it and then, immediately afterward, put the abbreviation in parentheses. Thereafter, you can use the abbreviation alone.

- Spain voted to continue as a member of the **North Atlantic Treaty Organization (NATO)**, to the surprise of other **NATO** members.

40E   What abbreviations can I use in addresses?

40F

You can use abbreviations for addresses such as *St.* for *Street* and *Blvd.* for *Boulevard*. You can also use abbreviations for *North* (*N.*), *South* (*S.*), *East* (*E.*), and *West* (*W.*). In the United States, use the two-letter postal abbreviations for state names in addresses: CA for California, IL for Illinois, and so on.

If you include a full address in a sentence, spell out all words except the two-letter postal abbreviation. Otherwise, spell out the name of the state.

I wrote to Mr. Hugh Lern, 7 Rule Road, Summit, **NJ** 07901, for the handbook. Unfortunately, he had already moved to Flagstaff, **Arizona**.

40F   When can I use *etc.* and other Latin abbreviations?

Avoid *etc.*, Latin for "and the rest," in ACADEMIC WRITING. Instead, use substitutes *and the like, and so on*—or use a more concrete description.

● **EXERCISE 40-1**   Revise these sentences for correct use of abbreviations. For help, consult this chapter.

1. Originally named the Geo. S. Parker Company, located in Salem, Mass., the toy co. changed its name to Parker Bros. when Chas. joined the business in 1888.
2. Sev. of their games have become quite famous, esp. Monopoly and Clue, both of which were released in the 20th cent.
3. The obj. of the game Monopoly (meaning "dominating the mkt.") is to get the most $ by purchasing, renting, & selling real est.
4. Clue, another pop. brd. game, is a murder mys. in which players move from 1 rm. to another, making accusations to reveal the i.d. of the murderer, the weapon used, and the room where the crime took place.
5. On a cold day in Jan., when the snow is 3 ft. deep and it's dark by early eve., passing the hrs. with your fam. and friends playing a board game is great fun. ●

41 Numbers

■ ■ ■ ■ ■ ■

41A

Quick Points   You will learn to

➤ Use spelled out numbers and numerals correctly.

MyWritingLab™ Visit mywritinglab.com for more resources on numbers.

41A   When should I spell out numbers in words?

If numbers occur often in your humanities paper, spell out *one* through *nine*; use numerals (*1, 9*) for all others. If numbers occur rarely in your paper, use words.

❶ **Alert:** Use a hyphen in the two-word numbers *twenty-one* through *ninety-nine.* ●

Spell out a number at the beginning of a sentence, or revise the sentence.

ACCEPTABLE   Six hundred forty-six dollars buys a Gucci tote.
BETTER   A Gucci tote costs $646.

Never mix spelled-out numbers and figures when they refer to the same thing. In the following example, all numbers referring to bids are in figures, but *four* is spelled out because it refers to days, not bids.

- In the past four days, $5 bids increased from 5 to 8 to 17 to 233.
- On Saturday morning, 59 bids arrived from 22 districts.

41B How should I write dates, addresses, times, and other numbers?

After plural numbers, use the singular form of *hundred, thousand,* and *million.* Add *-s* only when no number comes before those words.

- **Five hundred** books were damaged in the flood.
- **Hundreds** of books were damaged in the flood.

Quick Box 41.1 models numbers in some common forms.

Quick Box 41.1   ■ ■ ■ ■ ■ ■

Using numbers

DATES	August 6, 1941 1732–1845 34 BCE to 230 CE
ADDRESSES	237 North Eighth Street [*or* N. 8th St.] Export Falls, MN 92025
TIMES	8:09 a.m., 4:00 p.m. [*but* four o'clock, *not* 4 o'clock; 4 p.m. *or* four in the afternoon, *not* four p.m. *or* 4 in the afternoon]
CHAPTERS AND PAGES	Chapter 27, page 245
ACT, SCENE, AND LINE	act 2, scene 2 (or act II, scene ii) lines 75–79
SCORES AND STATISTICS	a 6–0 score a 5-to-3 ratio [*or* a 5:3 ratio] 29 percent
IDENTIFICATION NUMBERS	93.9 on the FM dial call (212) 555-3930

continued >>

41B

Quick Box 41.1   Using numbers (continued) ▪ ■ ▪ ▪ ▫ ▫

MEASUREMENTS	2 feet 67.8 miles per hour 1.5 gallons, 3 liters 8-by-10-inch photograph
TEMPERATURES	–5°F, 3°C, 43° Celsius
MONEY	$1.2 billion $3.41 25 cents
DECIMALS AND FRACTIONS	5.55 98.6 3.1416 7/8 12 1/4 3/4 (three-quarters *but not* 3-quarters)

● **EXERCISE 41-1**   Revise these sentences so that the numbers are in correct form, either spelled out or as figures.

1. The 102-story Empire State building, which is one thousand two hundred and fifty feet tall, is struck by lightning on an average of five hundred times a year.
2. If you have three quarters, four dimes, and 4 pennies, you have $1 and nineteen cents, but you still can't make even change for a dollar.
3. Lake Tahoe is the second deepest lake in the United States with a maximum depth of five hundred and one meters (1,645 ft).
4. 37 percent of Americans have passports, which means that nearly 2 out of 3 US citizens cannot fly to Canada.
5. On March 2nd, nineteen sixty two, Wilt Chamberlain, playing basketball for the Philadelphia Warriors, scored 100 points.
6. Some people trace the origin of the knock-knock joke back to act two, scene three of Shakespeare's sixteen-eleven play *Macbeth*.
7. If you place a vertical stick in the ground on the Equator, it will cast no shadow at 12 o'clock p.m. on March twenty first.
8. Bamboo plants can grow up to one hundred centimeters every 24 hours, and they grow best in warm climates, but some species can survive in temperatures as low as twenty degrees below zero Fahrenheit.
9. The Boston Marathon, which began in 1897, is the world's oldest annual marathon and is held the 3rd Monday of every April.
10. 500,000 spectators watch the Boston Marathon every year as an average of twenty thousand runners each try to complete the twenty six point two mile run. ●

41B

Part 6
Tips for Multilingual Writers

CHAPTERS
42–47

A Message to Multilingual Writers

Learning a new language is like learning to play a musical instrument. Few of us play fluently without first making many errors. This experience applies when you're learning a new language—as you speak, listen, read, and especially as you develop skill with writing. We know that absorbing the rules of American English grammar takes time. Be patient with yourself and never get discouraged.

Most college essays and research papers in the United States use a straightforward structure and a direct tone. Typically, a THESIS STATEMENT (the central message of the paper) comes at the end of the introductory paragraph. Each paragraph that follows, which is called a BODY PARAGRAPH, relates in content directly to the essay's thesis statement. TOPIC SENTENCES usually begin most body paragraphs and state the main point of that particular paragraph. Then the sentences in each body paragraph support the point made in the topic sentence. The concluding paragraph of an essay arrives at a reasonable ending for the content because it grows out of what has been written in the entire essay.

As you get used to this structure for essays, we recommend that you recall how you learned to present ideas in your written native language. If you consider the differences, you can better clarify how American English works. In this book, we offer special features designed specifically for you as a multilingual learner. (For help with idiomatic usage, you may also wish to consult *The American Heritage English as a Second Language Dictionary* or *Merriam Webster's Learner's Dictionary* online.) This section of the book, Chapters 42–47, explains challenging issues in grammar that may trouble you as a multilingual writer. In other chapters, we offer you ESOL Tips, which are helpful hints about non-US cultural references and grammar issues.

As teachers and authors, we wish you success as you become a writer in the United States. As this happens, we hope that you will always treasure that as a multilingual writer, you bring a wealth of experience and knowledge to your written ideas. You're fortunate to know a culture and language that's different from ours. You possess a richness that most US students can't draw on. We extend our warmest wishes to you as you learn American English.

Lynn Quitman Troyka
Doug Hesse

42

42 Singulars and Plurals

■ ■ ■ ■ ■ ■

Quick Points   You will learn to

➤ Distinguish between count and noncount nouns (pp. 431–432 and 433).
➤ Use the proper determiners with singular and plural nouns (pp. 432–434).

MyWritingLab™   Visit mywritinglab.com for more resources on singulars and plurals.

42A   What are count and noncount nouns?

Count nouns name items that are counted: *phone, fingernail, idea*. **Noncount nouns** name things that aren't counted: *sand, rain, traffic*.

Count nouns can be SINGULAR (*phone*) or PLURAL (*phones*), so they may use singular or plural VERBS. Noncount nouns (see Quick Box 42.1) are used in singular form only, so they use only singular verbs.

Quick Box 42.1

■ ■ ■ ■ ■ ■

Uncountable items represented by noncount nouns

- Groups of similar items making up "wholes": *clothing, equipment, furniture, luggage, mail, money*
- Abstractions: *guilt, fun, health, justice, peace, respect*
- Liquids: *blood, coffee, gasoline, water*
- Gases: *air, helium, oxygen, smog, smoke, steam*
- Materials: *aluminum, cloth, cotton, ice, wood*
- Food: *beef, bread, butter, macaroni, meat, cheese*
- Collections of particles or grains: *dirt, dust, hair, rice, salt, wheat*
- Languages: *Arabic, Chinese, Japanese, Spanish*
- Fields of study: *biology, computer science, history, literature, math*
- Natural phenomena: *electricity, heat, moonlight, sunshine, thunder*

---

❶ **Alert:** If you're unsure whether a noun is count or noncount, check a dictionary such as the *American Heritage English as a Second Language Dictionary.* ●

Some nouns can be count or noncount, depending on their meaning in a sentence. Most of these nouns represent things that can be meant either individually or as "wholes" made up of individual parts (see Quick Box 42.1).

COUNT	**Two hairs** lay on his collar.
NONCOUNT	**His hair** was cut very short.

When EDITING your writing, make sure you haven't added the plural *-s* ending to any noncount nouns, which are always singular in form.

! **Alert:** Use a singular verb with any noncount noun that functions as a SUBJECT in a CLAUSE. ●

42B   Which determiners should I use with singular and plural nouns?

DETERMINERS tell *which, how much*, or *how many* about NOUNS. You choose the correct determiner to use with a noun, depending on whether the noun is noncount or count. For count nouns, you also need to decide whether the noun is singular or plural (see Quick Box 42.2).

! **Alerts:** (1) *Many, most*, and *some* require *of the* before a noun that is specific but not before a noun that is a generalization.

- **Most** supervisors are well qualified.   [general]
- **Most of the** supervisors **here** are well qualified.   [specific]

(2) The phrases *a few* and *a little* convey the meaning "some": *I have **a few** rare books* means "I have *some* rare books." *They are worth **a little** money* means "They are worth *some* money." Without the word *a, few* and *little* mean "almost none": *I have **few** books* means "I have *almost no* books." *They are worth **little** money* means "They are worth *almost no* money."

(3) The phrase *one of the* is always followed by a plural noun or pronoun. *One of the conference rooms is* [not *are*] *empty.* (See 18G.) *She is one of the people I still trust.* ●

42C   What forms are correct for nouns used as adjectives?

Some words can function as nouns and as ADJECTIVES. In English, adjectives don't have plural forms. If you use a noun as an adjective, don't add *-s* or *-es* to the adjective, even when the noun or PRONOUN it modifies is plural.

- Many American students are basketball fans.
- My nephew likes to look at picture books.

Quick Box 42.2

Using determiners with count and noncount nouns

GROUP 1: DETERMINERS FOR SINGULAR COUNT NOUNS
With singular count nouns, use any of the determiners on the left.

a, an, the	**a** house, **an** egg; **the** house, **the** egg
one, any, some, every, each, either, *neither, another, the other*	**any** book; **each** person; **another** year
my, our, your, his, her, its, their, nouns with *'s or s'*	**your** father; **its** cover; **Connie's** car
this, that	**this** week; **that** desk
one, no, the first, the second, and so on	**one** example; **no** reason; **the fifth** chair

GROUP 2: DETERMINERS FOR PLURAL COUNT NOUNS
All of the following determiners can be used with plural count nouns. Plural count nouns can also be used without determiners (see 43B).

the	**the** bicycles; **the** rooms; **the** ideas
some, any, both, many, most, few, *fewer, the fewest, a number of,* *other, several, all, all the, a lot of*	**some** people; **many** jobs; **all** managers
my, our, your, his, her, its, their, nouns with *'s or s'*	**our** coats; **her** books; **students'** grades
these, those	**these** days; **those** computers
no; two, three, four, and so on; *the first, the second, the third,* and so on	**no** exceptions; **four** students; **the first** months

GROUP 3: DETERMINERS FOR NONCOUNT NOUNS
All of the following determiners can be used with noncount nouns (always singular). Noncount nouns can also be used without determiners (see 43B).

the	**the** rice; **the** electricity
some, any, much, more, most, other, *the other, little, less, the least,* *enough, all, all the, a lot of*	**enough** snow; **a lot of** equipment; **more** food
my, our, your, his, her, its, their, nouns with *'s or s'*	**their** fame; **India's** heat; **your** leader's smile
this, that	**this** sugar; **that** fog
no, the first, the second, the best, and so on	**no smoking; the first** rainfall; **the best** vocabulary

42C

● **EXERCISE 42-1**   Consulting all sections of this chapter, select the correct choice from the words in parentheses and write it in the blank.

EXAMPLE

It can be tricky to bake (bread, breads) <u>bread</u> in Denver, Colorado, because of that city's high (elevation, elevations) <u>elevation</u>.

1. Denver has an elevation of 5,280 (foot, feet) _____, and changes must therefore be made to baking (recipe, recipes) _____.
2. The 5,280-(foot, feet) _____ elevation lowers the boiling point of (water, waters) _____.
3. The leading (American, Americans) _____ expert in high-altitude baking recommends adding more (flour, flours) _____ to bread recipes.
4. If your recipe includes different kinds of (liquid, liquids) _____, the expert recommends adding additional (liquid, liquid) _____ to combat dryness.
5. One of the (effect, effects) _____ of the high altitude is that the crust of a loaf of (bread, breads) _____ will cook faster. ●

43 Articles

■ ■ ■ ■ ■ ■

Quick Points   You will learn to

➤ Use articles correctly.

43   MyWritingLab™   Visit mywritinglab.com for more resources on articles.

Articles (*a, an, the*) are one type of DETERMINER. They signal that a NOUN will follow and that any MODIFIERS between the article and the noun refer to that noun (see Quick Box 43.1).

● **a** chair, **the** computer, **an** easy test

Quick Box 43.1

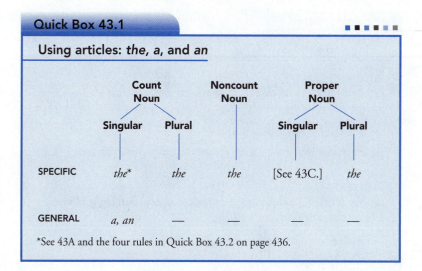

Using articles: *the*, *a*, and *an*

	Count Noun		Noncount Noun	Proper Noun	
	Singular	Plural		Singular	Plural
SPECIFIC	*the**	*the*	*the*	[See 43C.]	*the*
GENERAL	*a, an*	—	—	—	—

*See 43A and the four rules in Quick Box 43.2 on page 436.

43A How should I use articles with singular count nouns?

When you use a singular COUNT NOUN (see Quick Box 43.2 on p. 436), you need to use a determiner, as shown for Group 1 in Quick Box 42.2 on page 433. If you have to choose between *a, an*, and *the*, decide whether the noun is specific or nonspecific. A noun is specific when a reader can understand from the context exactly what the noun is referring to. Quick Box 43.2 can help you decide when a singular count noun is specific and requires *the*.

Alerts: (1) One common exception affects rule 3 in Quick Box 43.2. A noun may still require *a* or *an* after the first use if one or more descriptive adjectives come between the article and the noun: *I bought a sweater today. It was a* [not *the*] *red sweater.*

(2) *An* is used before words that begin with a vowel sound; *a* is used before words that begin with a consonant sound. Words that begin with *h* or *u* can have either a vowel or a consonant sound; check your dictionary. Choose *a* or *an* based on the sound, not the spelling, of the first word after the article.

- **an** idea, **a** good idea
- **an** umbrella, **a** useless umbrella
- **an** honor, **a** history book

Quick Box 43.2

Using *the* with singular count nouns

RULE 1

A noun is specific and requires *the* when it names something either unique or commonly known.

- **The** sun has risen above **the** horizon.

  Because only one *sun* and one *horizon* exist, they are specific nouns.

RULE 2

A noun is specific and requires *the* when it names something used in a representative or abstract sense.

- Benjamin Franklin favored **the** turkey as **the** national bird of the United States.

  Because *turkey* and *national bird* are representative references rather than references to a particular turkey or bird, they are specific nouns in this context.

RULE 3

A noun is specific and requires *the* when it names something that is defined elsewhere in the same sentence or in an earlier sentence.

- **The** ship *Savannah* was the first steam vessel to cross **the** Atlantic Ocean.

  Savannah names a specific ship, and *Atlantic Ocean* is a specific ocean.

- **The** carpet in my bedroom is new.

  In my bedroom defines exactly which carpet is meant, so *carpet* is a specific noun in this context.

- I have an iPad and a printer in my office. **The** printer is often broken.

  Use *the* in the second sentence to refer to that specific printer.

RULE 4

A noun is specific and requires *the* when it represents something that can be inferred from the context.

- **I need an expert to fix the problem.**

  If you read this sentence after the example about a printer in Rule 3, you understand that *problem* refers to the broken printer, and so *problem* is specific in this context. Here the word *the* is similar to the word *this*.

43A

43B How should I use articles with count and noncount nouns?

Like singular count nouns, plural count nouns and NONCOUNT NOUNS that are *specific* usually use *the* according to the rules in Quick Box 43.2 (p. 436). When a noun has a *general* meaning, it usually does not use *the*.

■ Using articles with plural count nouns

- Geraldo planted tulips and roses this year. **The** tulips will bloom in April.

By the second sentence, *tulips*, a plural count noun, has become specific, so *the* is used. See Rule 3 in Quick Box 43.2.

■ Using articles with noncount nouns

- Kalinda served rice and chicken to us. She flavored **the** rice with curry.

Rice is a noncount noun. By the second sentence, *rice* has become specific, so *the* is used. This example is related to rule 3 in Quick Box 43.2.

■ Generalizing with plural and noncount nouns

Omit *the* in generalizations using plural or noncount nouns.

- ~~The~~ tulips are ~~the~~ flowers that grow from ~~the~~ bulbs.

Compare this sentence to a generalization with a singular count noun.

- **A** tulip is **a** flower that grows from **a** bulb.

43C How should I use *the* with proper nouns?

PROPER NOUNS represent particular people, places, or things. Most proper nouns do not require articles: *We visited Lake Mead* [not **the** *Lake Mead*] *with Asha and Larry*. However, certain types of proper nouns do require *the*.

Nouns with the pattern *the . . . of . . .* : *the United States of America, the president of Mexico* [not the Mexico]

Plural proper nouns: *the Johnsons, the Chicago Bulls, the United States*

Collective proper nouns (nouns that name a group): *the Society of Friends, the AFL-CIO*

Some, but not all, geographical features: *the Amazon, the Gobi Desert, the Indian Ocean*

43C

● **EXERCISE 43-1**   Consulting all sections of this chapter, decide which of the words in parentheses is correct and write it in the blank. If no article is needed, leave the blank empty.

EXAMPLE

In (a, an, the) _____ United States of America, (a, an, the) _____ highways are labeled with (a, an, the) _____ number that indicates (a, an, the) _____ highway's direction.

In (a, an, the) <u>the</u> United States of America, (a, an, the) <u>[no article]</u> highways are labeled with (a, an, the) <u>a</u> number that indicates <u>the</u> highway's direction.

1. If (a, an, the) _____ highway runs north and south, then it is designated with (a, an, the) _____ odd number, but (a, an, the) _____ highways that run east and west are given (a, an, the) _____ even number.

2. For example, (a, an, the) _____ highway that runs north and south along (a, an, the) _____ coast of California is called (a, an, the) _____ Highway 1.

3. (A, An, The) _____ interstate highway that runs east-to-west is given (a, an, the) _____ low even number if it is in (a, an, the) _____ southern U.S., such as (a, an, the) _____ Interstate 10.

4. (A, An, The) _____ three-digit freeway usually encircles (a, an, the) _____ major city.

5. One of (a, an, the) _____ America's most famous highways is (a, an, the) _____ Route 66, which is (a, an, the) _____ road that runs from Los Angeles to Chicago. ●

44 Word Order

44

Quick Points   You will learn to

➤ Use appropriate English word order (pp. 438–440).
➤ Place adjectives and adverbs in the proper places in sentences (pp. 439–441).

MyWritingLab™ Visit mywritinglab.com for more resources on word order.

44A   What are standard and inverted word orders?

Standard word order is the most common sentence pattern in English. The SUBJECT comes before the VERB: *That book* [subject] *was* [verb] *heavy.*

Inverted word order, with a verb coming before the subject, is common for DIRECT QUESTIONS in English: *Was* [verb] *that book* [subject] *heavy? Were* [verb] *you* [subject] *close to it when it fell?*

A common way to form questions is to use inverted order with a form of the verb *do* as an AUXILIARY VERB before the subject and the SIMPLE FORM of the main verb after the subject: ***Does she want** her book?*

Use *do* with inverted order when a question begins with a question-forming word such as *what, why, when, where,* or *how:* ***When do** you **read?***

When a question has more than one auxiliary verb, put the subject after the first auxiliary verb: ***Would you** have replaced the book?*

🛑 **Alert:** Do not use inverted word order with INDIRECT QUESTIONS: *She asked where I saw the book* [*not* She asked where did I see the book]. ●

Verb–subject word order is also required by initial ADVERBS.

- Only once [two adverbs] **did she** ask my advice.
- Never [adverb] **have I** seen such a mess!

Verb–subject word order rules also apply to exclamations: ***Was** that **book** heavy!* ***Did she** ever enjoy that book!*

44B   Where should I place adjectives?

In English, an ADJECTIVE ordinarily comes directly before the NOUN it modifies. Quick Box 44.1, page 440, shows the most common order for positioning several adjectives that modify the same noun.

44C   Where should I place adverbs?

ADVERBS and adverbial PHRASES modify verbs, adjectives, other adverbs, or whole sentences. They can go in three different places in a CLAUSE: first, middle, or last. ("Middle" usually means just after the auxiliary verb, if any.) See Quick Box 44.2 (pages 440–441).

🛑 **Alert:** If a sentence begins with a negative adverb of frequency (*never, rarely, only once, seldom*), the subject–verb word order must be inverted (see 44A). This creates emphasis.

- **Seldom** has Nick been bitten by a dog. ●

44C

Quick Box 44.1

Word order for adjectives

1. Determiner, if any: *a, an, the, my, your, Jan's, these*, and so on
2. Expressions of order, if any: *first, second, next, last*, and so on
3. Expressions of quantity, if any: *one, two, few, each, some*, and so on
4. Adjectives of judgment or opinion, if any: *smart, happy, interesting, sad, boring*, and so on
5. Adjectives of size or shape, if any: *big, short, round, oval*, and so on
6. Adjectives of age or condition, if any: *new, young, broken*, and so on
7. Adjectives of color, if any: *red, green, beige, turquoise*, and so on
8. Adjectives that can also be used as nouns, if any: *French, metal, Protestant, cotton*, and so on
9. The noun

1	2	3	4	5	6	7	8	9
A		few		tiny		red		ants
The	last	six					Thai	drums
My			fine		old		oak	table

Quick Box 44.2

Types and positions of adverbs

ADVERBS OF MANNER
Describe how something is done. Usual position: middle or last.

- Nick **carefully** groomed the dog.
- Nick groomed the dog **carefully**.

ADVERBS OF TIME
Describe the order or length of an event. Usual position: first or last.

- **First**, Nick shampooed the dog.
- Nick shampooed the dog **first**.

ADVERBS OF FREQUENCY
Describe how often an event takes place. Usual position: middle to modify a verb, first to modify an entire sentence.

- Nick has **never** been bitten by a dog.
- **Occasionally**, Nick is scratched while shampooing a cat.

continued >>

44C

Quick Box 44.2

Types of adverbs (continued) ■ ■ ■ ■ ■ ■

ADVERBS OF DEGREE OR EMPHASIS

Indicate *how much* or *to what extent* about other modifiers. Usual position: directly before the word they modify.

- Nick is **rather** quiet around animals.
- Nick wears protection **only** when examining an exotic pet.

    See 24A on the placement of *only*.

SENTENCE ADVERBS

Modify an entire sentence. They include transitional words and expressions, as well as such words as *maybe, probably, possibly, fortunately*, and *incredibly*. Usual position: first.

- **Incredibly**, Nick was once asked to groom a squirrel.

● **EXERCISE 44-1**   Consulting all sections of this chapter, find and correct any errors in word order.

1. A beautiful few flowers began to bloom in my garden this week.
2. A neighbor asked me, "You did grow all these yourself?"
3. "Yes," I replied, "roses are my favorite husband's; tulips are mine."
4. My neighbor, who extremely was impressed with my gardening efforts, decided to grow some flowers of her own.
5. Weeks later, as I strolled by her house, I saw her planting happily seeds from her favorite type of plant—petunias. ●

45 Prepositions
■ ■ ■ ■ ■ ■

45

Quick Points   You will learn to

➤ Use *in*, *at*, and *on* to show time and place (p. 442).
➤ Use prepositions correctly (pp. 442–444).

MyWritingLab™   Visit mywritinglab.com for more resources on prepositions.

Prepositions and their OBJECTS form PREPOSITIONAL PHRASES, which often describe relationships in time or space. When prepositions are combined with certain VERBS, they are called **phrasal verbs** (see 45B). In some cases, phrasal verbs take on idiomatic meanings. A dictionary such as the *Oxford Advanced Learner's Dictionary* is helpful for finding the correct preposition for certain **idioms**.

45A How should I use *in, at,* and *on* to show time and place?

To Show Time

- *in* a year or a month (*during* is also correct but less common): *in 1999*, *in May*
- *in* a period of time: *in a few months* (*seconds, days, years*)
- *in* a period of a day: *in the morning* (*evening*), *in the daytime* but *at night*
- *on* a specific day: *on Friday*, *on my birthday*, *on May 12*
- *at* a specific time or period: *at noon*, *at 2:00*, *at dawn*, *at nightfall*, *at takeoff* (the time a plane leaves), *at breakfast* (the time a specific meal takes place)

To Show Place

- *in* a location surrounded by something else: *in my car*, *in Utah*
- *at* a specific location: *at your house*, *at 376 Oak Street*, *at home*
- *on* a street: *on Oak Street*, *on Third Avenue*, *on the road*

45B How should I use prepositions in phrasal verbs?

Phrasal verbs are verbs that combine with prepositions to deliver their meaning. The meaning of many phrasal verbs is idiomatic, not literal; *pick on*, for example, means "annoy" or "tease." Also, many phrasal verbs are more appropriate for conversation than for ACADEMIC WRITING. For a research paper, for example, *propose* or *suggest* is a better choice than *come up with*.

In some phrasal verbs, the verb and the preposition must always stay together: ***Look at*** *the moon* [not ***Look*** *the moon* ***at***].

In other phrasal verbs, called *separable phrasal verbs*, words can separate the verb and the preposition without interfering with meaning: *I **threw away** my homework* [or *I **threw** my homework **away***].

When a separable phrasal verb has a PRONOUN object, that object should be placed between the verb and the preposition: *I **threw it away*** [not *I **threw away** it*]. Object PHRASES or CLAUSES with more than four or five words usually come after the preposition: *I **threw away** the quiz from last week*.

Here's a list of some common phrasal verbs. The ones that can't be separated are marked with an asterisk (*).

SELECTED PHRASAL VERBS

ask out	fill up	keep up with*	make up
break down	find out	leave out	run across*
call back	get along with*	look after*	speak to*
call off	get back	look around*	speak with*
drop off	get off	look into*	throw out
figure out	go over*	look out for*	turn down
fill out	hand in	look over	

● **EXERCISE 45-1**   Consulting the preceding sections of this chapter and using the list of phrasal verbs in 45B, write a one- or two-paragraph description of a typical activity in which you use at least five phrasal verbs. After checking a dictionary, revise your writing, substituting for the phrasal verbs any more formal verbs that might be more appropriate for academic writing. ●

45C How should I use prepositions with the passive voice?

VERBS used in the PASSIVE VOICE usually follow the pattern *be* + PAST PARTICIPLE + *by*: *The child **was frightened by** a snake.* However, many passive constructions require other prepositions instead of *by*: *The child **is afraid of** snakes.* Here's a list of some of these passive expressions with their prepositions. Look in a dictionary for others. (See 46A on using GERUNDS after some of these expressions.)

SELECTED VERBS AND PREPOSITIONS
USED IN PASSIVE CONSTRUCTIONS

be accustomed to	be interested in
be acquainted with	be known for
be composed of	be located in
be concerned about	be made of (*or* from)
be disappointed with (*or* in)	be married to
be discriminated against	be prepared for
be done with	be satisfied with
be excited about	be tired of (*or* from)
be finished with	be worried about

45C

45D How should I use prepositions in expressions?

Different prepositions convey great differences in meaning in many common expressions. For example, *agree **to**, agree **about**, agree **on**,* and *agree **with*** have different meanings. Check a dictionary if you're unsure of the precise differences.

Many adjectives also require certain prepositions: *afraid of, familiar with, famous for, friendly toward* (or *with*), *guilty of, patient with, proud of.*

46 Gerunds and Infinitives

Quick Points   You will learn to

➤ Use gerunds correctly (pp. 444–447).
➤ Use infinitives correctly (pp. 444–447).

MyWritingLab™ Visit mywritinglab.com for more resources on gerunds and infinitives.

Gerunds and **infinitives** are VERBALS, which are verb forms that function as NOUNS or MODIFIERS. When used as direct objects, gerunds follow some verbs, and infinitives follow others. A few verbs may be followed by either gerunds or infinitives, while other verbs change meaning depending on which verbal follows them.

46A What verbs use a gerund, not an infinitive, object?

Certain verbs use gerunds, not infinitives, as direct objects: *Yuri denied **calling*** [not *to call*] *the mayor.*

VERBS THAT USE GERUND OBJECTS

acknowledge	delay	have trouble	recall
admit	deny	imagine	recommend
advise	detest	include	resent
anticipate	discuss	insist on	resist
appreciate	dislike	keep (on)	risk
avoid	dream about	mention	suggest
cannot help	enjoy	mind	talk about
complain about	escape	object to	tolerate
consider	evade	postpone	understand
consist of	favor	practice	
contemplate	finish	put off	
defer from	give up	quit	

■ Using a gerund after *go*

Although *go* is usually followed by an infinitive object (*We can **go to see*** [not *go seeing*] *a movie*), *go* is followed by a gerund in such phrases as *go swimming, go fishing, go shopping,* and *go driving: I will **go swimming*** [not *go to swim*] *tomorrow.*

■ Using gerunds after *be* + complement + preposition

A COMPLEMENT often follows a form of *be*. Some complements require certain PREPOSITIONS (see 45C).

SELECTED *BE* + COMPLEMENT + PREPOSITION EXPRESSIONS

be (get) accustomed to	be prepared for	be tired of (*or* from)
be angry about	be responsible for	be (get) used to
be bored with	be capable of	be worried about
be excited about	be committed to	
be interested in	be concerned about	

- We are excited about **voting** [not *to vote*] in the election.
- They were interested in **hearing** [not *to hear*] the candidates' debate.

46A

 Alert: Always use a gerund, not an infinitive, as the object of a preposition. Be especially careful when the word *to* functions as a preposition: *We are committed to **saving*** [not *committed to save*] *the elephants.* ●

46B   What verbs use an infinitive, not a gerund, object?

Certain verbs can be followed by infinitives, not gerunds, as direct objects:
Three people decided **to question** [not *decided questioning*] *the speaker.*

VERBS THAT USE INFINITIVE OBJECTS

afford to	claim to	intend to	refuse to
agree to	consent to	know how to	seem to
aim to	decide to	learn to	struggle to
appear to	decline to	like to	tend to
arrange to	demand to	manage to	threaten to
ask to	deserve to	mean to	try to
attempt to	expect to	offer to	volunteer to
be able (unable) to	fail to	plan to	wait to
be left to	give permission to	prepare to	want to
beg to	hesitate to	pretend to	would like to
care to	hope to	promise to	

■ Using infinitives after *be* + some complements

- We are eager **to go** [*not* going] to the mountains.
- I am ready **to sleep** [*not* sleeping] in a tent.

■ Using unmarked infinitive objects

Some verbs take an unmarked infinitive, an infinitive without the word *to*. Common verbs followed by unmarked infinitives are *feel, have, hear, let, listen to, look at, make* (meaning "compel"), *notice, see,* and *watch*. In the following examples, *take* is shown first as an unmarked infinitive, then as a marked infinitive.

- Please **let** me **take** [*not* to take] you to lunch.

  Take is an unmarked infinitive after *let*.

- I want **to take** you to lunch.

  To take is a marked infinitive after *want*.

46C   How does meaning change if an infinitive object or a gerund follows *stop, remember,* or *forget*?

Here are some examples of what happens when a verb is followed by either a gerund or an infinitive. Followed by a gerund, *stop* means "finish, quit": *We stopped eating* means "We finished our meal." However, followed by an infinitive, *stop* means "stop or interrupt one activity to begin another": *We stopped to eat* means "We stopped doing something [such as driving or painting the house] to eat."

Followed by a gerund, *remember* means "recall a memory": *I remember talking to you last night.* However, followed by an infinitive, *remember* means "not to forget to do something": *I must remember to talk with Isa.*

Followed by a gerund, *forget* means "do something and not recall it": *I forget having put my keys in the refrigerator.* However, followed by an infinitive, *forget* means "not do something": *If you forget to put a stamp on that letter, it will be returned.*

46D Do sense verbs change meaning with a gerund or an infinitive object?

Sense verbs such as *see, notice, hear, observe, watch, feel, listen to,* and *look at* usually don't change meaning whether a gerund or an infinitive is used as an object. *I saw the water rising* and *I saw the water rise* (unmarked infinitive—see 46B) both deliver the same message.

46E How should I choose between *-ing* and *-ed* forms of adjectives?

Deciding between the *-ing* form (PRESENT PARTICIPLE) or the *-ed* form (PAST PARTICIPLE) of an ADJECTIVE in a sentence can be difficult. For example, *I am amused* and *I am amusing* are both correct, but their meanings vary.

- **I am amused** at the circus.

  I experience amusement.

- **I am amusing** at the circus.

  I cause the amusement of other people.

To make the right choice, decide whether the modified NOUN or PRONOUN is causing or experiencing what the participle describes.

Use a present participle (*-ing*) to modify a noun or pronoun that is the cause of the action. This meaning is in the ACTIVE VOICE.

- Mica explained your **interesting** plan.

  The noun *plan* caused interest, so *interesting* is correct.

- I find your plan **exciting**.

  The noun *plan* causes excitement, so *exciting* is correct.

46E

Use a past participle (*-ed* on regular verbs) to modify a noun or pronoun that experiences or receives whatever the MODIFIER describes. This meaning is in the PASSIVE VOICE.

- An **interested** committee wants to hear your plan.

  The noun *committee* experiences interest, so *interested* is correct.

- **Excited** by your plan, I called a board meeting.

  The pronoun *I* experiences excitement, so *excited* is correct.

To choose between these frequently used participles, decide whether the noun or pronoun *experiences* or *causes* what the participle describes.

annoyed, annoying	frightened, frightening
appalled, appalling	insulted, insulting
bored, boring	offended, offending
confused, confusing	pleased, pleasing
depressed, depressing	reassured, reassuring
disgusted, disgusting	satisfied, satisfying
fascinated, fascinating	shocked, shocking

● **EXERCISE 46-1** Compose complete sentences, using either a gerund or infinitive object, beginning with the words below. For help, consult 46A–46E.

EXAMPLE

Never begin.

Never begin to doubt the value of your own intelligence.

1. Think about
2. Flexible schedules allow (or let) us
3. No one favors
4. We can no longer afford
5. Will you consider ●

● **EXERCISE 46-2** Choose the correct participle from each pair in parentheses. For help, consult 46E.

EXAMPLE

It can be a (satisfied, satisfying) <u>satisfying</u> experience to learn about the lives of artists.

1. The artist Frida Kahlo led an (interested, interesting) _____ life.
2. When Kahlo was eighteen, (horrified, horrifying) _____ observers saw her (injured, injuring) _____ in a streetcar accident.

3. A (disappointed, disappointing) _____ Kahlo had to abandon her plan to study medicine.
4. Instead, she began to create paintings filled with (disturbed, disturbing) _____ images.
5. Some art critics consider Kahlo's paintings to be (fascinated, fascinating) _____ works of art, though many people find them (overwhelmed, overwhelming) _____. ●

47 Modal Auxiliary Verbs

■ ■ ■ ■ ■ ■

Quick Points   You will learn to

➤ Use modal auxiliary verbs to help main verbs convey information.

MyWritingLab™   Visit mywritinglab.com for more resources on modal auxiliary verbs.

Modal auxiliary verbs suggest how actions are viewed. These auxiliaries include *can, could, had better, may, might, must, should, ought, will,* and *would.*

47A   How do modal auxiliary verbs differ from *be, do,* and *have?*

47A

Modal auxiliary verbs are always followed by the SIMPLE FORM of a main verb: *I **might go** tomorrow.*

One-word modal auxiliary verbs do not have an *-s* ending in the third-person singular: *She **could** go with me, it **must** be cold outside.*

Two modals that have forms that end in *-s* are *have to* and *need to* in the third-person singular: *She **has** to stay; he **needs** to smile more.*

47B   Which modal auxiliary verbs express ability, necessity, advisability, or probability?

■ Expressing ability

Can means "able in the present." The modal auxiliary verb *could* sometimes means "able in the past."

- You **can work** late tonight.

  This means "You are able to work late tonight."

- I **could play** the piano when I was younger.

  This means "I was able to play the piano when I was younger."

The modal auxiliary verb *could* often expresses some condition that is required to be fulfilled before another condition.

- If you **could** come early, we can start on time.

  This means "We can't start on time unless you come early."

- I **could** have gone to bed at 10:00 if I had finished my homework.

  This means "I couldn't go to bed at 10:00 because I had not finished my homework."

Adding *not* between a modal auxiliary verb and the main verb makes the sentence negative: *I could **not** work late last night.*

■ Expressing necessity

Must, have to, and *need to* express a requirement to do something. *Must* implies only future action. *Have to* and *need to* imply action in all verb tenses.

- You **must leave** before midnight. She **has to leave** when I leave.
- We **needed to be** with you last night. You **will need to be** here before dark tonight.

■ Expressing advice or the notion of a good idea

Should and *ought to* express a suggestion or an obligation. Their PAST-TENSE FORMS are *should have* and *ought to have*, followed by the PAST PARTICIPLE.

- You **should call** your dentist tomorrow. I **ought to have** gone to my dentist last week.

The modal *had better* expresses the meaning of good advice or warning or threat.

- You **had better see** a doctor before your cough gets worse.

47B

■ Expressing probability

May, might, could, and *must* usually express probability or possibility.

- We **might** see a tiger in the zoo. We **could** go this afternoon.

The past-tense forms for the modal auxiliary verbs *may, might, could,* and *must* add *have* and the main verb's past participle to the modals.

- I'm hungry; I **must have neglected** to eat breakfast.

47C Which modal auxiliary verbs express preference, plan, or past habit?

■ Expressing preferences

Would rather (present tense) and *would rather have* (past tense) express a preference. In the past tense, the modal is also followed by a past participle.

- I **would rather text** you. I **would rather have received** text messages than calls.

■ Expressing a plan or obligation

A form of *be* followed by *supposed to* and the simple form of a main verb, in both present and past tense, means something planned or an obligation.

- I **was supposed to meet** them at the bus stop.

The word *supposed* may be omitted with no change in meaning.

- I **was to meet** them at the bus stop.

■ Expressing past habit

Used to and *would* mean that something happened repeatedly in the past.

- I **used to hate** getting a flu shot. I **would dread** the injection for weeks beforehand.

❗ Alert: Both the modal auxiliary verbs *used to* and *would* can be used for repeated actions in the past, but the modal auxiliary verb *would* cannot be used for a situation that lasted for a period of time in the past.

> used to
> I ~~would~~ live in Arizona. ●
>   ^

● **EXERCISE 47-1**   Select the correct choice from the words in parentheses and write it in the blank. For help, consult 47A through 47C.

EXAMPLE

When I was younger, I (would, used to) <u>used to</u> love to go bicycle riding.

1. You (ought to have, ought have) _____ called yesterday as you had promised you would.
2. Large puddles outside indicate that it (must be rained, must have rained) _____ all night.
3. Ingrid (must not have, might not have been) _____ as early for the interview as she claims she was.
4. After all the studying he did, Pedro (should have, should have been) _____ less frightened by the exam.
5. I have to go home early today, although I really (cannot, should not) _____ leave before the end of the day because of all the work I have to do. ●

47C

Part 7
Special Writing Situations

CHAPTERS
48–55

An Overview of Writing Across the Curriculum

Quick Points You will learn to

➤ Adapt your writing to various college courses.

➤ Use cue words to tell what your college writing needs to accomplish.

MyWritingLab™ Visit mywritinglab.com for more resources on writing across the curriculum.

48A What is writing across the curriculum?

Writing across the curriculum refers to the writing you do in college courses beyond first-year composition. (A related term is "writing in the disciplines," which usually refers to writing that is specific to individual majors.) Good writing in courses as different as history, biology, and psychology has many common features. However, there are also important differences. A lab report for a chemistry course, for example, differs from a paper for a literature course. Quick Box 48.1 summarizes different types of writing across the curriculum.

Quick Box 48.1

Comparing the disciplines

Discipline	Types of Assignments	Primary Sources	Secondary Sources	Usual Documentation Styles
HUMANITIES history, languages, literature, philosophy, art, music, theater	essays, response statements, reviews, analyses, original works such as stories, poems, auto-biographies	literary works, manuscripts, paintings and sculptures, historical documents, films, plays, photographs, artifacts from popular culture	reviews, journal articles, research papers, books	Modern Language Association (MLA), Chicago Manual of Style (CM)

continued >>

Quick Box 48.1   Types of writing (continued)   ■ ■ ■ ■ ■ ■

Discipline	Types of Assignments	Primary Sources	Secondary Sources	Usual Documentation Styles
SOCIAL SCIENCES psychology, sociology, anthropology, education	research reports, case studies, reviews of the literature, analyses	surveys, interviews, observations, experiments, tests and measures	journal articles, scholarly books, literature reviews	American Psychological Association (APA)
NATURAL SCIENCES biology, chemistry, physics, mathematics	reports, research proposals and reports, science reviews	experiments, field notes, direct observations, measurements	journal articles, research papers, books	often Council of Science Editors (CSE) but varies by discipline

48B   How do audience and purpose work across the curriculum?

The AUDIENCE for ACADEMIC WRITING consists of scholars, professors, and students in particular fields. As a result, you need to use the kind of sources and follow the kinds of conventions that are expected in each discipline. Conventions include format and organization, types of evidence, tone and style, and documentation style. They can vary considerably from writings for more general and popular readers. We suggest you study examples of the kinds of writing you've been asked to produce.

PURPOSES can vary widely. Some tasks mainly require explaining information you acquire from readings or other data. Other tasks require making an argument supported by evidence and reasoning. Most assignments contain **cue words** that tell what your writing needs to accomplish. Quick Box 48.2 presents some common cue words.

Quick Box 48.2   ■ ■ ■ ■ ■ ■

Some common cue words

Cue Word	Meaning
ANALYZE	Separate into parts and discuss each, often including how it contributes to a meaning or implication.
CLASSIFY	Arrange in groups based on shared characteristics or functions.

continued >>

48B

Quick Box 48.2   Cue words (continued)   ■ ■ ■ ■ ■ ■

Cue Word	Meaning
CRITICIZE	Give your opinion and explain why you approve or disapprove of something.
COMPARE	Show similarities and differences.
DEFINE	Tell what something is to differentiate it from similar things.
DISCUSS	Explain and comment on, in an organized way, the various issues or elements involved.
EXPLAIN	Make clear a complex thing or process that needs to be illuminated or interpreted.
INTERPRET	Explain the meaning or significance of something.
REVIEW	Evaluate or summarize critically.
SUMMARIZE	Lay out the major points of something.
SUPPORT	Argue in favor of something.

49 Writing in the Humanities
■ ■ ■ ■ ■ ■

Quick Points   You will learn to

➤ Understand the different types of papers in the humanities.

MyWritingLab™ Visit mywritinglab.com for more resources on writing in the humanities.

49A   What are the humanities?

Disciplines in the humanities seek to represent and understand human experience, creativity, thought, and values. These disciplines include literature, languages, philosophy, and history, although some colleges group history with the social sciences. Also, many colleges include the fine arts (music, art, dance, theater, and creative writing) as part of the humanities.

49A

49B   What are types of writing in the humanities?

Because the humanities cover an impressively broad range of knowledge, writing in the humanities covers many types and purposes.

■ Summaries

Occasionally your instructor will request an objective summary of a text; you might need to tell the plot of a novel or present the main points of an article (see Chapter 13). Generally, however, a summary is a means to a greater end. For example, writing an interpretation often requires you to summarize parts of the source so that your points about it are clear.

■ Syntheses

SYNTHESIS relates several texts, ideas, or pieces of information to one another (see Chapter 13). For example, you might read several accounts of the events leading up to the Civil War and then write a synthesis that explains what caused that war. Or you might read several philosophers' definitions of morality and write a synthesis of the components of a moral life.

■ Responses

In a response, you give your personal reaction to a work, supported by explanations of your reasoning. For example, do you think Hamlet's behavior makes sense? Do you agree with Peter Singer's philosophical arguments against using animals in scientific experiments? Before you write a response, clarify whether your instructor wants you to justify it with references to a text. (See Chapter 11.)

■ Interpretations

An interpretation explains the meaning or significance of a particular text, event, or work of art (see Quick Box 49.1, p. 458). For example, what does Plato's *Republic* suggest about the nature of a good society? What was the significance of the 9/11 tragedy for Americans' sense of security? Your reply isn't right or wrong; rather, you present your point of view and explain your reasoning. The quality of your reasoning determines how successfully you convey your point.

■ Narratives

When you write a narrative, you construct a coherent story out of separate facts or events. In a history class, for example, you might examine news events, laws, diaries and journals, and related materials to create a chronological version of what happened. You might do the kind of work that a

Quick Box 49.1

■ ■ ■ ■ ■

Selected analytical frameworks used in the humanities

RHETORICAL	Explores how and why people use LOGICAL, EMOTIONAL, and ETHICAL APPEALS to create desired effects on specific audiences, in specific situations (see 2B).
CULTURAL OR NEW HISTORICAL	Explores how social, economic, and other cultural forces influence the development of ideas, texts, art, laws, customs, and so on. Also explores how individual texts or events provide broader understandings of the past or present.
DECONSTRUCTIONIST	Assumes that the meaning of any given text is not stable or "in" the work. Rather, meaning always depends on contexts and the interests of the people in power. The goal of deconstruction is to produce multiple possible meanings of a work, usually to undermine traditional interpretations.
FEMINIST	Focuses on how women are presented and treated, concentrating especially on power relationships between men and women.
FORMALIST	Centers on matters of structure, form, and traditional literary devices (plot, rhythm, imagery, symbolism, and others).
MARXIST	Assumes that the most important forces in human experience are economic and material ones by focusing on power differences between economic classes of people and the effects of those differences.
READER-RESPONSE	Emphasizes how the individual reader determines meaning. The reader's personal history, values, experiences, relationships, and previous reading all contribute to how he or she interprets a particular work or event.

biographer does by gathering information about isolated events in people's lives, interviews with those people or others who knew them, letters or other writings, and related SOURCES, all to form a coherent story of their lives. (See also Chapter 7.)

Some writing assignments in the humanities may ask you to write about your memories or experiences (see Chapter 7). Generally, such writings involve not only effectively telling a story but also some reflection on or analysis of that story.

■ Textual and literary analyses

Chapter 11 explains common features of textual and literary analysis. The humanities use a number of analytical frameworks, or systematic ways of investigating a work. Quick Box 49.1, on page 458, summarizes some common analytical frameworks used, most notably in literary analysis. Nearly all writing in the humanities depends on analysis to some extent.

49C What documentation styles are common in the humanities?

Most fields in the humanities use the Modern Language Association (MLA) documentation style (see Chapter 14). Some disciplines in the humanities use *Chicago Manual* (CM) style. A few have begun to use the American Psychological Association (APA) documentation style (see Chapter 15).

Writing in the Social Sciences
50

Quick Points You will learn to

➤ Understand the different types of papers in the social sciences.

50A What are the social sciences?

The social sciences focus on the behavior of people as individuals and in groups. This includes disciplines such as economics, education, anthropology, political science, psychology, sociology, and sometimes history. In the social sciences, PRIMARY SOURCES include surveys and questionnaires, observations, interviews, and experiments. Surveys and questionnaires systematically gather information from a representative number of individuals. To prepare a questionnaire, use the guidelines in Quick Box 12.6 on p. 146. For advice on

50A

collecting information through observation, see 12H, where we also explain interviewing strategies, especially in Quick Box 12.7 on p. 147.

The social sciences sometimes use data from experiments as a source. For example, if you want to learn how people react in a particular situation, you can set up that situation artificially and bring individuals (known as "subjects") into it to observe their behavior. With all methods of inquiry in the social sciences, you are required to treat subjects fairly and honestly, not in ways that could harm their body, mind, or reputation.

Use APA documentation style (see Chapter 15) for papers in the social sciences.

50B What are different types of papers in the social sciences?

The social sciences often involve the same kinds of writing as in the humanities (see 49B). Four additional types of papers are case studies, ethnographies, research reports, and research papers (or reviews of the literature).

■ Case studies

A **case study** is an intensive study of one group or individual. Case studies are important in psychology, social work, education, medicine, and similar fields in which it's useful to form a comprehensive portrait of people to understand them and, in some cases, to help them. For example, if you learn that a certain teaching style is effective, you might do a case study of a student to understand how that style works in a particular instance.

A case study's specific parts and their order vary. Most case studies contain the following components:

1. Basic identifying information about the individual or group

2. A history of the individual or group

3. Observations of the individual's or group's behavior

4. Conclusions and perhaps recommendations as a result of the observations

■ Ethnographies

Ethnographies are comprehensive studies of people interacting in a particular situation. Ethnographies commonly are written in courses in business, education, or the social sciences, with anthropology and sociology being prime examples. A sociologist might compose an ethnography of a classroom, for instance, to understand the interactions and relationships among students. The level of details needed in ethnographies has been described by anthropologist Clifford Geertz as "thick description." The more details you have, the better because you can't be sure which ones will be important until you analyze and reflect on the information.

◼ Research reports

Research reports explain your own original research based on PRIMARY SOURCES. These may result from interviews, questionnaires, observations, or experiments. Research reports in the social sciences often follow a prescribed format:

1. Statement of the problem

2. Background, sometimes including a review of the literature

3. Methodology

4. Results

5. Discussion of findings

◼ Research papers (or reviews of the literature)

Very often, social science research requires you to summarize, analyze, and synthesize SECONDARY SOURCES (see 12A). These sources are usually articles and books that report or discuss the findings of other people's primary research. To prepare a review of the literature, comprehensively gather and analyze the sources that have been published on a specific topic. *Literature* in this sense simply means "the body of work on a subject." Sometimes a review of the literature is a part of a longer paper, usually in the "background" section of a research report. Other times, the entire paper might be an extensive review of the literature.

51 Writing in the Natural Sciences

◼ ◼ ◼ ◼ ◼ ◼

Quick Points   You will learn to

➤ Understand the different types of papers in the natural sciences.

MyWritingLab™   Vist mywritinglab.com for more resources on writing in the natural sciences.

51A   What are the natural sciences?

The natural sciences include disciplines such as astronomy, biology, chemistry, geology, and physics. The sciences seek to describe and explain natural phenomena. The *scientific method*, commonly used in the sciences to make discoveries, is a procedure for gathering information related to a specific hypothesis. Quick Box 51.1 gives guidelines for using this method.

Documentation styles differ among the various sciences. A common style is that of the Council of Science Editors (CSE).

Quick Box 51.1

Guidelines for using the scientific method

1. Formulate a tentative explanation (a *hypothesis*) for a scientific phenomenon.
2. Read and summarize previously published information related to your hypothesis.
3. Plan a method of investigation to test your hypothesis.
4. Experiment, following exactly the investigative procedures you have outlined.
5. Observe closely the results of the experiment, and write notes carefully.
6. Analyze the results. Do they confirm the hypothesis?
7. Write a report of your research. At the end, you can suggest additional hypotheses that might be investigated.

51B   What are different types of papers in the natural sciences?

Two major types of papers in the sciences are reports and reviews.

■ Science reports

Science reports tell about observations and experiments. When they describe laboratory experiments, as is often true in academic settings, they're usually called lab reports. Formal reports feature the eight elements identified in Quick Box 51.2. Less formal reports, which are sometimes assigned in introductory college courses, might not include an abstract or a review of the literature. Ask your instructor which sections in Quick Box 51.2 to include in your report.

Quick Box 51.2

Parts of a science report

1. **Title.** Precisely describes your report's topic.

2. **Abstract.** Provides a short overview of the report to help readers decide whether or not your research is of interest to them.

3. **Introduction.** States the purpose behind your research and presents the hypothesis. Any needed background information and a review of the literature appear here.

4. **Methods and materials.** Describes the equipment, material, and procedures used.

5. **Results.** Provides the information obtained from your efforts. Charts, graphs, and photographs help present the data in a way that is easy for readers to grasp.

6. **Discussion.** Presents your interpretation and evaluation of the results. Did your efforts support your hypothesis? If not, can you suggest why not? Use concrete evidence in discussing your results.

7. **Conclusion.** Lists conclusions about the hypothesis and the outcomes of your efforts, paying particular attention to any theoretical implications that can be drawn from your work. Be specific in suggesting further research.

8. **List of references.** Presents references cited in the review of the literature, if any. Its format conforms to the requirements of the DOCUMENTATION STYLE in the particular science that is your subject.

■ Science reviews

A science review discusses published information on a scientific topic. The purpose of the review is to summarize for readers all the current knowledge about the issue. Sometimes the purpose of a science review is to synthesize to present a new interpretation of previously published material. In such a review, the writer presents EVIDENCE to persuade readers that the new interpretation is valid. In a science review, you want to

1. Choose a very limited scientific issue currently being researched

2. Use information that is current—the more recently published the articles, books, and journals you consult, the better

3. Accurately paraphrase and summarize material (see Chapter 13)

4. Document your sources

If your review runs longer than two or three pages, you might want to use headings to help readers understand your paper's organization and idea progression.

51B

52 Creating Multimedia Texts

Quick Points   You will learn to

➤ Plan and organize an oral presentation (pp. 464–466).
➤ Use visual and multimedia aids in an oral presentation (see pp. 466–470).
➤ Create video and sound recordings (see pp. 468–470).

MyWritingLab™ Visit mywritinglab.com for more resources on multimedia texts.

52A   What are multimedia texts?

Multimedia texts combine words with nonverbal items such as photographs, drawings, videos, slides, audio recordings, and so on. Through the Internet and computers, multimedia texts have become common in work, public, personal, and academic settings. Preparing a multimedia text and writing a paper involve similar thought and writing processes (see Chapters 4–6). This chapter provides additional information about preparing oral presentations with multimedia aids and video and sound recordings. To see examples of creative multimedia texts created by college students, visit the online journal The Jump.

52B   How do I plan and organize an oral presentation?

When planning a presentation, you need first to think about your audience and purpose. Then you can go on to organize your ideas and presentation accordingly.

■ Thinking about audience and purpose

You need to adjust presentations to fit PURPOSES, AUDIENCES, roles, and any special considerations. Consider three different situations.

- You want to address a group of students to inform them about a film club you're starting.
- You need to persuade a management group at work to adopt a new set of procedures for making purchasing decisions.
- You plan to give a toast at a friend's wedding to express your feelings and to entertain the wedding guests.

Different approaches will be successful in each instance because your purpose and audience are different.

Adapting your presentation to your listeners means holding their interest and being responsive to their viewpoints. Consult the strategies for analyzing AUDIENCES in Quick Box 4.4 on p. 28. Especially consider your listeners' prior knowledge of your topic. Are they *uninformed, informed*, or *mixed*? Quick Box 52.1 suggests how to adapt your message to each type of audience.

Quick Box 52.1

■ ■ ■ ■ ■ ■

Adapting a presentation to your audience

UNINFORMED AUDIENCE	Start with the basics and then move to a few new ideas. Define new terms and concepts and avoid unnecessary technical terms. Use visual aids and give examples. Repeat key ideas—but not too often.
INFORMED AUDIENCE	Never give more than a quick overview of the basics. Devote most of your time to new ideas and concepts.
MIXED AUDIENCE	In your introduction, acknowledge the more informed audience members who are present. Explain that you're going to review the basic concepts briefly so that everyone can build from the same knowledge base. Move as soon as possible toward more complex concepts.

■ Organizing your presentation

As with essays, an oral presentation has three parts: introduction, body, and conclusion. Within the body, you present your major points, with support for each point. Drafting a SENTENCE OUTLINE (see 4G) gets you close to your final form and forces you to sharpen your thinking.

INTRODUCING YOURSELF AND YOUR TOPIC

All audiences want to know three things about a speaker: Who are you? What are you going to talk about? Why should I listen? To respond effectively to these unasked questions, try these suggestions.

- Grab your audience's attention with an interesting question, quotation, or statistic; a bit of background information; a compliment; or an anecdote. If it is necessary to establish your credibility—even if someone has introduced you—briefly and humbly mention your qualifications as a speaker about your topic.

52B

- Give your audience a road map of your talk: Tell where you're starting, where you're going, and how you intend to get there. Your listeners need to know that you won't waste their time.

FOLLOWING YOUR ROAD MAP

Listening to a presentation is very different from reading an essay. Audiences generally need help following the speaker's line of reasoning. Try these strategies:

- Signal clearly where you are on your road map by using cue word transitions such as *first, second*, and *third; subsequently, therefore*, and *furthermore;* or *before, then*, and *next*.
- Define unfamiliar terms and concepts, and follow up with strong, memorable examples.
- Occasionally tell the audience what you consider significant, memorable, or especially relevant and why. Do so sparingly, at key points.
- Provide occasional summaries at points of transition. Recap what you've covered, and say how it relates to what's coming next.

WRAPPING UP YOUR PRESENTATION

To demonstrate that you haven't let key points simply float away, try ending with these suggestions.

- Do not introduce new ideas at the last minute.
- Signal that you are wrapping up your presentation using verbal cues, such as "In conclusion" and "Finally." When you say "finally," mean it!
- Make a dramatic, decisive statement; cite a memorable quotation; or issue a challenge. Allow a few seconds of silence, and then say "Thank you."

52C   How do I use multimedia in presentations?

Multimedia elements such as visual aids, sound, and video can reinforce key ideas in your presentation by providing illustrations or concrete images for the audience. See also Chapter 6 for ideas about designing documents.

■ Using traditional visual aids

Various types of visual aids can enhance your presentation. Always make the text or graphics large enough to be read easily at a distance.

- **Posters** can dramatize a point, often with color or images.
- **Dry-erase boards** are preferable to chalkboards because colors on them are visually appealing. Use them to roughly sketch an illustration or to emphasize a technical word.

- **Handouts** are useful when the topic calls for a longer text or when you want to give your audience something to refer to later. Short, simple handouts work best during a presentation, but longer, more detailed ones are more effective at the end. Remember to wait until everyone has one before you begin speaking about it. Always include DOCUMENTATION information for any SOURCES used in preparing the handout. A handout can be an all-important backup in case other technologies are missing or broken.

Using presentation software

PowerPoint, the most widely used presentation software, can create digital slides. (Similar programs, such as Prezi and Impress, are available free on the Internet.) These slides can contain words, images, or combinations of both (see Figure 52.1).

Never present so much information that your audience spends more time reading than listening to you. Also, never simply read large amounts of text from your slides; your audience will quickly—and rightfully—become bored. People have coined the phrase "death by PowerPoint" in despair at presenters who simply repeat what's written on slides. For advice on designing presentation slides, see Quick Box 52.2 on p. 468.

Figure 52.1   A sample PowerPoint slide.

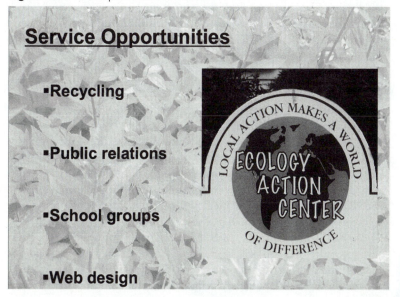

52C

Quick Box 52.2

Guidelines for designing PowerPoint or similar presentation slides

- **Keep slides simple.** Use only a few very short lines of text on each slide. (Use the old rule "six by six": no more than six lines, each with no more than six words.)

- **Keep slides readable.** Make sure text and images are large enough to be read by everyone in the room (find out in advance the room size). Contrast is important, so use black or very dark colors for text on a white background, or use white text on a very dark background.

- **Keep slides interesting.** A single well-chosen image can enhance a slide. Sometimes a slide that consists only of an image (a photograph, a chart, or other graphic) can be quite effective.

- **Keep slides few.** It's far more effective to have five well-chosen and designed slides for a short talk than to have twenty. "Death by PowerPoint" results mainly from endless streams of slides.

■ Using sound or video clips

A brief sound file (for example, a sentence or two from a speech) or a video clip (perhaps 20 to 30 seconds of footage from an event) can occasionally help you illustrate a point. Always keep them brief, and be absolutely sure that your audience will recognize immediately that they enhance your message and aren't just for show.

52D   How do I create video and sound recordings?

As you probably know from YouTube, short online videos can be an excellent source of entertainment (or, depending on your point of view, a major waste of time). However, videos and sound recordings, such as radio essays or podcasts, can be effective ways to deliver information, tell stories, or even make arguments. Also, videos often present complicated how-to directions more effectively than words alone. Documentaries, such as Ken Burns's famous series on baseball, the Civil War, the national park system, or jazz, vividly convey the sights and sounds of people and places.

Despite their advantages, video and sound projects can take considerable time and expertise to do well. Just like written texts, they require planning, drafting, and revising, so make sure you have sufficient time before you take one on. Quick Box 52.3 offers guidelines for recordings.

52D

Quick Box 52.3

Guidelines for producing sound and video recordings

- **Plan your recording.** A good video or podcast has a beginning, middle, and end. Decide what elements you need to record for each.

- **Create and practice a script.** If your project has a narrator, write a script that contains what the person needs to say, what will be shown when someone is speaking, and what music or sound effects you'll need. Practice the script with whomever is involved before you record.

- **Create a storyboard for visual projects.** A storyboard is a series of rough sketches (you can use stick people, for example) that show the major scenes or elements in your video. It helps to plan the sequence and keep track of what shots you need to make.

- **Arrange to interview and record people** who will appear in your recording. Set up a time and place to record or film people. Have anyone appearing in your work sign a release, which is a form you can create that gives you permission to circulate their voice and images.

- **Find an appropriate place to record.** Unless you're trying to capture a real atmosphere such as the crowd at a ball game or a protest, find a quiet place with good acoustics and no background noise, especially for narrations or interviews.

- **Use the best equipment available.** A dedicated video camera will generally produce better quality than a regular digital camera that has video capacity, for example. A dedicated microphone records better than a laptop's built-in microphone. Your college may have equipment you can borrow.

- **Edit what you've recorded or shot.** The real work of producing an effective recording comes in editing the raw footage. To get the best result, you'll need to shorten some elements and move them around. You'll need to add transitions. You may even need to shoot new material that you don't find you need until you're in the middle of the project. Learn how to use free or cheap sound editing programs like Audacity or video editing programs like MovieMaker or iMovie.

Figure 52.2 shows the opening to a documentary video that student Siena Pinney created about a forest fire in Colorado.

52D

Figure 52.2 Opening shot of documentary video.

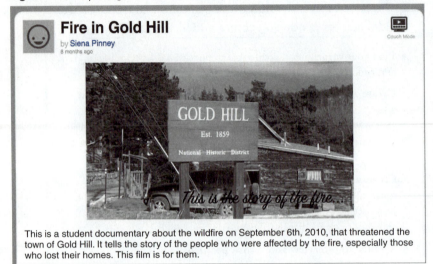

This is a student documentary about the wildfire on September 6th, 2010, that threatened the town of Gold Hill. It tells the story of the people who were affected by the fire, especially those who lost their homes. This film is for them.

53 Writing in Online Environments

■ ■ ■ ■ ■ ■

Quick Points   You will learn to

➤ Understand how to write for online using blogs and wikis.

MyWritingLab™   Visit mywritinglab.com for more resources on writing in online environments.

53A   What is writing for online environments?

Writing for digital environments means producing texts that can best—or perhaps that can only—be read through computers, generally online. Examples include status updates, blogs, wikis, videos, and podcasts. Online environments:

- allow instant publication so that readers far and wide can read texts online and online texts can reach real audiences

- allow interactions, so that readers can share comments on what they've read or even collaborate in different times and places to compose a text together

- allow writers easily to incorporate photographs, images, and colorful graphics, without the expense of printing

- allow writers to create or incorporate recordings, either sound or visual

- allow links to other sources available online, to enrich the content of a text

Online environments can also present challenges or complications that you need to avoid.

- They require so much time and energy to design that they take attention away from writing.

- They raise copyright or ownership concerns by circulating found images without getting proper permission.

- They allow work to be made public that isn't of the highest quality, potentially hurting its author's reputation.

The one problem you cannot prevent is people posting inappropriate or reckless comments on other peoples' work.

53B How do I write for a blog?

A Web log, or **blog**, is a Web site that displays a series of posts, or items. Posts are usually diarylike entries or observations, but may also be images, videos, audio files, and links. Blogs generally focus on a particular topic.

Most blogs have a similar design. The main content, a post about a particular topic, is in the center of the screen. The most recent post appears at the top of a page, followed by previous ones as a reader scrolls down. Many blogs contain a comment feature that allows others to respond to the original blog post. Some blogs also have a blogroll, which is a list of links to other blogs that focus on similar topics. Figure 53.1 shows a typical blog design.

Many instructors require students to contribute to a class blog. This is like having students write in journals as a regular way of writing about course content with the twist that other class members are required to read and comment on each person's postings. If you're assigned to write on a course blog, follow your instructor's specific directions.

If you'd like to create your own blog, decide on a type and PURPOSE. You need to find an AUDIENCE who cares about your perspective. You might participate in blogs and network with others, eventually gaining the attention of people who are interested in what you have to say. Most important, have something interesting to say. Easily available software allows you to start blogging almost immediately with little trouble. For example, Blogger is a popular online community that gets you started with only a few mouse clicks. Quick Box 53.1 contains guidelines for writing for a blog.

53B

Figure 53.1 Typical blog design.

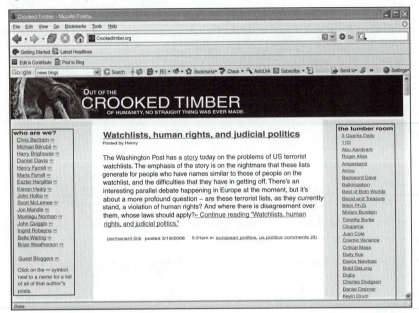

Quick Box 53.1

Guidelines for writing your own blog

- **Pick a unique title for your blog.** People and Internet search engines will recognize your blog if it has a good title.

- **Decide whether to use your own name or a made-up username.** You can protect your privacy to some degree if you have a pseudonym (literally, a "false name") or username. Especially if you're writing about controversial topics or taking controversial positions, you might not want employers, instructors, or even relatives to know your identity. Of course, an anonymous username doesn't give you license to be irresponsible or unethical. On the other hand, the advantage of your real name is that you get credit (and, we suppose, blame) for your writings. Think carefully about this decision.

- **Link, show, and share.** Include links in your posts to other, similar posts or items from the Web. Post images, videos, or audio files, but do respect copyrights. And share your posts and blog with others through the use of a blogroll or by participating on other blogs.

53B

53C How do I write for a wiki?

A wiki is a technology that allows anybody to change the content of a Web page without using special Web writing or uploading software. *Wiki* is a Hawaiian word meaning "fast," and the name refers to how quickly people using this technology can collaborate and revise information. One of the more popular wiki applications is the online encyclopedia, Wikipedia.

Wikis can be useful tools for collaborative writing projects because group members can all view a draft at the same time. Individuals can easily make contributions and changes. However, as you can imagine, this can also lead to complications. If you're using a wiki for a college project, you'll want to review strategies for writing with others. If you want to create a new wiki, setting one up is fairly easy. Simple software like Pbwiki will allow you quickly to do so without worrying about server space. Quick Box 53.2 offers guidelines for writing for a wiki.

Quick Box 53.2

Guidelines for writing in a wiki

- **Revise with respect for others.** The strength of a wiki is its ability to allow people to share their expertise, so try to maintain what others have said. Instead of deleting material, you might add qualifications, for example, words like "possibly" or phrases such as "in some cases" or "some have argued." You might add a section entitled "Opposing Arguments" (see 9C) that suggests an alternative viewpoint.

- **Cite your sources whenever possible.** Whenever possible, cite your sources, and in some cases, find corroborating sources. Any addition to a wiki entry that contains references to reputable sources is less likely to be deleted or revised later, making your influence more lasting.

- **Post images, videos, and audio files.** Include links and references from other sources on the Web, but in every case, respect copyrights.

53C

Quick Points   You will learn to

➤ Identify the unique features of workplace writing.

MyWritingLab™   Visit mywritinglab.com for more resources on workplace writing.

54A   What is workplace writing?

Writing infuses most workplaces, from corporate offices and healthcare facilities to farms and factories. People write to coworkers, customers, vendors, or service providers using e-mails and letters.

54B   How do I write effective business e-mails and letters?

The purpose of business e-mails and letters is to relay information in a professional manner. Resist using the informal tone you use when you write to friends and family. As you plan your business writing, remember that the recipient can forward e-mails and smartphone texts, and copy letters for others to see, even though doing so is considered unethical. Remember, too, that a business document can take on legal significance; even your most casually written messages can become official evidence in court. You therefore want to write without gossip, put-downs, sarcasm, and any statements that can be misinterpreted now or in the future. Also, edit thoroughly and patiently for correct grammar (see Chapters 16–20) and punctuation (see Chapters 30–37) and always use GENDER-NEUTRAL LANGUAGE. Here's specific advice about the main types of business writing.

Business-Related E-Mails (For a sample, see Figure 54.1.)

- Emphasize key points with your choice of words, not with capital letters (which are read as shouting).
- Avoid slang, texting abbreviations, and informal words or expressions.
- Refrain from using all lowercase letters or all capital letters.
- Plan ahead to keep your content brief and concise, with short paragraphs.
- Address your e-mail to the correct person to prevent its needing to be forwarded.

Figure 54.1 Business e-mail.

To:	sherrel.ampadu@jpltech.com
From:	Chris Malinowitz <cmalinowitz@chateauby.com>
Subject:	Confirming Meeting Arrangements
Cc:	dmclusky@chateauby.com
Bcc:	
Attached:	C:\Documents and Settings\Desktop\Chateau Menus.doc

Dear Ms. Ampadu:

I am writing to confirm the final arrangements for your business meeting on June 17, 2013, at our conference center.

As you directed, we will set the room in ten round tables, each seating six. We will provide a podium and microphone, an LCD projector and screen, and a white board with markers. I understand that you will be bringing your own laptop. Our technician can help you set it up.

You indicated that you would like to provide lunch and refreshments at two breaks. Attached please find our menus. Please send me your lunch selections at least 48 hours in advance.

If you have questions or wish to make changes, I would be pleased to accommodate your needs. Thank you for choosing The Chateau at Brickyard.

Sincerely,

Chris Malinowitz
Catering Director, The Chateau at Brickyard

- Use the "cc" line to send your message to people who need to see your message but aren't expected to respond.
- Avoid sending "blind copies" ("bcc") because it's unprofessional and can easily be forwarded to others.
- Write a specific, not general, topic on the subject line.
- Start with a paragraph of only one or two sentences that directly and clearly express your main message; don't assume your subject line does this job.
- Use the next paragraph to present the details of your message, including any related background information.
- Conclude in the next paragraph by asking for a specific action or additional information, or if none is needed, very briefly recap your message.
- End with a complimentary closing (*Sincerely, Cordially*), followed by your full name and title.
- Forward an e-mail you receive only if you have asked permission of the writer to do so.

54B

Business-Related Letters (For a sample, see the job application letter in Figure 54.2.)

- Use 8½-by-11-inch white paper, unless your company has its own stationery. Fold it horizontally into thirds to fit a standard number 10 business envelope.
- Center your letterhead at the top of the page, including your full name, address, e-mail, and telephone number, unless your company has its own letterhead. Use the same font as in the body of your letter, though it can be one or two points larger.

Figure 54.2 Job application letter.

Monica A. Schickel
1817 Drevin Avenue
Denver, CO 80208
Cell phone: (303) 555-7722
E-mail: mnsschl@wordnet.com
Professional portfolio: www.schickelgraphics.net

May 3, 2012

Jaime Cisneros
Publications Director
R.L. Smith Consulting
2000 Wabash Avenue
Chicago, IL 60601

Dear Mr. Cisneros:

Please consider my application for the graphic designer position currently being advertised on your company's Web site. I believe that my professional experiences, education, and skills prepare me well for this opportunity.

Currently I am completing a paid internship at Westword, a weekly features and entertainment magazine in Denver, CO. My responsibilities have included designing advertisements, laying out sections, and editing photographs. My other related experience includes commissions as an illustrator and photographer. My professional portfolio at my Web site demonstrates the range and quality of my work. As my enclosed resume notes, I have additional experience in business environments.

Next month I will earn a BA in graphic design from The University of Denver, where my course of study has included extensive work in graphic design, photography, drawing, and illustration. My minor is in digital media studies and has included courses in Web design, video editing, and sound editing. I am expert at all the standard software applications that would be relevant to your position.

I would be pleased to provide my references and to interview at your convenience. The opportunities at R.L. Smith closely match my background and goals, and the prospect of joining your team in Chicago is exciting.

Sincerely,

Monica A. Schickel

Monica A. Schickel

54B

- Place the date flush left a double space below the letterhead.

- Place the full name and address of your recipient one double space below the date, also flush left. Use the exact name of your recipient. If you don't know the name, use the Internet or telephone to try to find it; if you can't locate it, use a gender-neutral title (never *Dear Sir* or *Dear Madam*), such as *Dear Sales Manager* or *Dear Human Resources Officer*.

- Format your paragraphs **block style**, single spaced within paragraphs and double spaced between paragraphs.

- Follow the pointers given above for business e-mails when you choose your words; craft clear, direct sentences; and end with a complimentary close.

Job Application Letters (For a sample, see Figure 54.2.)

- Follow the format and content pointers given above for business-related letters.

- Remember that this serves as a cover letter for your resume, so don't repeat what your resume says.

- Restrict it to one page.

- State in your first sentence the position for which you're applying.

- Explain in the next paragraph the precise benefit you will bring to the company; this will impress your reader by showing that you're familiar with the organization.

- Describe your qualifications and key attributes as they're directly relevant to the position you want, but don't repeat your resume. For example, you might say that you're energetic, self-disciplined, punctual, and eager to work hard.

- Tell the reader that you can easily be reached, that you have references to submit immediately upon request, and—with as much flexibility as possible—when you'd be available for an interview.

ESOL Tip: In some cultures, work-related correspondence is often sprinkled with elaborate language, many descriptive details, and even metaphors. Most American organizations, however, prefer correspondence that is clear and gets to the point quickly. ●

54C How do I write an effective resume?

A resume details your accomplishments and employment history. Its purpose is to help a potential employer determine whether you'll be a suitable candidate for the open position. Today, many employers have applicants upload their

54C

resumes to an employment Web site or send them as an e-mail attachment. Sometimes employers use software to scan electronic resumes, looking for keywords. For a sample resume, see Figure 54.3.

To make a favorable impression, here's specific advice for composing an effective resume that employers can receive in an e-mail, at a Web site, or as regular mail.

Scannable or plain-text resume

- Place your name, address, e-mail address, and telephone number centered at the top.
- Target the resume to the position you want. Help employers see your most significant attributes quickly and easily. If you're applying for a job as a computer programmer, you'll want to emphasize different facts than you would if you were applying for a job selling computers in an electronics store.
- Use headings to separate blocks of information, as appropriate: "Position Desired" or "Career Objective"; "Education"; "Experience"; "Licenses and Certifications"; "Related Experience"; "Honors and Awards," if any; "Publications and Presentations"; "Activities and Interests"; and "Special Abilities, Skills, and Knowledge."
- Start every line of text at the left margin.
- Try to fit all of the information on one page. If you need a second page, make sure the most important information is on the first page.
- Use high-quality paper that is white or off-white for print resumes.
- Make the resume easy to read. Label the sections clearly.
- Place your most recent job first in your work experience; list your most recent education degree, certificate, or enrollment first. Include only relevant information.
- Do not mention your religion or marital status. (However, such details are sometimes expected by cultures outside the United States.)
- Write telegraphically by starting with verb phrases, not with the word *I;* omit *a, an,* and *the.*
- Tell the truth. An employer who discovers you lied will most probably fire you.
- Include names of references, or state that you can provide them on request.
- Proofread carefully; even one spelling error or one formatting error can eliminate you from consideration.
- Be aware that scannable resumes are designed to be scanned by machines that digitize their content. This means that sophisticated software searches the content to match key terms to position requirements. As a result,

Figure 54.3   Sample resume.

MONICA A. SCHICKEL
1817 Drevin Avenue
Denver, CO 80208
Cell phone: (303) 555-7722
E-mail: mnsschl@wordnet.com
Professional portfolio: www.schickelgraphics.net

OBJECTIVE: Entry level position as a graphic designer or publications assistant

EXPERIENCE

9/12–present: Publications Intern (half-time; paid), *Westword* (Denver, CO)
• Design advertisements
• Prepare photographs for publications
• Lay out "Tempo" section
• Fact-check, edit, and proofread articles

6/10–8/12: Customer Service Representative, Wells Fargo Bank (Aurora CO).
• Sold accounts to customers; made all sales goals
• Created promotional posters

4/07–8/09: Evening Assistant Manager, McDonalds Restaurant (Longmont, CO).
• Supervised 7 cooks and counter workers
• Assured food and service quality

EDUCATION

8/12–present: Bachelor of Arts, The University of Denver, expected June 2014
Major: Graphic Arts; Minor: Digital Media Studies

8/10–5/12: AA General Education, Front Range Community College, May 2012

SKILLS AND SELECTED EXPERIENCES

• Expert in complete Adobe Creative Suite and complete Microsoft Office Suite
• Excellent Spanish language skills
• Illustrator and photographer; have completed several commissions, posted on my Web site given above
• Vice President, Student Residence Halls Association
• Cartoonist and Designer, *The DU Clarion* (campus newspaper)
• Excellent customer service skills

REFERENCES: Available on request

scannable resumes need a very simple design: don't use columns, different fonts, lines, graphics, or bold or italic fonts. Choose a clean sans serif font such as Arial or Geneva in a 10–12 point size. Include keywords that the computer can match to the job. Here is the keyword list Monica Schickel created for her scannable resume in Figure 54.3:

54C

SAMPLE OF KEYWORDS FOR RESUMES

Publications experience, graphic design, editing, photography, supervisor, customer service, digital media, excellent Spanish, Adobe creative suite, Photoshop, InDesign, Quark, CSS, Dreamweaver, Web design, illustrator, proofreader, Excel, Access, Publisher, newspaper, layout, sales, willing to relocate.

55 Writing with Others

■ ■ ■ ■ ■ ■

Quick Points   You will learn to

➤ Collaborate with other writers (pp. 480–483).
➤ Work with peer-response groups (pp. 481–483).
➤ Give useful feeback and benefit from others' help (pp. 481–484).

MyWritingLab™   Visit mywritinglab.com for more resources on writing with others.

55A   What is writing with others?

Although writing may often seem like a lonely act, a surprising amount of it depends on people working together. Any time you ask someone else to give you feedback for revision, you're working with others. The other person could be a friend, a classmate, a campus writing center tutor, or an instructor.

A more direct kind of writing with others happens when two or more people collaborate (work together) to complete a single project. Collaborative writing assignments are popular in college courses; small groups are commonly asked to brainstorm a topic together before individual writing tasks, to discuss various sides of a debatable topic, to share reactions to a reading, or so on. Collaborative experience you gain in college is a skill that employers value.

🚫 **Alert:** Some instructors and students use the terms *peer-response group* and *collaborative writing* to mean the same thing. In this handbook, we assign the terms to two different situations. We use *collaborative writing* (see 55B) for students writing a paper together in a group. We use *peer-response group* (see 55C) for students getting together in small groups to help one another write and revise. ●

55A

55B   How can I collaborate with other writers?

Three qualities are essential to collaborative writing.

1. **Careful planning.** Your group needs to decide when and how it will meet (in person, in a telephone call, in an online discussion); what steps it will follow and what the due dates will be; what technology you'll use; and who will be responsible for what. You'll also probably find it useful to assign people basic roles such as leader (or facilitator) and recorder (or secretary).

2. **Clear communication.** Open and honest communication is vital, and people need to build a productive and trusting atmosphere. Keep notes for every meeting. If people disagree over the group's decisions, the group should resolve that disagreement before moving on. You'll also find it effective to ask for regular brief reports from each group member.

3. **A fair division of labor.** Almost nothing causes bad feelings more quickly than when some group members feel like they're doing more than their share. There are two basic ways to divide tasks: (1) Divide according to the different steps in the writing process. (2) Assign part of the project to each person.

55C   How can I give useful feedback to others?

There are two main ways to give feedback to other writers. One is in a small group of three to five people (usually), who together discuss each group member's draft out loud. Another way is to work in pairs, providing oral or written comments for each other.

■ Working in peer-response groups

A peer is an "equal": another writer like you. Participating in a **peer-response group** makes you part of a respected tradition of colleagues helping colleagues. Professional writers often seek comments from other writers to improve their rough drafts. As a member of a peer-response group, you're not expected to be a writing expert. Rather, you're expected to offer responses as a practiced reader and as a fellow student writer who understands what writers go through.

   Peer-response groups are set up in different ways.

1. Students pass around and read one another's drafts silently, writing down reactions or questions in the margins or on a response form created by the instructor.

2. Students read drafts aloud, and then others respond orally or in writing.

55C

3. In yet another arrangement, students provide focused responses to only one or two features of each draft (perhaps each member's thesis statement, or topic sentences and supporting details, for example).

If your instructor gives you directions, follow them carefully. The guidelines in Quick Box 55.1 will also help you.

Quick Box 55.1

Guidelines for participating in peer-response groups

Always take an upbeat, constructive attitude, whether you're responding to someone else's writing or receiving responses from others.

- Think of yourself as a coach, not a judge.

- Consider all writing by your peers as "works in progress."

- After hearing or reading a peer's writing, summarize it briefly to check that both of you are clear about what the peer actually wrote. (It's useful to know when you thought you were saying one thing but people thought you meant something else.)

- Start with what you think is well done. No one likes to hear only negative comments.

- Be honest in your suggestions for improvement.

- Base your responses on an understanding of the writing process, and remember that you're reading drafts, not finished products. All writing can be revised.

- Give concrete and specific responses. General comments such as "This is good" or "This is weak" don't offer much help. Describe specifically what is good or weak.

- Follow your instructor's system for recording your comments so that your peer can recall what you said. For example, one group member might take notes from the discussion; the group should take care that they're accurate.

■ Giving peer response as an individual

Often an instructor will have two people exchange drafts and provide responses and suggestions to each other. All the general guidelines for peer response in groups apply to situations when you're the only person giving feedback, especially being helpful, specific, and polite.

You might find it useful to play a role if you feel awkward about giving reactions or suggestions to a classmate—especially if you think that some critical comments will help revision. For example, instead of responding as yourself, pretend that you're a skeptical member of the writer's target audience. Respond as that person would, even in his or her voice. However, you should still aim to be constructive. Of course, you could also take the opposite role, responding as someone who agrees with the writer; that role can be particularly helpful if you personally disagree with a draft's position. If you're playing a role as you respond, you should make that clear to the writer.

As with peer response, your instructor may have you use a response form or follow a set of questions. Here are some specific questions you might find useful for giving peer feedback:

- What part of the paper was most interesting or effective?
- If you had to remove one paragraph, which would you sacrifice, and why?
- If you had to rearrange two parts of the paper, which would you move, and why?
- What is one additional fact, argument, or piece of information that might improve the paper?

Another good strategy is for the writer to generate a couple of questions that he or she would particularly like the reviewer to answer. Avoid questions that require only a *yes* or *no* response. For example:

| **NOT HELPFUL** | Is paragraph two on page three effective? |
| **HELPFUL** | How can I improve paragraph two on page three? |

| **NOT HELPFUL** | Do you like my tone in the paper? |
| **HELPFUL** | How would you describe my tone in this paper? |

Instead of answering specific questions, the instructor might ask you simply to write to the author about the strengths and weaknesses of the draft. Such responses can take the form of a letter to the author. Our students usually find that if they're thoughtful while writing open responses to others, they get useful responses in return.

55D   How can I benefit from others' help?

We offer you four pieces of advice from our own experiences.

1. Keep in mind that most students don't like to criticize their peers. They worry about being impolite or inaccurate, or losing someone's friendship. Try, therefore, to cultivate an attitude that encourages your peers to respond as freely and as helpfully as possible. It's particularly important to show that you can listen without getting upset or defensive.

55D

2. Realize that most people can be a little defensive about even the best intentioned and most tactful criticism. Of course, if a comment is purposely mean, you and all the others in your peer-response group have every right to say so.

3. Listen and resist any urge to interrupt during a comment or to jump in to react. A common rule in many writing workshops is that the paper's author must remain silent until the group has finished its responses and discussion.

4. Ask for clarification if a comment isn't clear or is too general.

Finally, no matter what anyone says about your writing, you keep ownership of your writing always, and you don't have to make every suggested change. Use only the comments that you think can move you closer to reaching your intended AUDIENCE and PURPOSE. Of course, if a comment from your instructor points out a definite problem and you choose to ignore it, that could affect your grade.

ESOL Tip: International students might feel especially uncomfortable about responding to peers. Please know, however, that peer-response groups are fairly common in US schools and at jobs because people usually think that "two heads are better than one." Sharing and questioning others' ideas—as well as how they are expressed in writing—is an honorable tradition in North American colleges, so please feel free to participate fully and politely. In fact, some instructors grade students on their participation in such activities. ●

TERMS GLOSSARY

Words printed in SMALL CAPITAL LETTERS in your *Quick Access Brief* indicate important terms that are defined in this glossary. The parenthetical references with each definition tell you the handbook sections where each term is most fully discussed. If you can't find a term's definition in this glossary, look for the term in the Index.

absolute phrase A phrase containing a subject and a participle that modifies an entire sentence: *The semester* [subject] *being* [present participle of *be*] *over, the campus looks deserted.* (16M)

academic writing The writing people do for college courses and as scholarship published in print and online journals. (Ch. 7)

action verb A verb that describes an action or occurrence done by or to the subject. (25E)

active reading Annotating reading to make connections between your prior knowledge and the author's ideas. (3B)

active voice When a verb shows that its action or the condition expressed is done *by* the subject. The *active voice* stands in contrast with the *passive voice*, which conveys that the verb's action or condition is done *to* the subject. (17G)

adjective A word that describes or limits (modifies) a noun, a pronoun, or a word group functioning as a noun: *silly* joke, *three* trumpets. (16E, Ch. 20)

adjective clause A dependent clause, also known as a *relative clause*, that modifies a noun or pronoun that comes before it. An adjective clause begins with a relative word (such as *who, which, that,* or *where*). Also see *clause*. (16N)

advanced searches Also called *guided searches.* Allow you to search by entering information in a form online. (12B)

adverb A word that describes or limits (modifies) verbs, adjectives, other adverbs, phrases, or clauses: *loudly, very, nevertheless, there.* (16F, Ch. 20)

adverb clause A dependent clause beginning with a subordinating conjunction that establishes the relationship in meaning between itself and its independent clause. An adverb clause can modify an independent clause's verb or an entire independent clause. (16N)

agreement The concept of matching number and person of a subject and verb (Ch. 18) and of a pronoun and its antecedent (19A–19E). See also *antecedent.*

analogy An explanation of the unfamiliar in terms of the familiar, often comparing things not usually associated with each other. Analogy is a rhetorical strategy useful for developing a paragraph (5E). Unlike a simile, which uses *like* or *as* in making a comparison, an analogy does not use such words. (28E)

analysis A process of critical thinking, sometimes called *division*, that divides a whole into its component parts that shows how the parts interrelate. Analysis is a rhetorical strategy useful for developing paragraphs. (5E)

annotated bibliography Bibliography in which listed sources are accompanied by summaries of, or comments about, each source. (13D)

antecedent The noun or pronoun to which a pronoun refers. (16B)

APA style *APA* is the abbreviation for the American Psychological Association. APA style specifies the format and the form of citation and documentation used in source-based papers in many academic disciplines, especially psychology and most other social sciences. (Ch. 15)

appositive A word or group of words that renames the noun or noun phrase coming immediately before or after it: *my favorite month, **October***. (16L)

argumentative writing Using rhetorical strategies to convince one's readers to agree with the writer's position about a topic open to debate. (Ch. 9)

articles Also called *determiners* or *noun markers*, the words *a, an*, and *the*. *A* and *an* are indefinite articles; *the* is a definite article. Also see *determiner*. (Ch. 43)

assertion A statement that expresses a point of view about a topic. Often used by writers to develop a thesis statement. (4F)

audience The readers to whom a written document is primarily directed. (4C)

auxiliary verb Also known as a *helping verb*, a form of *be, do, have*, or one of the modal verbs. Auxiliary verbs combine with main verbs to express tense, mood, and voice. Also see *modal auxiliary verbs*. (17C)

balanced sentences Sentences consisting of two short independent clauses that serve to compare or contrast. (27D)

bias Material that is slanted toward beliefs or attitudes and away from facts or evidence. (2A)

blog Shortened form of "Web log," an online journal usually updated on a fairly regular basis. (53B)

body paragraphs Paragraphs in an essay or other document that come between the introductory and concluding paragraphs. (5D)

Boolean expressions Words such as *AND, OR*, and *NOT* that researchers can use in a search engine to create keyword combinations that narrow and refine their searches. (12B)

brainstorming Listing all ideas that come to mind on a topic, and then grouping the ideas by whatever patterns emerge. (4E)

call number Identification number, usually according to the Dewey Decimal System, used to store and retrieve an individual book or other library material. (12B)

case The form of a noun or pronoun that shows whether it's functioning as a subject, an object, or a possessive in a particular context. Nouns change form in the possessive case only (*city* can be a subject or object; *city's* is the possessive form). Also see *pronoun case*. (19J–19S, 33A)

case study Research that relies on the careful, detailed observation and analysis of one person or a small group of people. (50B)

cause and effect The relationship between outcomes (effects) and the reasons for them (causes), which is a rhetorical strategy for developing paragraphs. (5E)

citation Information that identifies a source referred to in a piece of writing. Also see *documentation*. (Chs. 14 and 15)

classical argument An argument with a structure consisting of introduction, thesis statement, background, evidence and reasoning, response to opposing views, and conclusion. (9A)

classification A rhetorical strategy that organizes information by grouping items according to their underlying shared characteristics. (5E)

clause A group of words containing a subject and a predicate. A clause that delivers full meaning is called an *independent* (or *main*) *clause*. A clause that lacks full meaning by itself is called a *dependent* (or *subordinate*) *clause*. Also see *adjective clause, adverb clause, nonrestrictive element, noun clause, restrictive element*. (16N)

cliché An overused, worn-out phrase that has lost its capacity to communicate effectively: *soft as a kitten, lived to a ripe old age*. (28D)

close reading The practice of reading carefully, analytically, and critically. (3B)

clustering Also called *mapping*, it is an invention technique based on thinking visually about a topic and drawing attached balloons for its increasingly specific subdivisions. (4E)

coherence The written or spoken progression from one idea to another using transitional expressions, pronouns, selective repetition, and/or parallelism to make connections between ideas explicit. (5D)

collective noun A noun that names a group of people or things: *family, committee*. (18H)

colloquial language Casual or conversational language. (28D)

comma splice Sometimes called a *comma fault*, the error that occurs when a comma alone connects two independent clauses. (Ch. 22)

common noun A noun that names a general group, place, person, or thing: *dog, house*. (38C)

comparative The form of a descriptive adjective or adverb that expresses a different degree of intensity between two things: *bluer, less blue; more easily, less easily*. Also see *positive, superlative*. (20D)

comparison and contrast A rhetorical strategy for organizing and developing paragraphs by discussing a subject's similarities (by comparing them) and differences (by contrasting them). (5E)

complement A grammatical element after a verb that completes the predicate, such as a direct object after an action verb or a noun or adjective after a linking verb. Also see *object complement* and *subject complement*. (16L, 17A)

complete predicate See *predicate*.

complete subject See *subject*.

complex sentence See *sentence*.

compound-complex sentence See *sentence*.

compound predicate See *predicate*.

compound sentence See *sentence*.

compound subject See *subject*.

compound word Two or more words placed together to express one concept, such as "fuel-efficient" or "proofread." (37C)

conciseness Writing that is direct and to the point. Its opposite, which is undesirable, is *wordiness*. (Ch. 25)

concluding paragraph Final paragraph of an essay, report, or other document. (5F)

conjunction A word that connects or otherwise establishes a relationship between two or more words, phrases, or clauses. Also see *coordinating conjunction, correlative conjunction, subordinating conjunction*. (16H)

conjunctive adverb An adverb that expresses a relationship between words, such as addition, contrast, comparison, and the like. (16F, Quick Box 16.5)

connotation Ideas implied, not directly stated, by a word giving emotional overtones. (28C)

contraction A word in which an apostrophe takes the place of one or more omitted letters: *can't, don't, I'm, isn't, it's, let's, they're, we've, won't*, and others. (33E)

coordinating adjectives Two or more adjectives that carry equal weight in modifying a noun (**big, friendly** dog). The order of coordinating adjectives can be changed without changing the meaning. Also see *cumulative adjectives*. (30E)

coordinating conjunction A conjunction that joins two or more grammatically equivalent structures: *and, or, for, nor, but, so, yet*. (16H)

coordination The use of grammatically equivalent forms to show a balance in, or sequence of, ideas. (26A)

correlative conjunction A pair of words that joins equivalent grammatical structures: *both . . . and; either . . . or; not only . . . but also*. (16H)

count noun A noun that names items that can be counted: *radio, street, idea, fingernail*. (42A)

critical reading A parallel process to critical thinking in which readers think about what they are reading during and after reading. (Ch. 3)

critical thinking A form of thinking in which you take control of your conscious thought processes by judging evidence, considering assumptions, making connections, and analyzing implications. (2A)

cue words   Words that tell what an assignment suggests that students accomplish in their writing. (48B)

cumulative adjectives   Adjectives that build up meaning from word to word as they get closer to the noun (*familiar rock tunes*). The order of cumulative adjectives cannot be changed without destroying the meaning. Also see *coordinating adjectives*. (30E)

dangling modifier   A modifier that illogically attaches its meaning to the rest of its sentence, either because it is closer to another noun or pronoun than to its true subject or because its true subject is not expressed in the sentence. (24E)

database   An electronic collection of citations and, frequently, articles or documents on a particular subject matter or field, or about a specific body of sources. (12A)

definition   A rhetorical strategy that defines or gives the meaning of terms or ideas. (5E)

deliberate repetition   A writing technique that uses the conscious repetition of a word, phrase, or other element to emphasize a point or to achieve a specific effect on readers. (5D)

denotation   The dictionary definition of a word. (28C)

dependent clause   Also called *subordinate clause*, a subordinate clause can't stand alone as an independent grammatical unit. If it tries to, it is a sentence fragment. Also see *adjective clause, adverb clause, noun clause*. (16N)

description   A statement that paints a picture in words. (5E)

descriptive adjective   An adjective that describes the condition or properties of the noun it is modifying and (except for a very few words, such as *dead* and *unique*) has comparative and superlative forms: *flat, flatter, flattest*. (16E)

descriptive adverb   An adverb that describes the condition or properties of whatever it is modifying and has comparative and superlative forms: *happily, more happily, most happily*. (16F)

descriptive writing   Paints a picture in words. (5E)

determiner   A word or word group, traditionally identified as an *adjective*, that limits a noun by telling whether a noun is general (**a** noun) or specific (**the** tree). (16E and Quick Box 16.4)

dialect   See *regional language*.

diction   Word choice. (28A)

direct address   Words naming a person or group being spoken to: *"The solution, **my friends**, is in your hands."* (19H)

direct discourse   Words that repeat speech or conversation exactly, always enclosed in quotation marks. Also see *indirect discourse*. (23E, 34C)

direct object   A noun, pronoun, or group of words functioning as a noun that receives the action (completes the meaning) of a transitive verb. (16K)

direct question   A sentence that asks a question and ends with a question mark: *Are you going to the concert?* (35B)

direct quotation   See *quotation*.

documentation   The acknowledgment of a source's words and ideas being used in any written document by giving full and accurate information about the source of the words used and about where those words can be found. Also see *documentation style*. (14A, 15A)

documentation style   Any of various systems for providing information about the source of words, information, and ideas that a writer quotes, paraphrases, or summarizes from any source other than the writer. Documentation styles discussed in this handbook are MLA (Ch. 14) and APA (Ch. 15).

document design   The arrangement of words, images, graphics, and space on a page or screen. (6A)

double negative   A nonstandard structure that uses two negative modifiers rather than one. (20B)

drafting   The part of the writing process in which writers compose ideas in sentences and paragraphs, thereby creating *drafts*.

A *discovery draft* is what some writers call an early, rough draft. (4A)

edited American English   Written usage of the American English language, expected in academic writing, that conforms to mainstream rules of grammar, sentence structure, punctuation, spelling, and mechanics. Sometimes it is referred to as *standard English*, but given the diversity of dialects in the United States today, the term *standard* is less descriptive than it once was. (28D)

editing   The part of the writing process in which writers check a document for the technical correctness in edited American English of its grammar, sentence structure, punctuation, spelling, and mechanics. (4A, 4J)

ellipsis points   Group of three or four spaced periods to help fit quotations smoothly into your sentences. Ellipsis points indicate that words have been omitted from the original source. When used, you want to be sure that the remaining words accurately reflect the source's meaning and that your sentences flow smoothly. (36D)

elliptical construction   A sentence structure that deliberately omits words that can be filled in because they repeat words already in the sentence. (23G)

emotional appeal   Rhetorical strategy intended to evoke empathy and compassion. Its Greek name is *pathos*. (2B)

ethical appeal   Rhetorical strategy intended to evoke confidence in your credibility, reliability, and trustworthiness. Its Greek name is *ethos*. (2B)

euphemism   Language that attempts to blunt certain realities by speaking of them in "nice" or "tactful" words. (28D)

evaluation   Examining new ideas independently and fairly, avoiding biases and prejudices that you might have accepted without question before. (3A)

evidence   Facts, data, and examples used to support a writer's assertions and conclusions. (12A)

example   Specific incident or instance provided to illustrate a point. (5E)

expletive construction   The phrase *there is (are), there was (were), it is (was)* at the beginning of a clause, which postpones the subject: *It is Mars that we hope to reach* (a better version would be *We hope to reach Mars*). (25C)

expletives   Words or phrases, such as *there are* or *it is*, that postpone the subject. (18H)

faulty predication   A grammatically illogical combination of subject and predicate: *The purpose of television was invented to entertain.* (23F)

field research   Primary research that involves going into, and taking notes on, real-life situations to observe, survey, interview, or be part of some activity. (12H)

figurative language   Words that carry other meanings in addition to their literal meanings, sometimes by making unusual comparisons. Also see *analogy, irony, metaphor, personification, overstatement, simile, understatement.* (28E)

first person   See *person*.

focused freewriting   Freewriting that starts with a set topic or builds on one sentence taken from earlier freewriting. (4E)

formal outline   An outline that lays out the topic levels of generalities or hierarchies and marks them with roman numerals, letters, and numbers indented in a carefully prescribed fashion. (4G)

frame   A guide that suggests how to develop or structure an essay or assignment. (Ch. 7)

freewriting   Writing nonstop for a period of time to generate ideas by free association of thoughts. (4E)

future perfect progressive tense   The form of the future perfect tense that describes an action or condition ongoing until some specific future time: *I will have been talking when you arrive.* (17E)

future perfect tense   The tense indicating that an action will have been completed or a condition will have ended by a specified point in the future: *I will have talked to him by the time you arrive.* (17E)

future progressive tense   The form of the future tense showing that a future action will continue for some time: *I will be talking when you arrive.* (17E)

future tense   The form of a verb, made with the simple form and either *shall* or *will*, expressing an action yet to be taken or a condition not yet experienced: *I will talk.* (17E)

gender   The classification of words as masculine, feminine, or neuter. In English, a few pronouns show changes in gender in third-person singular: *he, him, his; she, her, hers; it, its, its;* also, a few nouns that define roles change form to show gender difference (*prince, princess*), but most no longer do (*actor, police officer, chairperson*). (28C)

gender-neutral language   Nonsexist language. (28C)

general reference work   The starting point for many college researchers that help identify keywords useful in searching for subject headings and catalogs—and for finding examples and verifying facts. (12D)

gerund   A present participle functioning as a noun: **Walking** *is good exercise.* Also see *verbal*. (16D, Quick Box 16.3, Ch. 46)

gerund phrase   A gerund, along with its modifiers and/or object(s), which functions as a subject or an object: **Walking the dog** *can be good exercise.* See also *gerund*. (16M)

helping verb   See *auxiliary verb*.

homonyms   Words spelled differently that sound alike: *to, too, two.* (29D)

idiom   A word, phrase, or other construction that has a different meaning from its usual or literal meaning: *He lost his head. She hit the ceiling.* (Ch. 45)

illustration   Provides support for the main idea of a paragraph by giving several examples, often ones that call on the five senses to picture them. (5E)

imperative mood   The grammatical form that expresses commands and direct requests, using the simple form of the verb and almost always implying but not expressing the subject: *Watch out.* (17F)

indefinite pronoun   A pronoun, such as *all, anyone, each*, and others, that refers to a nonspecific person or thing. (18E, 19D)

independent clause   A clause that can stand alone as an independent grammatical unit. (16N)

indicative mood   The grammatical form of verbs used for statements about real things or highly likely ones: *I think Grace will be arriving today.* (17F)

indirect discourse   Reported speech or conversation that does not use the exact structure of the original and so is not enclosed in quotation marks. (23E, 34C)

indirect object   A noun, pronoun, or group of words functioning as a noun that tells to whom, or for whom, the action expressed by a transitive verb was done. (16K)

indirect question   A sentence that reports a question and ends with a period, not a question mark: *I asked if you are going.* (35A)

indirect quotation   A quotation that reports a source's words without quotation marks, unless any words are repeated exactly from the source. It requires documentation of the source to avoid plagiarism. See *indirect discourse*.

infinitive   A verbal made of the simple form of a verb and usually, but not always, preceded by the word *to*. It functions as a noun, an adjective, or an adverb. (16D, Ch. 46)

infinitive phrase   An infinitive, with its modifiers and/or object, which functions as a noun, an adjective, or an adverb. (16M)

informal outline   Outline that doesn't follow the rules of a *formal outline*. (4G)

intensive pronoun   A pronoun that ends in *-self* and that intensifies its antecedent: *Vida **himself** argued against it.* Also see *reflexive pronoun*. (19S)

interjection   An emotion-conveying word that is treated as a sentence, starting with a capital letter and ending with an exclamation point or a period: *Oh! Ouch.* (16I)

in-text citation Source information placed in parentheses within the body of a research paper. Also see *citation, parenthetical documentation.* (Chs. 14 and 15)

intransitive verb A verb that does not take a direct object. (17A)

introductory paragraph Opening paragraph of document that orients readers and generates interest in the topic or ideas that follow. (5B)

inverted word order In contrast to standard order, the main or auxiliary verb comes before the subject in a sentence: *In walks* [verb] *the president* [subject]. Most questions and some exclamations use inverted word order: *Did* [verb] *you* [subject] *see the circus?* (18H, 27H, Ch. 44)

irony Using words to imply the opposite of their usual meaning. (28E)

irregular verb A verb that forms the past tense and past participle other than by adding *-ed* or *-d.* (17B)

jargon Specialized vocabulary of a particular field or group that is not familiar to a general reader. (28D)

keywords Main words in a source's title, or that the author or an editor has identified as central to that source. Sometimes keywords are called *descriptors* or *identifiers.* (12B)

levels of formality The degrees of formality of language, reflected by word choice and sentence structure. A formal level is used for ceremonial and other occasions when stylistic flourishes are appropriate. A semiformal level, which is neither too formal nor too casual, is acceptable for most academic writing. (28D)

library catalog A database that lists all books and other items owned by a particular library. (12A)

linking verb A main verb that links a subject with a subject complement that renames or describes the subject. Linking verbs convey a state of being, relate to the senses, or indicate a condition. (Quick Box 17.1, 18H)

logical appeal Rhetorical strategy that intends to show readers that the argument depends on formal reasoning, including providing evidence and drawing conclusions from premises. Its Greek name is *logos.* (2B)

logical fallacies Flaws in reasoning that lead to illogical statements that need to be rejected in logical arguments. (2D)

long quotation A direct quotation that in an MLA-style source-based paper occupies, if it is prose, more than four lines of type, and if it is poetry, more than three lines of the poem. In an APA-style source-based paper, if it is more than forty words of prose. Long quotations are block indented on the page. Also see *short quotation.* (34B)

main clause See *independent clause.*

main verb A verb that expresses action, occurrence, or state of being and that shows mood, tense, voice, number, and person. (16C)

mechanics Conventions governing the use of capital letters, italics, abbreviations, and numbers. (Chs. 38–41)

metaphor A comparison implying similarity between two things: *a mop of hair.* A metaphor does not use the words *like* or *as,* which are used in a simile to make a comparison explicit: *hair like a mop.* (28E)

misplaced modifier Describing or limiting words that are wrongly positioned in a sentence so that their message either is illogical or relates to the wrong word(s). (Ch. 24)

mixed construction A sentence that unintentionally changes from one grammatical structure to another incompatible grammatical structure, so that the result is garbled meaning. (23F)

mixed metaphor Inconsistent metaphors in a single expression: *You'll get into hot water skating on thin ice.* (28E)

MLA style *MLA,* the abbreviation for the Modern Language Association, specifies the format and the form of citation and documentation in source-based papers in English and some other humanities courses. (Ch. 14)

modal auxiliary verb   A group of auxiliary verbs that communicate possibility, likelihood, obligation, permission, or ability: *can, might, would.* (17C, Ch. 47)

modifier   A word or group of words functioning as an adjective or adverb to describe or limit (modify) another word or word group. (16L)

mood   The attribute of verbs showing a writer's orientation to an action by the way the verbs are used. English has three moods: imperative, indicative, and subjunctive. Also see *imperative mood, indicative mood, subjunctive mood.* (17F)

narrative writing   Writing that tells a story. (5E)

noncount noun   A noun that names "uncountable" things: *water, time.* (42A)

nonrestrictive clause   A clause that is not essential to the sentence's meaning. (30F)

nonrestrictive element   A descriptive word, phrase, or dependent clause that provides information not essential to understanding the basic message of the element it modifies; it is therefore set off by commas. Also see *restrictive element.* (30F)

nonsexist language   See *gender-neutral language.*

noun   A word that names a person, place, thing, or idea. Nouns function as subjects, objects, or complements. (16A)

noun clause   A dependent clause that functions as a subject, object, or complement. (16N)

noun phrase   A noun along with its modifiers functioning as a subject, object, or complement. (16M)

number   The attribute of some words indicating whether they refer to one (singular) or more than one (plural). (18A, 19A, 23A)

object   A noun, pronoun, or group of words that receives the action of the verb

(*direct object;* 16K); tells to whom or for whom something is done (*indirect object;* 16K); or completes the meaning of a preposition (*object of a preposition;* 16G).

object complement   A noun or adjective renaming or describing a direct object after certain verbs, including *call, consider, name, elect,* and *think:* Some *call* daily **joggers** [object] **fanatics** [object complement]. (16L)

objective case   The case of a noun or pronoun functioning as a direct object, an indirect object, an object of a preposition, or a verbal. A few pronouns change form to show the objective case (for example, *him, her, whom*). Also see *case.* (19J)

outline   A technique for laying out ideas for writing in an orderly fashion that shows levels of generality. An outline can be formal or informal. (4G)

overstatement   Deliberate exaggeration for emphasis; also called *hyperbole.* (28E)

paragraph   A group of sentences that work together to develop a unit of thought. (5A)

paragraph development   Rhetorical strategies for arranging and organizing paragraphs using specific, concrete details (RENNS) to support a generalization in the paragraph. (5D)

parallelism   The use of equivalent grammatical forms or matching sentence structures to express equivalent ideas: *singing* and *dancing.* (5D, 27A)

paraphrase   A restatement of a source's ideas in language and sentence structure different from that of the original. (13I)

parenthetical documentation   Citation of source information enclosed in parentheses that follows quoted, paraphrased, or summarized material from another source. Such citations alert readers that the material comes from a source other than the writer. Parenthetical documentation and a list of bibliographic information at the end of a source-based paper together document the writer's use of sources. (Chs. 14 and 15)

participial phrase   A phrase that contains a present participle or a past participle and any modifiers and that functions as an adjective. Also see *verbal*. (16M, 27G)

participle   A verb form that indicates the present tense (*-ing* ending) or the past tense (*-ed, -d, -n,* or *-t* ending). A participle can also function as an adjective or an adverb. Also see *present participle, past participle*. (Chs. 16–17)

parts of speech   The names and definitions of types of words that give you a vocabulary for identifying words and understanding how language works to create meaning. (16A–16I)

passive voice   The *passive voice* emphasizes the action, in contrast to the *active voice*, which emphasizes the doer of the action. If the subject is mentioned in the sentence, it usually appears as the object of the preposition *by: I was frightened by the thunder* (the active voice form is *The thunder frightened me*). (17G)

past participle   The third principal part of a verb, the past participle is formed in regular verbs by adding *-d* or *-ed* to the simple form to create the past tense. In irregular verbs, past and past participle formation varies by adding a letter or two to the simple form: *break, broke, broken*. The past participle functions as a verb only with an auxiliary verb as its partner. (17B)

past perfect progressive tense   The past-perfect-tense form that describes an ongoing condition in the past that has been ended by something stated in the sentence: *Before the curtains caught fire, **I had been talking***. (17E)

past perfect tense   The tense that describes a condition or action that started in the past, continued for a while, and then ended in the past: *I had talked to him before*. (17E)

past progressive tense   The past-tense form that shows the continuing nature of a past action: *I was talking when you walked in*. (17E)

past-tense verb   The second principal part of a verb. In regular verbs, the past tense is formed by adding *-d* or *-ed* to the simple form. In irregular verbs, the formation of the past tense varies from merely adding a letter or two to the simple form: *break, broke; see, saw*. (17B)

peer-response group   Groups of students in your class who gather together to read and constructively react to each other's writing. (55C)

perfect tenses   The three tenses—the present perfect (*I have talked*), the past perfect (*I had talked*), and the future perfect (*I will have talked*)—that help to show complex time relationships between two clauses. (17E)

periodicals   Magazines, newspapers, and journals published on a regular basis. (12B)

person   The attribute of nouns and pronouns showing who or what acts or experiences an action. *First person* is the one speaking (*I, we*); *second person* is the one being spoken to (*you*); and *third person* is the person or thing spoken about (*he, she, it, they*). All nouns are third person. (18A, 23A)

personal pronoun   A pronoun that refers to people or things: *I, you, them, it*. (19K)

personification   Assigning a human trait to something not human. (28E)

phrasal verb   A verb that combines with one or more prepositions to deliver its meaning: *ask **out**, look **into***. (Ch. 45)

phrase   A group of related words that does not contain a subject and predicate and thus cannot stand alone as an independent grammatical unit. A phrase can function as a noun, a verb, or a modifier. (16M)

plagiarism   A writer's presenting another person's words or ideas without giving credit to that person. Writers use documentation systems to give proper credit to sources in standardized ways recognized by scholarly communities. Plagiarism is a serious offense, a form of intellectual dishonesty that can lead to course failure or expulsion from an institution. (13G)

planning   Early part of the writing process in which writers gather ideas. (4A)

plural   See *number*.

possessive case   The case of a noun or pronoun that shows ownership or possession. Also see *case*. (19J, 33A)

possessive pronoun   A pronoun that shows ownership: *his, hers*, and so on. (33C)

predicate   The part of a sentence that contains the verb and tells what the subject is doing or experiencing or what is being done to the subject. A *simple predicate* contains only the main verb and any auxiliary verb(s). A *complete predicate* contains the verb, its modifiers, objects, and other related words. A *compound predicate* contains two or more verbs, modifiers, objects, and other related words. (16J)

prefix   Letters added at the beginning of a root word to create a new word: *pre-test*. (37B)

preposition   A word that conveys a relationship, often of space or time, between the noun or pronoun following it and other words in the sentence: *under, over, in, out*. The noun or pronoun following a preposition is called the *object of the preposition*. (16G, Ch. 45)

prepositional phrase   A group of words beginning with a preposition and including a noun or pronoun, which is called the *object of the preposition*. (16M)

present participle   A verb's *-ing* form: *talking, singing*. Used with auxiliary verbs, present participles function as main verbs. Used without auxiliary verbs, present participles function as nouns or adjectives. (17B)

present perfect progressive tense   The present-perfect-tense form that describes something ongoing in the past that is likely to continue into the future: *I have been talking for a while.* (17E)

present perfect tense   The tense indicating that an action or its effects, begun or perhaps completed in the past, continue into the present: *I had talked to her before you arrived.* (17E)

present progressive tense   The present-tense form of the verb that indicates something taking place at the time it is written or spoken about: *I am talking to her right now.* (17E)

present tense   The tense that describes what is happening, what is true at the moment, and/or what is consistently true. It uses the simple form (*I talk*) and the *-s* form in the third-person singular (*he talks, she talks, it talks*). (17E)

present-tense participial phrase   A verbal phrase that uses the *-ing* form of a verb and functions only as a modifier (whereas a gerund phrase functions only as a noun). (16M)

primary sources   Also called *primary evidence*, these sources are "firsthand" work such as written accounts of experiments and observations by the researchers who conducted them; taped accounts, interviews, and newspaper accounts by direct observers; autobiographies, diaries, and journals; and expressive works such as poems, plays, fiction, and essays. They stand in contrast to *secondary sources*. (12A)

process writing   Presents instructions, lays out steps in a procedure, explains how objects work, or describes human behaviors. (5E)

progressive forms   Verb forms made, in all tenses, with the present participle and forms of the verb *be* as an auxiliary. Progressive forms show that an action, occurrence, or state of being is ongoing: *I am singing; he was dancing.* (17E)

pronoun   A word that takes the place of a noun and functions in the same ways that nouns do. Types of pronouns are demonstrative, indefinite, intensive, interrogative, personal, reciprocal, reflexive, and relative. (16B)

proofreading   Carefully scrutinizing your final draft to fix typing errors and missing/repeated small words. (4A)

pronoun–antecedent agreement   The match required between a pronoun and its antecedent in number and person, including personal pronouns and their gender. (19A)

pronoun case The way a pronoun changes form to reflect its use as the agent of action (*subjective case*), the thing being acted upon (*objective case*), or the thing showing ownership (*possessive case*). (19J–19S)

pronoun reference The relationship between a pronoun and its antecedent. (19F–19I)

proper adjective An adjective formed from a proper noun: *Victorian, American.* (16E)

proper noun A noun that names specific people, places, or things; it is always capitalized: *Tom Thumb, Buick.* (38C)

purpose Purposes for writing vary: to narrate, give information, analyze a text, argue or persuade, and evaluate. (4C)

quotation Repeating or reporting another person's words. *Direct quotation* repeats another's words exactly and encloses them in quotation marks. *Indirect quotation* reports another's words without quotation marks except around any words if they are repeated exactly from the source. Both direct and indirect quotation require documentation of the source to avoid plagiarism. (13H)

References The title of a list of sources at the end of a research paper or scholarly article or other written work used in many documentation styles, especially that of APA. (15D, 15E)

reflexive pronoun A pronoun that ends in *-self* and that reflects back to its antecedent: *They claim to support **themselves**.* (19S)

regional language Language specific to a particular geographic area. (28D)

regular verb A verb that forms its past tense and past participle by adding *-ed* or *-d* to the simple form. Most English verbs are regular. (17B)

relative adverb An adverb that introduces an adjective clause: *The garage **where** I usually park my car was full.* (16F)

relative clause See *adjective clause.*

relative pronoun A pronoun—such as *who, which, that, whom, whoever,* and a few others—that introduces an adjective clause or sometimes a noun clause. (16N)

RENNS A memory aid for the specific, concrete details used to support a topic sentence in a paragraph: reasons, examples, names, numbers, and the five sentences. (5D)

research A systematic process of gathering information to answer a question. (13A)

research log A diary of your research process; useful for keeping yourself organized and on track. (13B)

research question A question that provides a clear focus for your research and a goal for your writing process. (13A)

restrictive clause A dependent clause that gives information necessary to distinguish whatever it modifies from others in the same category. In contrast to a nonrestrictive clause, a restrictive clause is not set off with commas. (30F)

restrictive element A word, phrase, or dependent clause that provides information essential to the understanding of the element it modifies. In contrast to a nonrestrictive element, a restrictive element is not set off with commas. Also see *nonrestrictive clause.* (30F)

revising A part of the writing process in which writers evaluate their rough drafts and, on the basis of their assessments, rewrite by adding, cutting, replacing, moving, and often totally recasting material. (4A, 4I)

rhetoric The art and skill of speaking and writing effectively. (2B)

rhetorical strategies Various techniques for presenting ideas to deliver a writer's intended message with clarity and impact, including logical, ethical, and emotional appeals. (2B) Rhetorical strategies involve stylistic techniques such as parallelism and planned repetition as well as patterns for organizing and developing writing such as illustration, description, and definition. (5E)

Rogerian argument An argument technique using principles developed by Carl Rogers in which writers strive to find common ground and thus assure readers who disagree with them that they understand others' perspectives. (9A)

run-on sentence A sentence in which independent clauses run together without the required punctuation that marks them as complete units. Also known as a *fused sentence*. (Ch. 22)

search strategy A systematic way of finding information on a certain topic. (13B)

secondary source A source that reports, analyzes, discusses, reviews, or otherwise deals with the work of someone else. It stands in contrast to a primary source, which is someone's original work or firsthand report. A reliable secondary source must be the work of a person with appropriate credentials, must appear in a respected publication or other medium, must be current or historically authentic, and must reflect logical reasoning. (12A)

second person See *person*.

sentence A group of words, beginning with a capitalized first word and ending with a final punctuation mark, that states, asks, commands, or exclaims something. A sentence must consist of at least one *independent clause*. A *simple sentence* consists of one independent clause. A *complex sentence* contains one independent clause and one or more dependent clauses. A *compound sentence* contains two or more independent clauses joined by a coordinating conjunction. A *compound-complex sentence* contains at least two independent clauses and one or more dependent clauses. (16O)

sentence fragment A portion of a sentence that is punctuated as though it were a complete sentence. (Ch. 21)

sentence outline A type of outline in which each element is a sentence. (4G)

shift An unnecessary change within a sentence in person, number, voice, tense, or other grammatical framework that makes a sentence unclear. (Ch. 23)

short quotation A direct quotation that occupies no more than four lines of type in an MLA-style source-based paper (for prose) or no more than three lines of poetry. In an APA-style source-based paper, a short quotation has no more than forty words of prose. Short quotations are enclosed in quotation marks. (34A)

simile A comparison, using *like* or *as*, of otherwise dissimilar things. (28E)

simple form Part of a verb, the simple form shows action, occurrence, or state of being taking place in the present. It is used in the singular for first and second person and in the plural for first, second, and third person. Simple forms divide time into past, present, and future. (17B, 17E)

simple predicate See *predicate*.

simple sentence See *sentence*.

simple subject See *subject*.

simple tenses The present, past, and future tenses, which divide time into present, past, and future. (17E)

singular See *number*.

slang Coined words and new meanings for existing words, which quickly pass in and out of use. Slang is inappropriate for most academic writing except when used intentionally as such. (34F)

slanted language Language that tries to manipulate the reader with distorted facts. (28D)

source A print or online book, article, document, CD, other work, or person providing information in words, music, pictures, or other media. (12A)

specialized reference work A reference work (such as a dictionary, encyclopedia, biographical compendium) covering a specific discipline or topic. (12D)

split infinitive One or more words coming between the two words of an infinitive. (24C)

squinting modifier A modifier that is considered misplaced because it isn't clear whether it describes the word that comes before it or the word that follows it. (24B)

standard English   See *edited American English*.

standard word order   The most common sentence pattern in English, which places the subject before the verb. (27H, Ch. 44)

subject   The word or group of words in a sentence that acts, is acted upon, or is described by the verb. A *simple subject* includes only the noun or pronoun. A *complete subject* includes the noun or pronoun and all its modifiers. A *compound subject* includes two or more nouns or pronouns and their modifiers. (16J)

subject complement   A noun or adjective that follows a linking verb, renaming or describing the subject of the sentence. (16L)

subject directories   Lists of topics or resources and services, with links to sources on those topics and resources. An alternative to keyword searches. (12B)

subjective case   The case of the noun or pronoun functioning as a subject. Also see *case*. (19J)

subject–verb agreement   The required match in number and person between a subject and a verb. (Ch. 18)

subjunctive mood   The verb orientation that expresses wishes, recommendations, indirect requests, speculations, and conditional statements: *I wish you were here.* (17F)

subordinate clause   See *dependent clause*.

subordinating conjunction   A conjunction that introduces a dependent clause and expresses a relationship between the word and the idea in the independent clause. (16H)

subordination   The use of grammatical structures to reflect the relative importance of ideas in a sentence. The most important information falls in the independent clause, and less important information falls in the dependent clause or phrases. (26C)

suffix   Letters added at the end of a root word to change function or meaning: *useless*. (29B, 37B)

summary   A critical thinking activity to extract the main message or central point of a passage or other discourse. (3A, 13I)

superlative   The form of an adjective or adverb that expresses the greatest degree of quality among three or more things: *bluest; most easily*. (20D)

synonym   A word that is close in meaning to another word. (28A)

synthesis   A component of critical thinking in which material that has been summarized, analyzed, and interpreted is connected to what one already knows (one's prior knowledge) from reading or experiences. (13F)

tag question   An inverted verb–pronoun combination added to the end of a sentence and creating a question that "asks" the audience to agree with the assertion in the first part of the sentence: *You know what a tag question is, **don't you?** A tag question is set off from the rest of the sentence with a comma. (30H)

tense   The time at which the action of the verb occurs: in the present, the past, or the future. (17E)

tense sequence   In sentences that have more than one clause, the sequencing of verb forms to reflect logical time relationships. (17E)

thesis statement   A statement of an essay's central theme that makes clear the main idea, the writer's purpose, the focus of the topic, and perhaps the organizational pattern. (4F)

third person   See *person*.

tone   The writer's attitude toward his or her material and sometimes to the reader, especially as reflected by word choice. (6A)

topic outline   An outline in which items are listed as words or phrases, not full sentences. (4G)

topic sentence   The sentence that expresses the main idea of a paragraph. (5C)

transition   The word or group of words that connects one idea to another in discourse. Useful strategies for creating transitions include transitional expressions, conjunctive adverbs, parallelism, and planned repetition of key words and phrases. (5D)

transitive verb A verb that must be followed by a direct object. (17A)

understatement Figurative language in which the writer uses deliberate restraint for emphasis. (28E)

verb A word that shows action or occurrence, or that describes a state of being. Verbs change form to show time (tense), attitude (mood), and role of the subject (voice). Verbs occur in the predicate of a clause. Verbs can be parts of verb phrases, which consist of a main verb, any auxiliary verbs, and any modifiers. Verbs can be described as transitive or intransitive, depending on whether they take a direct object. (16C, Ch. 17)

verb phrase A main verb, along with any auxiliary verb(s) and any modifiers. (16M)

verbal A verb form that functions as a noun, adjective, or adverb. (16D, Quick Box 16.3)

verbal phrase A group of words that contains a verbal (an infinitive, participle, or gerund) and its modifiers. (16M)

voice Attribute of verbs showing whether the subject acts (active voice) or is acted upon (passive voice). (17G)

wordiness Writing that is full of words and phrases that don't contribute to meaning. The opposite of *conciseness*. (Ch. 25)

word order The order in which words fall in most English sentences. Usually, the subject comes before the predicate. Inverted word order can bring emphasis to an idea. Multilingual writers are often accustomed to word orders in sentences other than those used in English. (Ch. 44)

working bibliography A preliminary annotated list of useful sources in research writing with a brief summary of each source. (12C)

Works Cited In MLA documentation style, the list of standardized information about all sources drawn upon in a research paper or other scholarly written work. (14D, 14E)

writing process Stages of writing in which a writer plans, drafts, revises, edits, and proofreads. The stages often overlap. (4A, Quick Box 4.1)

writing situation Elements for writers to consider at the beginning of the writing process: their writing topic, purpose, audience, context, role, and special requirements. (4D)

USAGE GLOSSARY

This usage glossary explains the customary manner of using particular words and PHRASES. As used here, *informal* and *colloquial* indicate that words or phrases occur commonly in speech but should be avoided in ACADEMIC WRITING. *Nonstandard* indicates that words or phrases should not be used in either standard spoken English or writing.

All grammatical terms mentioned here are defined in the Terms Glossary. Also consult the commonly confused words listed in Quick Box 29.1.

a, an   Use *a* before words that begin with a consonant (*a dog, a grade, a hole*) or a consonant sound (*a one-day sale, a European*). Use *an* before words or acronyms that begin with a vowel sound or a silent *h* (*an owl, an hour, an MRI*). American English uses *a*, not *an*, before words starting with a pronounced *h*: *a* [*not* an] *historical event.*

accept, except   The verb *accept* means "agree to, receive." As a preposition, *except* means "leaving out." As a verb, *except* means "exclude, leave out."

> The workers were ready to **accept** [verb] management's offer **except** [preposition] for one detail: They wanted the no-smoking rule **excepted** [verb] from the contract.

advice, advise   *Advice*, a noun, means "recommendation." *Advise*, a verb, means "recommend, give advice."

> I **advise** [verb] you to follow your car mechanic's **advice** [noun].

affect, effect   As a verb, *affect* means "cause a change in, influence." (*Affect* also functions as a noun in the discipline of psychology.) As a noun, *effect* means "result or conclusion"; as a verb, it means "bring about."

> Loud music **affects** people's hearing for life, so some bands have **effected** changes to lower the volume. Many fans, however, don't care about the harmful **effects** of high decibel levels.

aggravate, irritate   *Aggravate* is used colloquially to mean "irritate." In formal writing, use *aggravate* to mean "intensify, make worse." Use *irritate* to mean "annoy, make impatient."

> The coach was **irritated** by her assistant's impatience, which **aggravated** the team's inability to concentrate.

ain't   *Ain't* is a nonstandard contraction. Use *am not, is not*, or *are not* instead.

all right   *All right* should be written as two words, never one (*not* alright).

allusion, illusion   An *allusion* is an indirect reference to something. An *illusion* is a false impression or idea.

> The applicant's casual **allusions** to many European tourist attractions created the **illusion** that he had seen them himself.

a lot *A lot* is informal for *a great deal* or *a great many;* avoid it in academic writing. Write it as two words (*not* alot) when you do use it.

a.m., p.m. These abbreviations may also be written as A.M., P.M. Use them only with numbers, not as substitutes for *morning, afternoon,* or *evening.*

> We will arrive **in the afternoon** [*not* in the p.m.], and we have to leave no later than **8:00 a.m**.

among, amongst, between Use *among* for three or more items and *between* for two items. American English prefers *among* to *amongst.*

> My three roommates discussed **among** [*not* between *or* amongst] themselves the choice **between** staying in school and getting full-time jobs.

amount, number Use *amount* for uncountable things (*wealth, work, corn, happiness*). Use *number* for countable items.

> The **amount** of rice to cook depends on the **number** of dinner guests.

an See *a, an.*

and/or This term is appropriate in business and legal writing when either or both of two items can apply: *The process is quicker if you have a wireless connection and/or a fax machine.* In the humanities, writers usually express the alternatives in words: *This process is quicker if you have a wireless connection, a fax machine, or both.*

anyplace *Anyplace* is informal. Use *any place* or *anywhere* instead.

anyways, anywheres *Anyways* and *anywheres* are nonstandard. Use *anyway* and *anywhere* instead.

apt, likely, liable *Apt* and *likely* are used interchangeably. Strictly, *apt* indicates a tendency or inclination. *Likely* indicates a reasonable expectation or greater certainty than *apt. Liable* denotes legal responsibility or implies unpleasant consequences.

> Alan is **apt** to leave early on Friday. I will **likely** go with him to the party. Maggy and Gabriel are **liable** to be angry if we do not show up.

as, as if, as though, like Use *as, as if,* or *as though,* but not *like,* to introduce clauses.

> This hamburger tastes good, **as** [*not* like] a hamburger should. It tastes **as if** [*or* as though *but not* like] it were barbequed over charcoal.

Both *as* and *like* can function as prepositions in comparisons. Use *as* to indicate equivalence between two nouns or pronouns. Use *like* to indicate similarity but not equivalence.

> Beryl acted **as** [*not* like] the moderator in our panel.

> Mexico, **like** [*not* as] Argentina, belongs to the United Nations.

assure, ensure, insure *Assure* means "promise, convince." *Ensure* and *insure* both mean "make certain or secure," but *insure* is reserved for financial or legal certainty, as in insurance.

> The agent **assured** me that he could **insure** my roller blades but that only I could **ensure** that my elbows and knees would outlast the skates.

as to   *As to* is nonstandard. Use *about* instead.

awful, awfully   Do not use *awful* or *awfully* in place of *terribly, extremely,* or *very.*

a while, awhile   As two words, *a while* (an article and a noun) can function as a subject or object. As one word, *awhile* is an adverb; it modifies verbs. In a prepositional phrase, the correct form is *a while: for a while, in a while, after a while.*

> The seals basked **awhile** in the sun after they had played for **a while** in the sea.

backup, back up   As a noun, *backup* is a copy of electronic data. *Backup* can also be used as an adjective to mean "alternative." *Back up* is a verb phrase.

> Many people recommend that you **back up** even your **backup** files.

bad, badly   *Bad* is an adjective; use it after linking verbs. (Remember that verbs like *feel* and *smell* can function as either linking verbs or action verbs.) *Badly* is an adverb and is nonstandard after linking verbs (see 20C).

> Farmers feel **bad** because a **bad** drought has **badly** damaged the crops.

beside, besides   *Beside* is a preposition meaning "next to, by the side of."

> She stood **beside** the new car, insisting that she would drive.

As a preposition, *besides* means "other than, in addition to."

> No one **besides** her had a driver's license.

As an adverb, *besides* means "also, moreover."

> **Besides**, she owned the car.

better, had better   Used in place of *had better, better* is informal.

> We **had better** [*not* We better] be careful.

between   See *among, amongst, between.*

bring, take   Use *bring* to indicate movement from a distant place to a near place or to the speaker. Use *take* to indicate movement from a near place or from the speaker to a distant place.

> If you **bring** a leash to my house, you can **take** the dog to the vet.

but, however, yet   Use *but, however,* or *yet* alone, not in combination with each other.

> The economy is strong, **but** [*not* but yet *or* but however] unemployment is high.

can, may   *Can* signifies ability or capacity; *may* requests or grants permission. In negations, however, *can* is acceptable in place of *may.*

> When you **can** get here on time, you **may** be excused early.

can't hardly, can't scarcely   These double negatives are nonstandard (see 20B).

censor, censure   The verb *censor* means "delete objectionable material, judge." The verb *censure* means "condemn or reprimand officially."

> The town council **censured** the mayor for trying to **censor** a report.

chairman, chairperson, chair Many prefer the gender-neutral terms *chairperson* and *chair* to *chairman; chair* is more common than *chairperson*.

complement, compliment Each term functions as both a noun and a verb. As a noun, *complement* means "something that goes well with or completes." As a noun, *compliment* means "praise, flattery." As a verb, *complement* means "bring to perfection, go well with; complete." As a verb, *compliment* means "praise, flatter."

> The president's **compliment** was a fine **complement** to our celebration.
> When the president **complimented** us, her praise **complemented** our joy.

comprise, include See *include, comprise*.

conscience, conscious The noun *conscience* means "a sense of right and wrong." The adjective *conscious* means "aware or awake."

> To live happily, be **conscious** of what your **conscience** tells you.

continual(ly), continuous(ly) *Continual* means "occurring again and again." *Continuous* means "occurring without interruption."

> Intravenous fluids were given **continuously** for three days after surgery, so nurses were **continually** hooking up new bottles of saline solution.

could care less *Could care less* is nonstandard; use *couldn't care less* instead.

could of *Could of* is nonstandard; use *could have* instead.

couple, a couple of These terms are informal. Use *a few* or *several* instead.

> Rest for **a few** [*not* a couple *or* a couple of] minutes.

criteria, criterion A *criterion* is "a standard of judgment." *Criteria* is the plural form of *criterion*.

> Although charisma is an important **criterion** for political candidates to meet, voters must also consider other **criteria**.

data This is the plural of *datum*, a rarely used word. Informally, *data* is commonly used as a singular noun requiring a singular verb. In academic or professional writing, it is more acceptable to treat *data* as plural.

> The researchers' **data** suggest that some people become addicted to e-mail.

different from, different than *Different from* is preferred for formal writing, although *different than* is common in speech.

> Please advise the council if your research produces data **different from** past results.

don't *Don't* is a contraction for *do not* but not for *does not* (use *doesn't*).

> She **doesn't** [*not* She don't] like crowds.

effect See *affect, effect*.

elicit, illicit The verb *elicit* means "draw forth or bring out." The adjective *illicit* means "illegal."

> The government's **illicit** conduct **elicited** mass protest.

emigrate (from), immigrate (to)   *Emigrate* means "leave one country to live in another." *Immigrate* means "enter a country to live there."

> My great-grandmother **emigrated** from the Ukraine in 1890. After a brief stay in Germany, she **immigrated** to Canada in 1892.

ensure   See *assure, ensure, insure.*

etc.   *Etc.* is the abbreviation for the Latin *et cetera*, meaning "and the rest." For writing in the humanities, avoid using *etc.* outside parentheses. Acceptable substitutes are *and the like, and so on*, and *and so forth.*

everyday, every day   The adjective *everyday* means "daily." *Every day* is an adjective-noun combination that can function as a subject or an object.

> Being late for work has become an **everyday** occurrence. **Every day** that I am late brings me closer to being fired.

everywheres   Nonstandard for *everywhere.*

except   See *accept, except.*

explicit, implicit   *Explicit* means "directly stated or expressed." *Implicit* means "implied, suggested."

> The warning on cigarette packs is **explicit**: "Smoking is dangerous to health." The **implicit** message is "Don't smoke."

fewer, less   Use *fewer* for anything that can be counted (with count nouns): *fewer dollars, fewer fleas, fewer haircuts.* Use *less* with collective or other non-count nouns: *less money, less scratching, less hair.*

finalize   Academic audiences prefer *complete* or *make final* instead of *finalize.*

> After intense negotiations, the two nations **completed** [*not* finalized] a treaty.

former, latter   When two items are referred to, *former* signifies the first one and *latter* signifies the second. Avoid using *former* and *latter* in a context with more than two items.

> Brazil and Ecuador are South American countries. Portuguese is the most common language in the **former**, Spanish in the **latter**.

go, say   *Go* is nonstandard when used for forms of *say.*

> After he stepped on my hand, he **said** [*not* he goes], "Your hand was in my way."

gone, went   *Gone* is the past participle of *go; went* is the past tense of *go.*

> They **went** [*not* gone] to the concert after Ira **had gone** [*not* had went] home.

good and   This phrase is an informal intensifier; omit it from writing.

> They were **exhausted** [*not* good and tired].

good, well   *Good* is an adjective. Using it as an adverb is nonstandard. *Well* is the equivalent adverb.

> **Good** maintenance helps cars run **well**.

hardly   See *can't hardly, can't scarcely.*

have, of   Use *have*, not *of*, after such verbs as *could*, *should*, *would*, *might*, and *must*.

> You **should have** [*not* should of] called first.

have got, have to, have got to   Avoid using *have got* when *have* alone delivers your meaning.

> I **have** [*not* have got] two more sources to read.

Avoid using *have to* or *have got to* for *must*.

> I **must** [*not* have got to] finish this assignment today.

he/she, s/he, his, her   To avoid sexist language, use *he or she* or *his or her*. A less wordy solution is to use plural pronouns and antecedents.

> Every mourner bowed **his or her** head [*not* his head *or* their head].
>
> The **mourners** bowed **their** heads.

humanity, humankind, humans, mankind   To avoid sexist language, use *humanity, humankind,* or *humans* instead of *mankind*.

> Some people think computers have influenced **humanity** more than any other twentieth-century invention.

i.e.   This abbreviation refers to the Latin term *id est*. In formal writing, use the English translation *that is*.

if, whether   At the start of a noun clause, use either *if* or *whether*.

> I don't know **if** [*or* whether] I want to dance with you.

In conditional clauses, use *whether* (*or* whether or not) when alternatives are expressed or implied.

> I will dance with you **whether or not** I like the music. I will dance with you **whether** the next song is fast or slow.

In a conditional clause that does not express or imply alternatives, use *if*.

> **If** you promise not to step on my feet, I will dance with you.

illicit   See *elicit, illicit*.

illusion   See *allusion, illusion*.

immigrate   See *emigrate, immigrate*.

imply, infer   *Imply* means "hint at or suggest." *Infer* means "draw a conclusion." A writer or speaker implies; a reader or listener infers.

> When the governor **implied** that she would not seek reelection, reporters **inferred** that she was planning to run for vice president.

include, comprise   The verb *include* means "contain or regard as part of a whole." The verb *comprise* means "to be composed of."

inside of, outside of   These phrases are nonstandard when used to mean *inside* or *outside*.

> She waited **outside** [*not* outside of] the dormitory.

In time references, avoid using *inside of* to mean "in less than."

I changed clothes **in less than** [*not* inside of] ten minutes.

insure   See *assure, ensure, insure.*

irregardless   *Irregardless* is nonstandard. Use *regardless* instead.

is when, is where   Avoid these constructions in giving definitions.

Defensive driving **requires that** [*not* is when] drivers stay alert.

its, it's   *Its* is a possessive pronoun. *It's* is a contraction of *it is.*

The dog buried **its** bone.

It's a hot day.

kind, sort   Use *this* or *that* with these singular nouns; use *these* or *those* with the plural nouns *kinds* and *sorts*. Also, do not use *a* or *an* after *kind of* or *sort of*.

Drink **these kinds of** fluids [*not* this kind of fluids] on **this sort of** [*not* this sort of a] day.

kind of, sort of   These phrases are colloquial adverbs. In formal writing, use *somewhat* instead.

The campers were **somewhat** [*not* kind of] dehydrated after the hike.

lay, lie   *Lay* (*laid, laid, laying*) means "place or put something, usually on something else" and needs a direct object. *Lie* (*lay, lain, lying*), meaning "recline," does not take a direct object (see 16K). Substituting *lay* for *lie* is nonstandard.

Lay [*not* Lie] the blanket down, and then **lay** the babies on it so they can **lie** [*not* lay] in the shade.

leave, let   *Leave* means "depart"; *let* means "allow, permit." *Leave* is nonstandard for *let*.

Let [*not* Leave] me use your car tonight.

less   See *fewer, less.*

lie   See *lay, lie.*

like   See *as, as if, as though, like.*

likely   See *apt, likely, liable.*

lots, lots of, a lot of   These are colloquial usages. Use *many, much*, or *a great deal* instead.

mankind   See *humanity, humankind, humans, mankind.*

may   See *can, may.*

maybe, may be   *Maybe* is an adverb; *may be* is a verb phrase.

Maybe [adverb] we can win, but our team **may be** [verb phrase] too tired.

may of, might of   *May of* and *might of* are nonstandard. Use *may have* and *might have* instead.

media   This word is the plural of *medium*, yet colloquial usage now pairs it with a singular verb.

The **media** saturates us with information about every fire.

morale, moral   *Morale* is a noun meaning "a mental state relating to courage, confidence, or enthusiasm." As a noun, *moral* means an "ethical lesson implied or taught by a story or event"; as an adjective, *moral* means "ethical."

> One **moral** to draw from corporate downsizings is that overstressed employees suffer from low **morale**. Unhappy employees with otherwise high **moral** standards may steal from their employers.

most   *Most* is nonstandard for *almost: Almost* [*not* Most] *all the dancers agree. Most* is correct as the superlative form of an adjective (*some, more, most*): *Most dancers agree.* It also makes the superlative form of adverbs and some adjectives: *most suddenly, most important.*

Ms.   *Ms.* is a women's title free of reference to marital status, equivalent to *Mr.* for men. For a woman who does not use *Dr.* or another title, use *Ms.* unless she requests *Miss* or *Mrs.*

must of   *Must of* is nonstandard. Use *must have* instead.

nowheres   Nonstandard for *nowhere.*

number   See *amount, number.*

of   Use *have* instead of *of* after the following verbs: *could, may, might, must, should,* and *would.*

OK, O.K., okay   All three forms are acceptable in informal writing. In academic writing, try to express meaning more specifically.

> The weather was **suitable** [*not* OK] for the picnic.

outside of   See *inside of, outside of.*

plus   *Plus* is nonstandard as a substitute for *and, also, in addition,* or *moreover.*

> The band will give three concerts in Hungary, **and** [*not* plus] it will tour Poland for a month. **Also** [*not* Plus], it may perform once in Vienna.

precede, proceed   *Precede* means "go before." *Proceed* means "advance, go on; undertake; carry on."

> **Preceded** by elephants and tigers, the clowns **proceeded** into the tent.

pretty   *Pretty* is an informal qualifying word; in academic writing, use *rather, quite, somewhat,* or *very.*

> The flu epidemic was **quite** [*not* pretty] severe.

principal, principle   *Principle* means "a basic truth or rule." As a noun, *principal* means "chief person; main or original amount"; as an adjective, *principal* means "most important."

> During the assembly, the **principal** said, "A **principal** value in this society is the **principle** of free speech."

proceed   See *precede, proceed.*

quotation, quote   *Quotation* is a noun; *quote* is a verb. Do not use *quote* as a noun.

> The newspaper **quoted** the attorney general, and the **quotations** [*not* quotes] quickly showed up in public health messages.

raise, rise   *Raise* (*raised, raised, raising*) means "lift" and needs a direct object. *Rise* (*rose, risen, rising*) means "go upward" and does not take a direct object (see 16K). Using these verbs interchangeably is nonstandard.

If the citizens **rise** [*not* raise] up in protest, they may **raise** the flag of liberty.

real, really   *Real* is nonstandard as an intensifier, and *really* is almost always unnecessary; leave it out.

reason is because   This phrase is redundant; use *reason is that* instead.

One **reason** we moved **is that** [*not* is because] we changed jobs.

regardless   See *irregardless*.

respective, respectively   The adjective *respective* relates the noun it modifies to two or more individual persons or things. The adverb *respectively* refers to a second set of items in a sequence established by a preceding set of items.

After the fire drill, Dr. Pan and Dr. Moll returned to their **respective** offices [that is, each to his or her office] on the second and third floors, **respectively**. [Dr. Pan has an office on the second floor; Dr. Moll has an office on the third floor.]

right   *Right* is a colloquial intensifier; use *quite, very, extremely*, or a similar word for most purposes.

You did **very** [*not* right] well on the quiz.

rise   See *raise, rise*.

scarcely   See *can't hardly, can't scarcely*.

seen   The past participle of *see* (*see, saw, seen, seeing*), *seen* is a nonstandard substitute for the past-tense form, *saw*. As a verb, *seen* must be used with an auxiliary verb.

Last night, I **saw** [*not* seen] the show that you **had seen** in Florida.

set, sit   *Set* (*set, set, setting*) means "put in place, position, put down" and must have a direct object. *Sit* (*sat, sat, sitting*) means "be seated" and does not take a direct object (see 16K). Using these verbs interchangeably is nonstandard.

Susan **set** [*not* sat] the sandwiches beside the salad, made Spot **sit** [*not* set] down, and then **sat** [*not* set] on the sofa.

should of   *Should of* is nonstandard. Use *should have* instead.

sit   See *set, sit*.

sometime, sometimes, some time   The adverb *sometime* means "at an unspecified time." The adverb *sometimes* means "now and then." *Some time* is an adjective–noun combination meaning "an amount or span of time."

Sometime next year we have to take qualifying exams. I **sometimes** worry about finding **some time** to study for them.

sort of   See *kind of, sort of*.

such   *Such* is an informal intensifier; avoid it in academic writing unless it precedes a noun introducing a *that* clause.

> The play got **terrible** [*not* such terrible] reviews. It was **such** a dull drama **that** it closed after one performance.

supposed to, used to   The final *d* is essential in both phrases.

> We were **supposed to** [*not* suppose to] leave early. I **used to** [*not* use to] wake up as soon as the alarm rang.

sure   *Sure* is nonstandard as a substitute for *surely* or *certainly*.

> I was **certainly** [*not* sure] surprised at the results.

sure and, try and   Both phrases are nonstandard. Use *sure to* and *try to* instead.

than, then   *Than* indicates comparison; *then* relates to time.

> Please put on your gloves, and **then** put on your hat. It is colder outside **than** inside.

that there, them there, this here, these here   These phrases are nonstandard. Use *that, them, this*, and *these*, respectively.

that, which   Use *that* with restrictive (essential) clauses only. *Which* can be used with both restrictive and nonrestrictive clauses; many writers, however, use *which* only for nonrestrictive clauses and *that* for all restrictive clauses (see 30F).

> The house **that** [*or* which] Jack built is on Beanstalk Street, **which** [*not* that] runs past the reservoir.

their, there, they're   *Their* is a possessive. *There* means "in that place" or is part of an expletive construction (see 25C). *They're* is a contraction of *they are*.

> **They're** going to **their** accounting class in the building **there** behind the library. **There** are twelve sections of Accounting 101.

theirself, theirselves, themself   These are nonstandard. Use *themselves* instead.

them   Use *them* as an object pronoun only. Do not use *them* in place of the adjective *these* or *those*.

> Buy **those** [*not* them] strawberries.

then   See *than, then*.

till, until   Both are acceptable; except in expressive writing, avoid the contracted form *'til*.

to, too, two   *To* is a preposition. *Too* is an adverb meaning "also; more than enough." *Two* is the number.

> When you go **to** Chicago, visit the Art Institute. Go **to** Harry Caray's for dinner, **too**. It won't be **too** expensive because **two** people can share an entrée.

try and, sure and   See *sure and, try and*.

type   *Type* is nonstandard when used to mean *type of*.

> Use that **type of** [*not* type] glue on plastic.

unique   *Unique* is an absolute adjective; do not combine it with *more, most,* or other qualifiers.

> Solar heating is **uncommon** [*not* somewhat unique] in the Northeast. A **unique** [*not* very unique] heating system in one Vermont home uses hydrogen for fuel.

used to   See *supposed to, used to.*

utilize   Academic writers prefer *use* to *utilize.*

> The team **used** [*not* utilized] all its players to win the game.

way, ways   When referring to distance, use *way* rather than *ways.*

> He is a long **way** [*not* ways] from home.

well   See *good, well.*

where   *Where* is nonstandard when used for *that* as a subordinating conjunction.

> I read **that** [*not* where] Bill Gates is the richest man alive.

> **Where** is your house? [*not* Where is your house at?]

whether   See *if, whether.*

which   See *that, which.*

who, whom   Use *who* as a subject or a subject complement. Use *whom* as an object (see 16K).

who's, whose   *Who's* is a contraction of *who is. Whose* is a possessive pronoun.

> **Who's** willing to drive? **Whose** truck should we take?

would of   *Would of* is nonstandard. Use *would have* instead.

your, you're   *Your* is a possessive. *You're* is the contraction of *you are.*

> **You're** generous to volunteer **your** time at the elementary school.

CREDITS

Google Inc. Reproduced with permission; **p. 134, Fig. 12.7b:** Google and the Google logo are registered trademarks of Google Inc. Reproduced with permission; **p. 135, Fig. 12.7c:** Reproduced by permission of EBSCO Publishing; **p. 136, Fig. 12.7d:** Reproduced by permission of EBSCO Publishing; **p. 157, Fig. 13.4:** Screenshot from NoodleTools, Inc. website; **p. 162, mid:** Margot Roosevelt, *Time* Magazine. New York: Time, Inc., 2004; **pp. 162–163:** "Global warming is affecting . . . beaches had thawed" by Devon Harris; **p. 163, mid:** Ronni Sandroff, "Too Many Choices," *Consumer Reports on Health*, 2007; **p. 163, bottom:** From "The Tyranny of Choice," *Chronicle of Higher Education* by Barry Schwartz. Copyright ©. Reproduced by permission of Barry Schwartz; **pp. 177 and 178:** Turkle, Sherry, *Alone Together: Why We Expect More from Technology and Less from Each Other*. New York: Basic Books, 2011; **pp. 180–181:** Leora Tanenbaum, *CatFight: Women and Competition*. Seven Stories Press, 2011; **p. 182, bottom:** Peter Wood, *Diversity: The Invention of a Concept*. Encounter Books, 2004; **p. 184:** Ann Hulbert, "Post-Teenage Wasteland?" New York: The New York Times Company, 2005; **p. 185:** Paul Fussell, *Uniforms: Why We Are What We Wear*, Houghton Mifflin Harcourt, 2003; **p. 202, Fig. 14.2:** Wan, Amy J. "In the Name of Citizenship: The Writing Classroom and the Promise of Citizenship." *College English* 74.1 (2011): 28–49. Copyright © 2011 by National Council of Teachers of English. Reproduced with permission; **p. 203, Fig. 14.3:** Reproduced by permission of EBSCO Publishing; **p. 207, Fig. 14.4:** Turkle, Sherry. *Alone Together: Why We Expect More from Technology and Less from Each Other*. New York: Basic Books, 2011; **p. 248, Fig. 15.2:** From *Journal of Clinical Psychology 63*(1). 23–30 by Agliata, A.K., Tantleff-Dunn, S., & Renk, K. Copyright © 2007. Reproduced by permission of John Wiley & Sons, Inc.; **p. 253, Fig. 15.3:** Turkle, Sherry. *Alone Together: Why We Expect More from Technology and Less from Each Other*. New York: Basic Books, 2011; **p. 358:** "By night, the litter and desperation disappeared as the city's glittering lights came on; by day, the filth and despair reappeared as the sun rose" by Jennifer Kirk. Copyright ©. Reproduced by permission; **p. 360:** Annie Dillard, *Pilgrim at Tinker Creek*, HarperCollins Publishers, 2009; **p. 390:** George F. Will, "Well, I Don't Love You, E.T." Washington: GFW, Inc.; **p. 399:** Anne Tyler, *The Accidental Tourist*; **p. 404:** Dick Gregory, *The Shadow That Scares Me*, Doubleday, 1968; **p. 405:** Carol Tavris, *Anger: The Misunderstood Emotion*, Simon and Schuster, 1982; **p. 406, top:** Peter Bonner, "Travel Rhythms," *Sky Magazine*, MSP Communication; **p. 406, mid:** Winifred Gallagher, *The Power of Place*, Harper Collins, 2007; **p. 416:** Joyce Maynard, *An 18-Year-Old Looks Back on Life*. New York: New York Times, 1972; **p. 470, Fig. 52.2:** Screenshot, Opening Shot of Documentary Video by Siena Pinney. Copyright ©. Reproduced by permission; **p. 472, Fig. 53.1:** Screenshot, Typical Blog Design from Crooked Timber. Copyright ©. Reproduced by permission of David Krewinghaus; **p. 476, Fig. 54.2:** Job Application Letter by Monica A Schickel.

PHOTOS

page 21: Peter Vadnai; **p. 22:** Paul Conklin/Getty Images; **p. 62, top:** Michael Krasowitz/Getty Images; **p. 62, bottom:** Michael Krasowitz/Getty Images; **p. 138:** Evgeny Shevchenko/Fotolia; **p. 141, top:** vgstudio/Fotolia; **p. 141, mid:** Robert Lerich/Fotolia; **p. 144, bottom:** Yuri Arcurs/Fotolia.

INDEX